Collaborative Computer Security and Trust Management

Jean-Marc Seigneur
Université de Genève, Switzerland

Adam Slagell
National Center for Supercomputing Applications, USA
University of Illinois at Urbana-Champaign, USA

A volume in the Advances in Information Security, Privacy, and Ethics (AISPE) Book Series

Director of Editorial Content:	Kristin Klinger
Senior Managing Editor:	Jamie Snavely
Assistant Managing Editor:	Michael Brehm
Publishing Assistant:	Sean Woznicki
Typesetter:	Michael Brehm, Jamie Snavely
Cover Design:	Lisa Tosheff

Published in the United States of America by
Information Science Reference (an imprint of IGI Global)
701 E. Chocolate Avenue
Hershey PA 17033
Tel: 717-533-8845
Fax: 717-533-8661
E-mail: cust@igi-global.com
Web site: http://www.igi-global.com

Library of Congress Cataloging-in-Publication Data

Collaborative computer security and trust management / Jean-Marc Seigneur and Adam Slagell, editors.
    p. cm.
  Includes bibliographical references and index.
  Summary: "This book combines perspectives of leading researchers in collaborative security to discuss recent advances in this burgeoning new field"--Provided by publisher.
  ISBN 978-1-60566-414-9 (hbk.) -- ISBN 978-1-60566-415-6 (ebook) 1. Computer security. 2. Public key infrastructure (Computer security) 3. Data protection. 4. Computer networks--Security measures. 5. Computer crimes--Prevention. I. Seigneur, Jean-Marc. II. Slagell, Adam, 1977-
  QA76.9.A25C6145 2010
  005.8--dc22
                                        2009019505

This book is published in the IGI Global book series Advances in Information Security, Privacy, and Ethics (AISPE) Book Series (ISSN: 1948-9730; eISSN: 1948-9749)

British Cataloguing in Publication Data
A Cataloguing in Publication record for this book is available from the British Library.

The views expressed in this book are those of the authors, but not necessarily of the publisher.

Advances in Information Security, Privacy, and Ethics (AISPE) Book Series

ISSN: 1948-9730
EISSN: 1948-9749

MISSION

In the digital age, when everything from municipal power grids to individual mobile telephone locations is all available in electronic form, the implications and protection of this data has never been more important and controversial. As digital technologies become more pervasive in everyday life and the Internet is utilized in ever increasing ways by both private and public entities, the need for more research on securing, regulating, and understanding these areas is growing.

The **Advances in Information Security, Privacy, & Ethics (AISPE) Book Series** is the source for this research, as the series provides only the most cutting-edge research on how information is utilized in the digital age.

COVERAGE

- Access Control
- Device Fingerprinting
- Global Privacy Concerns
- Information Security Standards
- Network Security Services
- Privacy-Enhancing Technologies
- Risk Management
- Security Information Management
- Technoethics
- Tracking Cookies

IGI Global is currently accepting manuscripts for publication within this series. To submit a proposal for a volume in this series, please contact our Acquisition Editors at Acquisitions@igi-global.com or visit: http://www.igi-global.com/publish/.

Titles in this Series

For a list of additional titles in this series, please visit: www.igi-global.com

Theory and Practice of Cryptography Solutions for Secure Information Systems
Atilla Elçi (Aksaray University, Turkey) Josef Pieprzyk (Macquarie University, Australia) Alexander G. Chefranov
(Eastern Mediterranean University, North Cyprus) Mehmet A. Orgun (Macquarie University, Australia) Huaxiong
Wang (Nanyang Technological University, Singapore) and Rajan Shankaran (Macquarie University, Australia)
Information Science Reference • copyright 2013 • 351pp • H/C (ISBN: 9781466640306) • US $195.00 (our price)

IT Security Governance Innovations Theory and Research
Daniel Mellado (Spanish Tax Agency, Spain) Luis Enrique Sánchez (University of Castilla-La Mancha, Spain)
Eduardo Fernández-Medina (University of Castilla – La Mancha, Spain) and Mario Piattini (University of Castilla
- La Mancha, Spain)
Information Science Reference • copyright 2013 • 390pp • H/C (ISBN: 9781466620834) • US $195.00 (our price)

Threats, Countermeasures, and Advances in Applied Information Security
Manish Gupta (State University of New York at Buffalo, USA) John Walp (M&T Bank Corporation, USA) and
Raj Sharman (State University of New York, USA)
Information Science Reference • copyright 2012 • 319pp • H/C (ISBN: 9781466609785) • US $195.00 (our price)

Investigating Cyber Law and Cyber Ethics Issues, Impacts and Practices
Alfreda Dudley (Towson University, USA) James Braman (Towson University, USA) and Giovanni Vincenti
(Towson University, USA)
Information Science Reference • copyright 2012 • 342pp • H/C (ISBN: 9781613501320) • US $195.00 (our price)

Information Assurance and Security Ethics in Complex Systems Interdisciplinary Perspectives
Melissa Jane Dark (Purdue University, USA)
Information Science Reference • copyright 2011 • 306pp • H/C (ISBN: 9781616922450) • US $180.00 (our price)

Chaos Synchronization and Cryptography for Secure Communications Applications for Encryption
Santo Banerjee (Politecnico di Torino, Italy)
Information Science Reference • copyright 2011 • 596pp • H/C (ISBN: 9781615207374) • US $180.00 (our price)

*Technoethics and the Evolving Knowledge Society Ethical Issues in Technological Design, Research, Development,
and Innovation*
Rocci Luppicini (University of Ottawa, Canada)
Information Science Reference • copyright 2010 • 322pp • H/C (ISBN: 9781605669526) • US $180.00 (our price)

www.igi-global.com

701 E. Chocolate Ave., Hershey, PA 17033
Order online at www.igi-global.com or call 717-533-8845 x100
To place a standing order for titles released in this series, contact: cust@igi-global.com
Mon-Fri 8:00 am - 5:00 pm (est) or fax 24 hours a day 717-533-8661

Table of Contents

Selected Readings

Chapter 13

Li Yang, University of Tennessee at Chattanooga, USA
Chang Phuong, University of Tennessee at Chattanooga, USA
Andy Novobilski, University of Tennessee at Chattanooga, USA
Raimund K. Ege, North Illinois University, USA

Detailed Table of Contents

Chapter 1

G. Scott Erickson, Ithaca College, USA
Helen N. Rothberg, Marist College, USA

Development of knowledge assets and protection of knowledge assets are both complementary and competing concerns for the contemporary business. Each has specific issues related to trust that need to be understood and addressed before an individual firm launches a knowledge management initiative. Further, with important contemporary trends such as enterprise systems, external knowledge management networks, and aggressive competitive intelligence efforts, decision-makers must increasingly evaluate their circumstances and establish the appropriate levels of trust between individuals and the organization and between cooperating organizations. This chapter reviews and elaborates on such issues. It then passes to a consideration of how these concerns might vary by industry, presenting selected data on knowledge development and knowledge protection conditions in a variety of industries.

Chapter 2

Rainer Bye, Technische Universität Berlin, Germany
Ahmet Camtepe, Technische Universität Berlin, Germany
Sahin Albayrak, Technische Universität Berlin, Germany

Collaborative methods are promising tools for solving complex security tasks. In this context, the authors present the security overlay framework CIMD (Collaborative Intrusion and Malware Detection), enabling participants to state objectives and interests for joint intrusion detection and find groups for the exchange of security-related data such as monitoring or detection results accordingly; to these groups the authors refer as detection groups. First, the authors present and discuss a tree-oriented taxonomy for the representation of nodes within the collaboration model. Second, they introduce and evaluate an algorithm for the formation of detection groups. After conducting a vulnerability analysis of the system, the authors demonstrate the validity of CIMD by examining two different scenarios inspired sociology where the collaboration is advantageous compared to the non-collaborative approach. They evaluate the benefit of CIMD by simulation in a novel packet-level simulation environment called NeSSi (Network Security Simulator) and give a probabilistic analysis for the scenarios.

Security often requires collaboration, but when multiple stakeholders are involved, it is typical for their priorities to differ or even conflict with one another. In today's increasingly networked world, cyber security collaborations may span organizations and countries. In this chapter, the authors address collaboration tensions, their effects on incident detection and response, and how these tensions may potentially be resolved. The authors present three case studies of collaborative cyber security within the U.S. government and discuss technical, social, and regulatory challenges to collaborative cyber security. They suggest possible solutions and present lessons learned from conflicts. Finally, tje authors compare collaborative solutions from other domains and apply them to cyber security collaboration. Although they concentrate their analysis on collaborations whose purpose is to achieve cyber security, the authors believe this work applies readily to security tensions found in collaborations of a general nature as well.

It is desirable for many reasons to share information, particularly computer and network logs. Researchers need it for experiments, incident responders need it for collaborative security, and educators need this data for real world examples. However, the sensitive nature of this information often prevents its sharing. Anonymization techniques have been developed in recent years that help reduce risk and navigate the trade-offs between privacy, security and the need to openly share information. This chapter looks at the progress made in this area of research over the past several years, identifies the major problems left to solve and sets a roadmap for future research.

Collaborative business applications are an active field of research and an emerging practice in industry. This chapter will focus on data protection in B2B applications which offer a wide range of business models and architecture, since often equal partners are involved in the transactions. It will present three distinct applications, their business models, security requirements and the newest solutions for solving these problems. The three applications are collaborative benchmarking, fraud detection and supply chain management. Many of these applications will not be realized if no appropriate measure for protecting the collaborating parties' data are taken. This chapter focuses on the strongest form of data protection. The business secrets are kept entirely secret from other parties (or at least to the degree possible). This also corresponds to the strongest form of privacy protection in many instances. The private information does not leave the producing system, (i.e., data protection), such that the information producer remains its sole owner. In case of B2B application, the sensitive data are usually business secrets, and not personally identifiable data as in privacy protection.

Chapter 6

Weiliang Zhao, Macquarie University, Australia
Vijay Varadharajan, Macquarie University, Australia

There have been many trust management systems which are exclusively based on credentials. In this chapter, the authors propose an approach with a unified framework for trust management that can address the above mentioned limitations of current trust management systems. The unified framework uses a consistent way to cover a broad variety of trust mechanisms including credentials, reputation, local data storage, and environment parameters.

Chapter 7

N. Sahli, Dhofar University, Sultanate of Oman
G. Lenzini, Telematica Instituut/Novay, The Netherlands

This chapter surveys and discusses relevant works in the intersection among trust, recommendations systems, virtual communities, and agent-based systems. The target of the chapter is showing how, thanks to the use of trust-based solutions and artificial intelligent solutions like that understanding agents-based systems, the traditional recommender systems can improve the quality of their predictions. Moreover, when implemented as open multi-agent systems, trust-based recommender systems can efficiently support users of mobile virtual communities in searching for places, information, and items of interest.

Chapter 8

Mohammed Hussain, Queen's University, Canada
David B. Skillicorn, Queen's University, Canada

Mobile agents are self-contained programs that migrate among computing devices to achieve tasks on behalf of users. Autonomous and mobile agents make it easier to develop complex distributed systems. Many applications can benefit greatly from employing mobile agents, especially e-commerce. For instance, mobile agents can travel from one e-shop to another, collecting offers based on customers' preferences. Mobile agents have been used to develop systems for telecommunication networks, monitoring, information retrieval, and parallel computing. Characteristics of mobile agents, however, introduce new security issues which require carefully designed solutions. On the one hand, malicious agents may violate privacy, attack integrity, and monopolize hosts' resources. On the other hand, malicious hosts may manipulate agents' memory, return wrong results from system calls, and deny access to necessary resources. This has motivated research focused on devising techniques to address the security of mobile-agent systems. This chapter surveys the techniques securing mobile-agent systems. The survey categorizes the techniques based on the degree of collaboration used to achieve security. This categorization resembles the difference between this chapter and other surveys in the literature where categorization is on the basis of entities/parts protected and underlying methodologies used for protection. This survey shows the importance of collaboration in enhancing security and discusses its implications and challenges.

Chapter 9

Like wired network security, wireless sensor network (WSN) security encompasses the typical network security requirements which are: confidentiality, integrity, authentication, non-repudiation and availability. At the same time, security for WSNs differs from traditional security designed for classical wired networks in many points because of the new constraints imposed by WSN technology. Many aspects are due to the limited resources (memory space, CPU ...) and infrastructure-less property of WSNs. Therefore traditional security mechanisms cannot be applied directly and WSNs are more prone to existing and new threats than traditional networks. Typical threats are the physical capture of sensor nodes, the service disruption due to the unreliable wireless communication. Parameters specific to WSN characteristics may help to reduce the effect of threats. Examples of existing measures are efficient WSN power management strategies that can dynamically adjust the node cycles (sleeping or awake mode) based on the current network workload or the use of redundant information to locally detect lying nodes. In addition to adjusting existing WSN characteristics that impact security, establishing trust and collaboration is essential in WSNs for many reasons such as the high distribution of sensor nodes or the goal-oriented nature of many sensing applications. This chapter emphasizes the need of collaboration between sensor nodes and shows that establishing trust between nodes and using reputation reported by collaborating nodes can help mitigate security issues.

Chapter 10

The term "trusted computing" refers to a technology developed by the Trusted Computing Group. It mainly addresses two questions: "Which software is executed on a remote computer?" and "How can secret keys and other security sensitive data be stored and used safely on a computer?". In this chapter the authors introduce the ideas of the trusted computing technology first and later explain how it can help us with establishing "trust" into a business partner (e.g., for B2B or B2C interactions). More precisely: the authors explain how to establish trust into the business partner's computing machinery. So in their chapter "trust" means, that one business partner can be sure, that the other business partner's computing system behaves in an expected and non malicious manner. The authors define "trust" as something that can be measured by cryptographic functions on one computer and be reported towards and evaluated by the business partner's computer, not as something that is derived from observations or built upon legal contracts.

Chapter 11

Rima Deghaili, American University of Beirut, Lebanon
Ali Chehab, American University of Beirut, Lebanon
Ayman Kayssi, American University of Beirut, Lebanon

In distributed computing environments, it is often needed to establish trust before entities interact together. This trust establishment process involves making each entity ask for some credentials from the other entity, which implies some privacy loss for both parties. The authors present a system for achieving the right privacy-trust tradeoff in distributed environments. Each entity aims to join a group in order to protect its privacy. Interaction between entities is then replaced by interaction between groups on behalf of their members. Data sent between groups is saved from dissemination by a self-destruction process. Simulations performed on the system implemented using the Aglets platform show that entities requesting a service need to give up more private information when their past experiences are not good, or when the requesting entity is of a paranoid nature. The privacy loss in all cases is quantified and controlled.

Selected Readings

Chapter 12

Bolanle A. Olaniran, Texas Tech University, USA

Trust and relational development represents a critical challenge in online collaboration groups. Often the problem is attributed to several factors including physical distances, time differences, cultures, and other contributing factors. The challenge in virtual teams centers on creating a successful cohort that functions as a team and develops a sense of trust and cohesion in the process of accomplishing respective group goals. However, the lack of trust in online groups hinders relational development. The author contends that while online collaboration can be clouded by problems with trust and relational synergy as a whole, the problem is exacerbated in international online or e-Collaborative groups. The development of trust is essential to relational synergy and warmth that fosters successful task and social goal accomplishment. After reviewing related and extant research in online communication, the author offers some practical suggestions for facilitating and sustaining trust and relational synergy in international online collaboration with information communication technologies (ICTs).

Chapter 13

Li Yang, University of Tennessee at Chattanooga, USA
Chang Phuong, University of Tennessee at Chattanooga, USA
Andy Novobilski, University of Tennessee at Chattanooga, USA
Raimund K. Ege, North Illinois University, USA

Most access control models have formal access control rules to govern the authorization of a request from a principal. In pervasive and collaborative environments, the behaviors of a principal are uncertain due to partial information. Moreover, the attributes of a principal, requested objects, and contexts of a request are mutable during the collaboration. A variety of such uncertainty and mutability pose challenges when resources sharing must happen in the collaborative environment. In order to address the above challenges, the authors propose a framework to integrate trust management into a usage control model in order to support decision making in an ever-changing collaborative environment. First, a trust value of a principal is evaluated based on both observed behaviors and peer recommendations. Second, the usage-based access control rules are checked to make decisions on resource exchanges. The authors' framework handles uncertainty and mutability by dynamically disenrolling untrusted principals and revoking granted on-going access if access control rules are no longer met. They have applied our trust-based usage control framework to an application of file sharing.

Foreword

TRUST, TRANSPARENCY AND COLLABORATION: THE ETHICAL CHALLENGE TO THE INFORMATION SOCIETY

E-Government and the E-Governed: The Challenge Ahead

2007 may come to be seen as a pivotal year for e-government. The pivot was that curse of politicians- unexpected and destabilizing events – anticipated by some experts, but unheeded in many ICT programme developments. It was the year that the drive for e-government services suffered a series of highly media-sensitive setbacks, despite the surge in people using the Internet for both public and private purposes, especially retail uses. In the public domain there is the UK Government, for example, scoring well in international benchmarking, and moving to consolidate its own dispersed websites into two, one for citizen services, the other for business services. But despite such advances, a series of data losses on a large scale, with some data turning up in the USA, raises questions about how citizens and their children can be fully protected in what has been an open, often outsourced data management culture. These problems are having a political effect also, with large-scale IT schemes, such as the national identity card project, and the on-going IT for Health project in the NHS, coming under closer scrutiny from all sides. Even in the private sector, the problems of on-line fraud, e-banking security concerns as exemplified by the Societe Generale affair, and identity theft risk denting the wider need for trust among customers. A realisation is emerging that citizens' needs and customers' demands are not quite the same thing. Questions are being asked about control, accountability, trust and security, not just at national and international level but within regions as well. These will assume an even greater urgency and political potency when the sharing of data across borders by public administrations is accelerated in the years ahead. People will demand even greater control over cross-border data management systems where their personal data is concerned. This has profound implications for political cultures within countries and within collaborative inter-state constructs such as the EU, demanding a new culture based on citizen-centric expectations understood, acted upon and protected by their e-government guardians.

REBUILDING THE BRIDGE OF TRUST

If 2007 was a pivotal year for data assurance management, 2008 and beyond will be years when a range of questions will be raised entwining technology and politics as never before, and with civic concepts such as trust, security, fairness and transparency bridging both technology and politics.

The following list of questions will inform the debate:

- How secure is the whole outsourcing process, when personal data is handled in India, the USA, or wherever?
- Should lower costs determine the outsourcing process?
- Should 'efficiency gains' continue to take priority over the needs for security and access?
- Under what rules and conditions are data held and exchanged in the countries and companies which handle data on EU citizens, and people from around the world visiting the UK?
- How accountable are companies, including non-EU companies working for EU governments, to the taxpayer and governments when major security leaks occur?
- How adequate and sufficient are financial penalties or criminal penalities to encourage robust baked in security from the outset? How fast can they be updated to keep pace with technological advances?
- How do parliaments scrutinize major e-government programmes? Is scrutiny enough to ensure real accountability or is accountability no longer possible?
- How can legitimate concerns among citizens be addressed?
- How can vulnerabilities in remote and online transactions be addressed to decrease fraud and the exponential rise in cybercrime?
- If current e-government projects are judged to be insecure within a national context, what chance is there of getting popular support for either exchanging data at the EU level or for automated European interoperability between public sector data systems?
- How can the socially excluded and disadvantaged, the disabled and an aging population be expected to keep in step with and collaborate with e-government procedures, if they fail to provide the essential requirement of trust and reliability in handling individuals' data?
- How does government restore confidence in its ability to manage large IT schemes, and create alliances with citizens on benefits of both cost and service?
- What can we learn from other countries, especially other EU member states and regions?
- What lessons might be learned from studying the CNIL in France, a national watchdog on the impact of Internet-based technologies on citizens' privacy?
- How will states cope with Article 8 of the Services Directive, which will implement Internet-based service provision cross-border?
- Should citizens be able one day to monitor and even control some key aspects of their data held by government?
- What are the objections to allowing citizens to be in control of access to and the release of their personal data?

NATIONAL AWARENESS ENHANCED BY EUROPEAN ENGAGEMENT

Just as research informs innovation and development in the private sector, so its effect in government needs to be understood and selectively utilized, where it brings benefit. But too often policymakers fail to appreciate the relevance and applicability of many research projects and recommendations. Instead, they seem to prefer the recommendations of private-sector consultants and miss, through lack of awareness or a tendency to seek the traditional private 'solution,' the evidence of research funded by government itself in universities and national research laboratories, or research funded by the EC often with key inputs from the UK's research community.

There has never been a better time to engage in a process of mutual learning. Most major government projects now involve large ICT commitments and components. The European Data Protection Supervisor regularly identifies and reports on privacy and data handling weakness and solutions. Governments and citizens are anxious about and perplexed by ICT-led developments in biometric identification in passports and other ID domains, data management, fraud and ID theft, never mind the future challenge of the Internet of Things at the very time when there has been a massive increase in international mobility. Rather than being surprised by events in the future, it is essential that, within the EU, governments are alert to, engage with and shape, not just the ICT, but also the citizen-centric implications of the implementation of Article 20 of the EU Treaty on diplomatic and consular protection for citizens, moves towards a Common Consular Space and an EU External Action Programme, cross-border healthcare provision, judicial and police collaboration, and convergent standards for EU passports and visas. The internal borders of the EU have been largely dismantled; now the electronic barriers need to be removed. But just as recent referenda indicate that EU citizens have often felt left behind or just ignored in the rush to implement the single market and the euro programme for business, so this next challenge must involve the security, well-being and trust of the citizen as a prerequisite not just of administrative success but of the e-governed's assent to extend their civic rights into regulatable cyberspace.

BETTER NATIONAL PROTECTION AND PERFORMANCE INFORMED BY EU PROGRAMMES AND PROJECTS

A number of initiatives funded by the EC demonstrate the capacity to test, criticise and question the ways governments tackle national challenges, by taking a wider, Europe-wide view informed by good practice from public-private consortia, experience and piloting. Often such projects involve the evidence of small countries with pioneering experience of e-government. Below are some EC national and regional projects from which other states and their regions can benefit in shaping their own domestic e-government programmes:

- The Burgerkarte and successful e-government projects of Austria
- The e-justice EC project (2004-6), and e-justice programme piloted again by Austria
- Secure e-voting in Estonia
- The FIDIS project and its implications for biometric identification
- The SecurEgov project into security for pan-European interoperability systems
- The Challenge project examining implications for e-governance on traditional democtaric institutions and procedures
- The eGovernet project led by Sweden into e-government research in the EU
- The recently launched STORK project into e-ID
- The R4eGov Integrated Project into secure e-government data exchange interoperability at scale between member states and agencies
- The Hadrian project in the North East Region of England, a private-public partnership approach to restoring trust in ICT-led business and bureaucracy

CONTROLLING TECHNOLOGY, RENEWING DEMOCRACY

This book addresses how we can meet some of the challenges mentioned above by using technology to create and sustain alliances within trust-based collaborative structures. Understanding the tools available, and how we can better harness them for such tasks means that much of this volume addresses the technical sphere. For this, no apologies, because it is only with better instruments, those which already exist and also those we need to invent, that we can advance the trusted agenda of the e-governed. The Internet has created wealth, mobilities, and opportunities for work, leisure and learning at an unparalleled scale. It has also spawned a rash of global threats and intrusions into our everyday lives, creating apprehension and insecurity. Research which can help decision-makers and governments to learn, constanty, how best to built collaborative trust between themselves and their citizens or clients is one important pillar in rebuilding trust in the Internet age. And it is not just trust in the process of data management which is at stake, but trust in the clear and stated ability and resolve of democracies to master for its peoples their entitlement to the widened, secure, and better life offered by the Information Age.

Andrew Robinson
European Consular and Commercial Office, UK
Member of the EC Integrated Project R4eGov (2006-9)
into eGovernment secure interoperability systems

Andrew Robinson *is Hon Consul for France in the UK, and adviser on European and international strategic opportunities to both private and public sectors. His wide experience with EC programmes extends over 20 years experience, including most recently major EC research projects such as eJustice and R4eGov, both of which inform his Preface to this book. He is Chairman of the European Consular and Commercial Office, and joint creator of the first Franco-German Consulate in the EU in 2004. He is also a Member of the Fraud Forum in NE England, introducing the importance of cross-border interoperability, trust and security, which informs much of his current professional work. He is a Chevalier (Knight) of the Order of Merit, and the Chevalier of the Academic Palms by the French Government for his services to Franco-British and European collaboration. His career spans senior posts in universities, government service, and the private sector.*

Preface

COLLABORATIVE SECURITY AND TRUST MANAGEMENT

Security is usually centrally managed, for example in a form of policies duly executed by individual nodes. An alternative trend of using collaboration and trust to provide security has gained momentum over the past few years. Instead of centrally managed security policies, nodes may use specific knowledge (both local and acquired from other nodes) to make security-related decisions. For example, in reputation-based schemes, the reputation of a given node (and hence its security access rights) can be determined based on the recommendations of peer nodes. As systems are being deployed on ever-greater scale without direct connection to their distant home base, the need for self management is rapidly increasing. Interaction after interaction, as the nodes collaborate, there is the emergence of a digital ecosystem that can be driven by trust. By guiding the local decisions of the nodes, for example, with whom the nodes collaborate, global properties of the ecosystem where the nodes operate may be guaranteed. Thus, the security property of the ecosystem may be driven by self-organizing mechanisms based on trust. Depending on which local collaboration is preferred, a more trustworthy ecosystem may emerge.

In more traditional computer environments, there is the need of increased sharing of security evidence, for example, concerning network logs that have to encompass several network domains in order to detect more quickly new types of network attacks. However, network administrators are still reluctant to share their network logs with external parties due to the risk of exposing their remaining network security holes through these network logs.

This book is a collection of recent scientific contributions to this emerging field of security through collaboration. The foreword by Dr. Andrew Robinson underlines the ethical challenges for security through collaboration in the information society. Then, the first chapter delves into the issues of sharing electronic assets within this knowledge economy. The second chapter focuses on another application domain, namely, collaborative intrusion detection. The third chapter underlines the tensions that may arise when sharing security evidence between different organisations and suggests potential solutions to mitigate these tensions. Chapter 4 presents how anonymisation techniques have been developed to help reduce risk and manage the trade-offs between privacy, security and the need to openly share network information. Chapter 5 introduces three applications in another application domain, namely, the collaborative business-to-business application domain: collaborative benchmarking, fraud detection and supply chain management. Many of these applications could not be realised if no appropriate measures for protecting the collaborating parties' data are taken. The protecting measure based on trust management is explained in the sixth chapter. In Chapter 7, trust management is applied to the specific application domain of recommender systems. The eighth chapter shows the importance of collaboration in enhancing security of mobile agents that migrate among computing devices to achieve tasks on behalf of users. Another particular application domain where trust-based collaboration is used for increased security, namely wireless sensors network security, is surveyed in chapter 9. Chapter 10 investigates how new hardware technologies such as trust computing can help regarding increased collaborative security given that trusted computing helps to establish trust into business partners' computing machineries. Chapter 11 discusses how to achieve the right trade-off between loss of privacy and increased security in distributed computing environments using credentials. We also suggest reading the two following paperschapters, included in the selected readings section, to get an overview of trust management for fostering collaborative environments: "A Proposition for Developing Trust and Relational Synergy in International e-Collaborative Groups" and "Trust-Based usage Control in Collaborative environment."

After reading the chapters, the readers will have a clear overview of security through collaboration and that it can be applied to many different application domains. We hope that it will foster further use of security through collaboration in other application domains.

Jean-Marc Seigneur
Université de Genève, Switzerland

Adam Slagell
National Center for Supercomputing Applications
University of Illinois at Urbana-Champaign, USA

Acknowledgment

This material is in part based upon work supported by the European Commission under its Framework Programs. Any opinions, findings, and conclusions or recommendations expressed in this publication are those of the authors and do not necessarily reflect the views of the European Commission.

This material is also in part based upon work supported by the National Science Foundation under Award No. CNS 0524643. Any opinions, findings, and conclusions or recommendations expressed in this publication are those of the authors and do not necessarily reflect the views of the National Science Foundation.

Chapter 1
Knowledge Assets, E–Networks and Trust

G. Scott Erickson
Ithaca College, USA

Helen N. Rothberg
Marist College, USA

ABSTRACT

Development of knowledge assets and protection of knowledge assets are both complementary and competing concerns for the contemporary business. Each has specific issues related to trust that need to be understood and addressed before an individual firm launches a knowledge management initiative. Further, with important contemporary trends such as enterprise systems, external knowledge management networks, and aggressive competitive intelligence efforts, decision-makers must increasingly evaluate their circumstances and establish the appropriate levels of trust between individuals and the organization and between cooperating organizations. This chapter reviews and elaborates on such issues. It then passes to a consideration of how these concerns might vary by industry, presenting selected data on knowledge development and knowledge protection conditions in a variety of industries.

BACKGROUND: KNOWLEDGE ASSETS AND E-NETWORKS

A number of components constitute the knowledge assets of the firm. Although the field of knowledge management generally limits itself to intellectual property and the now fairly well-understood and well-accepted concept of intellectual capital, the basic framework can be easily extended to information and raw data with potential to become

intellectual capital. This view is important, as both knowledge management systems and enterprise systems for Enterprise Resource Planning (ERP), Supply Chain Management (SCM), and Customer Relationship Management (CRM) typically extend throughout a firm and reach outward to all the members of its e-network. All aspects of intellectual property, knowledge, information, and data are routinely shared through these extended networks, a practice raising important questions about trust between organizations and among the individuals within them.

DOI: 10.4018/978-1-60566-414-9.ch001

Table 1. Definition of terms

Data	"Observations or facts out of context" (Zack, 1999b, p.46)
Information	"Data within some meaningful context" (Zack, 1999b, p. 46)
Knowledge	"That which we come to believe and value on the basis of the meaningfully organized accumulation of information (messages) through experience, communication, or inference" (Zack, 1999b, p. 46). Also sometimes termed know-how, learning that takes place leading to individual expertise (Zander & Kogut, 1995).
Knowledge assets	Valuable, intangible assets of the firm. Personal knowledge, corporate culture, intellectual property or any other valuable organizational knowledge.
Intellectual property	Formalized knowledge assets, qualifying for a patent, copyright, trademark or other institutionalized protection mechanism.
Intellectual capital (IC)	Identified knowledge assets of the firm. The field of intellectual capital focuses on the identification, measurement, and management of these intangible assets. Includes IP and less formalized knowledge (Edvinsson & Malone, 1997).
Knowledge management	The practice of managing knowledge assets, focused on identification, capture, organization, sharing, and analysis. Closely related to IC, the differences are more in emphasis on measurement (IC) and management (KM).
Tacit knowledge	Knowledge assets that are personalized and hard (perhaps impossible) to communicate (Nonaka & Takeuchi, 1995; Polanyi, 1967).
Explicit knowledge	Knowledge assets that are captured by the organization, more easily communicated, perhaps stored in a formalized manner in an IT system or elsewhere (Choi & Lee, 2003).

Source: Erickson & Rothberg, 2008b

The discipline of knowledge management (KM) arose out of an increasing recognition that often the most critical source of competitive advantage is found in the people of an organization and what they know (Zack, 1999a, Grant, 1996). Intellectual property such as patents, copyrights, and trademarks is formalized knowledge and has been recognized for quite some time as being of value to an organization. KM developed as scholars and practitioners realized that firms possess countless examples of less formal knowledge assets that are also of value. Just because an innovative product or process isn't protectable by a patent doesn't mean it isn't worth something to the owner. From this basis came the related fields of knowledge management and intellectual capital (IC). IC is largely concerned with categorizing and measuring knowledge assets while KM focuses more on their identification, use, and sharing. These concepts and other definitions are summarized in Table 1 (Erickson & Rothberg, 2008b).

In the literature of the fields, several themes have been developed which are central to this paper. Initially, a well-known distinction exists between tacit and explicit knowledge (Nonaka & Takeuchi, 1995; Polanyi, 1967). Tacit knowledge is more personal, harder to express, and harder to share. Explicit knowledge is more structured, easier to express, and easier to share. In general terms, these distinctions have important implications for knowledge management systems as the processes for identifying critical knowledge, encouraging individuals to reveal it, expressing it, storing it, and distributing it can be quite different (Choi & Lee, 2003; Boisot, 1995). Although purely tacit and purely explicit pieces of knowledge are rare extremes, all of the variations of knowledge along a continuum anchored by these descriptors need management appropriate to their type. Generally, more explicit knowledge assets can be captured in digital form and stored in the KM systems run by information technology (IT) departments. Knowledge assets more tacit in nature are more likely to be identified by less structured means and are better shared person to person, when possible.

Another major theme in the literature, particularly on the intellectual capital side, is a breakdown of knowledge assets between human capital, structural capital, and relational capital (Bontis, 1999; Edvinsson & Malone, 1997). In simple terms, human capital is knowledge concerning an individual's job (whether production, service delivery, any level of management, finance, marketing, or any other function); structural capital is firm-specific and can include aspects of corporate culture, information technology, organizational structure, or other such items that persist throughout the entity; and relational capital has to do with knowledge about external relationships, whether with customers, suppliers, vendors, regulators, or any other friendly or neutral outsiders. Competitive capital, knowledge assets concerning competitors and their behaviour, is sometimes discussed as a fourth type of intellectual capital (Rothberg & Erickson, 2002). These distinctions are important to the process of recognizing knowledge that is valuable, trying to assess it, and, once again, then managing it more effectively.

Finally, this definitional foundation has enabled scholars and practitioners to observe, discover, and employ a range of strategies and tools for better managing knowledge assets, for managing this intellectual capital. One range of techniques looks to better measure these knowledge assets which are by definition intangible, often poorly defined, and admittedly hard to value. The well-known Balanced Scorecard (Kaplan & Norton, 1992) isn't related to IC directly but is a closely related system addressing some of these problems while the Skandia Navigator is an example of an explicit IC reporting device (Edvinsson & Malone, 1997). With measurement come attempts to manage, and everything from fairly substantial IT installations for managing KM (Matson, Patiath & Shavers, 2003) and digital expert identification systems (Forelle, 2005) to more personable techniques such as communities of practice (Wenger, 1998) or storytelling (Brown, et. al., 2004) can be utilized in managing these knowledge assets. Indeed, a

major direction of research in the KM field is seen in examining best practices in firms measuring and managing knowledge (Gupta & Govindarajan 2000b; Davenport, et. al., 1998).

This basic description of KM theory and practice raises a number of issues concerning trust that we'll address shortly. But some less discussed aspects suggest additional complications. Initially, firms looking to better manage their own knowledge assets must typically extend practices beyond their own boundaries. Not only are firms more collaborative with networks of partners in today's world, but it makes sense to draw knowledge assets from more places and leverage them by making them available to all potential users, internal and external, who can benefit the larger network by employing them. Hence, we have the tendency to extend KM systems to full organisational networks rather than limiting them to a single core firm.

Further, such networks of collaborating firms are probably even more likely to routinely share information and data through the contemporary enterprise systems mentioned earlier. Through such installations, digital data and information are constantly passed from one part of the e-network to another. While not as developed as what we normally deem knowledge assets, such data and information have the potential to become knowledge. With some analysis applied to them, these "preknowledge" assets can be just as valuable as more recognized knowledge assets such as intellectual capital or intellectual property. Clearly, a case can be made that organizations regularly exchange not only knowledge but also critical preknowledge assets through digital channels such as KM and enterprise systems (Rothberg & Erickson, 2005).

A further issue to consider is the similarly rapid growth in practice in the field of competitive intelligence (CI) over the past two decades (Herzog, 2007; ASIS, 1999). Just as one firm's proprietary knowledge and preknowledge assets may be valuable to it, so they may be valuable (perhaps even more so) to competitors. Sometimes substantial CI operations exist with the explicit objective of gathering information and/or knowledge about or from competing firms. KM systems, enterprise systems, and any other data interchange system are much more susceptible to CI activity because of the way in which they make available the full knowledge and preknowledge assets of the firm to many more people, in digital form, both inside and outside the organization (Rothberg & Erickson, 2005). As we'll see, the presence of CI, along with all the other factors we've discussed, creates unique and important trust issues for companies engaged in managing knowledge of one sort or another.

BACKGROUND: KNOWLEDGE MANAGEMENT & TRUST

Knowledge management is a concept and practice based on trust. Initially, the whole system is based on an exchange of knowledge taking place (Teece, 1980). Exchange generally requires some degree of trust. In this case, an individual is surrendering knowledge to the entity and/or taking knowledge from the entity. Across firm boundaries, organizations do the same thing, contributing to and/or taking from the e-network knowledge base. Thus, someone or something must be willing to give up knowledge if others are to benefit from it (Bakker, et. al., 2006). Willingness is predicated on getting something back in return. "Communication and trust are critical success factors" for such exchanges to take place (Choi & Lee, 2003, p. 406). And research suggests that conditions favorable to effective exchange include accessibility, value expectancy, motivation, and combinative capability (Nahapiet & Ghoshal, 1998).

All of this is based on the idea of social capital (Vainio, 2005). Individuals develop social capital by building relationships with others. Either more relationships or increasingly deeper relationships increase an individual's social capital (Nahapiet

& Ghoshal, 1998). In other terms, social capital is based on a structural component (network centricity) and a relational component. The relational component is directly related to trustworthiness, others' assessment of the integrity and reliability of the exchange partner (Tsai, 2000). This definition is obviously squarely in line with the mainstream view of trust, that an exchange participant will not engage in opportunistic behaviors (Chiles & McMackin, 1996). In an exchange, trust is based on capability, benevolence, and integrity, essentially the belief in the opposite party to be able to perform as expected (capability), to wish to perform as expected (benevolence), and then to actually perform as expected (integrity) (Bakker, et. al., 2006; Collins & Smith, 2006; Marshall, et. al., 2005). In terms of contributing variables, trust is built in environments with strong relationships (Collins & Smith, 2006; Foos, et. al., 2006), when partners share fields of experience (Lin, 2006), and when power can be employed to ensure compliance (Collins & Smith, 2006; Nielsen, 2005).

Individual to Organization

In relating this broader concept of trust specifically to knowledge management, it's useful to consider the specific nature of the exchanges taking place. First and foremost, there is the surrender to the organization of personal knowledge held by individuals. Within a firm, personal knowledge is often a source of power. Individuals possessing unique knowledge have special value to the firm, often resulting in increased job security, higher compensation, respect from peers, and other benefits. In surrendering knowledge, individuals may be giving up some of this power—if anyone can now know what they know and do what they do, the initiating individual is no longer special. As a result, individuals must be convinced to participate by contributing their expertise to KM systems and, in effect, the company (Gupta & Govindarajan, 2000a; 2000b). An exchange must take place, and the individual must trust in the firm to complete a fair exchange, even if the payback is sometime further in the future. As a consequence, clear incentives (Hansen & von Oetinger, 2001) and motivational systems (Davenport, et. al., 1998) generally must be employed to gain the individual cooperation necessary to make KM work.

Alternatively, on the other end of the system, users of the knowledge must believe that it's worth their effort to search it out within the system. They must trust the knowledge will be applicable and useful as they must contribute time and effort to discover, understand, and employ whatever they find. Similarly, back on the originating side of things, the individuals contributing knowledge must put forth time and effort to feed the knowledge into the system. In some cases, this is a relatively minor task, as in expert systems which simply identify individuals within the network with particular expertise. In other cases, the requirement is substantial as knowledge details, case histories, or other substantive knowledge must be codified within the KM system. Again, incentives must be in place so that individuals trust the exchange will be fair, i.e. that their time and effort to contribute information (presumably at the expense of other tasks) will be appreciated and rewarded. And firms must take particular care not to have disincentives in place that punish contributions (Prusak & Cohen, 2001). If knowledge contributions can potentially make individuals redundant or result in jobs being shipped to another location, the potential exists for negative effects flowing from use of a KM system. KM systems can't be employed to put originators out of work. Such scenarios obviously pose a potent threat to trust in the system and would pretty much end the willingness of individuals to contribute their personal knowledge assets to the company.

Organization to Individual

Within this structure, however, the trust implications do not flow only in one direction. Organizations implementing KM systems, enterprise systems, or other network wide applications must have trust in employees to use the tool properly and, most importantly, to protect the valuable proprietary knowledge assets within. The proper use issue is often not a major concern as few individuals would go to the trouble of searching for knowledge they had no intent to use (and use effectively). But the protection issue is a major one, especially in light of the competitive intelligence environment we discussed earlier. To reiterate, there are competing firms out there, often employing aggressive competitive intelligence techniques, seeking to get their hands on proprietary knowledge and preknowledge. Within this threatening environment, many more individuals within a targeted firm have access to a much greater percentage of the entity's knowledge assets, through digital means, both inside and outside the core firm. Thus, if there is a security breach and knowledge assets are lost, the potential loss is much greater in terms of volume (more assets, digital transfer) and in terms of being uncovered (with a digital removal, there is no "missing" file). And, of course, with so many individuals with access to the system, the threat of successful incursion goes up. CI operations have many more potential targets because of the use of e-networks.

So the firm trusts individuals to follow proper security procedures in protecting the knowledge assets in all types of systems. From formal intellectual property to identified intellectual capital to raw data and information, the knowledge and preknowledge flowing through IT systems in these various cross-boundary systems needs to be safeguarded. Organizations obviously know this, fear leakage, and establish procedures to protect vulnerable assets (Liebeskind, 1996; Zander & Kogut, 1993). But as the form of knowledge asset gets less formal and less traditionally recognized, individual concern for the security of the knowledge often dips. Everyone knows how to protect patented knowledge. Not everyone knows how to protect tacit human capital. From the standpoint of technical security, standard procedures such as limited access, firewalls, encryption, and all the usual techniques can usually minimize hacking or other unwanted incursions. But when the knowledge (or especially preknowledge) hasn't been identified as critical or proprietary, the attention given to protection may not be as great. And, again, these newer types of knowledge assets are not necessarily recognized as proprietary or valuable, and, indeed, they may not be intellectual property or intellectual capital as we commonly define them. But they often have potential to become valuable, particularly if they fell into the wrong hands. Further, soft incursion techniques employed by CI professionals such as social engineering, pretexting, monitoring public presentations or conversations, and others, can get right around the most sophisticated technical security structures. With so much knowledge in so many hands, organizations need to have a high level of trust in those to whom it provides access. Many show too high a level of trust and pay the price by having valuable proprietary knowledge walk right out the door and into competitive hands.

Organization to Organization

In a very similar manner, organizations contributing knowledge or preknowledge to KM or enterprise systems will trust organizational partners to have proper safeguards in place to protect the assets. Firms that are very careful about protecting their own knowledge with internal controls may not recognize the need to demand the same of network partners. CI operatives know this, of course, and typically seek out the weak link in the network—the partner with the loosest security standards. Firms giving up their knowledge will trust partners to install and administer appropriate protection systems, both technical and social, and establish security levels similar to their own.

Each of these dyadic relationships; individual-organization, organization-individual, and organization-organization; have clear and present trust issues, with one entity relying on he other(s)

to peform in some manner in response to an action. The basic trust issues such as capability, benevolence, and integrity, as well as the basic social capital concepts of relationships, fields of experience, and power are all important to understanding how the relationship dynamics work out. We have discussed those issues in more depth in previous work (Erickson & Rothberg, 2008a; 2008b). In this paper, we want to address the question of whether and how the circumstances of trust regarding KM and CI might vary by circumstances. In particular, is trust in this application environment-specific?

Knowledge Assets, Industries, and Trust

We have constructed a database to measure two aspects of environmental circumstance regarding managing knowledge assets: potential for developing knowledge and threat of competitive intelligence. Any single firm may have atypical amounts of knowledge assets and/or may face a singularly aggressive competitive intelligence operation by a competitor. But arranged by industry, some of the extreme individual variations average out. As a result, we can identify industries in which the development of knowledge assets seems particularly important to success. We can also identify industries where aggressive CI activities are prevalent, with the obvious threats to the security of proprietary knowledge assets. With such information at hand, particular firms in particular industries can better evaluate how much trust they might extend to individuals and other organizations. They can also better determine how much trust they need to instil in employees in order to encourage contributions to a KM system. If industry conditions make it critical to aggressively develop knowledge assets in order to be competitive, managers will need to develop high levels of trust among individual contributors and users of the system. And if industry conditions suggest that competitors are intent on relieving a firm of its knowledge by means of CI, then managers will need to develop high levels of trust in individuals and collaborators about protecting the knowledge assets. We believe we can measure each condition.

In the first case, that of establishing the importance of knowledge development, measuring knowledge assets or intellectual capital is a core issue in the field, and a number of approaches exist (Tam, et. al., 2007). Tobin's q was one of the earliest attempts, however, and in many ways is still the most compelling because of its simplicity and robustness. It also makes a lot of sense in studies such as ours in which numerous firms must be evaluated across numerous industries without necessarily using more precise internal firm data. Tobin's q employs public data to measure intangible assets of the firm by comparing market capitalization to replacement value of physical assets. As the latter value is often hard to capture, a common variation is to simply look at stockholders' equity. This relationship can be treated as a remainder or a ratio, we have chosen the latter approach since our database includes only large firms, so an outlier ratio from a small firm with very few physical assets will not be present and will not bias the results. This ratio, which we'll refer to as the KM Ratio, reflects the amount of knowledge in the firm, relative to physical assets. Intangible assets are a common and useful proxy for intellectual capital as most intangibles have some basis in the common IC categories—brand equity has to do with relational capital from customers; new product success is driven by human capital in the R&D, engineering, and marketing areas; and so forth. More intangible assets relative to physical assets is generally indicative of success in growing intellectual capital or knowledge assets.

For an industry, the average KM Ratio will illustrate the average level of intangible assets generated by participating firms in the field. And there are widely different values between industries, indicating that KM is more or less important.

In industries with high ratios, it would appear that knowledge assets are much more important to success. Knowledge development would be a priority for firms in such an industry. Our KM Ratio database covers 1993-1996 and almost 600 firms, including the Fortune 500 and a number of other large firms active in CI (included for the reasons that follow).

In measuring competitive intelligence activity, we obtained the membership list of the Society of Competitive Intelligence Professionals (SCIP). Industries here differ by the average number of SCIP members per firm. Although the absolute numbers are relatively small, CI operations can be run by a single individual who might be the SCIP member with quite a number of non-members working under him or her. So the difference between a single member, multiple members, or no members can indicate quite substantial differences in CI activity. For this value, which we'll refer to as CI Risk, a high value will indicate considerable CI activity in the industry, posing particular security threats to member firms. A firm that is part of an industry in which most competitors have active CI programs would obviously need to be much more concerned about protecting its knowledge assets.

This paper is not a full report on the database but, rather, a presentation of some of the numbers of interest as a prelude to a deeper discussion of trust. As such, selected industry figures follow, mainly to illustrate that very different industry conditions do exist. Different levels of KM are prevalent in different industries, strongly suggesting that a more aggressive approach to KM development is necessary for success in some fields. Similarly, very different CI values are present, clearly demonstrating that the threat of CI incursion varies by industry, (Table 2). A further report on the database is available from the authors and/or available in other venues (Erickson & Rothberg, 2009).

Not surprisingly and as expected, values vary dramatically by industry. The selected industries

Table 2. Sampling of KM/CI industry scores

Industry (SIC)	KM Ratio	CI Value
208 Beverages	7.87	0.83
26 Paper & Allied Products	3.24	0.98
2834 Pharmaceutical Preparations	5.54	2.88
2835 In Vitro, In Vivo Diagnostics	7.25	0.35
371 Motor Vehicles	3.43	1.48
372 Aircraft & Parts	3.26	0.81
45 Air Transportation	1.02	0.38
4813 Telephone Services	3.95	3.23
491 Electric Services	1.39	1.25
52-9 Retail	3.33	0.13
62 Security and Commodity Brokers	8.72	0.40
7372 Prepackaged Software	5.81	0.82

are representative of the spread of values of the full data set. The value of knowledge assets can be as high as eight times the value of physical assets, illustrating industries very dependent on intellectual capital and techniques to manage it. In the full database, there are a few industries with even higher values though they are not represented by a large number of firms and so not included here. Alternatively, some industries show very low values, in and around 1.0, suggesting virtually no valuable knowledge within the firms at all. Basically, sometimes KM and its trust demands is necessary for success and sometimes it isn't. Firms need to judge their industry and the trust requirements, managing systems, individuals, and collaborators accordingly.

Similarly, CI can vary from values near 0.00 to averages above 3.00, showing almost no interest in or threat from competitive intelligence to a high degree of competitor activity. As with KM, in some cases, protection measures need to be almost draconian as knowledge is critical to success, and competitors are extremely aggressive about uncovering it. In other cases, competitive interest is very low, perhaps because the knowl-

edge is hard to transfer or it just won't help that much even if obtained. Once again, it is up to firms to evaluate conditions in their industry and manage the trust issues accordingly, both inside and outside the core firm.

What are the implications for trust? In industries with relatively high KM ratios, knowledge must be developed and shared, otherwise firms will find it hard to compete with competitors who have aggressively built their knowledge assets. Thus, knowledge and preknowledge must be taken in and it must be shared out at high rates. In such situations, including beverages, pharmaceuticals, diagnostics, and security dealers above, high degrees of trust will need to exist. Individuals must be willing to contribute their knowledge at a relatively high level, organizations must distribute knowledge to individuals at a high level, and organizations must share with each other as well. Alternatively, in industries with low KM ratios, intellectual capital does not need to be built as aggressively, and so less complete knowledge collection and sharing could occur and yet not place a firm at a huge marketplace disadvantage. Illustrated by electrical services and air transportation above, there is not as much to be gained from knowledge sharing between all the partners, so the levels of trust don't need to be as high.

In terms of CI, in industries with high CI values in the table, the threat of competitor incursions is higher. In these industries, firms must either have very high levels of trust in the individuals and organizations with whom they share or, based on low trust, they will refuse to share any more than is necessary. Employees and business partners must demonstrate the proper security systems have been installed and administered if they are to be allowed to share in the knowledge assets. As noted, this would include both technical security such as firewalls and encryption and more social measures such as training and public presentation clearances. So in cases like pharmaceuticals and telecommunications services, potential partners would need to install the technical security pieces and follow good operating procedures in guaranteeing that the technical tools are effective. When combined with a need to develop knowledge, as with pharmaceuticals once again, the firms have almost no choice but to share knowledge widely but also build the highest levels of trust in employee and partner security. Telecommunications does not have the same knowledge demands and does not need to spread knowledge as widely. As a result, its firms can probably choose not to trust some of their more questionable potential partners. In cases where the CI value is low, the industry faces little threat of CI incursions and so the need for trust with individuals and other organizations in relation to security is minimized. If knowledge development is of value, it can be conducted in an almost carefree manner. Security and commodity brokers, for example, don't appear to need a high level of trust in network partner security because there just isn't that much interest in the knowledge assets these firms hold.

CONCLUSION

Within the field of knowledge management, a certain attitude exists among most scholars that knowledge assets should be collected and then spread through ever more hands, fully leveraging their impact. There is an implicit assumption that all network partners are trustworthy, both individuals and organizations, and that fuller distribution of knowledge is always better. As suggested in this paper, that may not always be the case.

Conditions for use of knowledge vary. This paper has looked at how they vary by industry. How much knowledge is useful in an industry, how much enterprise systems can be deployed, and how much competitive intelligence activity is occurring all have implications for the manner in which knowledge should be gathered and distributed. Further, there are trust factors that vary by these situations and, in return, that influence

what standard practices can and should be. When individuals trust the organization to engage in a fair exchange for their personal knowledge assets, organizational knowledge can be more effectively developed—provided that such a move makes sense in that industry. When organizations trust individuals and other organizations to install and execute appropriate security measures, knowledge can also be more fully developed as the risk of competitive intelligence incursions drops. But the higher the CI risk in an industry, the higher that level of trust will need to be before organizations can safely share their valuable proprietary knowledge.

Future research would look more fully into the variables behind the industry KM and CI scores noted here, helping managers to determine their potential, risk, and required levels of trust in a given situation. The makeup of knowledge assets of the firm and/or industry, be they full-bore intellectual property, intellectual capital, or some of the preknowledge we discussed would probably contribute something to the discussion. So would the distinction between tacit and explicit knowledge (harder/easier to share or protect and harder/easier to trust?) and between the types of intellectual capital (human, structural, relational, competitive). Again, different proportions may have important implications for KM potential, CI risk, and requisite levels of trust. Other variables noted in the literature but not mentioned in this paper, such as complexity and teachability might hold similar potential to contribute to the discussion.

REFERENCES

American Society for Industrial Security (ASIS)/ PriceWaterhouseCoopers. (1999). *Trends in Proprietary Information Loss*. Alexandria, VA: ASIS.

Bakker, M., Leenders, R., Gabbay, S., Kratzer, J., & Engelen, J. (2006). Is trust really social capital? Knowledge sharing in product development projects. *The Learning Organization, 13*(6), 594–605. doi:10.1108/09696470610705479

Boisot, M. (1995). Is your firm a creative destroyer? Competitive learning and knowledge flows in the technological strategies of firms. *Research Policy, 24,* 489–506. doi:10.1016/S0048-7333(94)00779-9

Bontis, N. (1999). Managing organizational knowledge by diagnosing intellectual capital: Framing and advancing the state of the field. *International Journal of Technology Management, 18*(5-8), 433–462. doi:10.1504/IJTM.1999.002780

Brown, J. S., & Duguid, P. (2000). Balancing act: how to capture knowledge without killing it. *Harvard Business Review, 78,* 73–80.

Chiles, T. H., & McMackin, J. F. (1996). Integrating variable risk preferences, trust, and transaction cost economics. *Academy of Management Review, 21,* 73–99. doi:10.2307/258630

Choi, B., & Lee, H. (2003). An empirical investigation of knowledge management styles and their effect on corporate performance. *Information & Management, 40,* 403–417. doi:10.1016/S0378-7206(02)00060-5

Collins, C. J., & Smith, K. G. (2006). Knowledge exchange and combination: The role of human resource practices in the performance of high-technology firms. *Academy of Management Journal, 49*(3), 544–560.

Davenport, T. H., DeLong, D. W., & Beers, M. C. (1998). Successful knowledge management projects. *Sloan Management Review, 39,* 43–57.

Edvinsson, L., & Malone, M. S. (1997). *Intellectual Capital: Realizing Your Company's True Value by Finding its Hidden Brainpower.* New York: Harper Business.

Erickson, G. S., & Rothberg, H. N. (2008a). Knowledge Management and Trust. In T. Kautonen & H. Karjaluoto (Eds.), *Trust and New Technologies: Marketing and Management on the Internet and Mobile Media.* Cheltenham, UK: Elgar.

Erickson, G. S., & Rothberg, H. N. (2008b). Knowledge Management and Trust in E-Networks. In L. Brennan & V. Johnson (Eds.), *Computer-Mediated Relationships and Trust: Managerial and Organizational Effects.* Hershey, PA: IGI Global.

Erickson, G. S., & Rothberg, H. N. (2009). Intellectual Capital in Business-to-Business Markets. *Industrial Marketing Management, 38*(2), 159–165. doi:10.1016/j.indmarman.2008.12.001

Foos, T., Schum, G., & Rothenberg, S. (2006). Tacit knowledge transfer and the knowledge disconnect. *Journal of Knowledge Management, 10*(1), 6–18. doi:10.1108/13673270610650067

Forelle, C. (2005, July 14). IBM tool dispatches employees efficiently. *Wall Street Journal,* pp. B3.

Grant, R. M. (1996). Toward a knowledge-based theory of the firm. *Strategic Management Journal, 17*(Winter), 109–122.

Gupta, A. K., & Govindarajan, V. (2000a). Knowledge flows within multinational corporations. *Strategic Management Journal, 21,* 473–496. doi:10.1002/(SICI)1097-0266(200004)21:4<473::AID-SMJ84>3.0.CO;2-I

Gupta, A. K., & Govindarajan, V. (2000b). Knowledge management's social dimension: lessons from Nucor Steel. *Sloan Management Review, 42,* 71–80.

Hansen, M. T., & von Oetinger, B. (2001). Introducing t-shaped managers: Knowledge management's next generation. *Harvard Business Review, 79,* 107–116.

Herzog, J. O. (2007). Why is there an increasing global demand for business intelligence? *Journal of Competitive Intelligence and Management, 4*(2), 55–70.

Kaplan, R. S., & Norton, D. P. (1992). The balanced scorecard: measures that drive performance. *Harvard Business Review,* (January-February): 71–79.

Liebeskind, J. P. (1996). Knowledge, strategy, and the theory of the firm. *Strategic Management Journal, 17,* 93–107.

Lin, H.-F. (2006). Impact of organizational support on organizational intention to facilitate knowledge sharing. *Knowledge Management Research & Practice, 4,* 26–35. doi:10.1057/palgrave.kmrp.8500083

Marshall, R. S., Nguyen, T. V., & Bryant, S. E. (2005). A dynamic model of trust development and knowledge sharing in strategic alliances. *Journal of General Management, 31,* 41–57.

Matson, E., Patiath, P., & Shavers, T. (2003). Strengthening your organization's internal knowledge market. *Organizational Dynamics, 32*(3), 275–285. doi:10.1016/S0090-2616(03)00030-5

Nahapiet, J., & Ghoshal, S. (1998). Social capital, intellectual capital, and the organizational advantage. *Academy of Management Review, 23,* 242–266. doi:10.2307/259373

Nielsen, B. B. (2005). The role of knowledge embeddedness in the creation of synergies in strategic alliances. *Journal of Business Research, 58,* 1194–1204. doi:10.1016/j.jbusres.2004.05.001

Nonaka, I., & Takeuchi, H. (1995). *The Knowledge-Creating Company.* New York: Oxford University Press.

Polanyi, M. (1967). *The Tacit Dimension.* New York: Anchor Day Books.

Prusak, L., & Cohen, D. (2001). How to invest in social capital. *Harvard Business Review, 79,* 86–93.

Rothberg, H. N., & Erickson, G. S. (2002). Competitive capital: A fourth pillar of intellectual capital? In N. Bontis (Ed.), *World Congress on Intellectual Capital Readings* (pp. 94-103). Woburn, MA: Butterworth-Heinemann.

Rothberg, H. N., & Erickson, G. S. (2005). *From Knowledge to Intelligence: Creating Competitive Advantage in the Next Economy.* Woburn, MA: Elsevier Butterworth-Heinemann.

Tam, H. P., Plowman, D., & Hancock, P. (2007). Intellectual Capital and Financial Returns of Companies. *Journal of Intellectual Capital, 9*(1), 76–95.

Teece, D. (1980). Economies of scope and the scope of the enterprise. *Journal of Economic Behavior & Organization, 1,* 223–248. doi:10.1016/0167-2681(80)90002-5

Vainio, A. M. (2005). Exchange and combination of knowledge-based resources in network relationships. *European Journal of Marketing, 39*(9/10), 1078–1095. doi:10.1108/03090560510610734

Wenger, E. (1998). *Communities of Practice: Learning, Meaning, and Identify.* Cambridge, UK: Cambridge University Press.

Zack, M. A. (1999a). Developing a knowledge strategy. *California Management Review, 41*(3), 125–145.

Zack, M. A. (1999b). Managing codified knowledge. *Sloan Management Review,* (Summer): 45–58.

Zander, U., & Kogut, B. (1995). Knowledge and the speed of transfer and imitation of organizational capabilities: An empirical test. *Organization Science, 6*(1), 76–92. doi:10.1287/orsc.6.1.76

Chapter 2
Teamworking for Security:
The Collaborative Approach

Rainer Bye
Technische Universität Berlin, Germany

Ahmet Camtepe
Technische Universität Berlin, Germany

Sahin Albayrak
Technische Universität Berlin, Germany

ABSTRACT

Collaborative methods are promising tools for solving complex security tasks. In this context, the authors present the security overlay framework CIMD (Collaborative Intrusion and Malware Detection), enabling participants to state objectives and interests for joint intrusion detection and find groups for the exchange of security-related data such as monitoring or detection results accordingly; to these groups the authors refer as detection groups. First, the authors present and discuss a tree-oriented taxonomy for the representation of nodes within the collaboration model. Second, they introduce and evaluate an algorithm for the formation of detection groups. After conducting a vulnerability analysis of the system, the authors demonstrate the validity of CIMD by examining two different scenarios inspired sociology where the collaboration is advantageous compared to the non-collaborative approach. They evaluate the benefit of CIMD by simulation in a novel packet-level simulation environment called NeSSi (Network Security Simulator) and give a probabilistic analysis for the scenarios.

INTRODUCTION

Teamwork– nowadays professional life as well as private life is hardly imaginable without teamwork. Above all, complex tasks are usually managed in teams. Ideally, each participant of a team can contribute in the area of his strengths. However, teams can also be homogeneous; dependent on the task a team is to fulfill, a heterogeneous set-up might not be necessary or may even be disadvantageous due to arising conflicts.

Intrusion detection is indisputably a complex task and there is no silver bullet coping with threats arising from malicious software or attackers. According to the 2008 Symantec Internet Security Threat Report, the security landscape was characterized by an "increasing professionalization of malicious code and the existence of organizations that employ

DOI: 10.4018/978-1-60566-414-9.ch002

programmers dedicated to the production of these threats" (Turner, 2008, p.46). That indicates the situation is even becoming worse.

Computer networks are exposed to a variety of threats: Zero-day attacks leave devices connected to the Internet susceptible to attacks because there are no appropriate signatures available during the vulnerability window. On the other hand, purely anomaly-based detection schemes capable of detecting new attacks are often of limited use due to a high false-positive rate.

Due to the shortcomings of conventional intrusion detection approaches we propose **CIMD (Collaborative Intrusion & Malware Detection)**, a scheme for joint intrusion detection approaches. We argue that teams respectively groups with a common purpose for intrusion detection and prevention provide improved protection from malware. An intrusion detection overlay is realized by enabling participants to state their *objectives*, i.e. the aim of a *detection group*, and *interests*, i.e. the desired properties of the team members. CIMD is collaborative, since for a common task, groups can be dynamically created in a heterarchical manner without pre-defined roles. After the **group formation** is complete, cooperative detection approaches can be carried out, i.e. tasks are divided between group members and roles are assigned. Nevertheless, in this phase a collaborative approach can be employed as well. In the following, the term joint intrusion detection is used when a differentiation between collaboration and cooperation is not necessary. CIMD is a part of ongoing research in the context of research activities aiming to develop autonomous intrusion detection and response techniques.

This work contributes a taxonomy-based data model reflecting relevant properties of the participants of the overlay. We discuss each category in the taxonomy with regard to their value for collaborative intrusion detection. Additionally, we also provide a group formation algorithm to establish these groups. Each participating node executes this algorithm that receives input objec-

tives and associated interests defined as instances of the **property taxonomy**. Moreover, it takes maximum group sizes into account. We examine different realization strategies for the system and discuss their characteristics.

Finally, we introduce the notion of homogeneous as well as heterogeneous detection groups analogous to the introductory example of teamwork in a sociological context. We consider a distributed anomaly detection approach as a scenario for homogeneous groups and discuss device similarity as a prerequisite. In the second scenario, we apply a signature mediation scheme wherein disparate NIDS (Network Intrusion Detection Systems) collaborate to reduce the vulnerability window. This is an example for a heterogeneous detection group enabling exchange of signatures between the devices. We conduct simulations for the latter scenario in a novel network simulation environment addressing the needs of security experts: NeSSi. Nevertheless, a distributed scheme like CIMD exhibits the danger of being compromised. Hence, we discuss security aspects of the system itself, provide adversary scenarios and discuss appropriate countermeasures.

This paper is organized as follows: subsequently, we introduce related work, present CIMD and show realization strategies of the system. We conduct a **vulnerability analysis** of CIMD and outline in the following the merits of an intrusion detection overlay based on the outlined scenarios. Subsequently, we simulate the "signature mediation" scenario as an example for collaboration in heterogeneous groups. Finally, we conclude and give an outlook on future work.

BACKGROUND

The initial group formation is an integral part in constructing the collaborative intrusion detection system. We give an overview of existing work in the area of group formation in **overlay networks**, joint intrusion detection and existing (interoperable) intrusion detection message exchange formats.

Semantic Group Formation in Overlay Networks

Semantic Group formation in overlay networks is not a new topic, but needs more attention to be applicable for a collaborative scheme like CIMD. Khambatti introduced the notion of interest-based communities in peer-to-peer networks (Khambatti *et al.*, 2004) to reduce the communication overhead of search operations. These communities are based on common attributes. The author distinguishes between group attributes like a domain name and personal claimed attributes. Bloom filter data structures are used to represent these properties due to their efficiency in determining inclusion relations.

Loeser *et al.* (2004) have introduced the concept of semantic overlay clusters (SOC). They use a hierarchical peer-to-peer system based on JXTA (https://jxta.dev.java.net), where the *Super Nodes*, dedicated nodes within such a peer-to-peer system, realize the clustering using a pre-defined policy. Participating peers in this network match their own properties by an *Information Provider Model* against the policy of the Super Node. In the case of a match, the peer is added to the group administrated by the Super Peer, whereas peers can join several groups.

Sripanidkulchai *et al.* (2003) have proposed interest-based shortcuts. This is an approach introducing the notion of interest-based locality, a principle expressing that if one peer has a piece of content another peer is interested in, it is very likely that the first peer has also other pieces of content that the second peer is interested in. These shortcuts are applied in pure peer-to-peer systems such as Gnutella in addition to the neighbor entries. The purpose is to increase the performance and the scalability by providing an improved search scheme.

The paradigm of structured **peer-to-peer networks** offers new opportunities for research. In this context, the application of DHTs (**Distributed Hash Tables**) enables exact mappings from resource names to peers, enabling fast and deterministic look-up operations. In this regard, Castro *et al.* realized an application-level multicast infrastructure on top of the DHT-based Pastry (http://research.microsoft.com/antr/Pastry/) framework (Castro *et al.*, 2002) where participating nodes can register for a subject administrated within an overlay. Notifications regarding the subject are subsequently distributed to all registrants.

In summary, the related work encompasses solutions for the grouping itself as well as approaches for the semantic clustering for different types of peer-to-peer networks (structured, unstructured purely decentralized and unstructured Super Node-based). The overall CIMD framework can exploit and enhance existing solutions for the purpose of intrusion detection and response. In this regard, further comments on implementation challenges are discussed later, whereas related work in the context of joint intrusion detection is discussed in the next section.

Cooperative Intrusion Detection

The DOMINO system uses overlay architecture of *axis nodes* exchanging intrusion-related information like black lists of IP addresses (Yegneswaran *et al.*, 2004). Each axis node forms the root of a hierarchy of distributed intrusion detection systems. In a retrospective analysis of the SQL-Slammer worm, the DOMINO system would have performed well for the purpose of early detection and prevention of this threat. This evaluation is based on the DSHIELD (http://www.dshield.org) data. For authentication, Yegneswaran *et al.* deem PKI mechanisms suitable for DOMINO, because the axis node overlay does not grow linear as a function of the aggregate number of nodes in the DOMINO system. No further information is given about the used peer-to-peer architecture, and there is no cooperation scheme except the grouping of axis nodes exchanging blacklists.

Indra is a peer-to-peer system, where participants of the overlay can exchange intrusion information between each other in a decentralized manner (Janakiraman et al., 2003). Indra proposes to use the multicast mechanism presented in (Castro *et al.*, 2002) to form interest-based groups with security-related topics like failed log-in attempts. The authors neither provided a scheme, how security-related topics can be organized, nor show simulation results about the benefits of that system. In the prototypical Indra version, central key servers are used for authentication. In the authors' opinion, the Web of Trust- approach is better suited for a decentralized peer-to-peer system.

Zhang *et al.* present a conceptual architecture for IDS agents on mobile devices in the context of mobile wireless networks (Zhang *et al.*, 2003). Such an agent also contains a module for cooperative detection that is able to interact with neighboring IDS agents and a global response module. The authors describe a basic majority-based, distributed intrusion detection algorithm based on exchanged anomaly status and apply a fixed scheme to detect abnormal routing table updates. Compared to CIMD, this approach follows a fixed objective and individual properties of the devices are not taken into account.

The notion of a cooperative **AIS (Artificial Immune System)**, inspired by the biological archetype, was presented by Luther *et al.* (Luther *et al.*, 2007). Here, an AIS component computes the probability of an anomaly on each participating node. The data processed by the AIS is statistical in nature, e.g. traffic measurements, and obtained by a monitoring component. The probability of an anomaly constitutes the status of a client and the cooperation between the participants takes place by sharing status levels. The cooperative aspect is realized via a hybrid, decentralized peer-to-peer system enabling the formation of a detection group and is prior work to CIMD. As a result, the false positive rate, one of the main challenges in anomaly detection, was lowered significantly in comparison to the non-cooperative scenario.

The presented schemes for intrusion detection differ from the contributions of CIMD, as they mostly aim for specialized scenarios. Indra follows a similar direction like CIMD, as the authors consider SCRIBE groups for security related topics. But here, neither properties of the participating nodes are taken into account nor is there an evaluation showing the benefit of the approach. CIMD even makes one step beyond: it aims to offer a generic scheme to enable a collaborative approach even for distinct IDS to exchange data. For this purpose, a common data format is needed.

Common Exchange Formats

Because of the huge variety of IDS, there were several attempts to standardize exchange formats and communication frameworks to enable interaction between distinct IDS. The first effort was the **CIDF** (Common Intrusion Detection Framework) funded by DARPA with the objective to enable various research projects (initially only DARPA projects) to exchange security-related information (http://gost.isi.edu/cidf/).

The initial result was the specification of the framework itself, wherein roles of the participating entities were defined; the different roles are *Event Generator*, *Event Analyzer*, *Event Database* and *Response Unit*. Second, the CISL (*Common Intrusion Specification Language*) was introduced basing on a prefix-based, recursive notation. This language enabled the exchange of GIDOs (*Generalized Intrusion Detection Objects*) that are either generated or consumed dependent on the aforementioned roles. CIDF was validated and tested in terms of (semantic) interoperability in the years 1998 and 1999. Although CIDF did not become a standard, it resulted in the creation of the IDWG (*Intrusion Detection Working Group*). This led to the development of **IDMEF**

(*Intrusion Detection Message Exchange Format*), which became experimental RFC 4765 (Deba *et al.*, 2007).

The main intention of the IDMEF is to provide communication standard enabling different intrusion detection analyzers from different origin (commercial, open source and research systems) to report to a managing entity (*Console*) in a single administrative domain. The XML-based language comprises of two message types: first, the Heartbeat message sent periodically to state a component in the distributed system is still alive. Next, there is an Alert message sent in the case a suspicious event occurs. These events can be associated with additional information in form of XML compound classes like the scanner type, timestamps and classifications in the case of an alert, or even self-defined attributes. Beside the language itself, there exists an experimental RFC (Feinstein & Matthews, 2007) for IDXP (*Intrusion Detection Exchange Protocol*) providing asynchronous communication between sensors and analyzers based on BEEP, an application protocol framework (Rose, 2007). Choosing an appropriate BEEP profile enables mutual authentication and ensures integrity as well as confidentiality of the communication channels.

In IDS practice, there exist IDMEF implementations for sensors, e.g. Snort (http://www.snort.org/), as well as for analyzers, e.g. Prelude IDS (www.prelude-ids.com), with an IDMEF communication interface. IDMEF can be extended in two ways: on one hand, the whole data model can be changed by inheriting existent classes; on the other hand an AdditionalData class enables incorporation of primitive data types as well as complete XML documents. The AdditionalData class is only associated directly with the message class however, i.e. other classes in the IDMEF data model are not extensible in this fashion.

In contrast, the **IODEF** (*Incident Object Description Exchange Format*), also an XML-based format, provides a more comprehensive extension mechanism. It is an RFC draft standard (Danyliw

et al., 2007). The main scenario for using IODEF is the exchange of incident reports between different **CSERT** (*Computer Security Emergency Response Teams*) in different administrative domains. To fulfill this role, IODEF uses only a single type of message: the incident message. This message type must contain a global unique identifier for the sender, an assessment of the incident as well as contact information of the involved parties. Supplementary optional data, e.g. time of detection, start or end time can also be added. For the sake of interoperability, IODEF offers additional extension strategies, because the XML schema must not be changed. First, each subclass in the IODEF is associated with the AdditionalData class. Second, there is a generic mechanism to add to the enumerated values of attributes; e.g. in the contact class the attribute type contains the values "person" or "organization" but can be extended by using an ext-value to integrate a type "department". IODEF maintains compatibility to IDMEF by allowing the encapsulation of IDMEF messages and by reusing IDMEF classes, e.g. Impact class or Confidence class.

The CIDSS (*Common Intrusion Detection Signatures Standard*) defines a common, XML-based data format to share signatures (CIDSS, n.d.). In doing so it primarily aims at IDS administrators to exchange signatures and evaluate their efficiency. Second, a future scenario is considered in which there exist independent contributors enabling the provision of signatures independent of a particular product or software. Each signature message is divided into two parts: the first part contains possible data elements of a signature such as source/destination addresses, protocol types or byte patterns. Second, in the Session class a stateful signature can be defined using the aforementioned data and logical expressions. Nevertheless, stateless signatures can also be realized by skipping attributes of the Session class. This approach seems suited for the signature mediation scenario presented in the scope of heterogeneous detection

Table 1. Evaluation of exchange formats with respect to key features valuable for CIMD

	CIDF	IDMEF	IOEDF	CIDSS	TIM
Inter-domain applicability	Is discussed	Not a focus, but possible	Good	Not a focus, but possible	Not a focus, but possible
Standard	No	RFC experimental	RFC draft	Expired IETF draft	Proprietary Cisco protocol
Still in use	No	Yes	Yes	No	Yes
Extensibility with respect to Compatibility	Limited	Limited	Good	Unclear	Unclear

groups. Nevertheless, the IETF-draft has not been completed and expired in November 2006.

There exist a variety of other formats that are either proprietary or have a very specialized objective: the **CVE** (*Common Vulnerability and Exposure*) represents a dictionary to name security vulnerabilities uniquely (http://cve.mitre.org). This goal is achieved by a central database coordinated by a consortium of representatives from industry, academia and government agencies, the *CVE Editorial Board*. This widely used industry standard offers an opportunity in the case of e.g. IODEF to relate to the same vulnerability from different CSERTs. The TIDP (*Threat Information Distribution Protocol*) is a proprietary protocol from Cisco to enable static grouping among the supporting products including authentication. On top, **TIM**s (*Threat Information Messages*) are distributed to specify suspicious traffic characteristics and associate Mitigation Enforcement Actions, i.e. to block or redirect the respective traffic.

With respect to the CIMD scenario, IOEDF provides better extension than IDMEF without changing the entire XML-schema. Otherwise, a change of the schema would lead to interoperability. A second advantage is that there exists an identifier for the sender in the message itself to associate it to an organization in a cross-domain scenario. In contrast, the usage scenario of IOEDF does not fit directly to the CIMD approach. Instead, it primarily focuses on the exchange of incident information between CSERT with mandatory attributes about involved parties in terms of orga-

nizations and personnel which is not in the scope of CIMD. The CIDSS is a specialized approach focusing on the signature exchange scenario. Supplementary, CVE can be used to uniquely reference vulnerabilities from different organizations. The results of the exchange format analysis are depicted in Table 1. Next, we introduce the CIMD architecture.

THE CIMD APPROACH

CIMD offers a scheme for the formation of **detection group**s based on an overlay network. In this section, we introduce the **collaboration model** as well as the decentralized group formation algorithm.

Collaboration Model

Every node in an overlay network needs to be able to express its interest regarding collaboration partners. In the CIMD architecture, these interests are expressed using terms from property taxonomy. They are used for the specification of potential collaboration partners in the look-up phase, but also for the description of the nodes itself. The collaboration model is depicted in Figure 1.

The model is at the moment based on five main categories *OS*, *Applications*, *Network Configuration*, *Detection* and *Hardware*, but remains extensible to new categories respectively within the categories itself. The first two categories are

Figure 1. The example taxonomy utilized for collaboration

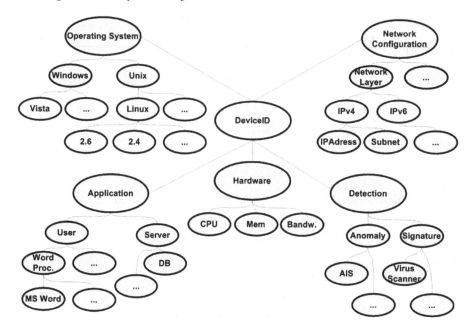

important because a lot of attacks target only a specific OS or a particular application. Additionally, they are essential for the determination of similarity between devices, a prerequisite for the formation homogeneous detection groups.

The category Operating System is modeled separately as it does not fit the User/Server subdivision of the application branch. Each of these two categories has several sub hierarchies wherein a number of applications respectively the operating system can be explicitly specified. In the example, the OS Linux is specified with the kernel version 2.4 or 2.6. Considering applications, for example the Microsoft Word program could be extended to specific versions like 2003 or 2007. The first two categories closely follow the attack taxonomy introduced by Hansman & Hunt (2005), while this structure is used to classify potential attack targets.

The third category deals with the network configuration of a device enabling the specification of the protocol stack configuration. IP address ranges or subnet masks can be set. In this manner, policy constraints by a system administration

entity can be modeled. Yegneswaran *et al.* (2004) have also shown that as "closer" (in terms of IP Address proximity) subnets are to each other, the more similar attacker blacklists become. Thus, a joint intrusion detection approach can be improved by local clustering. Additionally, mobile device characteristics such as mobile IP settings are included in this taxonomy branch.

The fourth category comprises of the available detection algorithms. The most basic distinction is between signature- and anomaly-based approaches. The model depicted in Figure 1 shows AIS (Luther *et al.*, 2007) as an example for anomaly detection or a virus scanner as an example for signature-based approach. For simplicity's sake, this branch contains a very flat hierarchy. However in the future, if advantageous, a more granular approach like the taxonomy from Axelsson (2000) could be applied here.

The fifth category is the hardware properties of a device, containing relevant attributes such as processing power or available memory. Again, the formation of homogeneous groups benefits from these attributes, depending on the used feature vectors. Additionally, bandwidth capabilities can be expressed here. This category, like the fourth, is also subject to future changes for new requirements. In the case of new scenarios the taxonomy will be adapted, e.g. active research is conducted in a collaborative scenario for Smartphone devices where an additional category reflecting the inherent mobile characteristics is put to the taxonomy. Next, we introduce an algorithm for the formation of the detection groups.

Group Formation

In this algorithm, we assume an overlay network providing search capabilities (in Algorithm 1 Search() is used). The Algorithm 1 (Figure 2) performs the grouping of the devices connected to the overlay. A device contains a property source p as described in the previous section. Additionally,

each device has several group formation objectives $r_{1..n}$ and interests $c_{1..n}$ associated with them. An objective is the purpose of the collaboration like "Blacklist IPs" or "Signature Exchange"; in contrast, interests are the desired properties of a group associated with the objectives. Each device has a notion of his groups $g_{1..n}$ related to an objective and contains a maximum size constraint $k_{1..n}$.

To increase the readability of the algorithm, we assume only one interest can be associated with an objective. A 1 to n relationship between objective and interest as well as group size is realized by verifying for each objective the corresponding interests and group sizes. An objective associated with more than one interest is necessary in the case of heterogeneous groups.

The Propagate() function in Algorithm 2 (Figure 3) enables a node A to state his search requests via the underlying overlay architecture

Figure 2. Algorithm 1--Message Handling in CIMD

```
1:    Input:
2:            p Property base of a device
3:            r_1..n Objective of group formation
4:            c_1..n Interests related to objectives r_1..n
5:            g_1..n Group related to r_1..n of a device
6:            k_1..n Maximum group size for g_1..n
7:            m Messages; contain interest m_c, objective m_r
8:            sender m_sender and a type

9:    Receive (message)
10:   switch type do
11:         case interest
12:                 foreach i = 1 to |r| do
13:                         if ( m_r==r_i and |g_i| < k_i and Matches(m_c,p)) then
14:                                 Send("hit",r_i, c_i, m_sender)
15:                         end
16:                 end
17:         end
18:         case confirm
19:                 Add m_sender to group g_x related to m_r
20:         end
21:         case hit
22:                 if Matches(m_c,p) and |g_x| related to m_rj| < k_x then
23:                         Send("confirm", |r_x|, m_sender)
24:                         Add m_sender to group g_x
25:                 end
26:         end
27:   end
```

Figure 3. Algorithm 2--Propagation method in CIMD; here, look-up for collaboration partners is triggered. The process is repeated until interests are satisfied.

```
1:      Input:
2:              r_{1..n} Objective of group formation
3:              c_{1..n} Interests related to objectives r_{1..n}

4:      Propagate()
5:              foreach i = 1 to |r| do
6:                      Search(r_i, c_i)
7:              end
```

and results in interest messages. A message can be processed by a node B if m_{sender} is compliant to an established security policy. This is already realized prior to message processing by the algorithm (c.f. "Vulnerability Analysis" for Access Control respectively security policies).

Upon receiving a message, we distinguish three cases: First, a node B may receive an interest message m of a node A containing an objective m_r and the interest m_c reflecting the desired properties. If the objective fits and the corresponding group has not reached the maximum member size, the interest m_c is matched against the own **property base**. We discuss the matching itself in the section discussing the realization strategies. In the case of a match, a hit message is sent to the requester A wherein the objective and the interest(s) of B regarding the objective are contained. When A receives this message, it is matched against its own property base and checked whether the corresponding group is still not complete. In this case, a confirm message is sent and A adds B to the appropriate group. Accordingly, after receipt of the confirmation, B also adds A to his group.

As a consequence, when each participating node in CIMD looks up its own groups, the resulting groups are non-equal sets for each node. This may be desirable in some cases, but for the sake of finding common groups, one peer in a group can take a leading role for the formation of the group. Additionally, this measure reduces communication overhead in the overlay. An illustrative example

for the group formation is given in Figure 4. The concrete implementation of CIMD is still work in progress. Hence, in the following section we give an overview, which technologies we consider promising for achieving this aim.

Realizing CIMD

The main aspects of CIMD are the taxonomy describing the device properties, the **grouping algorithm** and the matching function(s). Above all, an overlay network providing search functionality and grouping support is necessary. Additionally, we argue that a common language to communicate between the participating nodes is beneficial for applied detection schemes.

The prototype realized in NeSSi (Bye *et al.*, 2008b) is based on an extension to the hybrid decentralized peer-to-peer protocol first presented in (Luther *et al.*, 2007). This protocol is based on the *Super Node* concept; i.e. in general all nodes in the system are equal in their opportunities, but after an election process a subset of peers is chosen to perform the role of the Super Node. Furthermore, these nodes often have other beneficial properties like long uptime, high bandwidths or a public IP address.

In CIMD, the Super Nodes fulfill special tasks such as carrying out the aforementioned grouping algorithm. Additionally, sample ontologies can be realized as EMF (Eclipse Modeling Framework) data models for the description of the participants

Figure 4. Group Formation Process divided in four phases a-d. The tuple entries below each node denote, which objectives (r) and interests (c) are pursued (for the sake of simplicity here, each node shown to have only one interest and associated objective) and p represents the property base of the node, where c_x matches p_x and c_y matches p_y. Node 1 propagates his objectives via the underlying search functionality (a) and sends interest messages. In the second step (b), the nodes 2-6 receive an interest message, where in (c) 2, 3 and 4 respond with a hit message, as their objective and their property base match to the stated objective as well as the stated interest. Finally, in (d) node 1 sends a confirmation message to the nodes 2 and 3 but it does not send to 4 as the interest of c_y cannot be fulfilled by the property base p_x of node 1.

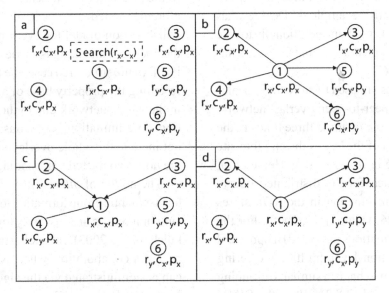

(http://www.eclipse.org/modeling/emf/). In the following, we will give two alternative realization strategies for CIMD and discuss their characteristics with respect to possible use cases.

Structured Overlay with Distributed Knowledge Base

We consider a structured overlay network as an interesting realization option for CIMD. These are peer-to-peer networks where the nodes are connected in a deterministic manner and resources can be looked-up fast, e.g. in logarithmic time. Often, these networks are implemented using a DHT-based (**Distributed Hash Table**) approach. In this context, one or more hash functions are used to arrange the participating nodes in an overlay to the co-domain of the used hash function(s), mak-

ing each node responsible for the administration of a fraction of the co-domain.

Next, a resource to be stored respectively their location is also hashed and forwarded to a node responsible for that fraction of the co-domain this value belongs to. Important representatives of this concept are CAN (Scalable Content Addressable Network), Chord and Pastry (Ratnasamy *et al.*, 2001; Stoica *et al.*, 2001; Rowstron & Druschel, 2001). The structured approach offers the advantage of fast and deterministic search, i.e. if the resource can not be looked up in the overlay, it is not available. This is an important difference to unstructured networks, where popular resources often can be looked up easily, but rare resources are difficult to find although they are available.

On top of the structured overlay, we consider peer-to-peer based RDF (Resource Description

Framework) stores (http://www.w3.org/RDF/). The RDF is a formal language to provide metadata in the context of *Semantic Web* and is based on statements about resources. Such statements are comprised of a subject, predicate and an object and are noted as triples, e.g. in the case of: *"the car has the color pink"*, *the car* is the subject, *has the color* the predicate and *pink* the object. In this way, the CIMD data model can also be mapped to RDF: an illustrative example is "Device x has Operating System Linux" and additionally to take also the kernel version into account "Device x has Kernel Version 2.6".

The RDF stores are used to store these triples in a DHT-based peer-to-peer overlay network. Therefore, each triple is stored three times in the hash table for each of the keys subject, predicate and object. Battré *et al.* as well as Heine *et al.* present an approach for the distributed querying of semantic information in the RDF stores (Battré *et al.*, 2006; Heine *et al.*, 2005). For the sake of group formation, the SCRIBE protocol offers an application-level multicast offering publish-subscribe mechanism similar to grouping concepts (Castro *et al.*, 2002). When the CIMD data model is stored in RDF triples and is put to a DHT, even uncommon objectives and interests can be satisfied.

Unstructured Overlay with Local Knowledge Base

In contrast, links in unstructured overlay networks are established arbitrarily. Here, different overlay networks exist which can be classified as *purely decentralized, partially centralized, and hybrid-decentralized* (Androutsellis-Theotokis & Spinellis, 2004). As mentioned in the main section *"Realizing CIMD"*, a hybrid-decentralized approach is realized in the NeSSi. Here, we will discuss the system to be based on a purely decentralized scheme: *Gnutella*. We consider the first available version 0.4 of the system (http://

rfc-gnutella.sourceforge.net/developer/stable/index.html).

In Gnutella, participating nodes are randomly connected to each other. In the case of a search, *Query* messages are flooded to all neighbors. This flooding is limited by application-level hop count (this is **not** TTL of Internet Protocol). When a node can match a query, it sends a *QueryHit* message to the originator of the search. In contrast to the aforementioned approach, the instance of the collaboration model for every node is stored on the node, i.e. matching is carried out via the node itself. In the structured case, the RDF triples- representing the property base of a node- are stored in the whole network due to the used hash function. One limitation is obvious: the search does not include the whole overlay network, but only the nodes contacted via flooding.

The notion of *interest-based shortcuts* facilitates semantic group formation to bring nodes with similar interests in the overlay together (Sripanidkulchai *et al.*, 2003), enhancing the look-up of new peers for collaboration, whereas the groups itself can be administrated via the algorithm presented in "Group Formation".

As an example matching technique, we adapt the approach proposed by Bauckhage *et al.* (2007) to CIMD. This work presents a fast algorithm for expert peering in web communities and constructs a large taxonomy reflecting different domains and their sub domains based on the inherent structure of the *Open Directory Project* (http://www.dmoz.org/). The whole taxonomy is converted into a large binary vector in DFS-tree representation. Then, each expert in the system can be identified by an instance of such a vector relating to his areas of expertise.

In the next step, users can formulate requests which a domain expert can answer. Those requests are also transformed to a binary vector representation and the scalar product of experts and requests is calculated as a measure of similarity. Additionally, weights for the entries in the taxonomy can be defined, e.g. as closer the leaves in the taxonomy tree are to the root node, the higher the associated weights. The CIMD approach can be directly transferred to such a system. The collaboration model can be encoded from top to bottom and left to right. Example: a peer has the *interest* to form a homogeneous detection group. The characterizing properties are encoded by the peer and submitted as a *Query* via the underlying overlay. Each peer contacted, in case it has the same *objective*, calculates the scalar product of his property base against the *interest* and if a threshold is crossed, the peer responds with a *QueryHit*.

On the one hand, the approach has the disadvantage that the underlying data model is hardly extensible. It is not sensible to match instances of different versions of collaboration models against each other. Furthermore, values can only be encoded with difficulties because the vectors are encoded in binary format. One approach is to convert a string to the binary representation, but then maximum length must be fixed. On the other hand, this approach is very fast due to using scalar product and also scales well.

Summary

We presented two realization alternatives for CIMD and briefly presented their advantages and shortcomings. In comparison, the extensibility of the first approach is much better than the second one, but it is not possible to look up directly similar devices. Here, the unstructured scheme enables a measure of similarity. This is a good fit to the homogeneous detection group scenario. In contrast, if exactly searched, every (rare) property can be found in the structured overlay network scenario. Additionally, the communication expenses for the first scenario should be less than in the unstructured scheme. However, if queries become too complex, e.g. joint queries of RDF-triples, communication overhead increases. The unstructured scenario has the advantage to be very robust against failures. In conclusion, we consider the structured scenario a good choice for fixed,

large networks, as the approach is scalable and has logarithmic look-up time. In contrast, the unstructured approach is well-suited for mobile nodes or ad-hoc networks. The overlay is robust and the matching not computationally expensive. Here, the property scheme needs to be fixed, but often mobiles have similar configurations compared to a desktop PC, e.g. similar hardware, similar set of applications etc.

Independent of the used approach, two more topics need to be mentioned: First, as the common exchange format, we consider IODEF the best solution due to is inherent, already presented characteristics. Furthermore, additional exchange formats like CIDSS or IDMEF can be incorporated for additional data. Second, we regard Trust Management an important topic in CIMD. Here, we refer to Donovan & Gil (2007). We foresee a static approach comprised of a priori trusted or non-trusted parties is not applicable for CIMD. Such a pre-trusted host may be compromised and attack the system. There must also be a dynamic component, based on feedback as presented by Kamvar *et al.* (2003). Regardless of the wide variety of implementation options, the choice for CIMD highly depends on the value of the system for the purpose of intrusion detection.

VULNERABILITY ANALYSIS

Above all, the application of an omnipresent overlay dedicated to intrusion detection and prevention enforces concerns about the security of the system itself. Important security topics when considering overlay structures respectively peer-to-peer networks are *Availability*, *Access Control*, *Anonymity* and the *Authenticity* of stored "documents", i.e. in this case the device defining properties. In the following, we will briefly discuss each topic, demonstrate two **adversary scenarios** and offer possible countermeasures.

First, access control is an important topic as CIMD provides knowledge about contained nodes and also enables peers to participate in a (possible) variety of intrusion detection measures. Here, a central login server respectively some central login servers like e.g. in the proprietary Skype (www. skype.com) system can be used. In the simulated scenario, the NSP can provide the login functionality for his private or business customers.

Second, preserving the authenticity of stored documents is not as challenging as in peer-to-peer file sharing networks where it is difficult to determine whether a document *A* existed before a document *B* and to decide which is "original". Here, the creator respectively originator of the device description is well-known: the device itself. In this regard, whether the properties are stored locally on the device or not –but e.g. in a DHT– it is sufficient to sign the properties by the device itself. In the case of a look up, the authenticity of those properties can be verified by comparison of the device public key.

Availability is highly affected by DDoS attacks or exploitation of protocol flaws. *Fiat et al.* presented a censor resistant peer-to-peer network that sustains the breakdown of up to 50% of the participating nodes (Fiat & Saia, 2002). Generally, availability depends on the underlying peer-to-peer overlay and as there are different implementation strategies for CIMD, we abstract from it here. We now consider two sample adversary scenarios:

In the first scenario, we assume a malicious peer managed to access the CIMD overlay and searches for devices exposing vulnerabilities. Due to the fact that vulnerabilities of e.g. a frequently used software or firmware are publicly known, an attacker may look up exploitable device configurations.

After entering the system, the attacker needs to obtain permission to read such information. Hence, data has to be associated with an authorization level. Thus, the formation algorithm can be extended to include security policies. Based on the implementation, the properties can directly be extended by a privacy value. Then, the sender needs to provide the necessary authorization level to read the classified information.

In the second scenario, we regard in special the signature exchange scheme as an application of CIMD. Here, the generator devices distribute signatures resulting in a DoS attack. For instance, in the case of a signature, the string "HTTP/1.1 200 OK" would result in blocking web server responses.

There exist two reasons for this scenario: (I) the used detection scheme in a device may result in a false positive, leading to the creation of an invalid signature. This is a general problem that especially affects anomaly-based detection schemes. Prior work from Luther *et al.* confronted this problem by enabling a cooperative anomaly status exchange affecting all participating detection units (Luther *et al.*, 2007). This scheme enabled a significant reduction of false positives. (II) The second reason for the distribution of wrong signatures is that such a device is compromised by an attacker with the clear intension to commit a DoS attack against the system. In both occasions, not relying on one, but at least *m* devices reporting a pattern is an option. Alternatively, (human) supervisors can be in charge of verifying signatures transmitted by the pattern generating machines and are the only entities "regular" devices accept signatures from.

SCENARIOS

A global detection overlay system like CIMD enables a variety of scenarios improving state of the art approaches as well as allowing the development of new detection schemes. As a result, we present here two sample scenarios: the first scenario considers **homogeneous detection groups** enabling joint anomaly detection, while the second examines a heterogeneous group of NIDS exchanging signatures.

Homogeneous Detection Group

We already introduced ongoing research in **cooperative AIS** in the context of collaborative intrusion detection. The AIS is, like the Biological Immune System, based on the distinction between self and non-self (Forrest el al., 1994). Initially, an n-dimensional feature space is covered by detectors (i.e., n-dimensional vectors of features: CPU utilization, memory usage, number of TCP connections...). In a training phase, these detectors are compared to feature vectors describing the self. In the case of a match the detectors are eliminated, while the remaining detectors are considered mature. They describe the non-self and are used for the detection of anomalies.

There are two challenges arising when dealing with anomaly detection schemes in general respectively with AIS in particular: on the one hand, anomaly detection often suffers from high false positive rates. Hence, we applied in (Luther *et al.*, 2007) a **cooperative intrusion detection** approach to lower the false positive rate. On the other hand, anomaly detection can become computationally expensive, depending on the number of deployed detectors. Essentially, in the training phase, computational costs depend on the covered feature space and the aimed density of detectors. In the **detection phase**, costs directly depend on the number of detectors to compare a feature vector with. Accordingly, a solution to lower computational costs is to partition the overall feature space and distribute different portions to several AIS nodes. In this way, each participating node is receiving a portion of the feature space and conducts the training generating distinct detectors describing the non-self. It is apparent that just preserving a fitting detector to an anomaly on one node comes with the danger of missing attacks. Accordingly, this results in a trade-off between desired redundancy on the one hand and performance constraints on the other. With combinatorial methods, a specified level of redundancy can be carried out deterministically in a decentralized manner. An illustrative example for Cooperative Detector Exchange is given in Figure 5. For further details we refer to (Bye *et al.*, 2008a).

The general assumption for such scenarios is that participating nodes have a common understanding of "normality". The nodes must, depending on the measured feature vector, be similar, i.e. have a common behavior, similar hardware etc. Otherwise an exchanged detector build by one AIS node is not suitable for another AIS node. For example, in the case of measuring network statistics as input for the AIS, a web server would most probably offer a different behavior than an "ordinary" client computer. To prevent such behavior, CIMD allows the formation of homogeneous groups by the specification of a similar node configuration, e.g. using the

Figure 5. In the first step, we divide the common feature space among the similar devices and each device trains, based on this portion of feature space, detectors for abnormal states. Afterwards, combinatorial design techniques are used for detector exchange to guarantee a defined level of redundancy (here: every detector exists two times).

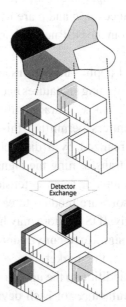

same operating system, having similar hardware resources or even fulfilling a server application role like SMTP or HTTP.

Heterogeneous Detection Group

Here we show how CIMD approach enables co-operation between different intrusion detection systems. As an example, consider three different IDS manufacturers A, B, C selling NIDS appliances. These systems are capable of detecting known malware by stored signatures provided centrally by their corresponding manufacturers. Accordingly, exclusively detecting known threats leaves the customer vulnerable to zero-day attacks and other unknown threats. As a result, the vulnerability window needs to be minimized. The companies A, B and C provide updates about new attacks independently of each other. Each individual appliance d_{ij} (i ϵ {a,b,c} and j ϵ {1..n}) connects in a fixed update interval (e.g. every hour) to its manufacturer checking whether new signatures are available.

Furthermore, we consider a large network service provider T connecting a set E of companies respectively business customers to the Internet, whereby each customer uses one of the afore-mentioned IDS appliances. In the first scenario (I), the appliances a, b and c are used to protect each customer in the NSP network independently of each other.

Secondly, T applies **mediator**s in the network capable of converting signatures between distinct formats, e.g. T has a contract with the different IDS manufacturers permitting this conversion. This can be realized by a distinct device that is capable of transforming the signatures to the according formats or as an extension hardware respectively software module to each appliance itself. Similarly, IDS vendors may have bilateral contracts for **signature conversion** to improve their position on the market.

Hence, in addition to the update of signatures from the manufacturer of each device type, the mediator devices are checked. This cooperation is initiated and realized via the CIMD detection overlay. The group objective is the mediation of signatures and the desired properties incorporate the different appliances. Hence, in scenario (II) the mediators are used to supply contracted devices with new signatures.

Last, in scenario (III) the NSP applies devices are capable of generating signatures based on suspicious traffic patterns. Hence, a device can also update the mediator and in this way deliver the self-generated signature to the other devices. Arising challenges regarding the specificity of the detection scheme respectively exploitation scenarios for this mechanism are discussed in Section "Vulnerability Analysis". Concerning CIMD, this is an extension to scenario (II) incorporating the signature-generators in the groups. The introduced variables are further used in the simulation part. There, we evaluate the benefit of CIMD for the scenario specified here.

SIMULATION

After motivating the application of CIMD, we define the **simulation** setup for the **heterogeneous detection group** scenario. At first, a novel network simulation environment tailored to security-related scenarios is presented: **NeSSi**.

NeSSi

The NeSSi is an agent-based network simulation environment built upon the JIAC (Java Intelligent Agent Componentware) framework (Fricke *et al.*, 2001). It is designed as a discrete, event-based, packet-level simulation tool where each device contains a network layer enabling IPv4 or IPv6 packet transmission. Above the network layer, end devices additionally contain transport layer functionality offering TCP and UDP as well as an application layer providing SMTP, HTTP and

IRC. The discrete time units in NeSSi are denoted as "ticks".

Foremost, NeSSi provides an API for the deployment and evaluation of detection units. These detection units can be well-known security solutions as standard virus scanners or new tools developed in scientific research projects. In NeSSi, both can be incorporated as long as they are adapted to a specified interface, and their performance can be compared for different traffic scenarios.

Furthermore, when a security framework composed of several detection units is to be evaluated, profiles can be used in NeSSi to simulate attacker behavior and attack patterns as well as user (email, HTTP) or system-inherent behavior. Thus, the profiles express characteristic traffic behavior that can be customized via port ranges, mean interval lengths and other distribution function dependent parameters. The cooperative AIS presented in (Luther *et al.*, 2007) was evaluated in the NeSSi environment. For further details about NeSSi we refer to (Bye *et al.*, 2008b).

Simulation Set-Up

Here, we define the simulation setup for the aforementioned scenario "Heterogeneous Detection Group". We consider the network of T providing Internet access to a set E of customers. Each customer network e_j is protected by a device d_{ij} ($i \in \{a,b,c\}$ and $j \in \{1..n\}$) monitoring all traffic on the gateway connected to T.

The simulated network topology is inspired by characteristics of **X-Win**, the backbone of Germany's National Research and Education Network (www.dfn.de); but it is not an exact replica. Originally, this backbone connects more than fifty research institutes all over Germany, whereby in this scenario a smaller set of 29 locations is used. The core network is depicted in Figure 6.

In addition, each e_j is modeled as an access network in NeSSi. In this regard, a core location is connected to an average of two customers

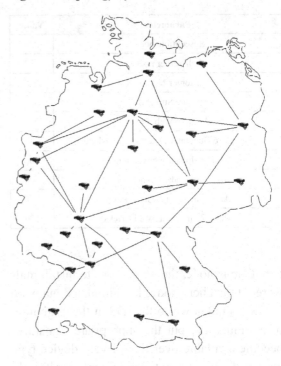

Figure 6. Topology of the simulated network

resulting in 58 access networks and therefore 58 used scanners. The different types of scanners a, b and c are equally distributed among the customers. Each customer is represented by an average of 12.5 clients and 5.5 servers, i.e. there are in total 726 susceptible clients and 322 web servers. The constant simulation settings are given in Table 2.

The attack vector is based on **drive-by downloads**, i.e. exploiting vulnerabilities in a user's client software like a web browser to install malicious code. According to the active Symantec Internet Security Threat Report (Turner, 2008) this attack pattern gained a considerable significance. Hence, we use the drive-by download for the infection of clients in this scenario.

The simulation variable p denotes the portion of malicious web servers. In this regard, the susceptible nodes randomly select an existing server IP address when initiating a request. Due to the random selection, a client might choose also a server from his "home" network. In the case of

Table 2. Simulation parameters

Parameter	Value
Susceptible nodes	726
Web Server nodes	322
Customer Networks	58
Average Susceptiple	12.5
Average Web Server	5.5
Signature Generator Detection Threshold	4
Scanner Update Interval in ticks	100
Minimum Update Time in ticks	600
Maximum Update Time in ticks	2000
Mean Request Interval in Ticks	100

a malicious node, the server tries to install malware on the client node. The simulated malware is always unknown to the IDS at the beginning of a simulation, but the appropriate signatures become available over time. Every device type has a different update time randomly (uniformly distributed) selected out of the interval between a fixed *Minimum Update Time* and *Maximum Update Time*. Hence, every device d_{ij} tries to update its threat database in a fixed *Scanner Update Interval* from a central server, administrated e.g. by T or the manufacturer.

Accordingly, if the scanner d_{ij} protecting e_j already possesses the signature for the attack, it prevents the infection of the client node; in case the malicious server is inside of the network e_j or the attack is still unknown, the node becomes infected. Additionally, if the cooperation is enabled, a detection device requests updates from the group members at the same time. We apply a grouping strategy building heterogeneous groups comprised of three members from different customer networks incorporating the disparate device types *a*, *b* and *c*. In addition, the generators monitor the network traffic and are capable of generating a signature for a new attack. In this regard, we model this functionality in NeSSi that a signature can be generated after observing it for a number of times denoted by *Signature Generator Detection*

Threshold. This functionality can be attached to a device, whereby from each group randomly one device is chosen.

Finally, this results in three different simulation options: first, there is the non-cooperative scenario (I) without using **signature generators**. Second, we apply cooperation but no generators (II); in the last scenario we apply in addition to the cooperative aspect signature generators (III). The scenarios were simulated with four different web server infection probabilities p = 0.005, 0.01, 0.025 and 0.05, where each scenario-infection probability combination was run 40 times, i.e. a total of 480 simulation runs. Each run ends after the expiration of the *Maximum Update* Time plus two times the *Scanner Update Interval* because then every scanner must have had received a signature update.

Results

The results are depicted in two different types of charts:

We show the total number of infections over time in detail for the infection probabilities 0.005 and 0.05 in Figure 7 and Figure 8 accordingly. The time units here are intervals of 100 ticks. It can be observed that both strategies exhibit similar infection behavior until approximately interval 7, after which both series diverge.

Furthermore, it can be seen that the signature generator approach "benefits" from a higher number of infected web servers, as the Signature Generator Detection Threshold is a constant value and a higher number of infected Web Servers results in a faster generation of a signature. Hence, in the case when ten times more web servers are infected, a signature is available earlier.

Figure 9 provides an overview of the simulation results, showing the total number of infections for all scenario-infection probability combinations neglecting the Minimum Update Time.

We do not count infections within the Minimum Update Time in this chart because the behavior in

Figure 7. Cumulated infections over time; 0.5% Web Servers infected

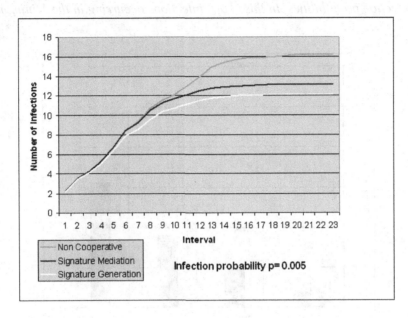

Figure 8. Cumulated infections over time; 5% Web Servers infected

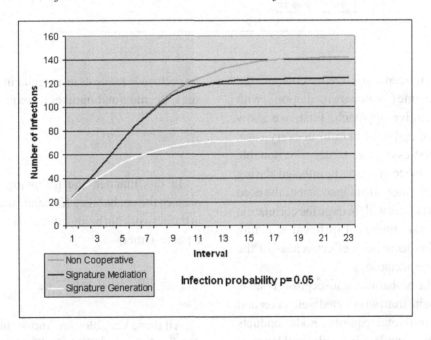

the beginning is always the same for *Non Cooperative* as well as *Signature Mediation* scenario. The average benefit in terms of fewer infections compared to the first scenario is 32 percent.

Analysis

The simulation results show the merits of the collaborative approach. In the following, we give a formal analysis for the Heterogeneous

Figure 9. Total number of infections for signature mediation and non-cooperative approach with respect to the different infection probabilities. In this chart, infections occurring in the Minimum Update Time are neglected.

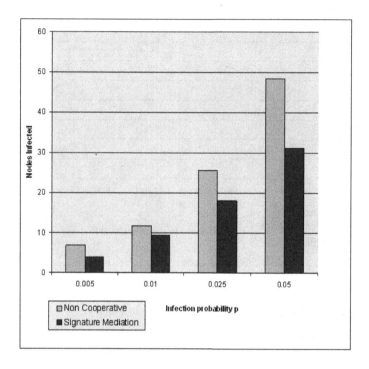

Detection Group scenario. Here we compare the cooperative scheme ("signature mediation") with the non-cooperative approach. First, we show that a signature update is helpful in every case, i.e. in the worst-case there exists a reasonable probability a device remains uninfected during the vulnerability interval independent of the used approach. Second, we will focus on the correlation between the total number of different scanning devices and the decreasing effectiveness of the non-cooperative scenario.

Let p_{inf} be the probability a susceptible node v_x requests a web site from an infected web server and n be the number of total requests a node conducts before a signature update is available. Hence, a node remains uninfected with the probability $p(v_x = not\_inf) = (1 - p_{inf})^n$.

In the worst-case scenario, signature updates are available at the Maximum Update Time T_{MUT}.

As each node requests in a regular interval T_{MI} web sites, the maximal number of requests is:

$$n_{max} = T_{MUT}/T_{MI}$$

In this manner, the following equation expresses the probability for each susceptible node in the network not being infected till the Maximum Update Time:

$$p(v_x = not\_inf) = (1 - p_{inf})^{T_{MUT}/T_{MI}}$$

All these variables are known in the scope of the simulation (cf. Table 2). Thus, the worst-case probability $p(v_x = not\_inf)$ ranges from 0.90 (0.5 percent infected web servers) to 0.36 (5 percent infected web servers).

This result show, that even in the most unlikely case signatures are available at the Maximum

Update Time and five percent of the web servers are infected, at least an average of one third of the susceptible nodes remains uninfected.

Second, we want to show the impact of the signature mediation scheme. In the simulation, we equally distribute the three different IDS appliances over the network, whereas each network is protected by exactly one device. Except for the case when the requested web server is inside the same network as the requesting client, the response passes two IDS. In the following, we assume to have n distinct appliances. In each network the probability a specific device is installed on a path is $(1/n)$. Thus, the probability an IDS is not installed on one gateway is $(1-1/n)$ and the probability it is not installed on a path between two different networks $(1-1/n)^2$ In this way, we receive the following equation denoting the probability a specific device type exists on a path between client and server: $p(d_{x\_exists}) = 1 - (1 -1/n)^2$.

In the case of the simulated scenario $p(d_{x\_exists})$ equals 0.56, whereas in the mediated one all appliances receive signatures. Considering the equation it is obvious, that the advantage of mediation compared to the non-cooperative scenario becomes bigger with the increasing number of distinct device types. In this way, it is clear that in the cooperative approach infections can be prevented faster than in the non-cooperative scenario. This correlates with the emerging trend simulation already provided. We neglect the case where a client sends a request to a server inside the same network as these just results in a constant factor (*1/CustomerNetworks*) for both schemes.

CONCLUSION AND FUTURE WORK

We presented CIMD, a collaborative scheme for realizing distributed intrusion detection approaches. Foremost, we presented a taxonomy reflecting security-related device properties as well as an algorithm enabling participating nodes to form groups based on their aims, objectives and associated interests. After providing different realization strategies for CIMD, we also introduced the notion of detection groups and presented example scenarios where heterogeneous as well as homogeneous "teams" are beneficial. Additionally, the security of the system itself was discussed. Furthermore, we simulated a cooperative signature mediation scheme in NeSSi, a novel simulation environment suited especially to evaluate security-related scenarios. The mediation scheme showed a better performance than the non-cooperative approach, although the third scenario, applying both signature generators and mediation, outperforms the others. Subsequently we gave a formal analysis for the scenario where we showed that the value of cooperation grows with the increasing number of distinct, collaborating devices.

The results indicate that collaborative security schemes and the CIMD approach are promising. In this regard, the next step will be an in-depth comparison of ontology matching techniques for the matching function used in the grouping algorithm. We believe CIMD should support not only one but a variety of techniques. Nodes in CIMD may be interested on the one hand in concrete parameter values, but on the other hand, more abstract notions of similarity can be beneficial for e.g. the homogeneous detection group scenario.

Regarding the implementation, a standardized interface description will enable different implementations of CIMD respectively components of it. Further, the automated gathering of the device defining properties is also an important task, as this can be, if done by hand, a time-consuming activity. Finally, we plan to carry out a more detailed vulnerability analysis.

REFERENCES

Androutsellis-Theotokis, S., & Spinellis, D. (2004). A survey of peer-to-peer content distribution technologies. *ACM Computing Surveys, 36*(4), 335–371. doi:10.1145/1041680.1041681

Axelsson, S. (2000). *Intrusion detection systems: A survey and taxonomy* (Tech. Rep. 99-15). Sweden. Guteborg, Chalmers University of Technology, Department of Computer Engineering.

Battré, D., Heine, F., & Kao, O. (2006). *Top rdf query evaluation in structured p2p networks.* Paper presented at 12th International Euro-Par Conference, Dresden, Germany.

Bauckhage, C., Alpcan, T., Agarwal, S., Metze, F., Wetzker, R., Ilic, M., & Albayrak, S. (2007). *An intelligent knowledge sharing system for web communities.* Paper presented at the IEEE International Conference on Systems, Man and Cybernetics, Montreal, Canada.

Bye, R., Luther, K., Camtepe, S. A., Alpcan, T., Albayrak, S., & Yener, B. (2008a). *Decentralized Detector Generation in Cooperative Intrusion Detection Systems.* Paper presented at 9th International Symposium on Stabilization, Safety, and Security of Distributed Systems, Paris, France.

Bye, R., Schmidt, S., Luther, K., & Albayrak, S. (2008b). *Application-level simulation for network security.* Paper presented at First International Conference on Simulation Tools and Techniques for Communications, Networks and Systems, Marseille, France.

Castro, M., Druschel, P., Kermarrec, A. M., & Rowstron, A. I. T. (2002). Scribe: a large-scale and decentralized application-level multicast infrastructure. *IEEE Journal on Selected Areas in Communications, 20*, 1489–1499. doi:10.1109/JSAC.2002.803069

CIDSS. (n.d.). *Common Intrusion Detection Signatures Standard (CIDSS).* Retrieved August 26, 2008, from http://xml.coverpages.org/appSecurity.html#cidss

Danyliw, R., Meijer, J., & Demchenko, Y. (2007). *The Incident Object Description Exchange Format* [RFC 5070]. Retrieved August 26, 2008, from http://rfc.net/rfc5070.html

Deba, H., Curry, D., & Feinstein, B. (2007). *The Intrusion Detection Message Exchange Format (IDMEF)* [RFC 4765]. Retrieved August 26, 2008, from http://rfc.net/rfc4765.html

Donovan, A., & Gil, Y. (2007). A survey of trust in computer science and the Semantic Web. *Journal of Web Semantics: Science . Services and Agents on the World Wide Web, 5*, 58–71. doi:10.1016/j.websem.2007.03.002

Feinstein, B., & Matthews, B. (2007). *The Intrusion Detection Exchange Protocol (IDXP)* [RFC 4767]. Retrieved August 26, 2008, from http://rfc.net/rfc4767.html

Fiat, A., & Saia, J. (2002). *Censorship resistant peer-to-peer content addressable networks.* Paper presented at Thirteenth Annual ACM-SIAM Symposium on Discrete Algorithms, San Francisco, USA.

Forrest, S., Perelson, A. S., Allen, L., & Cherukuri, R. (1994). *Self-nonself Discrimination in a Computer.* Paper presented at 1994 IEEE Symposium on Research in Security and Privacy, Los Alamos, USA.

Fricke, S., Bsufka, K., Keiser, J., Schmidt, T., Sesseler, R., & Albayrak, S. (2001). Agent-based telematic services and telecom applications. *Communications of the ACM, 44*, 43–48. doi:10.1145/367211.367251

Hansman, S., & Hunt, R. (2005). A taxonomy of network and computer attacks. *Computers & Security, 24*, 31–43. doi:10.1016/j.cose.2004.06.011

Heine, F., Hovestadt, M., & Kao, O. (2005). *Processing complex rdf queries over p2p networks.* Paper presented at the 2005 ACM workshop on Information retrieval in peer-to-peer networks, New York, USA.

Janakiraman, R., Waldvogel, M., & Zhang, Q. (2003). *Indra: A peer-to-peer approach to network intrusion detection and prevention.* Paper presented at the Twelfth International Workshop on Enabling Technologies, Washington, DC, USA.

Kamvar, S. D., Schlosser, M. T., & Garcia-Molina, H. (2003). *The eigentrust algorithm for reputation management in p2p networks.* Paper presented at 12th international conference on World Wide Web. New York, USA.

Khambatti, M., Ryu, K., & Dasgupta, P. (2004). Structuring Peer-to-Peer Networks Using Interest-Based Communities. In *Databases, information systems, and peer-to-peer computing* (LNCS 2944, pp. 48-63). Berlin, Germany: Springer.

Loeser, A., Naumann, F., Siberski, W., Nejdl, W., & Thaden, U. (2004). *Semantic overlay clusters within super-peer networks.* Paper presented at International Workshop On Databases, Information Systems and Peer-to-Peer Computing, New York City, USA.

Luther, K., Bye, R., Alpcan, T., Albayrak, S., & Müller, A. (2007*). A Cooperative AIS Framework for Intrusion Detection.* Paper presented at IEEE International Conference on Communications, Glasgow, Scotland.

Ratnasamy, S., Francis, P., Handley, M., Karp, R., & Schenker, S. (2001). *A scalable content-addressable network.* Paper presented at 2001 SIGCOMM conference on Applications, Technologies, Architectures and Protocols for computer communications, San Diego, USA.

Rose, M. (2007). *The Blocks Extensible Exchange Protocol Core* [RFC 3080]. Retrieved August 26, 2008, from http://rfc.net/rfc3080.html

Rowstron, A. I. T., & Druschel, P. (2001). *Pastry: Scalable, decentralized object location and routing for large-scale peer-to-peer systems.* Paper presented at IFIP/ACM International Conference on Distributed Systems Platforms (Middleware), Heidelberg, Germany.

Sripanidkulchai, K., Maggs, B. M., & Zhang, H. (2003). *Efficient content location using interest-based locality in peer-to-peer systems.* Paper presented at the 22nd Annual Joint Conference of the IEEE Computer and Communications Societies, San Francisco, USA.

Stoica, I., Morris, R., Karger, D., Kaashoek, M. F., & Balakrishnan, H. (2001). *Chord: A scalable peer-to-peer lookup service for internet applications.* Paper presented at 2001 SIGCOMM conference on Applications, Technologies, Architectures and Protocols for computer communications, San Diego, USA.

Turner, D. (2008). *Symantec Internet Security Threat Report* (Tech.l Rep. Vol. XIII). Symantec Corporation.

Yegneswaran, V., Barford, P., & Jha, S. (2004). *Global intrusion detection in the DOMINO overlay system.* Paper presented at Network and Distributed System Security Symposium (NDSS), San Diego, USA.

Zhang, Y., Lee, W., & Huang, Y.-A. (2003). Intrusion detection techniques for mobile wireless networks. *Wireless Networks, 9,* 545–556. doi:10.1023/A:1024600519144

Chapter 3

Tensions in Collaborative Cyber Security and how They Affect Incident Detection and Response

Glenn Fink
Pacific Northwest National Laboratory, USA

David McKinnon
Pacific Northwest National Laboratory, USA

Samuel Clements
Pacific Northwest National Laboratory, USA

Deborah Frincke
Pacific Northwest National Laboratory, USA

ABSTRACT

Security often requires collaboration, but when multiple stakeholders are involved, it is typical for their priorities to differ or even conflict with one another. In today's increasingly networked world, cyber security collaborations may span organizations and countries. In this chapter, the authors address collaboration tensions, their effects on incident detection and response, and how these tensions may potentially be resolved. The authors present three case studies of collaborative cyber security within the U.S. government and discuss technical, social, and regulatory challenges to collaborative cyber security. They suggest possible solutions and present lessons learned from conflicts. Finally, the authors compare collaborative solutions from other domains and apply them to cyber security collaboration. Although they concentrate their analysis on collaborations whose purpose is to achieve cyber security, the authors believe this work applies readily to security tensions found in collaborations of a general nature as well.

DOI: 10.4018/978-1-60566-414-9.ch003

BACKGROUND

Until recently, especially in government, "need to know" dominated the approach to data sharing and discouraged collaborative efforts. Such a system implicitly presumes that the danger of inadvertent disclosure outweighs the benefits of sharing. Since September 11, 2001, the U.S. government has been painfully learning that "need to know" prevents useful collaboration and makes organizations unnecessarily vulnerable (9-11 Commission, 2004).

But in the modern "need to share" or even "need to collaborate" environment, top-down approaches to incident detection and response are unlikely to be successful. It is necessary to consider other practical approaches that can support protection of shared assets within a collaboration. In this chapter, we discuss exemplar goals of collaboration stakeholders (both within an organization and among multiple cooperating organizations), how conflicts arise among protection goals, how these tensions affect the efficacy of the cooperating parties, and ways that these conflicts may be resolved. We will draw upon examples from the experience of several Department of Energy (DOE) laboratories and their successes and challenges in cooperative cyber security.

The DOE provides a particularly rich environment for discussion of collaboration, because DOE missions often require international scientific collaboration. In contrast to "need to know" environments, DOE scientists must collaborate closely, often sharing unique scientific resources across international boundaries. Even the newer "need to share" approach of transferring information among stakeholders is not sufficient for scientific collaboration: joint development of a shared understanding or new knowledge is not the same as sequential or even parallel knowledge discovery or analysis. Further complicating matters, the DOE contains both some of the most sensitive and most open computing resources in the world.

THE HISTORY AND PROBLEMS OF COLLABORATIVE CYBER SECURITY

On November 2, 1988, a 99-line program changed the world. That program, written by Cornell graduate student Robert Morris, stalled mail servers across the nascent Internet and motivated the first ever multi-organizational, international cooperative computer security effort. The implications of the worm led directly to the founding of the federally funded Computer Emergency Response Team Coordination Center (CERT/CC) at Carnegie-Mellon University.

Another pivotal cyber security wake-up call was the distributed denial of service (DDoS) attacks of February 2000. On Monday, February 7, the first of these high profile DDoS attacks was launched against Yahoo. Buy.com, eBay, CNN, and Amazon were also attacked that week. On Wednesday, February 9, the last day of the attacks, the amount of bandwidth consumed by these attacks (some servers received as much as 1 gigabit per second of incoming traffic), combined with curious internet users seeking online information about these attacks resulted in a 26.8 percent performance drop, as compared to the previous week's performance (Garber, 2000). Today, websites are better prepared to handle DDoS attacks partly because of increased cyber security collaborations with their ISPs.

In the past several years, identify theft, phishing, pharming, spyware, and online extortion have become more prevalent, and the economic impacts of cyber crime are more significant than many conventional crimes (Kshetri, 2006). Cyber crimes differ from other crimes because they require technological skills, they have a high degree of globalization, and they are relatively new (Kshetri, 2006). The newness and global reach of these crimes has outpaced traditional law enforcement's ability to detect, deter, and prosecute these crimes. Part of the reason law enforcement seems unable to cope with cyber crime is because there exists very little means for law enforcers to collaborate across jurisdictional or international boundaries.

Recently, cyber security has taken a more serious turn with the incidents in Estonia and Georgia. In Estonia, reported by some to be the first instance of "cyber war" (Thompson, 2007; Economist, 2007; Traynor, 2007), highly coordinated cyber attacks from botnets orchestrated by Russian bloggers, partially disabled the country's infrastructure in three waves of attacks over a period of weeks. It is unlikely that this was a state-sponsored act of war, and there was no declaration of war or overt war activity. Estonia pulled together an *ad hoc* collaboration of cyber experts from all over the world, including persons with expertise who just happened to be traveling in the country at the time. Still, this was a minor skirmish since no gunfire erupted and probably, only the economy of Estonia was seriously injured in the long run.

In former Soviet Georgia, cyber war ominously preceded gunfire by several weeks (Markoff, 2008) and could have been an early indicator of a shooting war. Cyber war also played a role during the conflict (Gaylord, 2008), although the effects on the nation were smaller than they would have been on a more technologically advanced nation such as the United States. Embattled Georgia reached out to the world for help in its cyber defense, but again the cooperation was rather *ad hoc*, depending partly on people who happened to be in Georgia at the time and their connections with the outside world. For example, the Georgian President's website was defaced by attackers but was moved to a server in Boston, Massachusetts because the website owner, a Georgian native, happened to be in Georgia at the time of the attacks.

Estonia and Georgia are prologues. *Ad hoc* cooperative defenses are not likely to prove successful as cyber attackers learn from these dress rehearsals to bring down the infrastructures of whole countries with greater efficiency. Cyber attack is inexpensive (Lesk, 2007), and cyber defense, especially when it depends on the very

infrastructures that are under attack, can often be very expensive (Dilley, 2008).

In 20 years since the Morris worm, computer worms have had their hey-day as icons of modern technological angst and have receded to be replaced in the public eye by identity theft, phishing, pharming, and spy-ware. But one fact has become increasingly obvious: the battle for control of our networks, computers, and data has begun in earnest. Security is required if the legitimate owners are to retain control of their property, and collaboration is needed to face the wide-spread threat.

The lesson is that we must learn to predict the likely targets of attack, proactively prepare collaborative relationships, and prevent cyber war before attackers can inflict costly damage to our systems. This chapter discusses how such collaborative cyber defenses may be organized, the frictions that make collaboration more difficult, and the benefits of successful collaboration.

In this chapter, we will examine the stakeholders in collaborations and their occasionally competing needs. We will study the types of collaboration and attempt to show how different types of collaboration give rise to different types of tension. We will discuss case studies from the DOE's cyber protection efforts and the lessons learned from them. Finally, we will discuss potential solutions (both technical and social) to the challenges we are faced with and the overall lessons learned.

INTRODUCTION

To understand collaborative cyber security, it is critical to understand who the stakeholders are and what kinds of collaboration are possible. In this section, we will briefly define terms to be used throughout the chapter and present the types of stakeholders and the types of collaboration.

Stakeholders

We consider four types of stakeholder groups: owning organizations, regulatory organizations, client organizations, and adversaries.

- **Owning organizations** are those directly responsible for appropriate operation and use of an asset. They own (or manage) and operate the assets to be defended and they have the primary interest in their continued secure operation. The following are some of the types of owners we consider:
  - *Employees* are persons who directly contribute to the mission of the organization to serve clients/customers. Employees are generally concerned with quality deliverables to clients and efficient job performance.
  - *Operators* are system designers, administrators, and support personnel who are charged with the smooth running of the systems.
  - *Upper management* forms the interface between the employees and external organizations. Managers often have higher liability and greater incentive to turn a profit than other employees.
  - *Defenders* protect the organization against cyber attack. Tactical defenders are most concerned with immediate threats to the computational infrastructure. Strategic defenders are more concerned with long-term threats to the enterprise, its information, and assets.
- **Regulatory organizations** are non-owners who have the right and obligation to ensure that owner organizations comply with established business processes or laws. This group may include higher headquarters (within a hierarchy of organizations), law enforcement, *etc.* They may periodically inspect owner organizations and may reward or punish them depending on the outcome of these audits.
- **Client organizations** are key cyber security stakeholders because their requirements may affect security at the owner's site. For example, a client could refuse to pay for cyber-security costs associated with the work they are funding, or a large customer could economically force a software supplier to produce more secure products. More indirectly, customer-driven growth may cause an organization to outgrow its cyber security capabilities while a decline in revenues can cause it to cut back necessary cyber security.
- **Adversaries** are atypical stakeholders because their stake in the system is not legally defensible. They may be anything from a curious teenager to a hostile nation-state. Adversaries have their own objectives that may include: gaining an economic or information advantage, exploiting systems for their own use, gaining access to classified information or intellectual property, intimidating or blackmailing organizations they attack, or simply causing trouble. Adversaries are always present and may, without any conscious collaboration, act in concert to destroy or degrade capabilities of defending organizations. Unfortunately, stakeholders do not always regard adversaries as their greatest threat.

Tensions in collaborative security often arise because of competing goals among the stakeholders. Obvious tensions include conflicts between adversaries and owners. However, other more interesting conflicts arise between owners and regulators, owners and clients, clients and regulators, and between subordinate groups within the same organization. Tensions can cause organizations to fail to detect or respond to cyber security incidents efficiently. Mitigating these tensions is

Figure 1. Taxonomy of kinds of collaboration

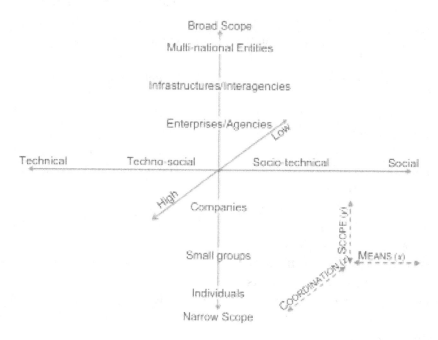

critical to establishing an effective cooperative cyber defense.

Types of Collaboration

Stakeholders may collaborate in a variety of ways. Although problems are similar across the entire scope of collaboration, small-scale collaborations (among individuals and small groups) experience different tensions than large-scale collaborations (among companies or nations). Collaborations may also be characterized by whether they are mostly technological collaborations, mostly social, or some mixture. A third way collaborations differ arises from the degree of interaction and coordination necessary among the collaborators to make it work effectively. Figure 1 shows a taxonomy of collaboration types used to define further discussion. In the figure, we call the size and scale of the collaboration its *scope*. We refer to the technical-social axis as the *means* of collaboration, and the amount of interaction required we call the degree of *coordination* required by the parties.

Collaborations based entirely on using shared tools would be purely technical. Those based on laws or policies without regard to implementation may be purely social. However, most collaborative efforts are based on a mix of social mores and technical means. Collaborations can be as narrow as those between individuals, broad enough to encompass multiple nations, or any degree in between. Collaborations may also require a great degree of interdependence and coordination among the parties or may be achievable without any overt coordination.

Some kinds of collaboration may span a broad range of the collaboration space depicted in this taxonomy. For instance, DShield (www.dshield.org) spans the entire spectrum of scope from narrow to large. Organizations and individuals contribute their firewall logs and the DShield project parses them and shares aggregated information about recently seen attacks with the whole world via their website. Collaborative clearinghouses like DShield and BugTraq (http://www.securityfocus.com/archive/1) require no coordination at all among their contributors, so they are broad-scope, purely technical, low-coordination collaborations.

The informal practice of system administrators sharing technical cyber-security tips across company boundaries requires nominal human coordination with few formal processes. We would describe this kind of collaboration as moderate scope, techno-social, medium-coordination collaborations. Finally, a company's collaboration with a managed-security firm typically would require legal documentation. A company-wide managed-security arrangement would be classified as a moderate scope, socio-technical, high coordination collaboration.

CASE STUDIES IN SECURITY COLLABORATION

In this section, we present three examples of collaborative security within the U.S. government and particularly DOE. Each of these examples is based on a working collaborative security system, but details have been omitted where sensitivities exist.

Case Study 1: The U.S. Government's Collaborative, Multi-Site Protection Systems

All federal agencies, their contractor-operated laboratories, and subordinate organizations participate in a nationwide, collaborative cyber security program. The program is a large socio-technical collaboration with a moderate to high degree of coordination. There are many stakeholders, and they participate in complex relationships. The program has its share of troubles, and resolutions are continually in progress. Figure 2 shows a notional view of how information is exchanged in this collaboration.

Site Security Teams: Each site employs security personnel to monitor its internal networks and to provide external network traffic data (*i.e.*, traf-

fic that passes between the organization and the outside world) to one or more of the analysis centers. Organizations do not share internal network traffic; however, operators at various sites often collaborate by sharing situational information with security teams from other sites.

Analysis Centers: Each analysis center exists to answer strategic security questions particular to some area of responsibility within the government. For instance, there might be an analysis center that is most concerned with nuclear nonproliferation or one whose responsibilities include network protection. Analysis centers typically store data streams from each site in separate repositories and send warnings back to each site from the perspective of the analysis center's area of responsibility. Further, some analysis centers may send reports to a public clearinghouse (such as the DOE's Computer Incident Advisory Capability, www.ciac. org). Reports sent to the clearinghouse are used to derive general warnings that are made available to the public via the web. Analysis centers collaborate with one another and provide reports on the protection state of their areas of responsibility to their owning agencies.

Agencies: The agencies use reports from the analysis centers for situational awareness and to rate the security of the various sites. Under the Federal Information Security Management Act of 2002 (FISMA) (FISMA, 2002; 44 U.S.C. § 3541 et seq.), all federal departments and agencies must adhere to information security best practices. Thus agencies use their own intrusion detection systems and network flow data[1] collections to help protect their computers, networks, and information. These security systems are deployed at the various agency sites, and the agency receives aggregated reports from security systems through the analysis centers it operates. Agencies, such as DOE, may also have their own programs in place to collaboratively secure their subordinate sites.

US-CERT: The United States Computer Emergency Readiness Team (US-CERT) was established in 2003 as part of the National Cyber

Figure 2. Notional diagram of the government's collaborative multi-site security arrangement

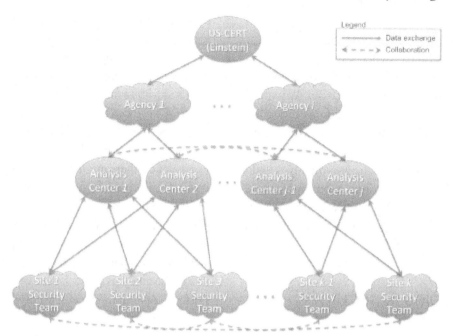

Security Division of the Department of Homeland Security (DHS). US-CERT is a partnership between the public and private sectors that protects the nation's Internet infrastructure and coordinates defense against and responses to cyber attacks across the nation. US-CERT's responsibilities include:

1. Analyzing and reducing cyber threats and vulnerabilities
2. Disseminating cyber threat warning information
3. Coordinating incident response activities

Issues and Challenges with the U.S. Government's Collaborative Systems

The primary problem with a monolithic federal-government-wide or agency-wide system is *scale*. The objective is to have a single point of cyber security control and monitoring for the entire nation. Ideally, US-CERT would be able to look at every packet on every network segment within the entire government. But, because of the sheer number of computers and network segments, this is impossible to attain in practice[2]. Even if all that traffic could be collected, it could neither be stored nor analyzed in a timely fashion. As a result, above the site level, mostly only network flow and intrusion alert data is ever collected, and even that cannot be stored long-term. US-CERT is unable to process the internal network data from every site, so it only collects data that flows between each site and the outside world.

Equally as important as the data loss above the site level is the loss of *context* that occurs once data leaves the site. For example, the DOE national laboratories participate in open science supporting a large constituency of foreign national researchers, some onsite and others abroad. Foreign-national scientists at a DOE laboratory are legitimately in frequent contact with their own embassies and others in their homelands. Not all the researchers abroad who legitimately access these open science systems belong to countries that are on equally good political terms with the

United States. Iran, for example, has a core of scientists that are internationally known for their expertise in energy science. The laboratory site security team knows which machines belong to or are accessed by international scientists, but at the analysis center level, all the site's machines look the same. As alerts traverse each layer up the chain, they lose contextual information that would indicate that a particular international scientist is a legitimate user accessing DOE systems. In fact, just looking at connection records without the data, it is impossible to tell who the user is, whether he is using legitimate credentials, or what he is doing on the system. From an analysis center's perspective, such an access can look like a dangerous data exfiltration.

Another type of context loss is that metadata containing the purpose and security plan for each monitored system is often not available outside the site. Within the site, metadata is available to tell what kinds of sensitive data may be stored on each system and what trust relationships exist among systems. Site security can contact individuals directly to gain a better understanding of what appears to be anomalous activity. Outside the site it is very difficult for analysts to be certain of the scope of a suspected attack. By default they may assume the gravest consequences. Usually the analysis centers retain knowledge of what is normal for the site as a whole, but the details are lost.

In the agency-level view, even site distinctions are lost and all that remains is an understanding of the missions of the analysis centers. DOE does not necessarily know which countries Pacific Northwest National Laboratory (PNNL) scientists will be interacting with. Further, at the US-CERT level, even distinctions between agencies are obscured. DOE is unusual in the government because it has a large science mission, but at that level, every machine is just an IP address. A machine owned by a DOE foreign-national scientist looks no different from a machine being used at a high-security defense site. To properly interpret the meaning of a detected incident, analysis centers must be in constant communication with site security personnel, and there must be a strong trust relationship. Similar trust and communication must exist between analysis centers and agencies and between agencies and US-CERT. Unfortunately the required communication and trust are not always in operation.

US-CERT could issue a mandate excluding communications with known miscreant websites or particular countries, but strange as it may seem at that high level, there are reasons to allow almost every type of interaction. Since all US-CERT has is IP addresses and TCP ports, it cannot easily make sweeping statements about which blocks of addresses everyone should avoid. There will always be exceptions, and granting exceptions on a case-by-case basis would be highly inefficient. This makes it difficult to coordinate site security policies.

Context loss is a problem, but it is also part of the solution to the scale problem. Level of detail should be commensurate with the type of oversight required. In fact, there should be an inverse relationship between breadth of responsibility (scope) and level of detail (Figure 3) if only to make management scalable. Site security teams need more detail to solve site-specific problems, while agency-level teams would require less specific context to address issues that span the entire agency. Two problems arise when amount of context and organizational scope do not match: (1) too little context may cause misclassification of events; (2) too much context may violate privacy of the monitored sites or individuals. Restating these problems in terms of scope, (1) a team that takes on a scope that requires more context than what is available to it will have insufficient information to perform accurate analysis, and (2) a team that attempts to operate at a lower scope than it should will require a commensurate amount of context and will end up micro-managing its subordinates.

Figure 3. Amount of data context and level of detail collected should be inversely proportional to the oversight scope of the organization.

Finally, even if all the data and context could be collected, stored, and analyzed in real-time, existing analysis tools can only do forensic analysis of past events. Analysis tools still cannot tell us what kinds of attacks to expect next. Worse, it can take days to pass all this data and analysis up and back down the chain, so events of interest that require agency or government-wide scope are typically several days old when the sites finally receive notice. By this time, effective site security teams may have already solved the problem at their level.

Numerous, high-profile data losses, especially of data containing personally identifiable information, have made the U. S. government leery of any cyber security incident that might further tarnish its reputation in the eyes of the public. In reaction to these cases, the U.S. Congress has enacted laws like the Federal Information Security Management Act (FISMA, 2002) ostensibly to increase security. An unintended side-effect of FISMA is that it overwhelms companies and agencies with compliance issues (Robinson, 2005), often at the expense of meaningful security. The apparent lack of visible improvement in government

cyber security is illustrated by continued poor performance on FISMA grades (Wait, 2006). Unfortunately, because of the extremely public nature of cyber security in the U.S. government (Aitoro, 2008b), agencies may choose to punish, fine, or otherwise censure sites that report security problems. This has a chilling effect on accurate reporting, making sites loath to admit when an intrusion has occurred.

Within DOE, the separation of site data and the regard for organizational privacy designed into the system contribute toward effective incident detection. But the sheer size of DOE and the large number of contractor organizations it supervises requires it to be split into multiple headquarters units with occasionally overlapping and conflicting goals. Conflicts at the headquarters level can dampen the effectiveness of DOE's otherwise very successful security system. Tensions can arise when US-CERT, DOE, or an analysis center attempts to operate within the scope that belongs to sites, circumventing standing agreements in the sites' operating contracts.

Finally, tensions can be caused by rules that prevent collaboration, especially between analysis centers and the sites they are monitoring. These rules may be put into place to protect privacy of individuals or organizations, but they can cause serious delays and miscommunications that negatively affect incident detection and response.

Design of a Multi-Site Collaborative Security Program

To mitigate the scale problem at the agency and analysis center levels, several agencies have fielded their own internal monitoring systems parallel to US-CERT that use mostly the same data. PNNL has been very active in the development and deployment of these monitoring capabilities. These systems mitigate some of the context loss problem by reporting certain metadata along with the raw network flows and intrusion alerts. Within-agency monitoring systems may also be effective at encouraging dialogue between analysis center and site security personnel.

To enable the analysis centers and higher headquarters to understand and evaluate site data accurately, PNNL has created a data guide that clearly articulates the contents of data sets, as well as contextual network information. Additionally, PNNL personnel provide analyst services that can help broker friendly relationships between analysis centers and monitored sites. All these improvements make the multi-site cooperative security system designed by PNNL one of the most effective in the world. Several design principles contribute to the success of this system:

1. The system monitors only data that travels between the site and the Internet, not traffic internal to the site. The latter is the responsibility of each site.
2. The data for each site is stored separately in a repository. Every site has access to a copy of its own monitoring data, but no site can access that of other sites.
3. None of the monitored sites owns the analysis centers or the repository.
4. A publicly available clearinghouse provides appropriately sanitized information to the public for the good of the community.

These design principles allow each site to maintain ownership of its own monitoring data while allowing the global monitoring of all the agency sites. PNNL's efforts at providing metadata and analyst services have helped alleviate many problems with off-site analysis while improving the performance of the system.

Case Study 2: The Radiation Portal Monitoring Project

Large collaborative projects involving the effort of many organizations working toward a common goal require cyber security, although it is not the primary goal of the project. A real-world example of this is the U.S. Department of Homeland Security's (DHS) Radiation Portal Monitoring Project (RPMP). This project is a large socio-technical collaboration with moderate coordination among a number of stakeholders. RPMP's key goal is interdicting nuclear material entering the United States of America.

RPMP is a joint project between U.S. Customs and Border Protection (CBP) and the Domestic Nuclear Detection Office. PNNL supports RPMP on behalf of the U.S. Department of Energy by providing deployment management and system integration expertise. Coordinating the effort of these government organizations has led to success, and RPMP clearly shows how multiple organizations may have both complementary goals and individual priorities.

Interdicting nuclear material is a law-enforcement function that must be supported by solid science. Law-enforcement personnel, nuclear scientists, radiation portal vendors' software developers, CBP software developers, CBP network administrators, and cyber-security professionals are stakeholders in this national sensor network.

Many law-enforcement functions naturally complement cyber-security functions. For example, the law-enforcement chain of custody is enhanced by strong user-authentication and auditing capabilities. However, tensions and trade-offs exist. Tension arose between cyber-security personnel and field users when increased user authentication and auditing capabilities were not as easy to use as the CBP officers desired. Reassessing the risks involved allowed another effective, but more usable solution to go forward. Adding the radiation portals to the CBP network entailed trade-offs. Placing the portals on the CBP network allowed its nuclear scientists near-real time access to portal data so they could better support the CBP officers in the field. But this action also had cyber security implications for the CBP network and the vendors of the radiation portal software.

Communication and cooperation has been important in RPMP. Mitigating security risks has required educational efforts to increase cyber security awareness for CBP's officers, scientists, and software developers as well as the radiation portal vendors' software developers. In turn, each of the stakeholders has been able to balance its individual priorities with the project's overall nuclear interdiction mission.

Case Study 3: PNNL Site Cyber Security Coordination

Cyber security incident detection and response at PNNL is an intra-company-scope socio-technical collaborative effort that requires a high degree of coordination. Three separate groups contribute to PNNL's successful cyber security program:

- A tactical cyber security group whose focus is on day-to-day protection of the network and computers.

- A strategic cyber security group that takes a long-range protection outlook to understand current cyber threats and to anticipate and mitigate new threats.

- The IT operations group whose primary goal is to provide the best possible IT infrastructure and services to PNNL's research and support staff.

All three groups have a common goal of keeping PNNL's cyber assets secure, but each group has individual priorities. From a tactical perspective, mitigating a cyber attack as soon as possible is most desirable. When tactical defenders halt a multi-step attack before it is finished, the network is protected but the ultimate target may remain unknown. Strategic defenders, on the other hand, may wish to allow an attack to continue so they can study the attacker and understand what he is after. This leads to a natural tension between tactical and strategic defenders: enabling strategic defenders to understand the motives and methods of attackers vs. enabling tactical defenders to prevent attacks from putting the network infrastructure at unnecessary risk.

A second kind of tension arises between the IT operations group and both types of defenders: the defenders require operational support that may cause extra work for the operations group. Defenders must place their sensors on the operational network, they must use bandwidth to collect data from the sensors, and they may require operations personnel to quickly reconfigure computer and network resources in response to a perceived attack. It is important for both defenders and operations personnel to respect each other's responsibilities and competence.

To improve the coordination and collaboration between each of the three groups that have cyber security responsibilities at PNNL, all parties devised and signed a joint memorandum of agreement. The agreement covers the following points:

- **Collective understanding:** The memorandum sets the tone for an effective collaborative effort by documenting each group's unique mission and how it contributes to PNNL's overall cyber security.

- **Data sharing:** The agreement prescribes how data may be shared to achieve each group's detection and analysis goals.
- **Event evaluation:** The agreement provides an evaluation framework to document an event's current risks and the risks associated with allowing the event to continue. This gives all parties the same risk-based criteria for when to allow an intrusion to proceed and when to intervene.
- **Incident response:** The memorandum provides a framework for identifying which of the three groups will take the lead for responding to a given event. It also identifies the first-responders in each group that must be notified of cyber incidents and the proposed cyber security responses.

The cyber security coordination memorandum has proven to significantly aid collaboration efforts at PNNL over the last several years. Perhaps the most significant impact of the agreement was that it formally captured the "tribal" knowledge that had previously existed within the three groups. And in so doing, it has set a positive collaborative tone for new and experienced staff within these groups.

CHALLENGES TO SUCCESSFUL COLLABORATION

Different kinds of collaborations are susceptible to different challenges. A purely technical collaboration within a small organization will be susceptible to different tensions than a purely social collaboration among many organizations. Similarly, collaborations that differ in level of coordination suffer different problems. Collaboration within a single organization or within a hierarchy of organizations under a unified chain of command generally requires more formal coordination and has a fundamentally different character from a voluntary collaboration among peer organizations. We would expect that large, mostly social, high-coordination collaborations would be the most complex and prone to tension while small, mostly technological, low-coordination collaborations would be relatively simple and would be hampered less by tension among stakeholders. In this section, we discuss the social and technical challenges to effective security collaboration. These challenges cut across all collaboration scopes and degrees of coordination, but they have different effects on collaborations that rely on different means.

Social/Regulatory Challenges

Every cyber system exists in a social context and is governed to some degree by applicable laws and organizational policies. Intellectual property protection and privacy are broadly felt needs. The legal framework regulating U.S. government (particularly Executive Order 12333 that regulates intelligence collecting activities) is even more restrictive to prevent violating the Constitution. Beyond the legal framework, law enforcement and several social challenges make security difficult for government and industry to accept as well.

Intellectual Property

Intellectual property protection applies to information that is being protected by patent, copyright, trade secret, or other legal means. In technical fields, patenting is so slow that it may take nearly a decade to obtain a patent. But the pace of technology can make most subject inventions (even when properly guarded) outdated in a matter of months. Prior to filing a patent application, the only protection this intellectual property has is its secrecy; private companies must protect their future revenues by protecting their intellectual property themselves.

At PNNL, a government lab run by a contractor (Battelle Memorial Institute), this problem is particularly thorny. If PNNL were a government agency, all of its intellectual property would belong to the citizenry. As a private company, intellectual property funded by a client belongs to that client first. But internal research can become the intellectual property of PNNL's contract operator, Battelle.

Intellectual property issues can spring up in unexpected places. For instance, if DOE monitors PNNL's networks (a reasonable expectation for DOE to perform for its labs), to whom does the monitoring data belong? At PNNL there are many projects that do not belong to DOE, and PNNL may wish to use that same data for its own research. Technically, the data only belongs to DOE if it is a specific project deliverable for a funded project. So then DOE would have to pay Battelle for data DOE gathered with its own sensors at its own laboratory. These difficult intellectual property questions are open issues for collaborative cyber security that have an effect on incident detection and response.

Privacy Concerns

At PNNL, suspected privacy breaches must be reported to higher headquarters within 45 minutes of detection. In contrast, a suspected compromise of Top Secret data or news of a death of a staff member must be reported only within 24 hours. The high-profile nature of identity theft drives the urgency of this policy. Although it may seem to be an unreasonable disparity that accidental release of an individual's mother's maiden name receives 32 times quicker response than compromise of classified material or news of an accidental death, the difference is somewhat supported by the base rate of occurrence of these phenomena. Privacy data is not afforded military-grade protection, so its theft should be quite a bit easier and accidental release should be expected to happen more frequently.

Protection of privacy impacts detection and response because it is impossible to know in advance whether a given stream of cyber data will contain personal information. Website and e-mail logins may contain usernames and even passwords in the clear; employees may reveal private information when interacting with associates over the Internet; machines may store cookies that happen to have privacy data in them. While this information stays with the employer, no harm is done, but it may constitute a violation of privacy to pass monitoring information containing privacy data on to government monitoring agencies. Privacy impacts incident detection and response because the parties with legitimate interest in analyzing the data may not be authorized by law to view it.

Legal Limitations

Limitations on intelligence gathering: Executive Order (EO) 12333 (1981) defines functions and limitations of United States government intelligence activities. While intelligence activities exist because of foreign powers, in the course of monitoring its own assets for intrusion, the government may inadvertently collect data on U.S. citizens. Worse yet, if a U.S. authority were to find out that the individual were breaking the law (for instance by downloading child pornography), then they would have to prosecute. But this would violate the Constitutional right of U.S. citizens not to be subject to searches without probable cause (U.S. Constitution, 1791). However, if the government does not monitor its own assets, it would be negligent (FISMA, 2002, sec 305(2)(c)(3)(C)(iii)).

This conundrum is difficult enough, but there are also many interpretations of the vagaries of EO 12333 and confusion over similar terms such as "U.S. Citizen" vs. "U.S. Person" (the latter may even be a foreign national). The result is very tricky legal grounds and less effective incident detection and response.

Law enforcement and lawsuits: Cybercrime's relative newness creates several challenges for the law enforcement community. Because it is unfamiliar to many judges, few attorneys will take small cyberfraud cases (Kshetri, 2006). The global reach of cyber crime means that multiple law enforcement jurisdictions must collaborate to solve and prosecute a crime. Strong industry participation will be required to solve cyber crime because the private sector owns most of the global cyber infrastructure. For example, 90% of the U.S. critical infrastructures are owned by the private sector and it is estimated that 80% of the world's email flows through global providers such as AOL, MSN, and Yahoo (Kshetri, 2006).

Cyber security collaboration can break down when one organization is compromised and its machines are used to attack another organization. The result can be costly lawsuits to find who is at fault. Organizations are required by U.S. law to take "reasonable" precautions against cyber crime or else risk being found negligent if someone should file a lawsuit against them. But "reasonableness" is not easy to define (Scher, 2006). Security technologies are changing all the time and organizations must keep up with or exceed changing accepted industry practices whether or not they actually enhance security. Following government compliance regulations such as FISMA, Sarbanes-Oxley, and HIPAA may not enhance actual security, and compliance is often quite expensive and time-consuming. However, following government regulations is part of the accepted meaning of "reasonableness." An organization may also be legally liable if it fails to follow its own security policies. Even following industry-standard "best practices" is not a guarantee against negligence if a court should find an entire industry's practice insufficient. Legal complexities such as these may seriously detract from organizational and inter-organizational cyber security collaboration.

Need to Know vs. Need to Share

Lee and Rao have analyzed the factors that influence sharing of inter-organizational information Anti/Counter-Terrorism (ACT) and Disaster Management (DM) agencies (Lee and Rao, 2007) and concluded that although information sharing has been mandated, the culture of agencies needs to change to promote sharing. ACT and DM organizations should share because it is in everybody's interest to share, but in the study, employees shared information only if they were satisfied that the receiver would safeguard the information and if a technical means existed to share the information. Agencies and employees need to be encouraged to share information via a complementary set of positive and negative incentives (Gao and Liu, 2005).

Vague classification guidelines and uncertainty about the sensitivity of information can prevent even critically necessary sharing. For example, a recent U. S. Government Accountability Office report discusses how inconsistent guidelines for designating information Official Use Only (OUO) create difficulties in sharing information (GAO, 2006).

In military coalition environments where sharing partners may range from active allies to traditional enemies, the risk is higher and the complexity of the system greater. Under these conditions, need to share is part of the military situational awareness and lives may be at stake. Gibson presents how the U.S. military implements secure networks internally and with multi-national alliance partners (Gibson, 2001). Zhang provides insight into the tradeoff between privacy protection and communication complexity in information sharing (Zhang, 2007).

Security as a Value Proposition

While legal concerns protect citizens from government and corporate intrusion, another social problem has no such benefit: it is very difficult to form a value proposition for cyber security because there is no accepted way to measure the value of what security *prevents* (Purser, 2004; Tsiakis, 2005; Anderson, 2008). Even if there were accepted valuations, people are risk-seeking when it comes to uncertain losses and risk-averse when it comes to certain loss. Thus, they may be more likely to risk a large loss (*i.e.,* a security breach) that seems unlikely than to pay for a smaller loss (*i.e.,* the cost of the security product/practice) that is certain (Schneier, 2008). Unfortunately, security is noticed most when it is conspicuously lacking, as when an incident is publicized.

Providing adequate levels of cyber security incurs significant costs—trained staff, specialized equipment, and time are all required. Allocating these resources can be difficult because it is hard to make an *a priori* evaluation of the value of good cyber security. In most industries, *annualized loss expectancy* is an accepted form of risk assessment. But in cyber security, the changing face of risk (including zero-day exploits) requires risk assessments to be more agile than an annualized model can provide. Discovering new methods of risk assessment that can address the dynamic nature of cyber security is an open area of research (Goranson, *et al.*, 2007).

Technical Challenges

Challenges to effective security collaboration can arise from absence of needed technology or from technical incompatibilities between parties. These technological shortfalls form a partial research agenda for collaborative cyber security.

Lack of Data Standards

Collaboration may be hindered by the lack of data standards. Without common formats and data processing tools, it is harder for an organization to share the data needed to support its collaborations. Additionally, data analysis tools must be updated to accept data from new cyber sensors.

Beyond low-level format issues, we have found that no two agencies describe their data the same way. Collaborations need a standard lexicon as a basis for a metadata ontology to enable translation between formats. This will require a great deal of long-term coordination. Probably a national or international standards body will need to define the ontology and then each agency or organization will need to accept and use the ontology. Of course, tackling this problem will take several years and a great deal of collaborative effort.

Another missing provision of metadata would be to provide tracking of data provenance and history. Data may be trusted or not depending on who collected it. Its value depends in part on why, where, and how it was collected. The modification history and chain of custody of the data is also important for processing with certainty. The most direct standard we have for attaching this metadata with any certainty is via digital signatures, but this implies additional overhead to distribute keys, compute hashes of large data files associated with cyber data, *etc*.

Limitation of Analysis Capabilities

So much cyber data exists that it simply defies analysis. In the government, analysis center personnel often rely on Analyst's Notebook software (www.i2inc.com), but this package cannot handle the sheer scope of data. Analysts we spoke to said that the tool becomes unwieldy at around 100,000 data items, while typically they are trying to correlate several orders of magnitude more information. Since government analysis centers are typically responsible for multiple sites, they must rely on scripts and data reduction techniques simply to get some of their data into an appropriate tool for analysis. The size of the data also protracts the time required to perform the analysis.

There are a bewildering variety of analysis tools available, but they are typically not interoperable, and they often fill only niche applications in the analysis process. Analysts need their tools to interoperate like a "mash-up" on the web. This implies the need to accept and generate data in a variety of formats and means. Analysts (especially above the site level) need tools that create geographic and temporal scaffoldings to file their data in and to create a cogent, true story from multiple sources where data may be uncertain, sparse, and possibly deceptive.

Unfortunately, Internet Protocol version 6 (IPv6) is about to make this problem much worse. Outside the United States, many governments and industries are switching to IPv6 from the widely used version 4 standard. Under the old standard, 32 bits of storage were allocated to store Internet addresses, but IPv6 allocates 128 bits to the address fields enabling 2^{96} times more addresses to be used—more than can possibly be displayed on any reasonable size screen, even if each address were only the size of a single atom (Radhakrishnan, *et al.*, 2007). Cyber security analysis technologies that today rely on classifying individual IP addresses as "good" or "bad" will utterly fail when IPv6 is widely accepted. Relatively few analytical tools are suited to IPv6. The new protocol is also much more complex than version 4, increasing its attack surface dramatically (Jeong-Wook, *et al.*, 2007). Analysts in the U.S. have relatively little experience with practical IPv6 security issues because there are few large installations that run IPv6. While relatively few attacks today exploit IPv6, when a sufficiently large installed base is established, attackers will turn more attention to IPv6 and will discover previously unknown deficiencies.

Lack of Strong Anonymization Techniques

Many organizations are reluctant to share their log files because these logs contain sensitive information about network infrastructure, computing systems, and business practices. Even when anonymized, valuable information may be gleaned from log files as demonstrated by the release of AOL's anonymized web search logs (Barbaro, 2006). Lack of data sharing hampers collaboration because attacks can only be described in high-level terms. The sender can only comment on the attack as he understands it but cannot provide the data that would allow him to benefit from external analysis.

Another problem introduced by current techniques is that the anonymization process may destroy important relationships latent in the data. For instance, a large raw packet trace gathered at the time of an attack may provide details about the internal structure of the network where it was gathered. These details could be used to make other attacks against that network much more efficient. By anonymizing the IP addresses in the trace, the provider can make it impossible to determine the structure of the internal network, but he also destroys evidence that makes it possible to analyze the behavior of the attacker. Because providers of public data can never be certain what use data will be put to, they must scramble everything, potentially making the data useless for most purposes.

One thing that is missing is a means to anonymously publish and compare details of intrusions across organizational boundaries in near real time. System administrators and security officers routinely share information with their friends and associates in the industry, but there is no permanent record of their exchanges, nor do third parties have access to this knowledge.

Existing forms of collaboration share only highly sanitized information describing attacks. Usually, only general information about the vulnerable software or the method of attack is revealed. A trusted third party that will not reveal the source of the information must host this information. Unfortunately, this process of receiving, anonymizing and publishing information is very slow. Analysts at PNNL say that it takes at least three days after the discovery of a new attack for details to be published in official sources.

Trust Management

Collaboration will be hindered if organizations do not have a technical means of access control that extends to collaboration partners who desire access to their sensitive data. Trust must be established between individuals who don't know each other very well and who collaborate in a high-stress environment. Trust management addresses both of these issues via policy-based and reputation-based approaches, respectively. Without trust management, it is difficult for data providers in one organization to know whether consumers in another organization can be trusted with their sensitive data.

Policy-based trust-management technologies use authorization credentials and attribute-based access control policies. They are most useful when two organizations do not share a common authentication system. Although authorization and access control technologies can protect sensitive data, they cannot guarantee that trusted individuals will continue to act in a trustworthy manner. Reputation-based trust management systems track the past behavior of collaborators to provide a basis for trust or distrust in future collaborations. However, if individuals give negative feedback on others' reputations, the trust-management system itself could easily cause loss of morale and trust. Implementing a system based on an award model, that collects only positive feedback, may avoid this pitfall.

Another issue is that the data provider has no absolute guarantee that a trusted consumer will not share the data with another person that the provider does not trust (*e.g.*, transitive trust). Digital Rights Management (DRM) technologies use encryption and identity management to try to make the data itself safe against abuse of transitive trust, but DRM schemes may be too cumbersome to use in the dynamic environment of cyber security. Defining appropriate trust management mechanisms for highly sensitive data of this nature will require ongoing research.

Data Uncertainty and Unreliability

Cyber data is subject to uncertainty because it is often collected from a diverse set of sensors each with its own independent clock. Milliseconds count when unraveling the forensic story told by cyber events, and even actively synchronized machines may have their clocks off by 200 milliseconds or more because of network latencies. Other forms of uncertainty arise from lack of precision. Software sensors may time-stamp events with different granularity or not at all. Standard Unix and Microsoft event loggers record with an accuracy of one second. Packet capture utilities such as tcpdump record messages with microsecond accuracy. Intrusion detection systems and firewalls usually keep timestamps with a granularity of at least a second. Blending data from different sources may require human judgment and sense-making that leaves room for analysis error.

Another source of uncertainty from shared data comes from the unknown reliability of shared summaries and data products. Organizations may edit data before releasing it to omit parts that are sensitive or not applicable. They may release summaries instead of actual data for these reasons. The summaries may be intentionally or unintentionally incomplete or inaccurate. Any redaction of analysis data is a source of uncertainty, especially in a collaborative environment. Further it may be unknowable whether source data has been edited at all.

Additionally, tools are needed that would help defenders determine the extent of data theft once a system has been compromised. For instance, if customer identity information were stored on a system that was compromised, it would be useful to know which records were actually stolen rather than assuming that all were. This would allow more efficient notification of affected parties, better valuation of both losses and security measures, and better collaborative analysis of intruder goals.

COLLABORATION SOLUTIONS

In this section, we discuss some social and technical solutions for effective security collaboration. While numerous kinds of security solutions exist, we concentrate only on those that are most applicable to collaborative security. As different kinds of collaborations are susceptible to different challenges, so there are many kinds of solutions with different applicability. Most solutions apply more to collaborations with particular scopes or degrees of coordination, but we strive to present the solutions in their most broadly-applicable form. Further solutions for collaboration are listed as lessons-learned in the following section.

Social and Regulatory Collaboration Solutions

In this section, we discuss the cyber security lessons we have learned from case studies of DOE collaborative cyber security systems. We also apply findings from other (noncyber security) domains where collaboration is critical to success. These other domains include public transportation, military counterinsurgency operations, and the collaborative environments engendered by internet applications.

Based upon our experience and the experience of other subject-matter experts at PNNL, developing and implementing solutions to overcome social/legal challenges to cyber security collaborations is a far more pressing and difficult concern than developing technical solutions. Perhaps this is because the technical challenges of data collection and analysis are mostly concerned with the volume and velocity of the information involved— straightforward technical problems. On the other hand, social and regulatory challenges present a very tricky minefield where small differences of opinion can quickly develop into serious issues of national/international scope.

Security as a Strategic Asset

Collaborative cyber security efforts must be viewed as a strategic asset. In the 1980's, some U.S. automotive manufacturers realized that they had to focus on quality to stay competitive and they instigated efforts to make quality a core requirement of every job. Likewise, in today's world, cyber security must become a core responsibility of every worker. Collaborations succeed when senior management recognizes that cyber security is a business enabler and then sets the tone that enables all workers to collaboratively strive for excellence.

The establishment of a Chief Information Security Officer (CISO) position can be an excellent start in this direction. Having a CISO in each organization also greatly enhances its ability to participate in collaborative cyber security. Without a single CISO, organizations may have multiple, divergent goals for their security programs. With a single CISO, an organization appoints a single person to represent and unify all subordinate security interests. The presence of CISOs also simplifies and may help standardize communication between cooperating organizations.

Education and Training

Most of the time, technical and managerial skills to lead collaborative efforts come as the result of education, training, and experience. Organizations need to invest in the professional development of their staff in both the technical and social skills needed to collaborate effectively on cyber-security issues. One useful mechanism is the rotation of staff across a variety of sub-organizations and roles. This allows individual staff members to gain a more complete perspective of each sub-organization's strategic goals, enabling increased coordination and rapid conflict resolution within the organization. Matrix management, where staff work on several projects independent of their home organization, may enable this valuable cross-training.

Additionally, rotational assignments of security personnel with other organizations can be very useful in establishing and maintaining trust, especially within an organizational hierarchy. Rotating site security personnel and analysis center personnel will improve broad organizational perspective, communication, and trust. Of course, establishing such a rotational program requires a measure of trust in the first place. Organizations must be willing to expose their internal structures, priorities, and data to temporary assignees from outside organizations. However, consider that few employees stay their entire careers in a single organization, and when an employee leaves, he takes his internal knowledge with him. Intentionally sharing this knowledge with members of other organizations that must be trusted anyway can be no more harmful, and may actually be quite helpful to the collaborative security of both organizations.

While we do not have direct experience of the utility of rotational assignments between peer companies, we suspect that they would improve security and collaboration there too. Of course, without the protection of formal hierarchical relationships between the organizations, peer organizations should employ other legal protections such as nondisclosure agreements to protect their proprietary information. We believe that the benefit of such rotations would far outweigh the risks.

Establishing Formal Partnerships

Informal and *ad hoc* partnerships have been used to overcome significant new issues in the past (e.g., the Morris worm, Estonia cyber-assault). While *ad hoc* methods may be more nimble than formal arrangements, formal arrangements allow organizations to bring their complete set of resources to bear on a problem efficiently. At PNNL, the tri-party memorandum of agreement between the

tactical defense, strategic defense, and network operations groups paved the way for an effective collaborative incident detection and response effort that meets the strategic goals of all three parties. The success of the memorandum is being used within DOE to help train cyber security staff at other DOE laboratories. While PNNL's tri-party agreement is not applicable to all organizations, the benefits to be gained by formalizing the parameters of a collaborative incident detection and response effort are worth the effort.

Formal partnerships can be difficult to establish, especially if the scope of the agreement is too broad. For the purposes of cyber security collaborations, simpler is better. Agreements should define the roles of the stakeholders, the kinds of data that will be exchanged, and the acceptable uses of that data. Additionally, any joint processes for incident evaluation and response should be outlined. Periodically, the parties should reevaluate the agreement since cyber security challenges are constantly changing.

Law and Policy Changes

Inter-organization policy and culture: The U.S. government's 9-11 Commission's final report recommended that, "Information procedures should provide incentives for sharing, to restore a better balance between security and shared knowledge" (9-11 Commission, 2004). While the Cold War mentality of "need to know" was prevalent, there were no penalties for over-classifying or over-compartmentalizing information and no incentives for sharing. Penalties for sharing, however, were clear and serious. We re-iterate the 9-11 Commission's recommendation and further appeal that even private industry should consider how incentives for sharing cyber security information might be implemented while preserving security.

Cyber crime collaboration: Cyber crime is relatively new in terms of case law, and cyber criminals are actively exploiting the holes in traditional regulations. Legislative bodies need to be educated about the danger posed by cyber crime so that national and international laws can be updated to address cyber crime and reward collaboration. Since private industry owns most of the cyber infrastructure, law enforcement and industry must collaborate to solve cyber crimes.

An example law enforcement collaboration is the Hillsboro (Oregon, USA) police department that started a reserve specialist program with a cyber crime focus (Harrison, *et al.*, 2004). Reservists with cyber security expertise in their civilian careers were taught about law enforcement objectives and acted as agents of the Hillsboro police. The reservists' technical expertise aided police with cyber crime investigations—areas where police chronically lag behind the criminals. The participating corporations benefited from law enforcement perspective and experience, and the resulting collaboration made both parties more successful in dealing with cyber crime. The long-term goals of the program include creating new case law that will contribute to better detection and prosecution of cyber crime.

TECHNICAL COLLABORATION SOLUTIONS

Technology may either assist or detract from the goals of collaborative security. In this section, we discuss research done by PNNL and others and present a brief research agenda for what remains to be done on the technical side of the solution space. Technical and techno-social collaborations of all sizes especially benefit from the development of new or the improvement of existing collaboration tools and standards.

Data Format and Access Standards

The United States government's 9-11 commission cited inability to share information as an impediment to terrorism prevention (9-11 Commission, 2004). Part of this inability to share stems from a lack of common data standards. Within small technical collaborations, common data standards are relatively simple to establish. Large technical collaborations within a common management or oversight hierarchy may also avoid data incompatibilities by mandating common data-export formats from security software such as firewalls and intrusion detection.

Unfortunately, other collaborations, especially large social/regulatory collaborations, may be unable to mandate a common data standard. This can be solved, in part, by developing mutual ontologies and data translators as needed. Common ontology is more difficult to achieve outside a common hierarchy, and standards bodies may be required. Within a hierarchy, the further away two organizations are, the less likely they are to share common semantics. At least within a hierarchy there is a way to enforce common semantics.

Further, we recommend that vendors of security tools design their software with application programming interfaces (APIs) that export data in forms suitable for use in a "mash-up." Mash-ups are hybrid web applications that take data from a variety of sources and fuse it together. Often, mash-ups are intended to be created by end-users, not programmers. Mash-up-compatible access standards would allow analysts to assemble data from many sources into new forms on the fly. Tools thus enabled would act as a distributed database that could be a powerful source of information for defenders. Of course, providers of this data must also protect themselves via access controls and anonymization techniques.

Data Anonymization

Anonymization obfuscates the sources and methods of data collection to protect the provider, the consumer, or both. Effective anonymization must retain the essential meaning of the data. The lack of adequate data anonymization techniques hinders the development of standard data sets that may be used to improve algorithms, compare security products, and train staff. For example, developing improved algorithms that can detect insider threats means real-world data is needed. But real-world data often "leaks" sensitive information when disparate data is correlated and aggregated (*i.e.*, the mosaic effect).

Unfortunately, the very act of anonymizing data can render it unusable for some purposes. Data providers must choose which features of the data to anonymize because obfuscating all features will make the data meaningless. Providers must have assurance that the users of their data will not violate their rights or pass data on to others who will.

Another approach to providing anonymous data is to take real data and derive parameters from it to generate synthetic data that resembles the original in form but not in content. Two problems with this promising approach are that the synthetic data may actually unintentionally reveal characteristics of the real data and synthetic data may not make sense. That is, the anonymization provided by the simulator may be either insufficiently obfuscated or too obfuscated for use. Anonymization is a hard problem and an open research area. Anonymization of data still requires the consumer to protect the provider to some extent.

Privacy-Preserving, Anonymous Collaboration

An alternative to anonymizing the data is to anonymize the provider instead. Web 2.0 technologies such as secure, anonymous blogs, and wikis could be employed to good effect. A real-time, anonymous cyber-security wiki could be an excellent means of multi-organizational cyber-security collaboration. To succeed, this kind of collaboration *must* ensure that the participants remain anonymous to protect them from legal, regulatory, and social reprisal, or from being identified as targets by adversaries. Information providers must also

take care not to reveal their identities accidentally through the data they publish.

Wikileaks (wikileaks.org) is an unofficial version of this collaboration approach. WikiLeaks uses the underlying anonymization technology of TOR (The Onion Router, www.torproject.org) to protect the identities of people who leak official documents about scandals, etc. to the Internet. While WikiLeaks is very controversial, the underlying technology could be used for collaborative cyber security. A superior approach would be for collaborating organizations to officially sanction the use of such a site while educating the contributors about the importance of operational security to avoid unintentional data extrusion.

For example, when a vendor discovers a software vulnerability it could work collaboratively in an open forum with its customers without the customers having to identify themselves. This would keep customers from revealing their vulnerabilities to attackers but would allow community members to share findings. The basic design could use a cross-domain (or multiple security level) wiki where the secure side was the organization that needed to patch the vulnerability and the open side was the Internet.

Another tool that could be modified to assist anonymous collaboration is Off-the-Record (OTR, http://www.cypherpunks.ca/otr/) that plugs in to chat programs and gives confidentiality and authentication coupled with deniability. While messages are authenticated as they are received by the chat host, the digital signatures are not attached, so after the conversation is over, no one can prove either side's contribution or involvement. OTR combined with the other tools may even allow collaboration between organizations that are direct competitors.

Risk Analysis and Damage Assessment

PNNL has developed the Risk Assessment Sensitivity Determination (RASD, O'Neil, 2005) system to allow employees to collaborate with defenders in the cyber security effort by providing and annual assessment of the capabilities and sensitivity of their systems. During an ongoing incident this information is valuable as the tactical and strategic defenders collaborate on possible incident responses.

FUTURE COLLABORATIVE TECHNOLOGIES

Several projects have addressed the technical need for collaborative security. There are four drivers that motivate research in this area:

1. Internet speeds require automated reaction times.
2. Dynamically changing strategy and tactics of adversaries require an adaptive cyber defense.
3. Humans are ultimately responsible for the actions of their automated systems.
4. An adaptive cyber defense that spans multiple organizations requires both human intelligence and automated rationality.

Much of the work on collaborative security to date has concentrated on the threat of Internet worms and the first two drivers alone. Examples of such systems are CRIM (Cuppens and Miege, 2002), Cossack (Papdopoulos, *et al.*, 2003), and Cooperative Response Strategies (Nojiri, *et al.*, 2003). Of these, only CRIM requires human analysts and provides them some form of workload savings. The others are intended to be fully automatic.

Smith et al. have developed the Yalta framework as a scalable, reliable application platform for distributed coalitions (Smith, 2003). This framework uses distributed tuplespaces for data sharing, threshold cryptography for high-throughput, intrusion tolerant public-key infrastructure, and scalable event notification for low-latency revocation. Yalta can help enable information sharing and trust management in a diverse environment as is needed in collaborative security.

The Institute for Information Infrastructure Protection (I3P) describes the potential benefit of better security through sharing of process control systems (PCS) security incident information (Eliopoulos, 2007) for the Oil & Gas industry. Communication among the members of these various organizations offers the potential benefit of better security but also carries with it the risks of lost competitive advantage, increased liability, and excessive loads on limited resources. The effort addresses the need for a secure, easy-to-use means of incident information sharing for members of the PCS community.

At PNNL, we seek to involve humans in detection and response without slowing the system down. We take a "mixed-initiative" (Haack, *et al.*, 2009) approach where humans and automated processes work together toward the common goal of defense. Collaborative security is inherently mixed-initiative with humans and automation from a variety of organizations sharing the lead, but we choose to limit the automation by defining the goals and roles it can take on.

One PNNL project intended for multi-organizational, mixed-initiative interaction is called the Cooperative Infrastructure Defense (CID, http://i4.pnl.gov/focusareas/as_projects/adaptive_agents.stm). CID defends infrastructures via rational and swarming agents led by human supervisors. The framework is designed to share information that may lead to discovery of an intrusion across multiple systems without compromising sensitive data.

The core of CID is a swarm of small mobile software agents that detect known problems or unusual differences between machines within an enclave. Each swarming agent, called a *Sensor*, has a classifier that employs a set of specific metrics (essentially a learning classifier system; Holland, *et al.,* 1999) on the hosts it visits. The Sensors act like digital ants and use ant-colony algorithms (Parunak, 1997) including depositing digital pheromone (Brueckner, 2000) to guide other Sensors to the host where troubles seem evident. Sensors each have unique classifiers, so with additional visiting Sensors, the system gathers more information on the alleged problem. When a Sensor finds evidence that a host may be compromised, it reports this to a stationary agent, the *Sentinel,* that monitors the host concerned. The Sentinel decides whether Sensors' alerts are of concern, based on its knowledge of the system. If the alert is valid, it will activate the Sensor and cause it go to other hosts leaving in its path a transient trail of digital pheromone that attracts other Sensors to the host where troubles were found.

Each enclave has a top-level software agent, the *Sergeant* that provides situational awareness to the human supervisor and receives guidance for the operation of the system from him or her. Through the Sergeant, the human supervisor may adjust parameters that govern the sensitivity and population of Sensors or define policies for the Sentinels. Sergeants may exchange attack information with Sergeants of other enclaves by passing along the classifiers of particularly successful Sensors.

We have implemented the CID system as a simulation model (Figure 4), and on a set of 64 virtual Linux machines. Simulation results showed that CID can control simulated attackers readily. The implementation showed how the approach was effective at detecting actual worms that were previously unknown to the system. While a multi-enclave implementation of CID is still future work at this writing, CID is an example of an approach that involves humans at an appropriate level and may foster collaboration while keeping sensitive data private.

LESSONS LEARNED

Lessons Learned from Collaborative Security in the DOE

In our experience, the tensions in collaborative security come primarily from the social/regulatory side. Although there are technical challenges, these are usually tractable. But the regulatory landscape where these monitoring programs must function, and the unusual combination of public and private resources at contractor-operated sites such as PNNL, amplify the social problems that exist in any large organization. Several key ideas that we have found effective in dealing with these problems are:

1. Remember who the real enemy is.
2. Trust your friends.
3. Collaboration is key to understanding the situation.
4. Reward the behaviors you wish to promote.

Remember the real enemy: Cyber security professionals have a serious job, but they must deal gently with each other and work together toward the common goal of defense. However, if security personnel at one site refuse to cooperate with those at another site, the ability to defend the whole will be diminished. Similarly, if distrust arises between levels of the hierarchy, the organization can become distracted by political maneuverings and lose focus on the activities of adversaries.

Micromanagement that violates site contract-operating agreements damages collaborative relationships particularly badly. Subordinates in the chain of command exist to make it possible to control the whole organization. When an agency-level inquiry violates the chain of command by trying to solve a site-level problem directly, it fosters distrust, overburdens agency staff and leaves site leadership uninformed. Violations of

Figure 4. CID's Cooperative Infrastructure Defense (CID) simulator

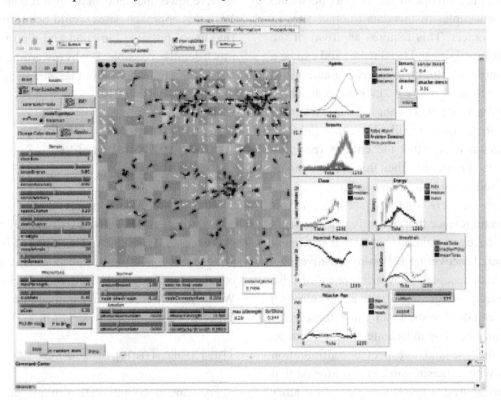

the chain of command should only be permitted to occur when serious harm (such as lives at risk) is imminent.

A common management approach in the government is to punish or fine organizations that show evidence of poor cyber security practices. This is a sound policy when the poor practices are uncovered as a result of an inspection. However, the typical outworking of this approach is that when an organization suffers a successful cyber attack, the higher headquarters uses that as evidence of poor practice and punishes the victim. By punishing subordinates when they are the victims of a real external attacker, higher headquarters becomes a more direct threat than the real enemy. This causes organizations to unduly concentrate on keeping superiors happy rather than actually protecting their systems.

Trust your friends: In a huge hierarchical meta-organization such as the U. S. government, or the

DOE, it is difficult for defenders to get to know and trust all the stakeholders with whom they must work. Analysts may believe that site security personnel are missing incidents or simply refusing to report them when in fact these "incidents" may actually have a reasonable explanation at the site level. Similarly, site security personnel may believe that the analysts don't add any value to the system and exist only to get the sites in trouble with their agency. Developing trust relationships, especially between personnel who interface at each level can help avoid these problems. Where no trust relationship exists, simply making a practice of assuming that the person on the other side is probably hard-working and reasonable helps tremendously.

There is no true substitute for developing and maintaining mature trust relationships between organizations. For example, much of the data being collected at sites is sensitive, but occasionally, it is in the interest of site security personnel to release samples of this data to other sites or analysis centers. This requires approval of the site's public affairs and legal teams and can be a lengthy process. But once approving authorities trust the site analysts (*e.g.*, they are reasonably sure they will not share data for purposes other than security, that they will release the minimum data necessary, and that the entities receiving the data can be trusted), then this process can be streamlined down to less than an hour.

Collaboration is key: Cyber security analysis is an inexact science that currently requires years of experience and training to master. It is in many ways an art. Discovering and tuning sensitive rules that have an acceptably low occurrence of false positives requires great skill, and simple changes to the monitored system can cause these rules to suddenly become inaccurate. Loss of context outside the site and unexpected configuration changes within the site can cause confusion that individual analysts cannot untangle alone. Rather than assuming that a sudden rash of alerts implies a serious incident, we believe that it is better to collaboratively examine the situation even if it takes longer. Of course, when sensitive information is at risk there is often not time to collaborate given the technical, social, and regulatory environment. This calls for better tools and processes such as written collaboration agreements and shared analysis tool suites.

Reward the behaviors you wish to promote: Although punishing sites for the intrusions they experience may make it appear that agencies are taking cyber security seriously, this practice provides an incentive for sites to perform minimal monitoring to meet regulatory requirements, rather than to do their best to detect and report every incident. Consider an alternative policy where agencies *expect* a certain frequency of incidents to occur and investigate when sites are not reporting enough incidents. The expected number of incidents would likely depend on the mission of the subordinate. Highly secure sites would be expected

to have fewer incidents than open research sites. With this approach, sites would be motivated to find every possible intrusion and report it in as much detail as possible. But by rewarding silence, agencies may be rewarding lax site security and dishonest reporting.

Lessons from other Domains Applied to Collaborative Cyber Security

In other domains, sharing lessons learned from both positive and negative experiences enhances everybody's experience. This applies in disciplines as diverse as public transportation, military counterinsurgency, and information sharing on the World Wide Web. It should apply equally well to cyber security.

The Public Transportation Sector

Every time a commercial airplane crashes, a train wrecks, or a commercial bus is involved in an accident, laws require a thorough analysis to determine the cause of the accident and how it can be prevented in the future. Once the cause has been determined, steps are taken to remediate the problem. This cycle of incident, analysis, and revision has made public transportation increasingly safer over time. Reporting requirements are codified in government regulations, and oversight agencies such as the Federal Aviation Administration (FAA) enforce these regulations.

Organizations that have cyber incidents would benefit greatly by following a similar cycle. For example, the state of California has created an office of Information Security and Privacy Protection (http://www.oispp.ca.gov/) under state law (CA Code § 11549-11549.6) to enact such a cycle. The mission of the office is, "to ensure the confidentiality, integrity, and availability of state systems and applications, and to promote and protect consumer privacy to ensure the trust of the residents of [California]." Government regulation is not the only means of achieving the benefits of sharing information, but it is a way to force it to occur. We believe it would be preferable for private companies and public agencies to establish conventions for information sharing and mutual defense. However, these kinds of partnerships can be difficult to motivate and maintain.

Military Counterinsurgency

In many ways, computer security resembles a war, but not one with clean fronts like World War II. Instead cyber security is a counterinsurgency war waged by loose coalitions, as is the war on terror. In the 1980's, the decade of the Orange Book (TCSEC, 1983), computer security professionals were just beginning to glimpse the implications of networking. Perimeter defense, firewalls, and access controls were seen as the answer to computer-security problems. But this is not the nature of the war we find ourselves in today. Just as today's militaries have had to graduate from trench warfare to asymmetric, counterinsurgency warfare, so our computer and network defenses must graduate from perimeter defense, and even defense-in-depth toward predictive, adaptive defenses that are more suited to protecting the complex computational infrastructures that are common in today's networked world (Frincke, *et al.*, 2006, and see i4.pnl.gov).

In an essay on the Iraq war, U.S. Army Lieutenant General David Petraeus (commander of the U.S. forces in Iraq) gave some advice on conducting a counterinsurgency war (Petraeus, 2006). The lessons learned are strikingly applicable to collaborative cyber security. Below are a few of Petraeus's lessons applied to collaborative cyber security:

- *Try to end each day with fewer enemies than when you started*—Defenders, regulators, and higher headquarters should first weigh the costs vs. benefits of every anticipated cyber security action from the

perspective of those affected. First, do no harm. Using force to ensure compliance will make enemies of those who are on the receiving end.

- *"Cultural awareness is a force multiplier."*—Security policy-makers must try to understand things from the site's point of view. Edicts from on high that do not take into account the specific needs of those they affect will ultimately be counterproductive. To collaborate, we must get out of the cloister and look at the situation from the perspective of others.

- *"Ultimate success depends on local leaders."*—No amount of force can produce as effective security as key site personnel in leadership positions who understand their user community and care about securing the system.

- *Equip and use junior leaders in the strategic rather than just the tactical fight*—Everyday, key site security personnel have the power to affect the security posture of the whole organization. To increase their positive effectiveness, we must mentor them in the long-term security issues faced by the whole organization.

- *"A leaders' most important duty is to set the right tone"*—By balancing priorities, a leader can make the whole organization more secure. Concentrating on defense to the exclusion of mission accomplishment, for instance, will backfire and ultimately reduce security and business.

Of course, Iraq and Afganistan are not the first counterinsurgency wars ever fought. Congressman Ike Skelton gave several other highly applicable lessons from the French and Indian war of the mid-18th century (Skelton, 2001). In this war, the British defenders were conducting conventional warfare against insurgent Indians. The British frequently relied on their infrastructure (particularly the telegraph) and their superior technology and armament. The Indians would attack the infrastructure by taking down miles of wire, or worse by replacing a few inches of wire somewhere along the hundreds of miles with a piece of blackened rawhide. Thus, the insurgents showed the conventional forces that technology cuts both ways. Adversaries use conventional means only when it best suits their purposes. Cyber defenders would do well to remember that our infrastructures are vulnerable and our methods of collaboration must be resilient and well defended.

Web 2.0: Wiki's, Blogs, etc.

Informal collaboration via the web has become a normal means of operation for many areas outside of computer security incident reporting. Several security vulnerability clearinghouses exist (most notably the Common Vulnerabilities and Exposures [CVE] public dictionary established by Mitre, http://cve.mitre.org/). Several anti-virus companies share anonymous information about computer viruses, worms, and vulnerabilities on the web as well. However, the information that appears there has generally been stripped of the context in which it was discovered to protect proprietary information. Numerous security blogs have appeared containing much useful information for securing computers.

The government is slowly accepting and utilizing the power of Web 2.0. (Walker 2007). In September of 2005, D. Calvin Andrus presented a paper entitled "The Wiki and the Blog: Toward a Complex Adaptive Intelligence Community" This paper turned into what is known today as Intellipedia, the intelligence community's version of wikipedia. Stephen Urquhart, a member of the Utah House of Representatives, was frustrated with the lack of participation in the benefits of the voucher system and as a result began blogging and eventually started an issues-based wiki, www.politicopia.com. The U.S Patent and Trademark Office is also attempting to utilize the "weapons of mass collaboration" (Wikinomics) by running

a pilot Peer to Patent Project that will make the patent process more open to the scientific community.

All these domains and many more show the value of open collaboration even when the risk of disclosure may be severe. Cyber security professionals involved in collaboration may benefit from lessons learned in these other disciplines.

CONCLUSION

Collaboration is the lifeblood of successful cyber security. In this chapter, we have presented a taxonomy of cyber-security collaboration types and described several key stakeholder types. We have presented case studies of how collaboration may work, what hinders it, and how it may be improved. Finally, we have presented some suggestions for improving collaboration from several non-cyber domains. The relatively brief history of cyber security has demonstrated that cyber attacks may be rapid, global, and coordinated. In the face of these dangers, *ad hoc* collaborations will be less effective than those based on shared understanding and agreement. Building successful collaborations in preparation for attacks requires forethought, well-defined stakeholder roles, and mutual respect.

Our research indicates that social and regulatory solutions are essential to the success of collaborative cyber security, and technical solutions enhance collaboration effectiveness. Non-technical solutions such as encouraging a "need to share" culture can provide excellent results even without new technologies. But new technologies that enhance information sharing, distributed analysis, and collaborative defense are also vital for enabling defenders to act at Internet speeds. Our adversaries are collaborating already, and the scope of cyber resources they control is truly staggering. Defenders from all kinds of organizations and backgrounds must collaborate to survive. By studying tensions in collaboration, how they affect incident detection and response, and how tensions may be mitigated, it is our hope to improve the safety, soundness, and security of our enterprises, infrastructures, and governments.

REFERENCES

Adams, A. A., & Sasse, M. A. (1999). Users are not the enemy. *Communications of the ACM, 42*(23), 40–46. doi:10.1145/322796.322806

Aitoro, J. R. (2008a, February 28). DHS gives itself a 'C' for cybersecurity. *Government Executive*. Retrieved from http://www.govexec.com/story_page.cfm?filepath=/dailyfed/0208/022808j1.htm

Aitoro, J. R. (2008b, March 2). OMB reports 60 percent increase in information security incidents. *Government Executive*. Retrieved fromhttp://www.govexec.com/story_page.cfm?filepath=/dailyfed/0308/030208a1.htm

Anderson, E. E., & Choobineh, J. (2008). Enterprise information security strategies. *Computers & Security, 27*(1-2), 22–29. doi:10.1016/j.cose.2008.03.002

Anderson, R. (1993). Why cryptosystems fail in. In *Proceedings of the 1st ACM Conference on Computer and Communications Security* (pp. 215-227). New York: ACM Press.

Barbaro, M., & Zeller, T., Jr. (2006, August). A Face Is Exposed for AOL Searcher No. 4417749. *The New York Times*.

Brueckner, S. (2000). *Return from the Ant: Synthetic Ecosystems for Manufacturing Control*. Unpublished doctoral dissertation, Humboldt-Universität: Berlin, Germany.

Caralli, R., & Wilson, W. (2004, July). *The Challenges of Security Management*. Carnegie Mellon University, Software Engineering Institute. Retrieved from http://www.cert.org/archive/pdf/ESMchallenges.pdf

Census Bureau. (2004). *Compendium of Public Employment: 2002 Census of Governments, Volume 3, Public Employment*. U.S. Census Bureau.

Cuppens, F., & Miege, A. (2002). Alert correlation in a cooperative intrusion detection framework. In *Proceedings of the 2002 IEEE Symposium on Security and Privacy*.

Dilley, C. (2008). *Air Force Cyber Command: Defending Cyberspace, or Controlling It?* Center for Defense Information. Retrieved from http://www.cdi.org/friendlyversion/printversion.cfm?documentID=4357

Economist. (2007, May 10). Estonia and Russia, a Cyber-Riot. *The Economist*.

Eliopoulos, C., Ibarguen, K., Thompson, P., Draelos, T., Mcintyre, A., Neumann, W., & Schroeppel, R. (2007, June). *Cross-Domain Information Sharing: Final Report* (I3P Research Report no. 10). Retrieved from http://www.thei3p.org/docs/publications/cdisresearchrep10.pdf Personal Information: Privacy, California Civil Code §1798.29 and §1798.82. Retrieved from http://info.sen.ca.gov/pub/01-02/bill/sen/sb_1351-1400/sb_1386_bill_20020926_chaptered.html

Executive Order 12333 of Dec. 4, 1981, in 46 FR 59941, 3 CFR, 1981 Comp., p. 200.

FBI. (2008). FY 2009 Budget Request Summary: A Pathway to Achieving Critical End-State Capabilities for the Federal Bureau of Investigation. In *Department of Justice FY 2009 Congressional Budget Submission*. Retrieved from http://www.usdoj.gov/jmd/2009justification/pdf/fy09-fbi.pdf

FISMA. (2002). *Title 44 USC Ch. 35, Federal Information Security Management Act of 2002.* Retrieved from http://csrc.nist.gov/drivers/documents/FISMA-final.pdf

Frincke, D. A., Wespi, A., & Zamboni, D. (2007). From Intrusion Detection to Self Protection. *Computer Networks, 51*(5), 1233–1238. doi:10.1016/j.comnet.2006.10.004

GAO. (2006). *Managing Sensitive Information: Departments of Energy and Defense Policies and Oversight Could Be Improved* (Report GAO-06-369). Retrieved from http://www.gao.gov/new.items/d06369.pdf

Gao, X., & Liu, W. (2005). Incentives for information sharing across branches in e-government. In *Proceedings of ICSSSM '05. 2005 International Conference on Services Systems and Services Management, 2005* (Vol. 2, pp. 1481-1483). Retrieved from http://ieeexplore.ieee.org/iel5/10017/32161/01500245.pdf

Garber, L. (2000). Denial-of-service attacks rip the Internet. *Computer, 33*(4), pp. 12-17. Retrieved from http://doi.ieeecomputersociety.org/10.1109/MC.2000.839316

Gaylord, C. (2008, August 13). *Anatomy of a cyberwar in Georgia, in Christian Science Monitor.* Boston, MA: The First Church of Christ.

Gibson, T. (2001). An Architecture for Flexible Multi-Security Domain Networks. In *Proceedings of the Network and Distributed Systems Security Symposium*, San Diego, CA. Retrieved from http://www.enhyper.com/content/gibson.pdf

Gooch, D. J., Hubbard, S. D., Moore, M. W., & Hill, J. (2001). Firewalls — Evolve or Die. *BT Technology Journal, 19*(3), 89–98. doi:10.1023/A:1011994416892

Goranson, C.A., Fink, G.A., & Kuchar, O.A. (2007). *Data Network and Policy Modeling, Year-end Report, FY07* (PNNL-16927 FY07) [Unpublished] . Pacific Northwest National Laboratory, Richland, WA.

Haack, J. N., Fink, G. A., Maiden, W. M., McKinnon, A. D., & Fulp, E. W. (2009), "Mixed-Initiative Cyber Security: Putting humans in the right loop." In *Proceedings of the 2009 Workshop on Mixed-Initiative Multiagent Systems* (MIMS '09), 2009. PNNL-SA-64635

Holland, J. H., et al. (1999). What Is a Learning Classifier System? In *Proceedings of Learning Classifier Systems '99*. Heidelberg, Germany: Springer-Verlag.

Iyer, S., & Thuraisingham, B. (2007). Design and Simulation of Trust Management Techniques for a Coalition Data Sharing Environment. In *Proceedings of the 11th IEEE International Workshop on Future Trends of Distrubuted Computing Systems (FTDCS '07)*. Retrieved from http://ieeexplore.ieee.org/iel5/4144597/4144598/04144616.pdf

Jeong-Wook, K. (2007). Experiments and Countermeasures of Security Vulnerabilities on Next Generation Network. In *Proceedings of the Future Generation Communication and Networking (fgcn 2007)*.

Kean, T. H., Hamilton, L. H., Ben-Veniste, R., Kerrey, B., Fielding, F. F., Lehman, J. F., et al. (2004). *The 9-11 Commission Report: Final Report of the National Commission on Terrorist Attacks Upon the United States*. Washington, DC: U. S. Government Printing Office. Retrieved from http://govinfo.library.unt.edu/911/report/index.htm

Kshetri, N. (2006). The simple economics of cybercrimes. *IEEE Security and Privacy, 4*(1), 33-39. Retrieved from http://doi.ieeecomputersociety.org/10.1109/MSP.206.27

Lee, J., & Rao, H. R. (2007). Exploring the causes and effects of inter-agency information sharing systems adoption in the anti/counter-terrorism and disaster management domains. In *Proceedings of the 8th Annual international Conference on Digital Government Research: Bridging Disciplines & Domains,* Philadelphia, PA (pp. 155-163). New York: ACM. Retrieved from http://portal.acm.org/citation.cfm?doid=1248460.1248485

Lesk, M. (2007). The New Front Line: Estonia under Cyberassault. *IEEE Security & Privacy,* *5*(4), 76–79. doi:10.1109/MSP.2007.98

Markoff, J. (2008, August 13). Before the Gunfire, Cyberattacks. *The New York Times.*

Nojiri, D., Rowe, J., & Levitt, K. (2003). Cooperative Response Strategies for Large Scale Attack Mitigation. In *Proceedings of DARPA Information Survivability Conference and Exposition (DISCEX 2003)* (pp. 293-302). Washington, DC: IEEE Press.

O'Neil, L. R. (2005). *PNNL Risk Assessment Sensitivity Determination (RASD) tool.* Paper presented at DOE Cyber Security Group conference 2005, Denver, CO.

Papadopoulos, C., Lindell, R., Mehringer, J., Hussain, A., & Govindan, R. (2003). Cossack: coordinated suppression of simultaneous attacks. In *Proceedings of the 2003 DARPA Information Survivability Conference and Exposition.* Retrieved from http://ieeexplore.ieee.org/iel5/8503/26875/01194868.pdf

Parunak, H. V. D. (1997). Go to the Ant: Engineering Principles from Natural Multi-Agent Systems. *Annals of Operations Research,* *75,* 69–101. doi:10.1023/A:1018980001403

Petraeus, D. H. (2006). Learning Counterinsurgency: Observations from Soldiering in Iraq. *Military Review.* Retrieved from http://usacac.army.mil/CAC/milreview/English/JanFeb06/Petraeus1.pdf

Purser, S. A. (2004). Improving the ROI of the security management process. *Computers & Security,* *23*(7), 542–546. doi:10.1016/j.cose.2004.09.004

Radhakrishnan, R., Jamil, M., Mehfuz, S., & Moinuddin, M. (2007). Security issues in IPv6. In *Proceedings of the ICNS. Third International Conference on Networking and Services.*

Robinson, T. (2005). Data security in the age of compliance. *NetWorker,* *9*(3), 24–30. doi:10.1145/1086762.1086764

Scher, M. (2006). On Doing 'Being Reasonable.' Retrieved from http://www.usenix.org/publications/login/2006-12/pdfs/scher.pdf

Simatupang, T. M., & Sridharan, R. (2002). The Collaborative Supply Chain. *International Journal of Logistics Management,* *13*(1), 15–30. doi:10.1108/09574090210806333

Skelton, I. (2001). America's Frontier Wars: Lessons for Asymmetric Conflicts. *Military Review,* 24-27. Retrieved from http://usacac.army.mil/CAC2/MilitaryReview/Archives/COINReaderII.pdf

Smith, T., Byrd, G. T., Xiaoyong, W., Hongiie, X., Thangavelu, K., Wang, R., & Shah, A. (2003). Dynamic PKI and secure tuplespaces for distributed coalitions. In *Proceedings DARPA Information Survivability Conference and Exposition.* Retrieved from http://ieeexplore.ieee.org/xpls/abs_all.jsp?arnumber=1194884

Specht, S. M., & Lee, R. B. (2004). Distributed Denial of Service: Taxonomies of Attacks, Tools and Countermeasures. In *Proc. 17th Int'l Conf. Parallel and Distributed Computing Systems (PDCS '04).*

TCSEC. (1983). *Department of Defense Trusted Computer System Evaluation Criteria.* Department of Defense Computer Security Center.

Thomson, I. (2007). *Russia 'hired botnets for Estonia cyber-war*. Retrieved from http://www.itnews.com.au/News/53322,russia-hired-botnets-for-estonia-cyberwar.aspx

Traynor, I. (2007, May 21). Russia accused of unleashing cyberwar to disable Estonia. *The Guardian*. Retrieved from http://www.guardian.co.uk/world/2007/may/17/topstories3.russia

Tsiakis, T., & Stephanides, G. (2005). The economic approach of information security. *Computers & Security*, *24*(2), 105–108. doi:10.1016/j.cose.2005.02.001

United States Constitution. (n.d.). *Amendment IV,1791*. Retrieved from http://www.law.cornell.edu/constitution/constitution.table.html

US-CERT. (2008). Privacy Impact Assessment for Einstein 2. Retrieved from http://www.dhs.gov/xlibrary/assets/privacy/privacy_pia_einstein2.pdf

Wait, P. (2006, April 3). Feds fumble with FISMA performance: Some doubt that grades give a true picture. *Government Computer News*. Retrieved from http://www.gcn.com/print/25_7/40277-1.html

Walker, R. (2007, May 21). Government taps the power of us. *Federal Computer Week*. Retrieved from http://www.fcw.com/print/13_16/news/102750-1.html

Yee, K.-P. (2004). Aligning Security and Usability. *IEEE Security & Privacy*, *2*(5), 48–55. doi:10.1109/MSP.2004.64

Zhang, N. (2007). On the Communication Complexity of Privacy-Preserving Information Sharing Protocols. In *Proceedings of the Intelligence and Security Informatics, 2007 IEEE* (pp. 289-295). doi: 10.1109/ISI.2007.379487

ENDNOTES

[1] The most common type of network flow data is the Cisco Netflow where each record summarizes a stream of TCP/IP packets that share the same source, destination, protocol, and type of service. Network flows contain only records of connections that were made, just as telephone pen/trap records contain only lists of dialed numbers, not call audio.

[2] The March 2002 Census of Government Employees (Census Bureau, 2004) estimates there were 2,426,000 full-time equivalent (FTE) federal employees: The inclusion of contractors may easily triple that number. Our experience in DOE indicates there is usually a 3:1 ratio of computers (including servers) to personnel yielding a very conservative estimate of 30 million computers, each responsible for tens to thousands of megabytes of traffic daily.

Chapter 4
Challenges in Sharing Computer and Network Logs

Adam Slagell
University of Illinois at Urbana-Champaign, USA

Kiran Lakkaraju
University of Illinois at Urbana-Champaign, USA

ABSTRACT

It is desirable for many reasons to share information, particularly computer and network logs. Researchers need it for experiments, incident responders need it for collaborative security, and educators need this data for real world examples. However, the sensitive nature of this information often prevents its sharing. Anonymization techniques have been developed in recent years that help reduce risk and navigate the trade-offs between privacy, security and the need to openly share information. This chapter looks at the progress made in this area of research over the past several years, identifies the major problems left to solve and sets a roadmap for future research.

INTRODUCTION

On March 20, 2004, the security incident response team at the National Center for Supercomputing Applications (NCSA) at the University of Illinois received an automated alert indicating that a particular NCSA machine was making an atypical number of outbound connections to external hosts. Often, when something like this happened in the past, it was because a machine had been infected with a worm or become part of a botnet. Naturally, the team investigated the anomaly, and they found

that unauthorized ports were open. By scanning the machine and reviewing their network flows, they found that the host was running a backdoor SSH client granting remote access to an unauthorized user. Worse yet, a subsequent scan of the network revealed that other machines had the same strange port open and were also compromised. Little did they realize that this was only the very smallest tip of the iceberg.

Rather quickly, it was discovered that the attacker, who later started identifying himself as "Stakkato," spread his attacks across much more than the NCSA network. He exploited a number of specific vulnerabilities across many of the TeraGrid

DOI: 10.4018/978-1-60566-414-9.ch004

sites. The TeraGrid was at the time the world's largest, most comprehensive distributed computing infrastructure for open scientific research, with high-performance computing resources spread across 11 institutions. While the attacks were expanding to encompass more and more institutions, they were also escalating in frequency. Because the attacker installed Trojaned SSH daemons on many infected machines, he was able to compromise accounts faster than they could be closed or have their passwords changed. This problem was exacerbated by the fact that many of the TeraGrid resources shared authentication credentials, as a typical user could run jobs on any of the TeraGrid supercomputers. Some of the sites were at times just trying to keep their heads above water to stay on top of this problem; eventually, all users were forced to change their passwords at these sites.

As the scope of the problem grew, even beyond TeraGrid, the FBI was brought in on the matter. A few key institutions became the points of contact between the FBI and the many other institutions involved with the case (which was named Major Case 216 by the FBI). Before the investigation was finally complete, the attacks had spanned 19 months and thousands of sites, including high-security military sites and federal research laboratories, university sites, private sector sites, and machines owned by individuals, both in the U.S. and in Europe. It was finally tracked back to a teenager in Sweden after whose apprehension the attacks suddenly stopped (Nixon, 2006).

Lessons Learned

We learned a great deal as one of the victim sites in this experience. First, not only can attacks be very large and sustained, but such attacks can be perpetrated by a single individual. In fact, if your organization is the target of a focused digital intrusion—not just worms or script-kiddies collecting bots—it is likely that your organization is just one of many involved in the same attack. Understanding the specific attack that we experi-

enced required a very broad picture of the incident and the cooperation and collaboration of many individuals at many different institutions. Achieving this collaboration and establishing trust were among the main challenges of the endeavor.

It was not uncommon for a large site to invest thousands of man-hours on handling this incident. One organization might find compromised hosts from hundreds of other organizations. When our incident response team contacted the other incident responders and system administrators, they gave them details on the compromised machines and offered our help with the investigations. Of course, the responses ran the gamut, from people completely unwilling even to acknowledge what was told to them to people openly asking for help and readily sharing data. However, most people were reluctant to cooperate too much. Usually they would only answer questions as to whether or not a particular machine had also attacked them, or perhaps would share high-level network data, like network flows, with our team. Nevertheless, even the limited traffic data we were able to obtain helped us better understand the scope and overall structure of the attack.

Reasons for the reluctance included legal issues, privacy concerns, concerns about leaking sensitive information, and a general inability to establish trust and secure communication channels. In fact, most communication was an ad hoc mixture consisting primarily of phone calls and PGP-encrypted e-mails. Luckily, there were already existing relationships with several other victim organizations through TeraGrid, Department of Energy (DOE) contacts, and contacts at other universities. The FBI also served as an intermediary in some places. That collaboration between the FBI and a small subset of the organizations involved in the attack was absolutely necessary to the traceback and eventual apprehension of the attacker. However, there is no doubt that efficiency could have been greatly improved had we overcome many more of the issues involved in sharing among the victims the logs relevant to the attack.

Why We need better Solutions to Log Anonymization

The Importance of Data Sharing

The case above illustrates a specific scenario in which log sharing and the difficulties associated with it were very important. However, the need for collaboration and sharing of network traces and computer logs is important to various communities for different purposes, including collaborative security, research, and education, among others. Industry is interested in sharing logs for multiple reasons. In general, corporations are interested in overall trends and activity on the Internet, and consequently, many subscribe and contribute to organizations like the Internet Storm Center and DShield. However, interest in more focused log sharing has also grown for industry; industrial entities were involved in FBI Major Case 216. That coordinated attack hit several companies as it crossed organizational and national boundaries. To understand an attack and get the big picture, companies need to collaborate and share information; otherwise they remain out of the loop. Unfortunately, without mechanisms and procedures in place for safe sharing of narrowly focused data of that level of detail, many companies choose to remain in the dark.

While the investigation of specific attacks targeted at the infrastructure supporting researchers is of concern to them—Major Case 216 hit many research labs and universities—the researchers themselves do not share the log data in those cases. It is the incident response team or system administrators at their labs who respond, and those people's motivations are similar to those of industry described above. However, researchers often do share logs and network traces for another purpose and on a much larger scale. Security researchers frequently need large data sets to run experiments. For example, those working on new intrusion detection systems and algorithms need to test their tools against real network traces for evaluation of false positive and negative rates. The network measurement community also needs large and diverse sets of network traces to evaluate the impact of changes in networking protocols. Other computer scientists have used web server logs to evaluate the effectiveness of different caching strategies on performance. The list of applications goes on and on.

While researchers can sometimes get away with generating data sets in-house, these are often not very representative samples. The data simply lack diversity because they were collected at a single vantage point. In addition to difficulties in generating diverse data, it is difficult to generate significant amounts of data, unless they are synthetically generated. While synthetic data are obviously useless for investigation of a specific intrusion for incident response, they can still be useful for some types of research. Unfortunately, they are not useful for all research. For example, even the best synthetic data sets for security research have been found to be problematic when intrusion detection systems are being evaluated (McHugh, 2000). Therefore, it is often the case that real data must be shared to accumulate the necessarily large and diverse data sets for computer science research. In fact, new repositories have been set up specifically to allow such sharing (e.g., the PREDICT repository[1]), though not without difficulties.

Log sharing has also become important to good pedagogy, and educators and those creating educational materials require logs and network traces to be shared. Professors want logs to create meaningful student projects. Institutions like SANS that train security professionals need logs and data for their classes focused on effective log analysis. Book publishers often need them for CD exercises they provide as companions to books. In all these cases, real log data are much more meaningful and desirable to students.

The importance of this kind of sharing has caught the government's attention, including that of the Department of Homeland Security, which has established Information Sharing and Analysis Centers (ISAC) to facilitate the storage and sharing of information about security threats (Slagell & Yurcik, 2005). Further, the importance of log sharing has been recognized in the National Strategy to Secure Cyberspace (NSSC), which explicitly lists sharing as one of its highest priorities—including data sharing within the government, within industry sectors, and between the government and industry. In fact, of the eight action items identified in the NSSC report, three are directly related to log data sharing: Item 2, "Provide for the development of tactical and strategic analysis of cyber attacks and vulnerability assessments"; Item 3, "Encourage the development of a private sector capability to share a synoptic view of the health of cyberspace"; and Item 8, "Improve and enhance public/private information sharing involving cyber-attacks, threats, and vulnerabilities."

The Importance of Data Sanitization

While all parties—educators, industry, government, and researchers—agree that we need to encourage sharing of computer and network logs for different uses, such sharing is still impeded for various reasons (Slagell & Yurcik, 2005). Chief among these reasons is the fact that data are often very sensitive. Logs and network traces can easily identify network topologies, services running, and the security architecture of the networks or machines they describe. At the very least, this makes reconnaissance easier for would-be attackers. At worst, it can reveal specific vulnerabilities and points of entry. Naturally, system administrators and network operators are thus reluctant to share such data without strong motivation.

There are also privacy issues about which network operators, particularly at Internet service providers, are concerned. Their customers have an expectation of privacy, often spelled out specifically in a corporate privacy policy, and the logs describe behaviors of those customers. It is thus in the providers' economic interest to consider the implications of sharing their logs, even if they have no official privacy policy. Furthermore, their customers may be afforded legal protection under several laws, even if there is no protection in the privacy policy (Sicker, Ohm, & Grunwald, 2007).

For effective data sharing, it is clear that we need to address the privacy concerns of data owners. In recent years, such concerns have been tackled through use of anonymization (also called *data sanitization*). The premise is simple: remove or modify information from the data set that could violate privacy. For instance, if a hospital plans to release medical logs, it would remove or modify sensitive information such as patient names and addresses. For network logs, the policy could be to obscure individual addresses.

Unfortunately, even if companies think they protect the privacy of their customers through sanitization mechanisms and are careful about meeting legal requirements, identifiable data may be released and lead to major embarrassment. Both AOL™ and Netflix™ have recently exposed themselves to such embarrassment by releasing large data sets they believed to be sufficiently anonymized, but were later found to be insufficiently protected. AOL™ released logs from their search engine (Hafner, 2006), and Netflix™ released information on user movie ratings and profiles (Narayanan & Shmatikov, 2006). One can be sure that both companies will be more hesitant to share such data in the future, as might other corporations that have taken notice of these events.

Consequently, there is a pressing need for research into anonymization mechanisms and the development of better anonymization tools. FBI Major Case 216 has given us the motivation to share data; the AOL™ and Netflix™ debacles have sounded a warning on the problems of sharing data. For collaborative security to move into the future, a solution must be reached between the extremes of all or nothing. It is this question of how to balance the needs of the different parties that we are tackling.

Log Anonymization Tools

When we began our research into log anonymization and created our position paper a few years ago (Slagell & Yurcik, 2005), the situation was very different. As we argued then, there were few tools performing anything beyond the most rudimentary forms of log anonymization. Tools were one-size-fits-all, with just a few options on how to do the anonymization. Log anonymizers would usually handle just one type of log and often anonymize only one field, typically IP addresses. Furthermore, there were only one or two types of algorithms for anonymization available for that one field.

There were several problems. First, one usually had to have a different anonymization tool for each type of log, even if it was just for different formats of the same kind of data. For many types of logs, there were no tools whatsoever available to anonymize them. That led to more substandard one-off tools that had few options and worked for only very specific data formats. Thus, people created a new tool for every anonymization task, rather than use one tool and change the policy or configuration. Last, the dearth of anonymization options meant that there was essentially only one level at which a log could be anonymized. However, depending upon the level of trust between two parties, the data owner might want to anonymize logs more or less. At the time, there was no granularity of choice, and anonymization tended to be superficial. Therefore, the tools available then were usually useful just for sharing with parties that were highly trusted.

Much has changed since then, and many researchers have answered the call we made for new log anonymization frameworks. In addition to

FLAIM (Slagell, Lakkaraju, & Luo, 2006), which is the anonymization framework we developed, several other anonymization tools have since been developed (Koukis, Antonatos, Antoniades, Markatos, & Trimintzios, 2006; Pang & Paxson, 2003; Pang, Allman, Paxson, & Lee, 2006; Ramaswamy & Wolf, 2007; Slagell, Li, & Luo, 2005; Slagell, Lakkaraju, & Luo, 2006; Yurcik, Woolam, Hellings, Khan, & Thuraisingham, 2007; Zhang & Li, 2006; Zhang, Wang, & Li, 2007). While most of them are still focused on network logs (FLAIM handles both network and system logs), many can anonymize almost any header field in a network log, and most of them support more than one type of basic anonymization primitive. So network owners now often have the raw tools necessary to sanitize their logs, but this solves only half the problem. For those tools are useless unless you know how to use them effectively.

Creating Effective Anonymization Policies

One of the major challenges now is not the creation of good log anonymization tools, but the creation of an anonymization policy to meet the needs of a given situation. At a minimum, there are always two parties involved in log sharing: the data owner, who typically is the person who generated the data, and the data analyst, who wants to use the data. The data analyst could be a researcher needing the data for experiments, an educator wanting to use them for a class project, or even a security incident investigator wanting details on a specific attack. Additionally, there is often a third party, the person(s) who are the object of the data set. Computer and network logs often describe behaviors of individual users, and they have a vested interest in this hypothetical log sharing as well.

Unfortunately, these parties do not always have interests that are aligned. The data owner is often concerned with security. The logs may contain sensitive information about their network, assets,

Figure 1. The data anonymization tradeoff

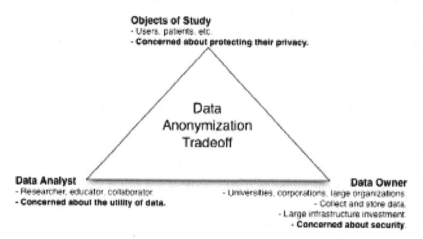

or security posture. Therefore, they do not want the logs to get into the hands of an adversary, and they know they lose control after they share the data. The person analyzing the data wants them to be as accurate as possible. Alterations of the data can change the results of any studies on the data. This is even more problematic if one does not even know how the data were altered through anonymization. Lastly, if the data are about the behaviors of specific people, they are likely to be interested in protecting their privacy. When they are customers of the data owner, their concerns may align with the data owner. However, that is not always the case, and if the data are not sensitive to the owner, the owner may lose the incentive to protect them adequately. Creating an anonymization policy is all about balancing the conflicting needs of these different actors.

Fundamentally, the problem comes down to what we have referred to as the *utility vs. security trade-off* in anonymizing logs (Slagell & Yurcik, 2005). The idea is rather straightforward. As you increase security or privacy requirements on the data, more anonymization must be performed. That means more information loss, which can never result in more utility to the one analyzing the data. At best, it can be a neutral change. So if one were to plot a function of information loss vs. utility—for any measure of utility—it would be a

monotonically non-increasing function. Of course, it isn't quite that simple, because information loss is not one-dimensional, and neither is any measure of security. At best, we can create partially ordered sets where one state is more secure than another, but not necessarily comparable to another state. For example, anonymization policy A may protect against adversary X, but not Y. Anonymization policy B may protect against adversary Y, but not X. In that case, one cannot say that either A or B is a more secure policy, unless one adversary's capabilities are a strict subset of the other. Furthermore, the information loss could be equal, but simply affect two different fields in the policies. All of this, plus the fact that there could be infinitely many kinds of valid utility measurement, make finding an optimal anonymization policy very challenging; it will never be as simple as sliding a rule to choose between two one-dimensional metrics in some sort of zero-sum game.

In the past few years we have learned that there is much more work still to be done in this area of research. While we have found solutions to some problems, we have created even more questions and discovered new challenges. The purpose of this chapter is to lay out the greatest open problems in the area of -and describe what we have learned in our initial attempts at solving these problems.

Figure 2. Static anonymization process

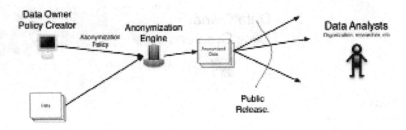

Our Vision

Current anonymization techniques usually assume a static anonymization process, one in which the data owner "pushes" anonymized data to clients. Figure 2 illustrates this process. The key steps are:

- Data owner chooses logs to anonymize.
- Data owner evaluates needs of a single or specific set of analysts.
- Data owner creates a specific anonymization tool/technique for this data analyst's needs.

The data owner is the primary agent in this static process; he or she is the one who decides which logs to anonymize and how to anonymize them. However, a static process provides only minimal interaction between the data analyst and the data owner.

The anonymization engine is tailored towards the analyst and data. It is usually created specifically for this sharing need; thus, it is not flexible and cannot be extended to other data sets.

While there have been significant results, the static anonymization process is inflexible and slow to implement. FBI Major Case 216 was a scenario in which data analysts needed quick access to a variety of logs anonymized at different levels for different organizations. The critical components missing from the static model of the anonymization process are

- Multiple clients,
- A variety of log types, and
- Multiple levels of anonymization.

To capture those aspects, we envision a dynamic anonymization process in which data owners and analysts dynamically interact. Figure 3 highlights this process. The key steps are:

1. Data analyst requests data from data owner.
2. Data owner evaluates the request, considering
   a. Relationship of the analyst to the data owner,
   b. Trustworthiness of the analyst, and
   c. What logs the analyst requires.
3. Based on those considerations, the data owner determines whether an anonymization policy exists that can meet the needs of both parties and generates one that minimally anonymizes the data, if such a policy exists.
4. The anonymization policy tailored to this request is applied to the relevant data.

The key aspect of this approach is the dynamic anonymization policy generation by the data owner predicated on the needs of an arbitrary data analyst.

Figure 3. A vision of dynamic log anonymization

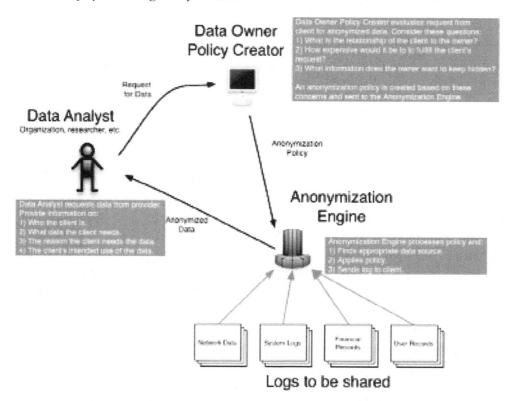

Challenges with a Model of a Dynamic Anonymization Process

To fully implement a dynamic anonymization system, we have to address many questions:

- How do we measure the utility of a log for a client?
- How can we describe the impact of anonymization on a log?
- How do we thwart de-anonymization and linking with other sources?

While there has been significant progress in this area of research since our position paper in 2005 (Slagell & Yurcik, 2005), there are still many challenges to effective sanitization of network traces and other computer log formats. These challenges can be categorized as either practical (engineering) or research challenges.

In terms of research challenges, the main questions to be answered are

- How do we measure the utility of a log, and
- How can de-anonymization be prevented?

Without a solid understanding of these fundamental issues, efficient data sharing will never take place. The practical challenges are

- To develop a production-quality, flexible, multi-log, multi-field, multi-level anonymization tool, and
- To negotiate anonymization policies automatically on the fly.

In this section, we discuss these four main challenges and describe the progress that has been made towards addressing them.

Practical Challenges

Better Tools

Log anonymization tools have improved in many ways. For example, most newer anonymization tools support more than one anonymization algorithm. Also, almost all of them support anonymization of several fields. Both FLAIM (Slagell et al., 2006) and AnonTool (Koukis, D., Antonatos, S., Antoniades, D., Markatos, E., & Trimintzios, P, 2006) are very flexible network log anonymization tools, although they make different trade-offs among usability, flexibility, and speed. Still, all of the log anonymization tools are deficient in some way.

One of the major drawbacks to all of these tools is that they are research prototypes and not commercial-quality software products. There is no official support, and after their supporting grants expire, such tools tend to fall into disuse. They are no longer updated to fix bugs, address newer log formats, or add requested features. While some, like FLAIM, are modular and allow expansion to handle new types of data (even more than network logs), none of these tools come with developer documentation to help those who would improve them. Few even have good documentation for users, let alone developers. Third parties have expanded FLAIM and created additional modules (Bezzi & Kounine, 2008), but this would have been difficult without the help they received from the original developers. *A strong commercial product would not only have good documentation for developers, but ideally would have a toolkit that would allow modules for new data formats to be quickly developed and new anonymization algorithms to be easily added.*

Furthermore, being research prototypes, those tools tend not to be optimized and suitable for use in a production environment. Most of the anonymizers cannot keep up with high data rates at line speed, and the ones that do sacrifice generality for speed. *None of the current anonymization tools make good use of multi-core technology by parallelizing anonymization operations.* While not all kinds of anonymization could be done in parallel (because of the special relationships between fields and records), in principle much of it could be parallelized to realize significant performance gains.

A problem that is more fundamental than the lack of optimizations and additional features (such as support for more types of data) is the lack of standards. *First, it would be of great benefit to researchers to have a standard meta data language to describe how a log or network trace was anonymized.* If they do not know how the data were anonymized, how can they know what effect that anonymization may have on their analysis? *Second, there are no standard formats for a policy language, and the existing policy languages are limited in many ways.* For example, while FLAIM's XML policy language is perhaps the most human-readable and flexible, it still lacks valuable features, such as a way to specify conditionals. One must anonymize all instances of a particular field with the same algorithm, regardless of any semantic information in that field. AnonTool addresses that problem in a fashion, but at the cost of creating a very opaque mechanism to specify how anonymization will be performed. A standard here would certainly make it simpler for one to use different anonymization tools to suit specific needs.

Negotiating Policies

The ability to measure utility and understand de-anonymization is really a prerequisite to solving the problem of creating sound anonymization policies. Now that there is actual choice, with the current-generation tools, in how one anonymizes a network trace or log, the issue remains of how to do so intelligently. As we have argued, this means balancing the requirements of three actors: the data provider, the data analyst, and the user (the one about whose behavior the data speak). The provider is interested mostly in security, the data analyst in some sort of measurement of utility, and the user in security as far as it concerns his or her privacy. The research questions we discuss in the sections that follow are about understanding the requirements of these parties, and are driven by the need to create anonymization policies that work for all parties.

As we come to better understand these utility and security requirements, this process of balancing different parties' requirements can be automated so that data providers do not simply have to guess whether or not anonymization has been sufficient. We have taken the first step towards this goal (King, 2008) with the creation of a predicate logic to describe the requirements and a mapping between a taxonomy of de-anonymization attacks and the predicate logic. This has been possible in part because we developed a taxonomy based upon attack preconditions. Thus, there is a natural mapping from the taxonomy to statements about what kinds of information must be removed, and these can be expressed as simple logical syllogisms in conjunctive normal form. For example, one requirement in plain English may be that *IP addresses must be anonymized so that pseudonyms are not consistent and the granularity of timestamps must be at the minute level, or IP addresses must be completely annihilated*. Statements such as those are a natural fit for a first-order predicate logic.

We can also create statements in this logic about what *cannot* be anonymized. Any utility requirement is really a statement about what cannot be anonymized. Therefore, the complete requirements of all parties in regard to their anonymization constraints can be expressed as a logical statement, and the variables are those things we can specify in a policy. By prototyping this predicate logic in Prolog, we have been able to load information about what makes a well-formed policy, a set of statements reflecting policy constraints, and a policy. Then Prolog can tell us whether or not the policy is well-formed and in compliance with the

requirements. Furthermore, we can query it to ask whether or not a policy meeting all the requirements even exists, and, with a simple enhancement, it can even generate a set of conditions for such a policy. Software could be created to take the set of values that makes the statement true and translate it into an explicit policy for software like FLAIM (Slagell et al., 2006).

Of course, a great deal of work needs to be done to reach the goal of automatic negotiation of policies. First, we have just created a research proof of concept implemented in Prolog. The bulk of the work was in creating the first-order predicate logic itself. A full implementation would have an interface that allows one to select an adversary to protect against (or part of the de-anonymization attack taxonomy) along with a set of utility constraints, translate that into the predicate logic, generate a set of minimally complex policies to choose from, and translate the user-chosen one into an actual XML policy for a tool like FLAIM. It would also allow policies for anonymization tools to be uploaded and validated against a set of constraints.

Another area for researchers to address is how we can negotiate policies more quickly. The full problem of finding policies that make the predicate true in this logic can be shown to be NP-hard. We have used some heuristics to scope the search and removed variables and statements in the predicate logic where appropriate to speed up the process, but this basic approach gets very complex as the policy language becomes complex. Specifically, the problem grows exponentially with respect to the number of fields and anonymization algorithms. Work needs to be done either to take an entirely different approach to negotiating these constraints that does not use a predicate logic, or to create heuristics that may not always lead to a minimal solution, but to a solution within less time.

One of the strengths of our approach to measuring the security of an anonymization policy is that our attack taxonomy (discussed in more detail below), and hence our adversarial model, map so well into the predicate logic. However, utility requirements must be manually specified in this logic. One reason is that the research on measuring utility is far less complete, and it is specific to the type of analysis to be done with the data. The security of a policy does not depend upon what is to be done with the data, only upon potential adversaries, and therefore is more universal. As people start to look at measuring utility for different applications, research should be done to find ways to map different utility levels or requirements into specific statements in the predicate logic.

Adversarial models may adapt, and new attacks may be discovered. With our approach, as new attacks are discovered, they must be put into the taxonomy, and a mapping must be manually created to connect it to the adversarial model. It would be far better if one could just map directly from the adversarial model into the predicate logic. The adversarial model would thus be much less likely to need constant updates than the taxonomy of known attacks. Furthermore, it would be fruitful to look at how one can map from other adversarial models into constraints specified in the predicate logic. We even envision better adversarial models that capture probabilistic statements. Ideally, in the future, we would want to specify that we need a certain probabilistic level of assurance that an adversary cannot de-anonymize something. That would require modification not only of the adversarial model, but potentially of the predicate logic as well.

Research Challenges

Measuring Utility

Critical to development of any anonymization policy is an understanding of the needs of the person(s) analyzing the data. If not done properly, anonymization can affect the result of experiments and make the data useless. Therefore, it is imperative to understand the constraints of what *cannot* be anonymized as imposed by the data analyst.

Unfortunately, there can be no single metric of utility. Depending upon the users and the tasks they wish to perform with the data, different fields within the data are of value. Furthermore, the same fields may need to be anonymized more or less. For example, a network researcher may need the TCP flags and TTL to remain untouched and the subnet structure to remain intact. Someone testing an intrusion detection system may not care about any of that and may even be satisfied with any random permutation of IP addresses. On the other hand, an incident response team may want to get logs from another organization that was attacked and to investigate what the attacker did on the other network. At a minimum, they cannot anonymize the attacker's IP address(es).

Very little has been done to examine how anonymization affects utility. We performed the first extensive investigation with the development of the *IDS Utility Metric* (Lakkaraju & Slagell, 2008), although we must note that the basic idea of analyzing the effect of anonymization on intrusion detection systems (IDSes) was presented earlier (Koukis, D., Antonatos, S., Antoniades, D., Markatos, E., & Trimintzios, P, 2006). The main idea of this our work was to investigate changes in false positive and negative rates as anonymization policies were changed, with the purpose of analyzing the effect that anonymization would have on collaborative intrusion detection and incident response. We tested hundreds of policies against the MIT Lincoln Labs DARPA data set (McHugh, 2000) and looked at the differentials of these metrics to determine what kinds of policies had more or less of an effect.

While that work was progress towards the goal of understanding how anonymization affects utility, it still just scratched the surface. Even while considering the task of intrusion detection, we varied only one field at a time. Initial experiments with more complex policies demonstrated that the effects of multi-field anonymization could not simply be inferred from data on single-field anonymization policies. Furthermore, we did not examine the effect of varying the type of intrusion detection system (anomaly vs. signature-based) or the signature set on the measure of utility.

Most importantly, studies to date have looked only at the effect of anonymization on just one type of analysis for one type of data: network traces. Even if we only consider network traces, we need to consider utility for the network measurement, security visualization, network forensics, and many other communities. Also, many other types of data are anonymized: firewall logs, network flows, process accounting logs, file system logs, web server logs, authentication logs, and more. Similar attention needs to be given to those other types of data, so that anonymization policies can be constructed that do not unduly diminish the data's utility for the communities that require those logs.

Understanding De-Anonymization

In recent years, several new attacks have been created to de-anonymize network traces and a couple other log types (Bethencourt, Franklin, & Vernon, 2005; Coull, Wright, Monrose, Collins, & Reiter, 2007; Coull, Collins, Wright, Monrose, & Reiter, 2007; Koukis, Antonatos, & Anagnostakis, 2006; Kohno, Broido, & Claffy, 2005; Ribero, Chen, Miklau, & Towsley, 2008). In fact, creating a new one-off de-anonymization attack seems to be the easiest and most popular way to get a result published in this field. What is harder, and has had very little effort put into it, is finding ways to protect against such attacks and create adversarial models that expand our understanding of these attacks on a more theoretical level.

As a first step towards understanding how anonymization can be attacked, we have worked to create a taxonomy of these attacks (King, 2008). Aside from one paper that listed 4 non-mutually exclusive categories of attacks (Pang & Paxson, 2003), ours is the only work of which we are aware that tries to relate common de-anonymization attacks. We decided to base our taxonomy upon

prerequisite conditions for an attack, as that would most naturally lend itself to mapping elements of the taxonomy to specific preventative measures that could be taken. Our approach was to take all the currently known attacks (about two dozen of them) and try to relate them to each other by means of common preconditions. Once we did that, we were able to construct a tree that grouped and generalized the current attacks. In that way, we have taken a very pragmatic approach that captures known attacks well, but also allows for expansion to include new attacks as they are discovered. The taxonomic tree simply grows in depth as the corresponding taxonomy becomes finer. *More research needs to be done in this direction, and it will take time to validate our approach and decide whether the taxonomy is ultimately useful.*

There have also been two approaches to creating formal adversarial models to better understand the threats posed by de-anonymization attacks. There have been very pragmatic approaches such as ours, which reverse-engineers our taxonomy into a set of adversarial capabilities and means (King, 2008), and there have been more theoretical approaches, such as that developed by Coull et al. (Coull, Wright, Keromytis, Monrose, & Reiter, 2008). Coull et al. have focused on a particular type of attack and modeled adversaries as a process that matches distributions of anonymized and unanonymized values. Using entropy metrics, they can thus find fields and records that are vulnerable to de-anonymization. This covers a large class of inference attacks, and can potentially be used to find new specific attacks. However, it cannot address a large range of attacks—for example, anything active rather than passive—and it does not address compositions of attacks. Its real strength is that it can expose sensitive fields and records that may be insufficiently anonymized and provide hard guarantees for this one type of attack primitive.

The other approach in the literature is ours, which is based in part upon the adversarial model of Avoine (Avoine, 2005). He modeled RFID identification attacks by creating a composable framework of means and capabilities. We did a similar thing, creating a set of means and capabilities that are necessary to perpetrate the attacks in our taxonomy. That made it rather straightforward to map adversaries to parts of the taxonomy, and vice versa. However, the adversarial model is even more generic and can incorporate new attacks as discovered. The main purpose of our taxonomy, was to allow translation between questions about whether or not a policy can stop a given attack to questions about whether or not it can stop a given adversary. That aim was, of course, predicated upon the assumption that our taxonomy is complete, something that has not been proven. This is one of the limitations of our very pragmatic approach: although the model and taxonomy are expandable, the approach is restricted to a universe of attacks that have already been discovered, whereas Coull et al.'s approach can potentially discover new attacks of a limited class.

Clearly, a lot of work remains to be done in the area of understanding de-anonymization and information leakage. *First, we would like to see a more powerful adversarial model that has the benefits of both approaches. That is, it can capture all of the current attacks, and it can potentially lead to discovery of new attacks. Another major breakthrough in this area of research would be to detect active attacks before releasing data.* Many attacks are what we call *data injection* attacks, ones that send probes that will be recorded and later released in the anonymized data set. By recognizing these injected probes, it is often possible to mount a sort of known-plaintext attack. Many of the specific attacks already described may be simple enough to detect, but in general they are not. The attack essentially creates a covert channel, and covert channels are very difficult to detect in large data sets. *In addition to investigating ways to detect these sorts of attacks, researchers should look at ways to prevent them.* Since almost any field can be used for the covert channel, often one

would have to anonymize almost all the fields to stop such an attack. However, there are alternative measures to anonymization as well. Changing how logs are released can affect attacks. For example, sampling of the data means that the attacker cannot depend on the assumption that his or her probe is in the data. Playing with the release schedule and spacing out releases can make data injection attacks too slow. Changing keys every time data are released makes mappings inconsistent between data sets and can also thwart an attacker. All of these solutions should be considered along with anonymization and investigated further.

CONCLUSION

FBI Major Case 216 is a portent of the future. As computers and devices become ever more connected through the Internet, the scope and complexity of cyber attacks will continue to increase unabated. To address this problem, those defending our computer systems must come together to share information, knowledge, and resources. However, at this time there are no effective, secure, and flexible ways of sharing between organizations even the most basic of data sets: computer and network logs.

Our vision is to develop a dynamic anonymization process in which clients negotiate with data owners to make appropriate tradeoffs between security, privacy, and utility. The potential benefits are tremendous, and would affect researchers, security engineers, and educators everywhere. The steps towards fulfilling this vision are taking place now; however, there are numerous important hurdles that must be overcome. First, we contend that there are three major research directions that must continue to be pursued for our vision to be realized:

- We must seek a better understanding of the relationship between anonymization and utility for the many different scenarios of sharing logs.

- We must create adversarial models that not only capture current de-anonymization attacks, but also reveal new ones.
- We must be able to map utility and security constraints from the adversarial models into a system able negotiate anonymization policies.

In addition to these research challenges, we have also noted that there are several engineering challenges to building such a system. Currently, even the best anonymization tools are still research prototypes, and they are not nearly as robust or reliable as they need to be for production use.

We have taken significant steps towards pursuing the challenges. Determining the utility of a log is a difficult endeavor, since utility is very context-dependent; it matters who is using the log, what information they have, and for what purpose they are using it. Instead of calculating an ambiguous and simplistic one-dimensional measure of utility (e.g., a simple entropy-based metric), we focused on measuring the change in utility resulting from anonymization through the use of the *IDS Utility Metric*. With that approach, we have exhaustively measured the loss in utility from anonymization for most single-field policies applied to network traces towards the task of intrusion detection. But other tasks, other logs, and even more complex policies must be evaluated by similar investigations.

While the research community has given much attention to creating new de-anonymization attacks, less work has actually looked at how to prevent de-anonymization in a proactive manner. Towards that goal, we have developed a taxonomy of de-anonymization attacks as well as created a formal adversarial model to better understand these threats. Like measures of utility, de-anonymization attacks are dependent upon context, and the likelihood of de-anonymization depends upon how the logs are anonymized, how they are released, to

whom they are released, and other outside information sources useful to inference attacks. Thus, it is only natural that our formal adversarial model focuses on attack preconditions by identifying the information a particular adversary would need to de-anonymize a particular type of log.

By modeling the preconditions through which de-anonymization takes place, we can identify "safe" anonymization policies. Thus, we have mapped our taxonomy and adversarial model into a predicate logic system that provides us with a means of creating appropriate policies for different situations. By adding to that logic constraints on what *cannot* be anonymized (i.e., utility constraints), we have taken a major step towards providing automatic policy negotiation.

Finally, a theoretical understanding of the issues surrounding anonymization is worthless without a framework with which one may act upon this understanding. FLAIM (Framework for Log Anonymization and Information Management) is a cutting-edge tool that we developed to realize that new vision of a dynamic anonymization process. Thus, FLAIM provides

- A core anonymization engine with many supported algorithms;
- An extensible, modular I/O system that allows new logs and data formats to leverage existing anonymization algorithms; and
- A powerful XML anonymization policy language that allows policies to be specified at run-time, rather than compile time.

FLAIM is vital to our vision. Unlike other anonymization tools, which have typically been developed specifically for one type of log or with very rigid anonymization policies, FLAIM is flexible and modular, and we hope that it will play a critical role in realizing our vision of dynamic anonymization.

To be effective, the security community must be able to collaborate efficiently. We have started down the right path with the work we have done to date, and we hope that our vision presented here will guide others and ourselves towards the realization of improved collaborative security.

REFERENCES

Avoine, G. (2005). Adversarial Model for Radio Frequency Identification. *Cryptology ePrint Archive* (Report 2005/049).

Bethencourt, J., Franklin, J., & Vernon, M. (2005). Mapping Internet Sensors with Probe Response Attacks. In *Proceedings of the 14th USENIX Security Symposium* (pp. 193-208).

Bezzi, M., & Kounine, A. (2008). *Assessing Disclosure Risk in Anonymized Datasets*. Paper presented at Flocon '08.

Coull, S., Collins, M., Wright, C. V., Monrose, F., & Reiter, M. (2007). On Web Browsing Privacy in Anonymized NetFlows. In *Proceedings of the 16th USENIX Security Symposium* (pp. 339-352).

Coull, S., Wright, C. V., Keromytis, A. D., Monrose, M., & Reiter, M. (2008). Taming the Devil: Techniques for Evaluating Anonymized Network Data. In *Proceedings of the 15th Network and Distributed Systems Security Symposium (NDSS '08)* (pp. 125-135).

Coull, S., Wright, C. V., Monrose, F., Collins, M., & Reiter, M. (2007). Playing Devil's Advocate: Inferring Sensitive Information from Anonymized Network Traces. In *Proceedings of the 14th Network and Distributed Systems Security Symposium (NDSS '07)* (pp. 35-47).

Hafner, K. (2006, August 23). Researchers Yearn to Use AOL Logs, but They Hesitate. *New York Times*.

King, J. (2008). *A Taxonomy, Model, and Method for Secure Network Log Anonymization*. Unpublished master's thesis, University of Illinois at Urbana-Champaign.

Kohno, T., Broido, A., & Claffy, K. C. (2005). Remote Physical Device Fingerprinting. *IEEE Transactions on Dependable and Secure Computing, 2*(2), 93–108. doi:10.1109/TDSC.2005.26

Koukis, D., Antonatos, S., & Anagnostakis, K. (2006). On the Privacy Risks of Publishing Anonymized IP Network Traces. In *Proceedings of the 10th IFIP Open Conference on Communications and Multimedia Security* (pp. 22-32).

Koukis, D., Antonatos, S., Antoniades, D., Markatos, E., & Trimintzios, P. (2006). A Generic Anonymization Framework for Network Traffic. In *Proceedings of the IEEE International Conference on Communications (ICC '06)* (Vol. 5, pp. 2302-2309).

Lakkaraju, K., & Slagell, A. (2008). Evaluating the Utility of Anonymized Network Traces for Intrusion Detection. In *Proceedings of the 4th Annual SecureComm Conference*.

McHugh, J. (2000). Testing Intrusion Detection Systems: A Critique of the 1998 and 1999 DARPA Intrusion Detection System Evaluations as Performed by Lincoln Laboratory. *ACM Transactions on Information and System Security, 36*(4), 262–294. doi:10.1145/382912.382923

Narayanan, A., & Shmatikov, V. (2006). How to Break Anonymity of the Netflix Prize Dataset (Technical Report cs/0610105). In *ACM Computing Research Repository*.

Nixon, L. (2006). The Stakkato Intrusions: What Happened and What Have We Learned? In *Proceedings of the Cluster Security Workshop (CCGrid '06)* (pp. 27).

Pang, R., Allman, M., Paxson, V., & Lee, J. (2006). The Devil and Packet Trace Anonymization. *Computer Communication Review, 36*(1), 29–38. doi:10.1145/1111322.1111330

Pang, R., & Paxson, V. (2003). A High-level Programming Environment for Packet Trace Anonymization and Transformation. In *Proceedings of the ACM SIGCOMM Conference* (pp. 339-351).

Ramaswamy, R., & Wolf, T. (2007). High-Speed Prefix-Preserving IP Address Anonymization for Passive Measurement Systems. *IEEE/ACM Transactions on Networking, 15*(1), 26-39.

Ribero, B., Chen, W., Miklau, G., & Towsley, D. (2008). Analyzing Privacy in Enterprise Packet Trace Anonymization. In *Proceedings of the 15th Network and Distributed Systems Security Symposium (NDSS '08)*.

Sicker, D., Ohm, P., & Grunwald, D. (2007). Legal Issues Surrounding Monitoring during Network Research. In *Proceedings of the Internet Measurement Conference (IMC '07)* (pp. 141-148).

Slagell, A., Lakkaraju, K., & Luo, K. (2006). FLAIM: A Multi-level Anonymization Framework for Computer and Network Logs. In *Proceedings of the 20th USENIX Large Installation System Administration Conference (LISA '06)* (pp. 6).

Slagell, A., Li, Y., & Luo, K. (2005). Sharing Network Logs for Computer Forensics: A New Tool for the Anonymization of Netflow Records. In *Proceedings of the Computer Network Forensics Research Workshop*.

Slagell, A., & Yurcik, W. (2005). Sharing Computer Network Logs for Security and Privacy: A Motivation for New Methodologies of Anonymization. In *Proceedings of the SECOVAL: The Workshop on the Value of Security through Collaboration*.

Yurcik, W., Woolam, C., Hellings, G., Khan, L., & Thuraisingham, B. (2007). Scrub-tcpdump: A Multi-Level Packet Anonymizer Demonstrating Privacy/Analysis Tradeoffs. In *Proceedings of the 3rd Workshop on the Value of Security through Collaboration (SECOVAL '07)* (pp. 49-56).

Zhang, Q., & Li, X. (2006). An IP Address Anonymization Scheme with Multiple Access Levels. In I. Chong & K. Kawahara (Eds.), *Revised Selected Papers from the International Conference on Information Networking (ICOIN 2006): Advances in Data Communications and Wireless Networks* (pp. 793-802). Berlin, Germany: Springer.

Zhang, Q., Wang, J., & Li, X. (2007). On the Design of Fast Prefix-Preserving IP Address Anonymization Scheme. In *Proceedings of the International Conference on Information and Communications Security (ICICS '07)* (pp. 177-188).

ENDNOTE

[1]   http://www.predict.org/

Chapter 5
Data Protection in Collaborative Business Applications

Florian Kerschbaum
SAP Research CEC Karlsruhe, Germany

ABSTRACT

Collaborative business applications are an active field of research and an emerging practice in industry. This chapter will focus on data protection in b2b applications which offer a wide range of business models and architecture, since often equal partners are involved in the transactions. It will present three distinct applications, their business models, security requirements and the newest solutions for solving these problems. The three applications are collaborative benchmarking, fraud detection and supply chain management. Many of these applications will not be realized if no appropriate measure for protecting the collaborating parties' data are taken. This chapter focuses on the strongest form of data protection. The business secrets are kept entirely secret from other parties (or at least to the degree possible). This also corresponds to the strongest form of privacy protection in many instances. The private information does not leave the producing system, (i.e., data protection), such that the information producer remains its sole owner. In case of B2B application, the sensitive data are usually business secrets, and not personally identifiable data as in privacy protection.

INTRODUCTION

Collaborative business applications are an active field of research and an emerging practice in industry. Collaborative business applications can be classified into business-to-consumer (B2C) and business-to-business (B2B) applications. Electronic B2C applications are of great interest with the advent of the Internet as an additional sales channel, but are usually restricted in their business model and architecture to classical client-server matching the buyer-seller relationship. B2B applications offer a much wider range of business models and architecture, since often equal partners are involved in the transactions. The security requirements resulting

DOI: 10.4018/978-1-60566-414-9.ch005

from these architectures therefore also span a much broader variety than in the B2C area.

This chapter will focus on data protection in B2B applications. It will present three distinct applications, their business models, security requirements and the newest solutions for solving these problems. The three applications are collaborative benchmarking, fraud detection and supply chain management. Each application has its own business model and architecture.

In each of these applications data protection is of the utmost importance. Many of these applications will not be realized if not appropriate measure for protecting the collaborating parties' data are taken. The involved data usually consists of business secrets whose revelation would impact the position of the company, e.g. its negotiation position or external recognition. This data is therefore associated with a risk of revelation, and the effect of data protection can be financially measured with risk analysis.

This chapter focuses on the strongest form of data protection. The business secrets are kept entirely secret from other parties (or at least to the degree possible). Each party is seen as an entity that is either entirely compromised or intact and can perform computations without being inspected. Then there is a protocol that relies on cryptographic protection run between the parties. One can show that (under certain assumptions) nothing can be inferred from the protocol except the result.

This also corresponds to the strongest form of privacy protection in many instances. The private information does not leave the producing system, i.e. data protection, such that the information producer remains its sole owner. In case of B2B application, the sensitive data are usually business secrets, and not personally identifiable data as in privacy protection. The value of business secrets can often be higher than that often irrationally low value of personal information as many studies suggest (Acquisti 2004, Cvrcek *et al.* 2006). Therefore the protection of data in collaborative

business applications can be much better economically motivated than its counterpart privacy.

The motivation for collaboration in these business applications stems from an economic benefit that cannot be achieved by a party by itself, i.e. the motivational factor is not enhanced security, but economics. Nevertheless as mentioned before many of these applications will not be realized, if not appropriate security measures are in place. In particular this chapter is concerned with the information gain, such applications can provide and that can be an effective obstacle to the realization of the application. The economic benefit is therefore tied to the security requirements which usually stem from the business model and so data protection enables an economic benefit.

Secure Multi-Party Computation

Secure Multi-Party Computation (SMC) (Ben-Or *et al.* 1988, Goldreich *et al.* 1987, Yao 1982) allows the joint computation of a function without any party revealing its input. What seems puzzling at first can be visualized with an example (Schneier 1996).

How can a group of people calculate their average salary without anyone learning the salary of anyone else? Let there be three people: Alice, Bob and Carol. Alice starts and adds a secret random number to her salary and tells Bob the result, such that Carol cannot hear it. Bob who only knows the sum does not know anything about Alice's salary. He then adds his salary and tells Carol the result without Alice hearing it. Carol does the same: adds her salary and tells it to Alice without Bob hearing it. Alice now remembers her secret random number and subtracts that from the result which is the sum of the three salaries. She announces the result and everybody can calculate the average by dividing by three, the number of people.

The intriguing fact about this simple protocol is that everybody learned the result, but no one else's input. The results from (Ben-Or *et al.* 1988, Goldreich *et al.* 1987, Yao 1982) show that this can be achieved for any computable function. It was first shown that this can be achieved for two parties in the cryptographic setting (Yao 1982) and then extended to the multi-party case in the cryptographic setting (Goldreich *et al.* 1987) and the information-theoretically secure setting (Ben-Or *et al.* 1988).

The constructions used in the completeness proofs are usually too expensive for real-world problems, such that special solutions for important problems are sought that improve the performance. There are two parameters that can be optimized: computation complexity and communication complexity. Computation complexity measures in the "big-O notation" the asymptotic running time of the protocol, while communication complexity measures the asymptotic communication effort in communication units (e.g. bits) also in the "big-O notation". Obviously it holds that computation complexity is greater or equal than communication complexity.

Another important metric for communication is the round complexity. Distributed system can often be reasonably well approximated by synchronous models (Lynch 1996). The round complexity is the number of steps it takes in a synchronous distributed system to complete the algorithm and it often dominates the communication time in real distributed systems.

Security Models

Seminal work has been performed in defining the security models for SMC (Goldreich 2004). A security model defines possible behaviors of attackers and outlines the strategy for proofs of security in those models. In general, a SMC protocol Π (called the real model) is compared to an ideal model. In the ideal model there is a trusted third party that receives the inputs from the parties, computes the function's results and returns those results to the parties. Loosely speaking, any attack possible in the real model (the execution of the protocol) must also be possible in the ideal model.

We now review briefly the most important security models.

Semi-Honest Model

In the semi-honest model attackers are passive, i.e. they conform to the protocol specification, but keep a record of all messages and try to infer as much information as possible. This corresponds to the simplest attacker who does not modify its software, but uses debuggers and sniffers to capture the exchanged information. Formally semi-honest security is defined via the view of a party during protocol execution.

Definition 1: The view of party X_i during protocol Π consists of his input x_i, his internal random number choices r_i and the t messages m_j $(j = 1, ..., t)$ received.

Let $x = (x_1, ..., x_n)$ be the input of the parties $X_1, ..., X_n$, $f(x)$ be the deterministic function computed and $f_i(x)$ be the output of party X_i. A subset $I = \{i_1, ..., i_j\}$ of the parties can behave adversarial. We denote with the subscript I the combined sets visible to the adversary: $x_I, f_I(x)$, $\text{VIEW}_I(x)$ and with subscript $\neg I$ the combined sets visible to the honest players. According to (Goldreich 2004) we can define semi-honest security.

Definition 2: We say that Π privately computes f (in the semi-honest model), if there exist a polynomial-time algorithm S (called simulator), such that for every I $S(I, x_I, f_I(x))$ is computationally indistinguishable from $\text{VIEW}_I(x)$.

A proof of security in the semi-honest model must show the existence of such a simulator. The simulator computes all "information" available in the view from the information available in the ideal model. It thereby shows that everything that can be computed from the view can be computed in the ideal model.

Malicious Model

In the malicious model attackers are active, i.e. they can deviate arbitrarily from the protocol. This corresponds to a much stronger attacker that reengineers the software given the protocol specification. Formally malicious security is defined via a (polynomial-time) transformation of an attacker in the real model into an "equivalent" one in the ideal model.

We use the notation from above and first define the possible attacks in the ideal model. The attacker can substitute his input before sending it to the trusted third party and can modify the output given the result from the trusted third party. These two attacks cannot be prevented even in the ideal model.

Definition 3: Let C be a family of polynomial-size circuits. An attacker (I,C) is admissible if $|I| < n/2$. The joint execution of (I,C) in the ideal model, denoted $\text{IDEAL}_{I,C}(x)$, is defined as $(C(x_I), f_I(C(x_I),x_{-I})), f_I(C(x_I),x_{-I}))$.

For completeness we also need to define the execution in the real model.

Definition 4: Let Π be an n-party protocol for computing f. The joint execution of Π under (I,C) in the real model, denoted as $\text{REAL}_{I,C}(x)$ is defined as the output sequence resulting from the interaction between the n parties where the messages of the parties in I are computed according to C and the messages of parties not in I are computed according to Π.

We can now define security against malicious attackers by comparing execution in the ideal and real model.

Definition 5: We say that Π securely computes f (in the malicious model), if there exists a polynomial-time computable transformation of polynomial-size circuit families A for the real model into polynomial-time circuit families B for the ideal model, so that for every I, such that $|I| < n/2$, the execution in the ideal model $\text{IDEAL}_{I,B}(x)$ is computationally indistinguishable from the execution in the real model $\text{REAL}_{I,A}(x)$.

A proof of security in the real model must show the existence of such a transformation. Fortunately, there exists a compiler, as shown in (Goldreich *et al.* 1987, Goldreich 2004) that transforms any protocol secure in the semi-honest model into a protocol secure in the malicious model.

Rational Model

There has been some criticism of the malicious model in the applied research community, since its construction is prohibitively expensive in most cases and the provided security does not meet the expectations of business users. It is still necessary in the malicious model to require somewhat honest behavior, since otherwise the result of the function computed can be destructively distorted, but the effects of this behavior are not taken into account for optimizing the protocol.

Some papers (Abraham et al. 2006, Halpern and Teague 2004, Shoham and Tennenholtz 2005) have examined SMC under rational players. A rational player acts according to some utility function trying to maximize its output, i.e. a player is no longer good (honest) or bad (malicious), but rather acts selfishly. The common thread among the papers is that they consider a player who, as a first preference, tries to obtain the (correct) result of f and, as a second preference, tries to withhold the result from as many other parties as possible.

In (Shoham and Tennenholtz 2005) a characterization of functions that are computable in this model is given. These functions are called non-cooperatively computable. For example sum or average is not non-cooperatively computable, since a player can provide false input and still compute the correct result (assuming other players do not do the same), but median is non-cooperatively computable, since deviation distorts the result.

It is not enough that the function itself is non-cooperatively computable, but also the protocol must implement the rational model. In particular is it difficult to perform the last step in many SMC protocols where each party holds a share of the output and the parties exchange those in order to obtain the result. The problem is that by sending one's share a party does not increase its chances to obtain the result, but only the others' and is therefore not inclined to do so. In (Abraham et al. 2006, Halpern and Teague 2004) the problem is solved by a protocol that randomizes the number of rounds and punishes deviation in all but the final round.

There is still much research necessary in order to formalize a full rational model that reflects the rationality of the players in all steps of a protocol, but the first steps have been taken.

Homomorphic Encryption

We use homomorphic encryption in many protocols. Homomorphic encryption maps one operation on the ciphertexts to an encryption of the result of a homomorphic operation on the plaintexts. We require in particular that the homomorphic operation is addition (modulo a key-dependent constant). Several such homomorphic encryption systems exist (Benaloh 1987, Damgard and Jurik 2001, Naccache and Stern 1998, Okamoto and Uchiyama 1998, Paillier 1999). Let $E_X(x)$ denote the encryption of x with X's public key and correspondingly, $D_X()$ the decryption with X's private key, then a homomorphic encryption system has the following property:

$$D_X(E_X(x) \cdot E_X(y)) = x + y$$

Using simple arithmetic the following property can be derived

$$D_X(E_X(x)^y) = x \cdot y$$

Privacy-Preserving Benchmarking

Benchmarking is an essential process for companies to stay competitive in today's markets. Benchmarking is the comparison of one's key performance indicators (KPI) to the statistics of the same KPIs of one's peer group. A KPI is a statistical quantity measuring the performance of some business process. Examples from different company operations are cash flow (financial), make cycle time (manufacturing), and employee fluctuation rate (human resources). A peer group is a group of (usually competing) companies that have an interest in comparing their KPIs based on some similarity measure of the companies. Examples formed along different characteristics are Fortune 500 companies in the United States (revenue and location), car manufacturers (industry sector), and airline vs. railway vs. haulage (sales market).

Privacy is utmost important in benchmarking. Companies are reluctant to share their KPIs due to the risk of losing a competitive advantage or being embarrassed. Imagine for example the cash flow of a non-public company. One could possibly infer if a company has payment difficulties which would result in an enormous loss of future orders.

Business Model

The main problem of collaborative benchmarking is identifying the right group to benchmark against (and convincing that group to collaborate). This can be solved in a community approach, where a central service provider offers a meeting place for companies willing to engage in collaborative benchmarking. As we will see later, the service provider might even facilitate the formation of effective peer groups.

As a benefit of engaging in collaborative benchmarking, each participant gets access to the statistics of his peer group. The service provider may now charge for its services of providing a platform and access to the peer group statistics. Ultimately, the service provider is offering a benchmarking service where one can compare to a peer group and pays a fee and, as an additional charge, participates in the peer group's statistics computation.

In this section we write the service provider as the central entity offering above described service, and subscribers as the participants in the platform and in the secure computation protocol.

Secure Computation Protocols

Several SMC protocols have recently been developed that can securely and privately compute the necessary statistics, e.g. (Atallah *et al.* 2004, Kerschbaum 2008, Kerschbaum and Terzidis 2006). SMC guarantees that no participant will learn more than what he can infer by the output of the protocol and his input, i.e. the other parties' inputs remain entirely confidential.

Requirements

The SMC protocol must fit into the architecture of the entire enterprise information system and we derive a number of requirements for the SMC protocol from the business model.

We first consider security against the service provider's platform. The benchmarking platform is not supposed to obtain the plaintext KPIs from the companies acting as a trusted third party, but rather the KPIs are to be kept private to the companies, even against the service provider. In the SMC protocol the benchmarking platform is a regular participant, just without any input.

We secondly consider the communication structure. The subscribers should only communicate with the service provider, but there should never be any communication amongst each other.

We thirdly require anonymity among the subscribers which can only be achieved, if they do not need to address messages to others, since

they otherwise need the destination address. The formal requirement for anonymity is that subscribers do not refer to or know any static identifier of any other subscriber (e.g. IP addresses, public keys, etc.).

Fourth the SMC protocols should have practical performance. The proposed protocols need to be optimized for computation and communication cost in order to keep them practical. All protocols have a constant number of rounds, but vary in their communication complexity.

Constrained Malicious Security

Another important goal of our benchmarking platform is to provide appropriate security against the service provider. For this purpose we define the constrained malicious security model. While semi-honest security is often a too strong assumption, malicious security rarely fits the business context. Security in the malicious model provides no security against protocol abortion (by the service provider) or the subscribers providing false input. A malicious subscriber can submit the maximum possible KPI value and invalidate the result of the maximum computation by locking it to the maximum value. Differently from auctions, where the maximum value or at the very least its submitter (Vickrey auctions) are revealed, this is not case in benchmarking.

Our main concern is secrecy of the KPIs. Consequently we assume a constrained malicious attacker that can still deviate from the protocol steps in order to obtain additional information (except what can be inferred by the local input and the result). The constraint is that the attacker has to deliver the (correct) result to the other parties. In the worst case such behavior can be enforced by contractual obligations, but more importantly it is economically motivated, since all subscribers and the service provider have a selfish interest in obtaining the correct result.

We formally define an attacker in the constrained malicious model.

Figure 1. Linear cost benchmarking protocol

Round 1:
$X_i \longrightarrow SP \quad E_{common}(x_i)$ $SP \longrightarrow X_i \quad E_{common}(c) = E_{common}(-1^? \cdot (r_1 \cdot (x_i - max) + r_2))$ $SP \xrightarrow{\pi} X_i \quad E^c = \begin{cases} E_{common}(x_i + r_4) & \text{if } c \geq 0 \;\; (r_3 = 0) \\ E_{common}(max + r_4) & \text{if } c < 0 \;\; (r_3 = 0) \end{cases}$ $X_i \longrightarrow SP \quad E_{common}(max') = E^c \cdot E_{common}(0)$ $SP \qquad E_{common}(max) = E_{common}(max' - r_4)$

Round 2:
$SP \longrightarrow X_i \quad E_{common}(sum) = E_{common}(\sum_{i=1}^n x_i)$ $\qquad E_{common}(max)$ $X_i \longrightarrow SP \quad sum$ $\qquad MAC(sum \| i, s_{common})$ $\qquad max$ $\qquad MAC(max \| i, s_{common})$ $\qquad E_{common}((x_i - \frac{sum}{n})^2)$

Round 3:
$SP \longrightarrow X_i \quad E_{common}(sum') = E_{common}(\sum_{i=1}^n (x_i - \frac{sum}{n})^2)$ $\qquad H(MAC(max \| 1, s_{common}), \ldots, MAC(sum \| n, s_{common}))$ $\qquad H(MAC(max \| 1, s_{common}), \ldots, MAC(max \| n, s_{common}))$ $X_i \longrightarrow SP \quad sum'$ $\qquad MAC(sum' \| i, s_{common})$

Round 4:
$SP \longrightarrow X_i \quad H(MAC(sum' \| 1, s_{common}), \ldots, MAC(sum' \| n, s_{common}))$

Definition 6: A pair *(I,C)* represents an adversary *A* in the real model. The joint execution of Π under *(I,C)*, denoted as $REAL_{I,C}(x)$, is defined as the output sequence resulting from the interaction between the *n* parties where the messages of the parties in *I* are computed according to *C* and the messages of parties not in *I* are computed according to Π. An adversary *A* is admissible (for the constrained malicious model) if the output sequence at the non-adversarial parties is $REAL_{-I-C}(x) = f(x)$.

Linear Cost Benchmarking Protocol

Linear Cost Benchmarking was the first attempt at designing protocols according to requirements described above. It computes the following statistics: mean, variance, maximum. Its main advantage is its low communication cost. The overall communication cost is linear ($O(n)$) resulting in a constant communication cost per subscriber ($O(1)$). It can therefore be considered the most practical of the protocols described here.

The protocol is very similar to the other benchmarking protocols and Figure 1 gives a detailed formal description. So, we omit a detailed textual description of the protocol as given for the benchmarking protocol.

Benchmarking Protocol

The benchmarking protocol is the second attempt at fulfilling the requirements described above. Its main advantage is that it also implements the statistics median and best-in-class. Best-in-class is the average of the top 25%. These statistics are less vulnerable to statistically outlying input, but provide similar information compared to average and maximum. They are more useful in practice, since it often happens that one party measures the KPIs incorrectly.

The benchmarking protocol is a composition of several SMC techniques. In the first round each subscriber X_i submits his input x_i encrypted under a commonly shared homomorphic key $E_{common}()$. Then the service provider chooses two random numbers r and r' for each input pair x_i, x_j, such that $r > 0$ and $r > r' \geq 0$ and computes a comparison value $c_{i,j}$ as

$$E_{common}(c_{i,j}) = (E_{common}(x_i) \cdot E_{common}(x_j)^{-1})^r \cdot E_{common}(r') = E_{common}(r \cdot (x_i - x_j) + r')$$

This computation can be performed on the ciphertexts due to the homomorphic encryption (Paillier 1998). As long as a wrap-around is prevented, it holds that $c_{i,j} < 0 \Leftrightarrow x_i < x_j$.

We assume that the value $c_{i,j}$ does not reveal the hidden values x_i, x_j or their difference, since it is hidden by the multiplicative factor r and furthermore in order to prevent factoring r' has been added. We have shown that this method of comparison is particularly efficient (Kerschbaum and Terzidis 2006).

In the second round, each subscriber X_i is given a random vector selected according to a permutation $\Phi(i)$ chosen by the service provider. Actually the service provider sends the ciphertext of the elements of the vector, but X_i can decrypt them. The number of non-negative comparison values in this vector indicates the rank of element $x_{\Phi(i)}$. Many of the sought-after quantities can be computed via the rank: The maximum has rank n, the median has rank $\lceil n/2 \rceil$, and the least element which is still included in the best-in-class computation has rank $\lceil (3n+3)/4 \rceil$. The service provider and the subscribers must now compute the value of these elements. Subscriber X_i has the rank of KPI $x_{\Phi(i)}$, but he does not know the value $x_{\Phi(i)}$. The service provider has $E_{common}(x_{\Phi(i)})$, chooses a random number r and prepares two values for sending in Oblivious Transfer (OT): $E_{common}(x_{\Phi(i)} + r)$ and $E_{common}(r)$. In this OT the subscriber X_i as receiver chooses $E_{common}(x_{\Phi(i)} + r)$ if $x_{\Phi(i)}$ has the sought-after rank, otherwise he chooses $E_{common}(r)$. Note that due to the secret sharing with the random number r, the subscriber X_i can learn nothing

about $x_{\Phi(i)}$ and returns the chosen ciphertext after re-randomization to the service provider. The service provider adds r using the homomorphic operation and sums up all received values after the round also using the homomorphic addition operation. He ends up with the ciphertext of the element with the sought-after rank. This is repeated for all three quantities: maximum, median and the least best-in-class element.

In the third round, the service provider performs the comparison operation again, but only against the least best-in-class element. In the same procedure using OT, this time all elements equal or larger to this least best-in-class element are selected and summed up. The service provider ends up with the ciphertexts of the results for each quantity, but he cannot decrypt, since he does not have the decryption key. If he submits, the ciphertext to only one subscriber, this subscriber can prevent all other subscribers from obtaining the correct result while still having obtained it himself by returning an incorrect value. A Zero-Knowledge-Proof of correct decryption would prevent this, but would not prevent the service provider from submitting to all subscribers different results. If he submits the result to all subscribers, the service provider can cheat and submit the original input back to each subscriber and compute the results from the returned plaintexts. He would have successfully broken the security of the protocol without modifying the result of the computation which makes it very difficult to detect. The service provider therefore sends a proof to all subscribers that he submitted the same value for decryption to all subscribers. The subscribers X_i sign the value with a (personalized) message authentication code and the service provider computes an aggregation that all subscribers can verify. This prevents the service provider from deviating from the protocol without modifying the result. In order for the median computation to work all KPI values need to be unique which is achieved by adding the subscriber number in the lower digits and the result is hidden before decryption using secret sharing, such that the service provider can round the result to an appropriate level for disclosure averaging out the lower digits.

Figure 2 gives a formal description of the entire protocol. It describes a two-party interaction between a subscriber X_i and the service provider SP subdivided into rounds. These interactions need to be completed by each subscriber X_i ($i = 1, \ldots, n$) in each round before any subscriber can engage in the next round. The order of the subscribers is not important.

Coalition-Safe Benchmarking Protocol

One drawback of the benchmarking protocol is that it uses a common key among all participants X_i that must remain unknown to the service provider SP. This section presents a protocol version that uses a threshold variant of this key and is secure against coalitions of up to $t - 1$ parties including the service provider. Note that the benchmarking protocol is secure against collusion of $n - 1$ subscribers in the semi-honest model and the constrained malicious model, but not against collusion with the service provider. Such security against collusion with the service provider provides the guarantee that if $t - 1$ parties (including the ser-

Figure 2. Benchmarking protocol

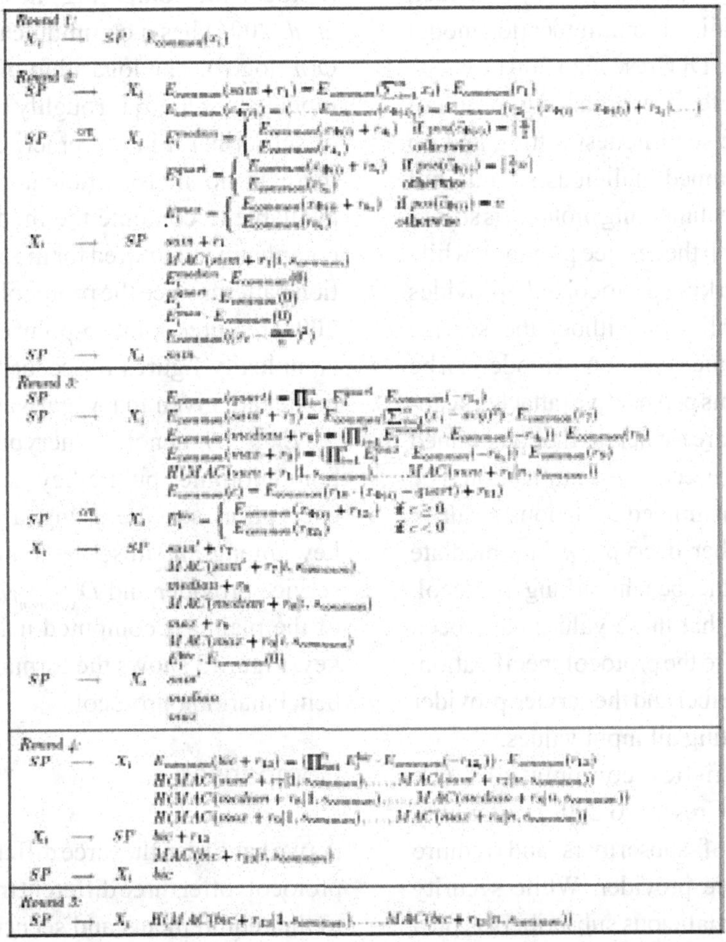

vice provider) get (passively) compromised the benchmarking platform can continue to operate, although with a reduced security level. It is not necessary to restart the entire system including key distribution, if one subscriber gets compromised. The benchmarking platform can continue to run, although with a reduced security level.

The coalition-safe benchmarking protocol requires global identifiers for each participant in order to reconstruct the plaintext during distributed decryption. The protocol is therefore at best pseudonymous and no longer anonymous, i.e. each party is statically identified by a pseudonym (to all subscribers) and no longer anonymous (among all subscribers). No other protocol for secure statistics computation or general secure multi-party computation currently considers anonymity. They all either require secure, authenticated channels between all parties or have unique keys for each subscriber in a centralized communication model (Di Crescenzo 2000, Di Crescenzo 2001).

The coalition-safe benchmarking protocol is only secure in the semi-honest setting and no longer in the constrained malicious setting, but the coalition-safe benchmarking protocol is secure against coalitions with the service provider, while the regular benchmarking protocol only provides security against coalitions without the service provider. Security in the semi-honest model can be motivated by a systems perspective (attackers cannot modify the software), whereas the constrained malicious model has an economic motivation. The main obstacle to constrained malicious security is that each subscriber decrypts n intermediate ciphertexts during the benchmarking protocol. Without guarantees that these values have been computed according to the protocol specification, a coalition of a subscriber and the service provider can cheat by decrypting all input values.

Centralized statistics computations (Di Crescenzo 2000, Di Crescenzo 2001) so far only consider collusion of subscribers and require a semi-honest service provider. While security against collusion of malicious subscribers is pro-

vided, no such security guarantee exists for collusion with the service provider. The protocols (Di Crescenzo 2000, Di Crescenzo 2001) are not secure against coalitions with the service provider for any number of subscribers even in the semi-honest model. A semi-honest service provider does not match the economic requirements of the application, since distrust in the service provider can be assumed and security is used a differentiating sales argument.

The computation and communication complexity of the coalition-safe benchmarking protocol is cubic ($O(n^3)$) as opposed to square ($O(n^2)$) as in the benchmarking protocol.

The complexity of the benchmarking protocol stems from the median computation, as can be seen from the linear cost benchmarking protocol. The only other secure multi-party computation protocol for computing the median (Aggarwal *et al.* 2004) has a communication complexity of $O(n^2 \log|x|)$. The logarithm of the domain of the input values $\log|x|$ is roughly equal to the number of subscriber n in our practical cases. Therefore there is no more efficient protocol than ours available to compute the median. No additional complexity is required for the central communication pattern, since the protocol in (Aggarwal *et al.* 2004) requires point-to-point communication. No complexity figures for security in the malicious model are given in (Aggarwal *et al.* 2004).

$E^t_{common}()$ denotes encryption in t-threshold homomorphic, public-key, semantically secure encryption scheme using a common (shared) key among all subscribers and unknown to the service provider and $D^i_{common}()$ denotes X_i's share of the plaintext computed using its share of the key. Figure 3 shows the formal description of the benchmarking protocol.

Comparison

As we have seen the three different benchmarking protocols offer three different trade-offs according to the requirements and security. The linear cost

Figure 3. Coalition-safe benchmarking protocol

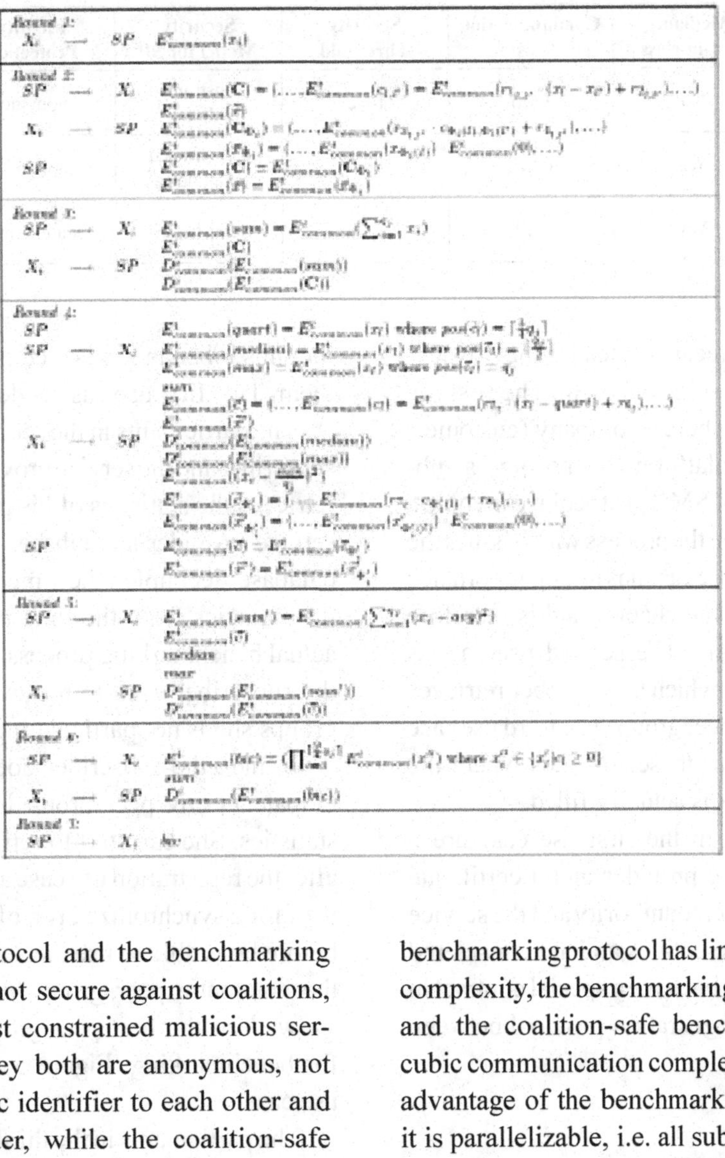

benchmarking protocol and the benchmarking protocol are both not secure against coalitions, but are safe against constrained malicious service providers. They both are anonymous, not providing any static identifier to each other and the service provider, while the coalition-safe benchmarking protocol is at best pseudonymous, where subscribers need to be identified by static (maybe pseudonymous) identifiers. The coalition-safe benchmarking protocol is also only secure in the semi-honest model, but safe against coalitions with the service provider. The three protocols also differ in the functionality offered. The linear cost benchmarking protocol only computes average, variance and maximum while the other two compute also median and best-in-class. The most important difference is in complexity. The linear cost benchmarking protocol has linear communication complexity, the benchmarking protocol quadratic and the coalition-safe benchmarking protocol cubic communication complexity. A further huge advantage of the benchmarking protocol is that it is parallelizable, i.e. all subscribers can access the service provider in parallel. This neither holds for the linear cost benchmarking protocol nor the coalition-safe benchmarking protocol.

Table 1 gives an overview over the differences of the three protocols.

System Architecture

We performed a detailed use case analysis for the benchmarking platform in order to structure the design and development of the platform. This

Table 1. Comparison of benchmarking protocols

	Median, Best-in-class	Communication Cost	Security Threshold	Security Model for SP	Identity Protection	Parallel-izable
Linear Cost Benchmarking	No	O(n)	t < 2	Constrained malicious	Anonymous	No
Benchmarking	Yes	O(n²)	t < 2	Constrained malicious	Anonymous	Yes
Coalition-Safe Benchmarking	Yes	O(n³)	t < k	Semi-honest	Pseudonymous	No

section describes three use cases for the privacy-preserving benchmarking platform. The first use case is registration where a company (customer) intends to join the platform and become a subscriber. To satisfy the SMC protocol we involve a certificate authority in the process which issues the common keys. This use case has minor importance in the remainder of the chapter and is therefore described only briefly. The second use case is statistics retrieval in which a subscriber retrieves the statistics for his peer group. The third use case is the computation of these statistics where the database of statistics is actually filled.

The participants in the first use case are a company, the service provider and a certificate authority. The certificate authority and the service provider are separate entities and are considered mutually distrustful, but have a special contract in order to execute a registration protocol between

the subscriber and the set consisting of the two of them. This first use case is depicted in Figure 4.

The participants in the second use case are one subscriber and the service provider. The subscriber retrieves the statistics of his peer group from the service provider's database. The storage in the database decouples the time of computation of the statistics from the time of retrieval, i.e. the actual benchmarking process. This would enable the subscriber even to retrieve statistics of peer groups she is not participating in.

In fact, the subscriber does not need to participate in any peer group in order to retrieve statistics. She can start to retrieve statistics right after the registration use case and does not have to wait for a synchronized run of the SMC protocol before he is able to use the service. Furthermore the automatic peer group formation algorithm shows him the best peer group in the platform for benchmarking. Figure 5 shows this second use case.

The participants in the third use case are a peer group of subscribers and the service provider. The exact relation between a subscriber and his peer group will be discussed later in this section on peer group models, but at least all members of a peer group need to participate. A candidate SMC protocol would be the benchmarking protocol. The statistics computation use case is depicted in Figure 6.

Figure 4. Registration use case

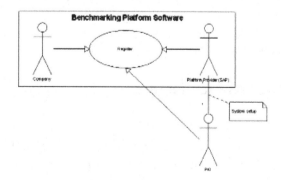

Figure 5. Registration use case

Figure 6. Statistics computation use case

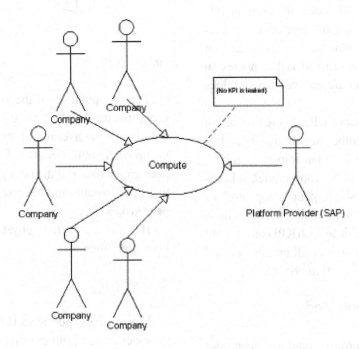

Peer Group Formation

As a result of the use case analysis it became clear that an important algorithm for the benchmarking platform is missing. The groups for the statistics computation need to be identified. The detailed description of this process can be found in (Kerschbaum 2007).

Peer group formation is the process of computing the peer groups and their participants from the set of subscribers at a given point in time. Peer group formation creates an injective and multi-valued mapping between subscribers and peer groups. A peer group has to be of a minimum size for its statistics to be meaningful in the benchmarking process. This minimum size is at least two, since a subscriber wants to compare to his competition and not just himself. Therefore a peer group always needs to contain multiple subscribers. A subscriber could be in one or more peer groups. So, two peer group models can be distinguished: single and multiple.

In the single peer group model a subscriber is part of exactly one peer group. In the multiple peer group model a subscriber can be part of more than one peer group. The peer group model has implications on the necessary number of parties in the statistics computation and the privacy of the KPIs.

Single Peer Group Model

In the single peer group model a subscriber maps to one and only one peer group. The privacy of the KPIs is maintained by the size of the peer group. If the statistics computation is done using a SMC protocol, no individual KPI is being leaked. The service provider may know the peer group a subscriber participates in without a privacy breach. The service provider only needs to communicate with the subscribers that are members of a peer group to compute its statistics, since the lack of communication with non-members does not reveal additional information the service provider does not already have.

Let k be the number of KPIs, p the number of peer groups, n the number of subscribers and m_i the number of subscribers participating in peer group i. In the single peer group model, it holds that $n = \Sigma_i^p m_i$. The single peer group model's SMC protocol has communication cost with a lower bound of $\Omega(nk)$, since each KPI is computed separately (k) and the sum of all members of all peer groups is n (see equation above).

Multiple Peer Group Model

In the multiple peer group model the subscriber can be part of more than one peer group. The privacy of the subscriber's KPI is at risk in the multiple peer group model, if the service provider knows which subscriber participates in which peer group.

Denote subscriber's X_i participation in peer group j by $\lambda_{i,j} = 1$, else $\lambda_{i,j} = 0$ (if he does not participate). Let Λ denote the p times n matrix of $\lambda_{0,0}, ..., \lambda_{n,p}$. Figure 7 shows an example of such a matrix, called peer group participation matrix.

Let $x_{i,k}$ be subscriber X_i's value of the k-th KPI. Let $\beta_{j,k} = (x_{1,k}, ..., x_{n,k})$ be the input vector of the j-th peer group. The computation of the sum (or average) of a KPI per peer group can be written as

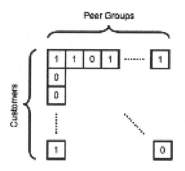

Figure 7. Peer group participation matrix

$$sum_k = \Lambda \, \beta_{j,k}.$$

The computation of the sum sum_k for a peer group for the k-th KPI is equivalent to the computation of the average, if the values in the peer group participation matrix Λ are divided by the peer group size or if the peer group size is known to all participants and the result is divided by the peer group size.

If Λ (or a selected subset of rows of Λ) are invertible, then

$$\Lambda^{-1} sum_k = \beta_{j,k}$$

Since sum_k is public and known to the service provider, Λ must either remain private for $\beta_{j,k}$ to remain private or all partial sub-matrices of Λ that contain all members (1s) of each contained peer group row (e.g. the intersections of columns 2, 3, 5 and rows 1, 4, 5, such that rows 1, 4, 5 have no 1's outside of columns 2, 3, 5) must be non-invertible.

Λ has to remain private to anyone, including the service provider. This implies that the communication pattern must not reveal Λ to the service provider and consequently every subscriber has to participate in the computation of every peer group. The multiple peer group model's SMC protocol has communication cost with a lower bound of $\Omega(nkp)$, since each KPI (k) must computed separately for each peer group (which now includes communication with all participants).

Comparison

A necessary condition for the peer group participation matrix Λ to be invertible (or pseudo-invertible) is $p \geq n$. This can never hold in the single peer group model. Also no partial sub-matrix that satisfies the condition above is invertible in the single peer group model, since for all KPIs of a peer group there is at most one equation. Peer group formation uses insensitive criteria that should even be public already, as input. A regular, non SMC computation of peer groups is preferable, since its computation and communication cost is significantly lower.

The single peer group model offers a better lower bound on the communication cost for the SMC protocol. We use data for evaluation considered realistic for real-world applications given today's business software and service market. Given this size requirement for the number of subscribers and $p = o(n)$, the multiple peer group model places a high burden on the practicality of the protocols. Assume that one ciphertext of size 256 bytes needs to be transferred per KPI, peer group and subscriber. For 200 KPIs and 100000 subscribers, one subscriber has to transfer over for 4 GB per peer group. Even under low assumptions this results in 16 TB per subscriber and 1600 PB for the service provider overall. This is clearly unpractical for a real-time enterprise system under current network conditions.

We conclude that a practical privacy-preserving benchmarking platform must work in the single peer group model.

Automatic Peer Group Formation

Peer group formation is a task of grouping related companies, very similar to data clustering. The task of peer group formation is performed by the platform provider alone in our benchmarking platform.

First each company is classified by a number of criteria; examples include continent of head-quarters, number of employees, revenue, industry sector, and legal form. Second each criterion is sub-divided into a fixed number of discrete classes, e.g. for number of employees: 0 to 10, 11 to 100, 101 to 1000, 1001 to 10000, more than 10000. Let m be the number of criteria, then each company forms a discrete data point in m-dimensional space. We can then use existing data clustering algorithms to form useful peer groups.

k,l-Means Clustering

We propose using the popular k-means clustering algorithm (MacQueen 1967), but it needs to be adapted to support a minimum cluster size. Recall that the minimum cluster size is necessary to create useful peer groups and to protect the privacy of the individual participants. Too small peer groups are not particularly useful for benchmarking and reveal the participants' KPI values (less than six members in the case of all five statistics). An adoption of k-means clustering called constrained k-means clustering using linear programming (LP) has been proposed in (Bennett *et al.* 2000). Unfortunately this solution does not scale to our problem sizes. Our example requirement of using 10000 companies and 1000 clusters leads to a LP model with 10^7 variables (and even more constraints). Such a large LP problem can only be solved using extensive computing power and we expect it to increase by a 100 for real-world applications. A more efficient algorithm is required.

The k-means algorithm starts by choosing k cluster centers at random. Then each data point (company) is assigned to the closest cluster center and the cluster center is recomputed as the mean of its assigned data points. The algorithm is continued until the cluster centers stabilize, i.e. the maximum distance of a cluster center between two iterations is below a certain threshold or the number of displaced cluster centers is below a certain threshold (or any combination of the two).

We propose a greedy algorithm as a small extension to k-means clustering. First, we choose a parameter *l* which represents the minimum cluster size. After each data point has been assigned to its cluster center, we process each cluster another time. If a cluster does not yet have *l* data points assigned, we assign it the closest data point that

- is not yet assigned to it
- has not been reassigned in this iteration

The second condition prevents infinite loops resulting from two cluster centers competing for a certain data point reassigning it in turn from one to the other. We continue to reassign data points until each cluster has at least *l* data points, and only then the cluster centers are recomputed. The pseudo-code of the final algorithm, which we call k,l-means clustering, is depicted in Figure 8. Our new addition to the regular k-means algorithm is confined to lines 8-20 and we described it in greater detail than the remaining algorithm which is well-known.

Complexity

The k,l-means clustering algorithm has three inner loops and one outer loop. The first inner loop (lines 5-7) runs *n*-times and searches for the nearest neighbor in the loop. We can use kd-trees (Bentley 1975) to optimally speed up the nearest neighbor search to $O(\log k)$. The time to build a kd-tree is $O(k \log k)$.

The third inner loop (lines 21-22) runs *k*-times, but overall at most *n* data points are being processed. Therefore by pre-processing the re-compute means operation, i.e. by creating linked lists for all data clusters in $O(n)$, the overall time of all loop iterations can be reduced to $O(n)$.

The loop added to regular k-means clustering (lines 8-20) consists of two nested loops. Nevertheless the main invariant is also that at most *n* data points get reassigned throughout those two loops. One of those reassignment takes at most a

Figure 8. k,l-Means Clustering Algorithm

```
1   means[] := random datapoint[k]
2   Do
3       size[] := 0[k]
4       flag[] := false[n]
5       for i := 1 to n
6           cluster[i] := index of closest means[]
7           size[i] := size[i] + 1
8       Do
9           reassign := false
10          for i := 1 to k
11              if size[i] < l
12                  min := index of closest datapoints[] with
13                      cluster[min] != i
14                      flag[min] == false
15                  size[i] := size[i] + 1
16                  size[cluster[min]] := size[cluster[min]] - 1
17                  flag[min] := true
18                  cluster[min] := i
19                  reassign := true
20      while reassign
21      for i := 1 to k
22          recompute means[]
23  until means[] stabilize
```

$O(n/k \log n)$ operation by searching for the n/k-th nearest neighbor in lines 12-14.

The number of iterations of the outmost loop depends on the stabilization criterion and is potentially unlimited. A good practical criterion limits the number of iterations by iteratively increasing the tolerated instability. E.g. increasing the threshold for displaced cluster means in each round by a constant limits the number of iterations to $O(k)$. The overall time complexity of the proposed algorithm is then $O(n^2 \log n)$. In comparison, the average complexity of constrained k-means clustering is $O(k n^3)$ (recall that $k = O(n)$) and its worst case complexity is exponential when using the simplex algorithm for LP.

The space complexity is dominated by the data structures linear in the number of data points ($O(n)$), e.g. cluster, flag or the data point kd-tree.

Incremental Peer Group Formation

k,l-means clustering provides sufficient quality and performance to form peer groups for our problem sizes, but operating on all data points at once potentially reassigns all subscribers. This would put an enormous statistics re-computation burden on the platform, since after just one clustering algorithm run all peer groups would need to be recomputed. Instead it is better to limit the re-computation to a set of affected subscribers only. Furthermore a customer benefits from retrieving a benchmarking result right after registration when he becomes a subscriber and may not want to wait for a re-clustering.

The solution for both problems is computing the peer groups incrementally. Every time a new subscriber arrives, he is assigned to an existing peer group (and can therefore immediately retrieve the statistics of this peer group). We set an upper bound on the peer group size, and when it has been reached, the peer group will be split into two. The k,l-means clustering algorithm is then used with $k=2$, $l=$upper limit/2 on the assigned peer group.

In our experiments the k,l-means algorithm converged for small data sets, even if the average cluster size was equal to l. As a result at most two peer groups need to be recomputed when a new customer subscribes. We set a lower time bound for the interval between re-computations, such that one can safely assume the KPIs have changed (and are now independent from the previous values), and therefore these multiple peer groups do not affect privacy as previously described.

Incremental peer group formation is favorable to k,l-means clustering on the entire data set due to the limit on the re-computation effort when a new customer subscribes.

Performance Evaluation

We evaluated an implementation of the benchmarking protocol in an experimental study. The service provider was deployed on a Pentium 4 3.2 GHz machine with 1.5 GB of memory. All subscribers were deployed on a Xeon Dual 3.6 GHz machine with 8 GB of memory. Between the subscribers' and service provider's machine we deployed a WAN emulator as an IP router. The WAN emulation software was the dummynet package for FreeBSD (Rizzo 1997). All machines were physically connected via a non-dedicated Gigabit Ethernet switch.

We independently modified two parameters in the study: We increased the number n of subscribers from 5 to 45 subscribers in steps of 5 and we increased the latency on the network connection from 0 to 100 milliseconds in steps of 25 milliseconds. The latency or delay simulates WAN conditions as over the Internet. A one-way delay of 100ms results in a round-trip time (RTT) of 200ms, which we estimated roughly corresponds to the RTT between Germany and Japan over the Internet. RTTs from Germany to destinations in the US are shorter and RTTs to destinations within Europe are even shorter than that.

The results are depicted in Figure 9. We can see from this picture that in this implementation the network performance plays a significant role. For 45 subscribers and a delay of 100ms the time spent for communication is almost half (precisely 45%) of the overall running time. The average for subscribers from 5 to 45 is 54% and constantly decreasing. We expected this, since the computational complexity is $O(n^2)$ while the number of connections to subscribers (incurring the delay) is $O(n)$. Therefore in the asymptotic limit the computational performance will be dominating. Nevertheless for our real-world number of subscribers the time spent on the network is significant.

In the next experiment we modified the service provider's implementation. Instead of sequentially calling each subscriber X_i in a loop, we create a thread for each subscriber that asynchronously handles the communication. This is possible only in the benchmarking protocol, since each round with each subscriber only requires input of the previous round, i.e. all subscribers can run concurrently. This means that the order of the subscribers does not matter for the protocol's semantics. We achieve the necessary synchronization using a barrier. The barrier synchronizes $n + 1$ threads: each thread communicating with a subscriber and the main thread. A thread calls the barrier's object method and sleeps until it is tripped. The last thread that reaches the barrier, trips it and all threads continue. The main thread continues to the next round while the other threads immediately terminate. The subscribers' threads have finished all communication before they reach the barrier. The barrier implementation is from Java's standard library module for concurrent utilities.

We conducted the same set of experiments with the concurrent implementation. We increased the number of subscribers and independently also increased the network delay.

The results are depicted in Figure 10. The impact of the network delay has significantly decreased and is now almost negligible compared

Figure 9. Running time of the protocol depending on number of subscribers and network delay

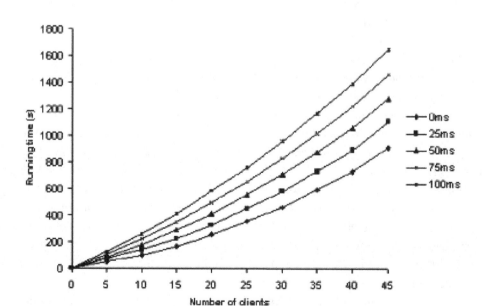

to the impact of the computational effort. For 45 subscribers and a network delay of 100ms the time spent for communication is only 6% of the overall running time.

The average percentage of communication time for subscribers from 5 to 45 is 14%. We conclude that the benchmarking protocol can be implemented, such that its performance is almost independent of the network performance, i.e. for the overall performance it nearly does not matter whether the subscribers are located on the same LAN or half-way around the world over the Internet.

The difference of the communication times can be explained with the different synchronization patterns of the sequential and concurrent implementation. In the sequential implementation for each subscriber a time period t_c is spent for communicating the request from the service provider to the subscriber and the response from the subscriber to the service provider. This time t_c is dominated by the delay of the network connection. During this time neither subscriber nor service provider can perform other computations or communications. A subscriber has to wait until all its predecessors have finished. Consequently the running time spent on the network is dominated by a linear number of delays due to the latency of the network. In our experiment using the sequential implementation the time spent on communication linearly increased with the number of subscribers supporting this hypothesis.

In the concurrent implementation the running time spent on one round is dominated by the slowest subscriber. Since, in our implementation all subscribers are identical (with identical network characteristics) the time is dominated by one subscriber. If the service provider is not able to schedule subscribers sufficiently fast, communications overlap only partially, but the communication with one subscriber may happen while another subscriber is computing. Therefore the communication time is only the delay as incurred in every round of the protocol.

Figure 10. Running time of the protocol depending on number of subscribers and network delay in concurrent implementation

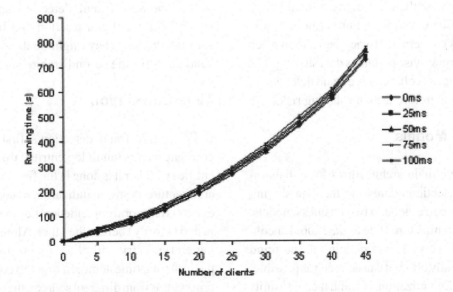

PRIVACY-PRESERVING FRAUD DETECTION

Not all cases of fraud can be detected by a company acting on its own. Imagine a fraudster that colludes with an outside supplier in order to create fake orders for supplies that are never delivered. Many internal controls, such as a good receipt in this case, can be circumvented, e.g. by ordering services. It is extremely difficult for one company to detect this fraud, but if both companies would collaborate and combine their data, they could detect that those services have never been provided.

There are other use cases with even higher impact where one party alone cannot detect the fraud case, in particular money laundering and organized crime. Therefore a new challenge is collaborative fraud detection where companies jointly search for fraud. Data sharing is the prerequisite for such collaboration and this brings along with it a number of new security and privacy challenges. In general no party is inclined to share its data unless the benefits exceed the risks and costs involved and in particular the perceived risks can be large. It is often difficult to decide the precise impact information may have on the operation of a company and therefore many companies are reluctant to share data very. Furthermore, if personal data is concerned privacy legislation often prohibits or otherwise regulates data sharing. The main obstacle for collaborative fraud detection to overcome is therefore the data sharing risk.

Business Models

There are two main architectures for collaborative fraud detection addressing the data sharing problem that correspond to two business models. In the first architecture (Lee *et al.* 2006, Lincoln *et al.* 2004) everyone participating in the fraud detection locally blinds it data as much as possible, e.g. by pseudonymization, etc. and then transmits it to a central entity that performs the combination

of all inputs non-interactively in order to detect the fraud cases. In the best case the central entity is supposed to be oblivious of the data (through the blinding), but in the worst case may be semi-trusted to handle the remaining data safely and also perform the detection honestly. This central entity acts a service provider offering the fraud detection service in the corresponding business model. In the second architecture (Atallah *et al.* 2004, Waters *et al.* 2004) the parties directly interact without a third party. They can use more powerful security techniques, such as SMC (Ben-Or et al. 1988, Goldreich et al. 1987, Yao 1982), to provably secure the data of each party. In the business model an independent software vendor would sell the application to perform the fraud detection to each company individually.

Comparing these two architectures a number of differences become apparent. The first architecture is currently more practical, since it requires less interaction and less complex computations. Therefore a few implementations have arisen recently (Parekh *et al.* 2006) following the first architecture. The second architecture is more secure and is able to provide provable security at the expense of more complex computations and a higher degree of interactions. Two party cases of collaborative fraud detection significantly simplify protocol construction and limit necessary interaction. They might be the first suitable candidates for the second architecture.

Time Correlation

Collaborative fraud detection's first step is to correlate events (audit log entries) from different entities whether it is done in the first or the second architecture. A strong indication of correlation of events is temporal coincidence, i.e. one event happened (shortly) before the other. Almost all event log entries carry with them time information in the form of a timestamp. In order to correlate two timestamps from different sources, the parties must have synchronized clocks. With the Network Time

Protocol (NTP) (Mills 1992) such synchronization is available over the Internet, but we can still improve and show how to get around it later.

Now we present a protocol that anonymizes (or better pseudonymizes) timestamps in the first architecture. Its goal is to leak to the central entity Trudy as little information as possible, but to still enable event correlation. Assuming two events that have occurred at time t and t', respectively, the main computation Trudy needs to perform is $|t - t'| < d$ where d is a pre-set threshold (Flegel and Biskup 2006).

Timestamp Pseudonymization

Let Alice and Bob be two users of Trudy's service. Then they can compare timestamps using the following algorithm. This algorithm guarantees that

- Trudy does not learn the value of the timestamp.
- Trudy can compute the distance between two timestamps, if the distance is below or equal to threshold d.
- Trudy cannot (directly) compute the distance between two timestamps, if the distance is above or equal to $2d$.

This can also be extended to 2-dimensional data points as shown in (Kerschbaum 2007a).

Setup

Alice and Bob commonly choose a shared secret s which is sufficiently hard to guess for Trudy. Then Alice and Bob also agree on a threshold value d for the maximum distance comparisons. Furthermore, they commonly choose a random value r in the range $0 \leq r < d$.

Timestamp Preparation

Alice and Bob perform the following steps for each timestamps t they own:

1. Compute a lower grid point $l = d \cdot \lfloor (t - r)/d \rfloor + r$.
2. Compute an upper grid point $u = l + d$.
3. Compute the difference m to l as $m = t - l$.
4. Compute the difference v to u as $v = t - u$.
5. Send the timestamp tuple $\langle t \rangle = \langle MAC(l, s), m, MAC(u, s), v \rangle$ to Trudy.

In this section we refer to both, l and u as well as their hashed counterparts as grid points.

Distance Computation

The third party Trudy can compute the distance $\delta = |t - t'|$ between two timestamps t and t' from the timestamp tuples $\langle t \rangle = \langle g_1, h_1, g_2, h_2 \rangle$ and $\langle t' \rangle = \langle g'_1, h'_1, g'_2, h'_2 \rangle$ with the following algorithm:

Case 1: $g_i \neq g'_j \ \forall \ i, j: \delta > d$
Case 2: $\exists \ g_c = g_i = g'_j: \delta = |h_i - h'_j|$

Visualization

Imagine the timestamps on a scale from left to right. The grid points then divide this scale into equal-sized sections. In the preparation step the algorithm computes the two grid points closest to the timestamp: the lower one l and the upper one u. The distance o the timestamp to the grid points is sent in plain-text to Trudy, i.e. the lower bits are leaked in some sense, but their exact values are also protected by r. Figure 11 depicts the timestamps t_1 and t_2 (as dots on the scale) with distance $\delta < d$ and common grid point g_c (grid points are depicted as line markers on the scale) and the timestamps t_3 and t_4 with distance $\delta' > d$ and without any grid point in common.

Figure 11. Distances of four timestamps

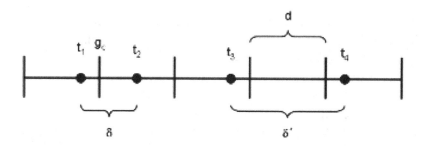

Attack on Timestamp Pseudonymization

The problem of timestamp pseudonymization is that the security it provides is limited and only holds in the case of two timestamps. This paragraph describes an attack on a set of timestamps where multiple timestamps are close and form clusters that allow an attacker to sequence the pseudonyms.

Assume Trudy has a black-box device that tells her for any two timestamp tuples the distance δ, if $\delta < d$ or indicates otherwise. This device is a less powerful abstraction of our algorithm, which actually computes the difference (and not just the distance) and sometimes allows the computation of differences $\delta > d$ (but $\delta < 2d$), i.e. everything an attacker can do with this black-box device he can do in our pseudonymization algorithm. Given a dense data set T of tuples $t_1, ..., t_n$ and this device, Trudy can align the timestamps on a linear scale by picking two tuples $\langle t \rangle$ and $\langle t' \rangle$ repeatedly querying the black-box device, until $|t - t'| = \delta \leq d$. She continues to search the remainder of the timestamp for a timestamp t'' (again by querying the black-box device), such that $|t - t''| = \delta' \leq d$. Now, she asks the device whether $\delta'' = |t' - t''| \leq d$. Then if $\delta = \delta' - \delta''$, she can conclude that $t < t' < t''$ or, if $\delta' = \delta - \delta''$, then she concludes $t < t'' < t'$.

If $t' - t'' > d$, she concludes that either $t' < t < t''$ or $t' > t > t''$ and that $\delta'' = \delta + \delta'$. Note that, she has computed a distance $\delta'' > d$ by inference

over two other distances $\delta < d$ and $\delta' < d$. Given enough data points Trudy can align all the timestamps along the scale. The direction ($<$ or $>$) remains unknown to Trudy, if only distances can be computed. We can achieve the same direction ignorance in our algorithm, if we flip a coin once and accordingly multiply each timestamp with -1 or not before preparing it.

The problem is even worse in our algorithm due to the availability of the grid points. Trudy only needs to align the grid points along the scale by comparing pairs and the timestamps will follow, but we showed above that this cluster alignment is unavoidable by any (non-interactive) solution to the problem.

Privacy-Preserving Logical Clocks

As mentioned above comparing timestamps from two different systems requires synchronized clocks on those systems. This requirement can be too strong in many practical systems and therefore logical clocks have been invented that relate to causality in distributed systems (Lamport 1978, Mattern 1989).

Vector clocks (Mattern 1989) are superior to Lamport's clocks (Lamport 1978) in that they allow to determine from the clock information whether an event x happened before an event y, vice-versa or if they are unrelated.

Each process maintains a logical clock estimate for each other process in the system in vector clocks. A process increments its local clock every time an event occurs (including receiving a message) which we call INC. If a process receives a message, it updates its estimation of the clocks of other processes. The sending process piggybacks his vector clock, i.e. its local clock and the estimates of the other's clocks, on the message and the receiving process stores the maximum of each sent clock entry and its local counterpart. We call this procedure MAX. Given two vector clocks a Timestamp Comparison Service (TCS) may want to infer which of them occurred before the other. We call this procedure COMP and we will later show how to realize each of these three operations in a privacy-preserving manner.

The security problems of vector and Lamport's clocks, such as forgery and denial have been addressed earlier (Reiter and Gong 1993), but the only solution so far that also achieves privacy requires trusted hardware (Smith and Tygar 1994). Privacy breaches by regular vector clocks may occur by process p_1 leaking information to p_2 about messages sent to other processes than p_2 while communicating with p_2. An example can be found in (Kerschbaum and Vayssiere 2007).

As a tool in our construction we use the same Yao's millionaires' comparison protocol on homomorphically encrypted values as in the benchmarking protocols. Note that some versions in the benchmarking protocols, e.g. the one in the Linear Cost Benchmarking protocol, are split-versions, such that after the protocol Alice and Bob hold a split (or shared) version of the result.

Proposed Protocol for Privacy-Preserving Vector Clocks

A process which keeps a virtual vector clock is a participant in the protocol. For simplicity we will limit ourselves to three participant processes Alice, Bob and Charlie, abbreviated as usual as A, B and C, although our protocols extend to an arbitrary number of parties. Each participant has its own public, private key pair, e.g. $E_A()$, $D_A()$.

During set-up, i.e. before the processes the protocols are executed, the participants have exchanged their public keys: $E_A()$, $E_B()$, ... As an additional primitive, we assume secure and authenticated pair-wise channels.

A privacy-preserving vector clock timestamp is represented as a tuple of individually encrypted regular vector clock timestamp entries:

$$E_A(t_A), E_B(t_B), E_C(t_C)$$

Each party's clock entry is encrypted under its party's public key, such that it is only readable in plaintext by itself, i.e. no clock entry value is being leaked to the other party.

Secure Increment

Incrementing a vector clock is done locally at either party's site. Since this party possesses the private decryption key, they could simply decrypt, add 1, and then encrypt again. For performance reason we recommend to operate on the ciphertext directly using the homomorphic addition. A secure INC would then be performed as, e.g. at Bob's

$$E_A(t_A), E_B(t_B) \cdot E_B(1) = E_B(t_B + 1), E_C(t_C)$$

Secure Maximum

Each time a party sends a message to another party, the receiving party updates its vector clock. As an example, assume Alice is sending a message to Bob. Let

A: $E_A(t'_A), E_B(t'_B), E_C(t'_C)$

denote the privacy-preserving vector clock of Alice at the time of sending the message, and

B: $E_A(t_A), E_B(t_B), E_C(t_C)$

denote Bob's vector clock. Then the update is

$$A \rightarrow B: E_A(max(t'_A, t_A)), E_B(t_B), E_C(max(t'_C, t_C))$$

Bob can simply take $E_B(t_B)$ from his timestamp without computing a maximum and Alice does not need to send Bob's logical time in her vector clock, but sends a placeholder $E_B(0)$ instead, since this may otherwise reveal unwanted causal information between two messages. This paragraph focuses on how Bob can compute $E_A(max(t'_A, t_A))$ and $E_C(max(t'_C, t_C))$.

Let's consider the first case of $E_A(max(t'_A, t_A))$. Bob has already received $E_A(t'_A)$ and privately holds $E_A(t_A)$. He can now engage in a split Yao's millionaires' protocol (see the benchmarking protocols) with Alice for computing $t'_A \leq t_A$:

$$A \leftrightarrow B: (c' \oplus c'') = (t'_A \leq t_A)$$

Afterwards Bob has c' and Alice has c''. Bob now uniformly chooses a random number r in the plaintext domain of $E_A()$ and prepares two values: $E_A(t'_A) \cdot E_A(r) = E_A(t'_A + r)$ and $E_A(t_A) \cdot E_A(r) = E_A(t_A + r)$. He numbers them according to his comparison result c':

$$B: \theta_{c'} = E_A(t_A + r) \quad \theta_{\neg c'} = E_A(t'_A + r)$$

Alice and Bob engage in an 1-out-of-2 OT protocol with Bob sending the pair $\{\theta_0, \theta_1\}$. Alice chooses $\theta_{c''}$ according to c''. One can easily verify that it follows that

$$A: \theta_{c''} = E_A(max(t'_A, t_A) + r)$$

Note, that Alice does not know which one is the larger timestamp, although she could decrypt $E_A(max(t'_A, t_A) + r)$, since she is blinded using secret sharing with r. Alice re-randomizes $\theta_{c''}$ to $\theta'_{c''}$ using homomorphic re-randomization, such that Bob cannot guess her choice c'' from the ciphertext, and then she sends $\theta'_{c''}$ to Bob.

$$A \rightarrow B: \theta'_{c''} = \theta_{c''} \cdot E_A \qquad (0)$$

Finally, Bob computes the desired (encrypted) maximum:

$$B: E_A(max(t'_A, t_A)) = \theta'_{c''} \cdot E_A(-r)$$

Bob repeats the same protocol with Charlie (replace all occurrences of Alice by Charlie in the protocol) and would do so for any other party in the system completing the vector clock.

Our protocol also supports networks with message reordering where messages, e.g. from Alice to Bob, are not always ordered FIFO. This can be for example the case over the Internet for UDP messages or multiple TCP connections in parallel. If the network guarantees FIFO delivery, the first maximum protocol with the sender Alice can be replaced by simply using $E_A(t'_A)$ as the maximum $E_A(max(t'_A, t_A))$, since Alice's local clock is always at least as large as its estimates. Then Bob has to execute only one maximum protocol with Charlie.

Secure Comparison

The TCS emulates a query to the system for the sake of convenience. It is not a trusted third party, since it requires the cooperation of all the participants to carry out its duties and does not have access to private keys and local vector clock information. The TCS receives two encrypted vector clock timestamps in order to determine the causality relationship between the two related events:

$$TCS: E_A(t'_A), E_B(t'_B), E_C(t'_C)$$

$$TCS: E_A(t_A), E_B(t_B), E_C(t_C)$$

As an example we assume that Alice sent the first timestamp and Bob the second. The following must hold for Alice's event to cause Bob's event

$t'_A \leq t_A \wedge t'_B \leq t_B$

The TCS engages in a split Yao's millionaires' protocol (again see the benchmarking protocols) with Alice for $t'_A \leq t_A$. Let c'_A be Alice's part of the result and c''_A be TCS's.

$A \leftrightarrow TCS: (c'_A \oplus c''_A) = (t'_A \leq t_A)$

The TCS engages in a similar protocol for $t'_B \leq t_B$ with Bob. Note that we need to use a variation of Yao's millionaires' protocol above to compute $t_B < t'_B$, where r' is chosen as a negative number $(0 \geq r' > -r)$. Afterwards Bob just negates his partial result and consequently the combined result equals $t'_B \leq t_B$. Let c'_B be Bob's part of the result and c''_B be the TCS's.

$B \leftrightarrow TCS: (c'_B \oplus c''_B) = (t'_B \leq t_B)$

Alice now forwards her partial result c'_A to Bob and Bob and the TCS need to compute the following formula

$c'_A \oplus c''_A \wedge c'_B \oplus c''_B$

This formula is similar to the main formula computed in (Goldreich 2004) for general SMC. We will use the same protocol except that we omit secret sharing of the output. Bob prepares four values for OT assuming each possible combination of the TCS's values.

$B: \lambda_0 = c'_A \oplus \wedge c'_B \oplus 0$ 0

$B: \lambda_1 = c'_A \oplus 1 \wedge c'_B \oplus$ 0

$B: \lambda_2 = c'_A \oplus 0 \wedge c'_B \oplus$ 1

$B: \lambda_3 = c'_A \oplus \wedge c'_B \oplus 1$ 1

Bob and the TCS then engage in 1-out-of-4 OT protocol with Bob as the sender of the four bits $\{\lambda_0, \lambda_1, \lambda_2, \lambda_3\}$ and the TCS chooses according to c''_A and c''_B the element with the number $2c''_B + c''_A$.

This completes the timestamp comparison operation. If the result is *false* (0), i.e. Alice's event did not cause Bob's event, the TCS computes again with the help of Alice and Bob the following formula for the inverse comparison to check whether Bob's event caused Alice's event.

$t_A \leq t'_A \wedge t_B \leq t'_B$

If the result of this formula is also *false*, the TCS concludes that the two events are concurrent.

Secure Supply Chain Management

It is a well-known fact that information exchange in supply chains reduces costs. This was first established in the seminal work of (Clark and Scarf 1960). Since then the negative effects of lacking information exchange have been shown, e.g. the so-called "bullwhip" effect (Padmanabhan and Whang 1997). Nevertheless practical adoption of information exchange faces major hurdles, since the data to be revealed is sensitive. It may negatively impact a company's position in future negotiations. Therefore companies are very reluctant to share this data.

Security technology and cryptography, and especially SMC, may help to overcome this problem. They can provide the necessary data protection during the computation, such that input data is protected while the result is available to the appropriate parties. This chapter will investigate a particular supply chain optimization problem central to medium-term production planning.

Business Model

The group formation process in supply chains has already solved when setting out to engage in secure supply chain management. All partners know each other and have a basic level of trust, e.g. they are willing to exchange messages. Therefore the most common architecture of SMC can be applied very well to the setting of secure supply chain management: all partners are treated equally and perform the same set of computations. The number of parties is limited as well, such that a smaller set of servers performing the computation to reduce the communication overhead is not mandatory.

The business model is therefore well-suited for a traditional software vendor that sells the applications in order to engage in secure supply chain management. The economy of scale is optimal for a software vendor that has essentially only development costs. The software business can be augmented with services for implementing the secure computation within a supply chain.

Other business models, such as the service model as in benchmarking, can be applied as well, of course. A suitable candidate might be a logistics provider that is in charge of transportation in the supply chain. He might gain an exclusive contract for the entire supply chain and thereby cross-finance the secure computation.

Supply Chain Master Planning

Supply Chain Master Planning (SCMP) is the collaborative, mid-term planning of production, warehousing and transportation. It strives to optimize the costs to a minimum still fulfilling the forecast demand. It is a centralized mechanism as opposed to the decentralized mechanism of upstream planning often observed in practice. SCMP aims for a global optimum rather than building on local optima as in upstream planning.

SCMP can be formulated as a Linear Programming (LP) problem. The objective function encompasses production costs, holding costs and shipping costs of finished products. The constraints ensure that the final customer demand is met, that finished and intermediate products are balanced, and that capacity is not exceeded. The outcome is a supply chain master plan that specifies production, warehousing and shipping

quantities across the entire supply chain for multiple planning periods.

Secure and Private Linear Programming

The trusted third party necessary for SCMP can be emulated using SMC. A protocol for computing LP is necessary. The most commonly used algorithm for LP is simplex (Dantzig and Thapa 1997). The problem with the simplex algorithm is that its worst case complexity is exponential. The running time of an algorithm may reveal additional information (even in the semi-honest model), such that a perfectly secure protocol would need to always run in exponential time, e.g. a circuit construction according to (Yao 1982) would be exponential in size.

The two protocols developed for secure LP (Li and Atallah 2006, Toft 2007) therefore take the approach to slightly leak information, namely the number of iterations in the simplex algorithm, while reducing the average complexity to that of simplex ($O(n^3)$). In (Li and Atallah 2006) a two-party algorithm that makes extensive use of homomorphic encryption is presented. It avoids leaking information about the pivot element of simplex by doubly permuting the matrix, such that no party knows the permutation. (Toft 2007) presents a solution based on the symmetric model of SMC. It can therefore compute multi-party problems. After deriving some basic building blocks it gives a construction for simplex. Instead of permuting the matrix it hides the pivot index by operations on the entire matrix using secretly shared values.

No implementations of the algorithms exist and one can only speculate about their performance on real-world problems. Many research problems need to be overcome before realizing secure supply chain management.

CONCLUSION

We have described three different B2B applications, their security requirements and their realization or first steps towards realization. We could show that data protection in these collaborative applications is important in order to protect vital business secrets and we showed that data protection is possible using a wealth of techniques mostly based on Secure Multi-party Computation (SMC). The architecture and business models of all three applications differ, such that the basic theoretic techniques of SMC need to be adapted or augmented with other techniques. We described a wealth of such techniques.

Privacy-Preserving Benchmarking is clearly the most advanced of the three applications and we can conclude that is not only theoretically feasible, but also practically. Special protocols based on homomorphic encryption have been developed to match the requirements of the business model a benchmarking platform as a service. These protocols have been thoroughly evaluated and their analysis in the constrained malicious model is based on the economic requirements of the application. This represents a major step forward in economically secure protocols.

The protocols have been embedded into a whole system architecture encompassing all steps from registration to statistics computation. A major hurdle for the adoption of secure computation was overcome by assigning peer groups first, delivering the statistics and then later engaging in the protocol for securely computing new statistics. It is therefore now possible to instantaneously deliver the benchmarking results after registration which is a major step towards customer acceptance.

The system architecture posed the problem of peer group formation as the first multi-group benchmarking platform. This was solved using a novel data mining technique that can efficiently cluster data points into clusters with a minimum size. This technique can also be applied incrementally with a negligible disadvantage in clustering performance. Using the combination of these techniques it is possible to build the benchmarking platform system.

We implemented and evaluated the benchmarking protocol using a prototypical system. The performance was shown to be reasonable in absolute terms. We could also show that using a parallel implementation, the benchmarking protocols become computation-bound rather than communication-bound which is good news, since we can expect an increase in available computation power due to Moore's Law.

In privacy-preserving collaborative fraud detection we investigated the problem of event correlation using time information. First timestamps were considered and a simple algorithm for pseudonymizing them was presented. This algorithm can be applied with a non-interactive third party. Unfortunately we could also show that any kind of such an algorithm can be attacked given a set of timestamps which serves as an example for the limitation of security in the non-interactive case.

We then showed how to perform privacy-preserving operations on logical time, such that synchronized clocks are unnecessary. We described an algorithm that uses a similar technique to the benchmarking protocol and therefore works quite efficiently, although its complexity is certainly higher than that of timestamp pseudonymization.

Last we gave an outlook on secure supply chain management using supply chain master planning. It can be reduced to secure computation of linear programs and we gave an overview over the current state-of-the-art. Clearly many research challenges lie ahead of us in this field.

Outlook

The advantages of collaborative business applications are apparent and their use is becoming more widespread every day. As such, the benefits are clear. On the downside there is the necessary data exchange and the full potential of the applications is often unused. This is particularly true in supply chain management where the need for information exchange has been recognized early on. The possible economic benefits are also the greatest in this field. Nevertheless it also faces the highest hurdles, since the necessary data is business vital and companies are very reluctant to reveal it.

We believe we will therefore see an increasing movement towards data protection in these applications. They widen the addressable market of the solutions and will eventually become a best practice, since given the possibility to perform the same application at the same service level privacy-preserving or using data sharing, one would also choose privacy-preserving.

Besides the presented three applications described here many applications will evolve. Examples currently put into practice include auctions (Bogetoft *et. al* 2008) and name correlation (IBM 2006). Theoretic work for many more exists.

REFERENCES

Abraham, I., Dolev, D., Gonen, R., & Halpern, J. (2006). Distributed Computing Meets Game Theory: Robust Mechanisms for Rational Secret Sharing and Multiparty Computation. In *Proceedings of the 25th ACM Symposium on Principles of Distributed Computing* (pp. 53-62).

Acquisti, A. (2004). Privacy in Electronic Commerce and the Economics of Immediate Gratification. In *Proceedings of the ACM Electronic Commerce Conference* (pp. 21-29).

Aggarwal, G., Mishra, N., & Pinkas, B. (2004). Secure Computation of the kth-Ranked Element. In *Proceedings of EUROCRYPT . Lecture Notes in Computer Science, 3027*, 40–55.

Atallah, M., Bykova, M., Li, J., Frikken, K., & Topkara, M. (2004). Private Collaborative Forecasting and Benchmarking. In *Proceedings of the ACM Workshop on Privacy in an Electronic Society* (pp. 103-114).

Ben-Or, M., Goldwasser, S., & Wigderson, A. (1988). Completeness theorems for non-cryptographic fault-tolerant distributed computation. In *Proceedings of the 20th ACM Symposium on Theory of Computing* (pp. 1- 10).

Benaloh, J. (1987). *Verifiable Secret-Ballot Elections*. Unpublished doctoral dissertation, Yale University.

Bennett, K., Bradley, P., & Demiriz, A. (2000). *Constrained K-Means Clustering* (Microsoft Technical Report).

Bentley, J. (1975). Multidimensional Binary Search Trees used for Associative Searching. *Communications of the ACM, 18*(9), 509–517. doi:10.1145/361002.361007

Bogetoft, P., Christensen, D., Damgard, I., Geisler, M., Jakobsen, T., Kroigaard, M., et al. (2008). *Multiparty Computation Goes Live*. Retrieved from http://eprint.iacr.org/2008/068

Clark, A., & Scarf, H. (1960). Optimal policies for a multi-echelon inventory problem. *Management Science, 6*(4), 475–490. doi:10.1287/mnsc.6.4.475

Cvrcek, D., Kumpost, M., Matyas, V., & Danezis, G. (2006). A study on the value of location privacy. In *Proceedings of the ACM Workshop on Privacy in the Electronic Society* (pp. 109-118).

Damgard, I., & Jurik, M. (2001). A Generalisation, a Simplification and some Applications of Pailliers Probabilistic Public-Key System. In *Proceedings of International Conference on Theory and Practice of Public-Key Cryptography* (LNCS 1992, pp. 119-136).

Dantzig, G., & Thapa, M. (1997). *Linear Programming 1: Introduction*. Berlin, Germany: Springer-Verlag.

Di Crescenzo, G. (2000). Private Selective Payment Protocols. In *Proceedings of Financial Cryptography* (LNCS 1962, pp. 72-89).

Di Crescenzo, G. (2001). Privacy for the Stock Market. In *Proceedings of Financial Cryptography* (LNCS 2339, pp. 269-288).

Flegel, U., & Biskup, J. (2006). Requirements of Information Reductions for Cooperating Intrusion Detection Agents. In *Proceedings of the International Conference on Emerging Trends in Information and Communication Security* (pp. 466-480).

Goldreich, O. (2004). *Foundations of Cryptography II: Basic Applications*. Cambridge, UK: Cambridge University Press.

Goldreich, O., Micali, S., & Wigderson, A. (1987). How to Play any Mental Game or A Completeness Theorem for Protocols with Honest Majority. In *Proceedings of the 19th ACM Symposium on Theory of Computing* (pp. 218-229).

Halpern, J., & Teague, V. (2004). Rational Secret Sharing and Multiparty Computation: Extended Abstract. *Proceedings of the 36th ACM Symposium on Theory of Computing* (pp. 623-632).

IBM. (2006). *IBM Anonymous Resolution Version 4.1 Technical Information*. Retrieved from http://ibm.com/db2/eas/

Kerschbaum, F. (2007). Building a Privacy-Preserving Benchmarking Enterprise System. In *Proceedings of the IEEE EDOC Conference* (pp. 87-96).

Kerschbaum, F. (2007a). Distance-preserving pseudonymization for timestamps and spatial data. In *Proceedings of the ACM Workshop on Privacy in the Electronic Society* (pp. 68-71).

Kerschbaum, F. (2008). Practical Privacy-Preserving Benchmarking. In *Proceedings of the 23rd IFIP International Information Security Conference*.

Kerschbaum, F., & Terzidis, O. (2006). Filtering for Private Collaborative Benchmarking. In *Proceedings of the International Conference on Emerging Trends in Information and Communication Security* (LNCS 3995, pp. 409-422).

Kerschbaum, F., & Vayssiere, J. (2007). Privacy-preserving logical vector clocks using secure computation techniques. In *Proceedings of the 13th International Conference on Parallel and Distributed Systems*.

Lamport, L. (1978). Time, clocks, and the ordering of events in a distributed system. *Communications of the ACM, 21*(7), 558–565. doi:10.1145/359545.359563

Lee, A., Tabriz, P., & Borisov, N. (2006). A privacy-preserving interdomain audit framework. In *Proceedings of the ACM Workshop on Privacy in the Electronic Society* (pp. 99-108).

Li, J., & Atallah, M. (2006). Secure and Private Collaborative Linear Programming. In *Proceedings of the International Conference on Collaborative Computing* (pp. 19-26).

Lincoln, P., Porras, P., & Shmatikov, V. (2004). Privacy-Preserving Sharing and Correlation of Security Alerts. In *Proceedings of the USENIX Security Symposium* (pp. 239-254).

Lynch, N. (1996). *Distributed Algorithms*. San Francisco: Morgan Kaufmann.

MacQueen, J. (1967). Some Methods for classification and Analysis of Multivariate Observations. In *Proceedings of 5th Berkeley Symposium on Mathematical Statistics and Probability* (pp. 281-297).

Mattern, F. (1989). Virtual Time and Global States of Distributed Systems. In *Proceedings of the International Workshop on Parallel and Distributed Algorithms* (pp. 215-226).

Mills, D. (1992). *Network Time Protocol (Version 3) -- Specification, Implementation and Analysis. IETF RFC 1305*. Retrieved from http://tools.ietf.org/rfc/rfc1305.txt

Naccache, D., & Stern, J. (1998). A New Public-Key Cryptosystem Based on Higher Residues. In *Proceedings of the ACM Conference on Computer and Communications Security* (pp. 59-66).

Okamoto, T., & Uchiyama, S. (1998). A new public-key cryptosystem as secure as factoring. In *Proceedings of EUROCRYPT* (LNCS, 1403, pp. 308-318).

Padmanabhan, H., & Whang, S. (1997). Information distortion in a supply chain. *Management Science, 43*(4), 546–558. doi:10.1287/mnsc.43.4.546

Paillier, P. (1999). Public-Key Cryptosystems Based on Composite Degree Residuosity Classes. In *Proceedings of EUROCRYPT* (LNCS 1592, pp. 223-238).

Parekh, J., Wang, K., & Stolfo, S. (2006). Privacy-preserving payload-based correlation for accurate malicious traffic detection. In *Proceedings of the SIGCOMM workshop on Large-scale attack defense* (pp. 99-106).

Reiter, M., & Gong, L. (1993). Preventing Denial and Forgery of Causal Relationships in Distributed Systems. In *Proceedings of the IEEE Symposium on Security and Privacy* (pp. 30-40).

Rizzo, L. (1997). Dummynet: a simple approach to the evaluation of network protocols. *ACM Computer Communication Review, 27*(1), 31–41. doi:10.1145/251007.251012

Schneier, B. (1996). *Applied Cryptography* (2nd ed.). New York: John Wiley & Sons.

Shoham, Y., & Tennenholtz, M. (2005). Non-Cooperative Computation: Boolean Functions with Correctness and Exclusivity. *Theoretical Computer Science, 343*(1-2), 97–113. doi:10.1016/j.tcs.2005.05.009

Smith, S., & Tygar, D. (1994). Security and Privacy for Partial Order Time. In *Proceedings of the International Conference on Parallel and Distributed Computing Systems* (pp. 70-79).

Toft, T. (2007). *Primitives and Applications for Multi-party Computation*. Unpublished doctoral dissertation, University of Aarhus.

Waters, B., Balfanz, D., Durfee, G., & Smetters, D. (2004). Building an Encrypted and Searchable Audit Log. In *Proceedings of the Internet Society Network Distributed Systems Symposium*.

Yao, A. (1982). Protocols for Secure Computations. In *Proceedings of the IEEE Symposium on Foundations of Computer Science* (pp. 160-164).

Chapter 6
An Approach to Unified Trust Management Framework

Weiliang Zhao
Macquarie University, Australia

Vijay Varadharajan
Macquarie University, Australia

ABSTRACT

In this chapter, the authors propose an approach with a unified framework for trust management with a consistent way to cover a broad variety of trust mechanisms including credentials, reputation, local data storage, and environment parameters. The trust request, trust evaluation, and trust consuming are handled in a comprehensive manner. The framework has a high extensibility to embrace established standards and new requirements. With the help of the proposed framework, the development of a trust management system in the real world can be automated to a substantially high level.

1. INTRODUCTION

There have been many trust management systems which are exclusively based on credentials. In these systems, credentials are the only type of trust evidence accepted. Before the clear concept of trust management, PKI and PGP have already used credentials to deal with trust management problems. PolicyMaker (Blaze, Feigenbaum, & Lacy, 1996), KeyNote (Blaze, Feigenbaum, & Keromytis, 1999), and REFEREE (Chu, Feigenbaum, LaMacchia, Resnick, & Strauss, 1997) belong to this kind of trust management systems. Normally,

these trust management systems include credential verification and security policies to restrict access to resources and services. G. Suryanarayana et al (Suryanarayana, Erenkrantz, Hendrickson, & Taylor, 2004) have pointed out that these systems are limited in the sense that they do not enable an entity to aggregate the perception of other entities in the system in order to choose a suitable reputable service.

The reputation of an entity can be used as a criterion to determine the restriction of access to resources and services. Some information systems such as e-Bay employ reputation as the exclusive evidence for trust. Reputation-based systems such as XREP (Damiani, Vimercati, Paraboschi, Samarati,

DOI: 10.4018/978-1-60566-414-9.ch006

& Violante, 2002), NICE (Lee, Sherwood, & Bhattacharjee, 2003), P-Grid (Aberer & Despotovic, 2001) provide the facilities to compute the reputation of an involved entity by aggregating the perception of other entities in the system. Some reputation systems like TrustNet (Schillo, Rovatsos, & Funk, 2000) and NodeRanking (Pujol, Sang, esa, & Delgado, 2002) utilize existing social relationships to compute reputations based on various parameters. M. Kinateder et al (Kinateder, Baschny, & Rothermel, 2005) proposed a generic model for trust based on reputation. Normally, these reputation systems are limited in the sense that they do not link the purpose of reputation to its evaluation.

All existing trust management systems focus on building up a new trust management layer and the concept of trust is normally assumed in a specific context. These systems normally support certain types of trust mechanisms exclusively. Most of them only support credentials or reputation exclusively. We believe that it is necessary to have a unified framework for trust management with the ability to put different trust mechanisms under the same umbrella.

In this chapter, we propose an approach with a unified framework for trust management that can address the above mentioned limitations of current trust management systems. The unified framework uses a consistent way to cover a broad variety of trust mechanisms including credentials, reputation, local data storage, and environment parameters. Different trust mechanisms can be assembled together easily when they are needed. The framework will embrace established standards and existing computing utilities/functions/systems in distributed information systems. A trust management architecture is proposed and the generic computing components in the architecture are described which can be used as enabling tools for the development of sub systems (or a separated layer) for trust management in distributed information systems.

The proposed unified framework for trust management is based on our formal model of trust relationship and unified taxonomy framework of trust proposed in (Zhao, Varadharajan, & Bryan, 2004, 2005b, 2007). The formal model of trust relationship can cover multiple and/or complex trust mechanisms in distributed information systems. The taxonomy framework can reflect the different forms of trust relationships based on their specific characteristics and a range of useful trust relationships can be expressed and compared. We have developed the general methodology for the analysis and modeling of trust relationships in (Zhao, Varadharajan, & Bryan, 2005a, 2006). These research results form a basis of the unified framework for trust management described in this chapter.

For a real trust management system, trust relationships must have been modeled and loaded into the trust management system before these trust relationships are requested by related applications. When a trust relationship is defined, any condition in a condition set must be assessable which means the condition can always be evaluated in the trust management system. The supporting trust mechanisms and condition constraints must be consistently considered in the analysis and modeling of trust relationships and the development of trust management systems. Our concerns in this chapter focus on the general characteristics of trust management systems. The computing components and processes in real systems will be abstracted to generic computing components and processes. We devise TrustEngine as a generic trust management system to express the unified framework. The unified framework for trust management is expressed by TrustEngine with its architecture, generic system components, generic system setting up, and typical operation sequences.

The rest of this chapter is organized as follows. Section 2 highlights major characteristics of trust management issues in distributed information systems. Section 3 provides an overview of our previous research result about unified taxonomy framework of trust. In Section 4, we propose a trust management architecture with a standard and high level design for trust management tasks that can be separated from distributed information systems. Section 5 describes the system components of our devised TrustEngine. Section 6 discusses system setting up and operations of trust management systems. Section 7 provides an application example for the implementation of our proposed unified trust management framework. Section 8 discusses some related work. Section 9 concludes this chapter and discusses some potential directions for future work.

2. CHALLENGES FOR TRUST MANAGEMENT

The migration from a centralized information system to a distributed information system means that some operations and transactions will span a range of domains, and multiple entities may be involved in these operations and transactions. The involved entities may have different levels of familiarity and information access. The entities may not be trusted to the same extent. The notion of trust must be introduced and it is beyond the traditional security requirements mentioned in last section. The trust between customers and the providers of the services is crucial in electronic commerce transactions on the Internet. There are multiple trust requirements when a service needs to be trusted as it claims, the privacy of customers needs to be protected, and the providers of the services need to be paid as expected. The trust decision must be made before a business transaction can be achieved, and it forms the basis for the customer's decision to choose the provided services and process the business transaction. Trust has become an intrinsic part of e-Business.

The issue of trust is one of the major concerns in distributed information systems in a range of research areas such as web services, grid computing, cooperative computing, and forensic computing.

Trust issues arise not only in business functions, but also in technologies used in the implementation of these functions. The business requirements and the technologies employed in target information systems are normally mingled with each other. The target distributed information systems must address all these trust issues.

Here we list some of the major characteristics of distributed information systems related with trust issues:

- **Multiple Trust Mechanisms: Closed information systems** have centralized control for security and trust. Trust is normally predefined and the related data is stored in the information system. Some distributed information systems and technologies only accept credentials to establish and broker trust relationships. At the same time, there is also an alternative trend of using reputation based trust for collaborations to satisfy security requirements in distributed information systems. Instead of centrally managed data and/or credentials, involved entities may use specific knowledge (both local and acquired from remote nodes or resources) to make trust decisions. In more complex cases, multiple trust mechanisms, such as credentials and reputation, can be required to work together for a single trust decision.
- **Open Nature: Business func**tions are normally open in modern distributed information systems. For example, everyone has the access to an online hotel booking service. The system is open to everyone and it can cover both known frequent customers and some previously unknown customers. Different trust relationships must be figured out in the system for various business operations and transactions. These distributed information systems have intrinsic requirements for appropriate trust management. Modern distributed information

systems are normally running over open networks, particularly over the Internet. The open nature of a distributed information system makes trust management a crucial part of the whole information system.

- **Multiple Domains: Modern distributed** information systems often span several networks, and there are multiple administrative or organizational boundaries. A typical distributed information system is composed of many interconnected heterogeneous resources that belong to multiple domains, and the relationship between these domains can be peer to peer or hierarchical, or a combination thereof. For example, a multi-enterprise financial trading system (Luckham, 2002) is distributed over various networks worldwide including the Internet. Various enterprises and organizations are simply the components of the system, and each of them has its own internal information processing system. There are multiple sub systems such as the stock market information system, brokerage houses, and online customers (or their workstations), the Federal Reserve, investment banks, and the networks through which all these components communicate with each other. There are multiple boundaries and domains in such a complicated information system. The trust relationships can be quite complex in such a system. There are many challenging trust issues in cross-boundary operations, management, and administration.

- **Real Time Trust: In many distribut**ed information systems, trust relationships must be evaluated and established in real time. Trust relationships are not static and they are continuously changing. The dynamic properties of trust must be included in many distributed information systems. Multiple evidences must be collected in real time for trust evaluation. The valid

period of the result of trust evaluation is also time relevant (for example, it can only be used in a fixed time period). The concept of time is an important concern in most trust issues in distributed information systems.

- **Scalability: Every distrib**uted information system has its specific scale. A distributed information system may have a large number of resources and a large number of users, or potential users. Some of these distributed information systems are required to scale up to the scope of the Internet. The scale of a distributed information system is crucial in trust management.

- **Complexity: Distributed** information systems can be very complicated. Modern distributed information systems can have complicated business functions and employ multiple advanced technologies. The trust management tasks can be very complex and challenging.

The above items describe the important challenges for trust management in modern distributed information systems.

3. TAXONOMY FRAMEWORK OF TRUST

This section provides a brief review of our previously proposed taxonomy framework of trust in general distributed information systems that can provide terminologies and enable tools for the analysis/modeling of trust relationships in distributed information systems. The taxonomy framework of trust is based on the formal definition of trust relationships and it includes the classification of trust; the properties of trust including trust direction, trust symmetry, scope and diversity of trust relationships; and operations and definitions about the relations of trust relationships. In this section, we only provide a high level description about the framework. More details about the elements of the taxonomy framework of trust can be found in published papers (Zhao et al., 2004, 2005b, 2007).

3.1 Formal Model of Trust Relationship

In the computing world, the concept of trust arises in many branches of computing systems. There is not a clear consensus about the meaning of trust. When the term of trust is used, its meaning must be judged based on the particular domain where it is used. Multiple notions of trust in computing make trust complex, multifaceted, and context-dependent. The broad generality of the term trust makes the concept of trust abstract and somewhat elusive. We believe that it is necessary to build up a solid taxonomy framework which can be used to describe the various characteristics of trust and clarify the difference between them. In order to capture the essence of trust, the starting point is to provide a formal definition of trust relationship. We propose a formal definition of trust relationship (Zhao et al., 2004) as follows:

Definition 1. A trust relationship is a four-tuple T =< R, E, C, P > where:

- *R is the set of trustors. It can not be empty.*
- *E is the set of trustees. It can not be empty.*
- *C is the set of conditions. It contains all conditions (requirements) for the current trust relationship. Normally, a trust relationship has some specified conditions. If there is no condition, the condition set is empty.*
- *P is the set of properties. The property set describes the actions or attributes of the trustees. It can not be empty. The property set can be divided into two sub sets:*
  - Action set: the set of actions which trustors trust that trustees will/can perform.
  - Attribute set: the set of attributes which trustors trust that trustees have.

When trust relationships are used, the full syntax (four-tuple < R, E, C, P >) must be followed. Trust relationship T means that under the condition set C, trustor set R trust that trustee set E have property set P. The proposed formal definition of trust relationship has a strict mathematical structure and a broad expressive power.

3.2 Classification of Trust

T. Grandison et al (grandison & Sloman, 2000) have given a bottom-up classification of trust and used the terms as resources access trust, service provision trust, certification trust, delegation trust and infrastructure trust. All the above trust types must build on a more basic trust relationship which is the authentication trust or identity trust. In our taxonomy framework of trust, trust relationships are categorized into two layers. Authentication trust is on layer one and other types are on layer two. Please see Figure 1.

At layer two, trust relationships can be classified in different ways. We provide a trust hierarchy based on the characteristics of tuples in trust relationships. Please see Figure 2.

3.3 Properties of Trust Relationships

The taxonomy framework of trust covers different properties of trust relationships. In our previous work, the properties of trust direction and trust symmetry, trust scope and trust diversity have been defined (Zhao et al., 2005b, 2007). In the taxonomy framework of trust, one-way trust relationship, two-way trust relationship, and reflexive trust relationship have been defined for the properties of trust direction. For the properties of symmetry of trust, we have defined symmetric trust relationships, symmetric two-way trust relationship, and the whole set of trust relationships. Trust scope label has been defined and a set of comparing rules for trust scope labels have been provided.

The definitions of properties of trust relationships cover a broad range of important and

Figure 1. Trust Layers

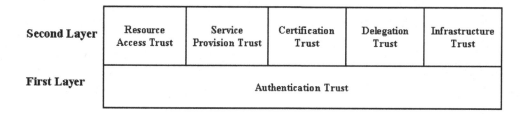

	Resource Access Trust	Service Provision Trust	Certification Trust	Delegation Trust	Infrastructure Trust
Second Layer					
First Layer	Authentication Trust				

popular situations in the real world. They provide standard terminologies and can be used as scenario examples for the analysis and modeling of trust relationships in information systems. More details can be found in (Zhao et al., 2005b, 2007).

3.4 Relations/Operations of Trust Relationships

The taxonomy framework of trust includes a set of operations and definitions for some relations of trust relationships (Zhao et al., 2004, 2007). There have been defined a set of operations to generate new trust relationships based on existing trust relationships. Definitions of equivalent, primitive, derived, direct redundant and alternate trust relationships have been proposed and the direct redundant trust relationships have been classified into different types. More details can be found in (Zhao et al., 2004, 2007).

4. TRUST MANAGEMENT ARCHITECTURE

Trust management architecture targets a standard, high level design for the development of trust management systems. Trust management architecture can be used as an auxiliary tool in the whole life cycle of the development of trust management systems, including specifications of requirements, preliminary design, active deployment, and maintenance. The architecture provides the basis for dependency and consistency analysis for trust management. As a general architecture, it can be reused in different systems.

The trust management architecture should have the ability to embrace frequently used mechanisms of evaluation of trust relationships and consumption of trust relationships. The architecture describes the high level design of the trust management system in terms of major computing components and their interrelationships. The details of its generic computing components provide guidelines and constrains for its implementation.

Figure 2. Trust Hierarchy

TrustEngine holds a set of trust related computing components that could be separated from applications. These computing components are generic. TrustEngine expresses a separated layer of trust management in distributed information systems. The formal definition of a trust relationship provides the starting point for the trust management architecture. TrustEngine addresses applications' trust requests like a database query engine. TrustEngine accepts a requested trust relationship, or a set of inputs, that could be used to determine the requested trust relationship. Depending on the form of the query, TrustEngine locates the requested trust relationship, evaluates the trust relationship, and manages the consumption of the evaluation result.

In TrustEngine, there is a data storage mechanism that is separated from other computing components. The finding of trust relationships based on the requests, the evaluation of trust relationships with the help of trust mechanisms, and the consuming management are separated and put into different computing packages. These computing packages have the flexibility to be extended for holding new trust components. Each component in TrustEngine performs some trust function or has some data storage to be used by other trust functions.

TrustEngine includes TrustDatabase for the storage of trust related data and component packages as LocatingTrust, EvaluatingTrust and ConsumingTrust. Figure 3 shows the top level components of TrustEngine.

4.1 TrustDatabase

TrustEngine includes a persistent storage mechanism for storing and retrieving information about trust. TrustDatabase is the data storage of TrustEngine that maintains trust relationships, instances of trust relationships, and trust parameters. These trust related data will only be used by

Figure 3. TrustEngine Package Hierarchy

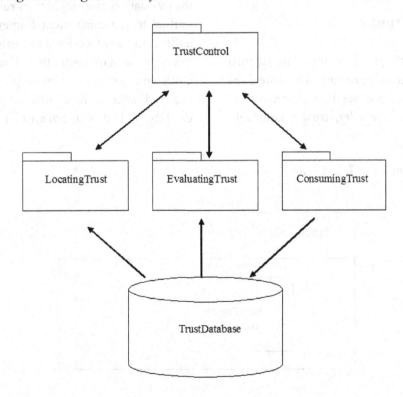

the computing components of TrustEngine. The storage mechanism can be a relational database or data profile.

For a real distributed information system, when an application is being developed, trust relationships required in the application must be analyzed and modeled. The trust relationships and trust related parameters must have been loaded into the TrustDatabase before they are involved at run time. The storage and retrieving mechanisms for instances of trust relationships, and other runtime parameters, must have been set up as well.

4.2 TrustControl

TrustControl is the package for the overall management and control of TrustEngine at run time. TrustEngine controller is the only computing component in this package. It is the general controller of TrustEngine that links applications and functional packages of TrustEngine (LocatingTrust, EvaluatingTrust and ConsumingTrust). See Figure 4.

4.3 LocatingTrust

LocatingTrust is the package for finding the trust relationship based on the request. There are three components in this package that are referred to as locating trust controller, trust relationship

locator, and authentication controller. Locating trust controller is the management component that receives the request from applications and it assigns tasks to the trust relationship locator and authentication controller. Trust relationship locator is the component that finds the requested trust relationship from the TrustDatabase. Authentication controller is the component that deals with authentication; normally it employs existing authentication services in the system to perform the tasks. See Figure 5.

4.4 EvaluatingTrust

EvaluatingTrust contains computing components required for the evaluation of trust relationships. The evaluation of a trust relationship involves checking whether the conditions of a trust relationship can be satisfied or not. The conditions of trust relationships take into account the risks from the evil actions of trustees, evil actions from other parties, and from unstable environments.

Multiple trust mechanisms can be involved in the evaluation of a single trust relationship. The unified trust management framework provides an integration place for these trust mechanisms to cooperate with each other. The existing standards and systems can be employed to support required tasks in the evaluation processes. Any existing system or mechanism for checking or

Figure 4. Components of TrustControl

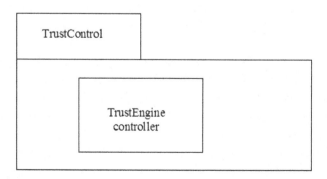

Figure 5. Components of LocatingTrust

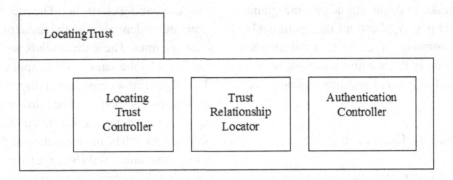

Figure 6. Components of EvaluatingTrust

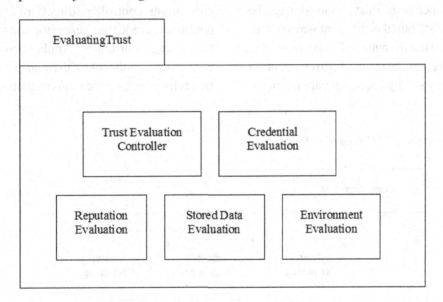

evaluating the evidence of trust could be included in the EvaluatingTrust package. For instance, the existing reputation-based systems and credential based systems can be employed to provide required information for trust evaluation.

In EvaluatingTrust, trust evaluation controller is the computing component that assigns the evaluation tasks to other functional components in this package. EvaluatingTrust has functional components for specific evaluating tasks, namely credential evaluation, reputation evaluation, stored data evaluation, and environment evaluation. In the implementation, the package of Evaluating-

Trust will be customized or extended based on the specific requirements. See Figure 6.

4.5 ConsumingTrust

ConsumingTrust contains the computing components for the control and management of trust consuming. Consuming trust deals with how to use the output of the evaluation of a trust relationship. ConsumingTrust contains the consuming controller and the two next level packages Application-Consuming and SystemConsuming. Consuming controller is the manager of trust consuming. It receives the result of trust evaluation and assigns consuming tasks to ApplicationConsuming and SystemConsuming. ApplicationConsuming deals with the consuming of trust by applications. SystemConsuming deals with the consuming of trust by TrustEngine and auditing system. See Figure 7.

4.5.1 ApplicationConsuming

In application consuming, the evaluation of an instance of a trust relationship is not always to be consumed immediately. The result of the evaluation of the instance of the trust relationship can be stored and/or distributed in different ways. There are three ways to use the output of trust evaluation. The first way is that the result of trust evaluation is immediately used by requesting applications.

The computing component for this way is direct trust consuming controller. The second way is to generate credentials with the result of trust evaluation as input. These credentials will be used in the future by the same or other applications. Credential generator consuming is the corresponding computing component. The third way is that the result of trust evaluation is stored in the database and the data will be retrieved and used by applications in the future. Data Storage Consuming is the corresponding computing component.

The package of ApplicationConsuming has four computing components, namely application consuming controller, direct trust consuming controller, credential generator consuming, and data storage consuming. Application consuming controller plays the role of the manager for application consuming. Application consuming controller

Figure 7. Components of ConsumingTrust

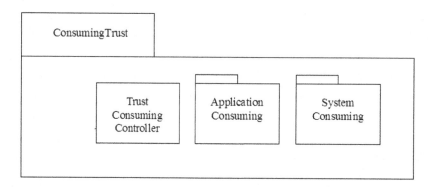

Figure 8. Components of ApplicationConsuming

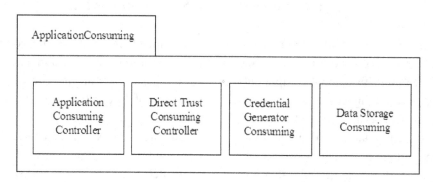

receives tasks from consuming controller and it assigns tasks to direct trust consuming controller, credential generator consuming, and data storage consuming. See Figure 8.

4.5.2 SystemConsuming

The package of SystemConsuming has three components that are system consuming controller, TrustEngine consuming controller, and auditing consuming controller. System consuming controller plays the role of the manager for system consuming. System consuming controller receives tasks from the consuming controller and it assigns tasks to the TrustEngine consuming controller and auditing consuming controller. TrustEngine consuming controller deals with the consuming of trust by TrustEngine. The Auditing consuming controller deals with the consuming of trust by the auditing system. See Figure 9.

5. SYSTEM COMPONENTS OF TRUSTENGINE

This section provides further details on the system components of the TrustEngine. The description of these system components will focus on their generic functions, interfaces, and inter-relationships with other system components. The existing computing standards, utilities, and systems are viewed as generic building blocks in these generic components.

These generic components cover the majority of required trust functions that can be separated from applications in a broad range of distributed information systems in the real world. These generic system components should have a high degree of comprehensibility and flexibility. They can provide guidelines or further information for the development of individual computing components of trust management systems in the real world.

The real trust management system must be developed based on specific business requirements, available technologies, and computing environments. The above generic description of system components provides a high level design for these system components. With the help of these generic components, the development of real system components in a trust management system becomes the implementation of business requirements with the considerations of available technologies and computing environments. These generic system components can bring benefits to reduce the cost and time of the system development. The following lists the generic system components and provides a high level description for each of them.

Figure 9. Components of SystemConsuming

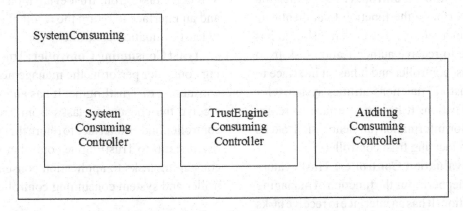

TrustEngine Controller: TrustEngine controller is a runtime controller of TrustEngine. It has an interface to receive trust requests from applications and an interface to return necessary feedback information from TrustEngine to request applications. It assigns tasks to locating trust controller, trust evaluating controller, and trust consuming controller. It receives returned information from locating trust controller, trust evaluating controller, and trust consuming controller. It performs management tasks for TrustEngine among the computing packages LocatingTrust, EvaluatingTrust, and ConsumingTrust.

Locating Trust Controller: Locating trust controller has an interface to receive requests from TrustEngine controller. It forwards the request to trust relationship locator for finding the related trust relationship. The locating trust controller has an interface to return the status of locating of the required trust relationship to TrustEngine controller. The locating trust controller assigns authentication controller to perform the task of authentication for the involved trustee. It has an interface to return information of trust locating to TrustEngine controller.

Trust Relationship Locator: Trust relationship locator performs the function to find the related trust relationship. It has an interface in connection with TrustDatabase where trust relationships are maintained. It has another interface to return the searching result to locating trust controller.

Authentication Controller: Authentication controller performs the function to authenticate the trustee in a required trust relationship. It has an interface to receive authentication task from locating trust controller and it has an interface to employ existing functions/utilities/systems for the authentication. It has an interface to return authentication information (authentication tokens or status) to locating trust controller.

Trust Evaluation Controller: Trust evaluation controller performs the function of managing trust evaluation. It has an interface to receive tasks of trust evaluation from TrustEngine controller. It assigns evaluation tasks to the computing components of credential evaluation, reputation evaluation, stored data evaluation, and environment evaluation. It has an interface to return evaluating results to TrustEngine controller.

Credential Evaluation: Credential evaluation is the computing component for credential evaluation. It includes multiple evaluating mechanisms for different credentials. It has computing functions and/or provides interfaces linking with existing computing utility of credential evaluation. It has an interface to receive tasks from trust evaluation controller and an interface to return the result of evaluation to trust evaluation controller.

Reputation Evaluation: Reputation evaluation looks after computing tasks in reputation evaluation. It includes computing functions for reputation calculation and/or interfaces to the existing utilities of reputation evaluation. It has an interface to receive the task from trust evaluation controller, and an interface to return the result of evaluation to trust evaluation controller.

Stored Data Evaluation: Stored data evaluation looks after the evaluation of trust against stored data. It has an interface to receive tasks from trust evaluation controller, and an interface to return the result of evaluation to trust evaluation controller.

Environment Evaluation: Environment evaluation looks after the evaluation of trust against environment variables. It has an interface to receive tasks from trust evaluation controller, and an interface to return the result of evaluation to trust evaluation controller.

Trust Consuming Controller: Trust consuming controller performs the management of trust consuming of TrustEngine. It has an interface to receive the consuming tasks from TrustEngine controller, and an interface to return the consuming result/status to TrustEngine controller. It assigns consuming tasks to application consuming controller and system consuming controller.

Application Consuming Controller: Application consuming controller performs the management of consuming of trust by applications. It has an interface to receive tasks from trust consuming controller, and an interface to return the consuming result/status to trust consuming controller. It assigns tasks to direct trust consuming controller, credential generator consuming, and data storage consuming.

Direct Trust Consuming Controller: Direct trust consuming controller looks after the consuming of trust when the evaluation of trust relationship is consumed immediately by the request application. It has an interface to receive the consuming tasks from the application consuming controller, and an interface to return the consuming status to application consuming controller. It has an interface for the consuming of trust relationship by the request application.

Credential Generator Consuming: Credential generator consuming looks after the consuming of trust when the evaluation of trust relationship is consumed by the generation of credentials. It has an interface to receive the consuming tasks from the application consuming controller, and an interface to return consuming status to application consuming controller. It has functions to generate and manage credentials. Existing standards and computing utility can be employed in the generation and management of the credentials.

Data Storage Consuming: Data storage consuming looks after the consuming of trust when the evaluation of trust relationship is consumed by storing related information in the database. The information stored in the database will be retrieved by applications in the future. It has an interface to receive the consuming tasks from the application consuming controller, and an interface to return consuming status to application consuming controller. It has functions to format data and has interfaces to save data with different data storage mechanisms such as local database, remote database, and profiles.

System Consuming Controller: System consuming controller performs the management of consuming of trust by system. It has an interface to receive tasks from trust consuming controller, and an interface to return the consuming result/status to trust consuming controller. It assigns tasks to the TrustEngine consuming controller and the auditing consuming controller. TrustEngine Consuming Controller: TrustEngine consuming controller looks after the consuming of trust by TrustEngine itself. It has an interface to receive the consuming tasks from the TrustEngine consuming controller, and an interface to return consuming status to TrustEngine consuming controller. It has functions for trust consuming by TrustEngine, and interfaces to save data in TrustDatabase.

Auditing Consuming Controller: Auditing consuming controller manages the consuming of trust for the auditing purpose. It has an interface to receive the consuming tasks from the TrustEngine consuming controller, and an interface to return consuming status to TrustEngine consuming controller. It has interfaces to link to auditing functions or database in the system.

6. SYSTEM SETTING UP AND OPERATIONS

In the development of a trust management system, the system components described in the last section will be customized based on specific requirements of the target information system. The implementation result of TrustEngine normally runs as a relatively independent system on a local server, or a logical local server, to serve one or multiple applications for their trust management tasks. It is also possible to embed the implementation result of TrustEngine into applications as a relatively independent software package. After the required computing components are installed, at runtime, a set of operations of these components will be activated based on the specific trust request from applications.

This section provides a generic description of system setting up and system operations. The description in this section provides high level guidelines for the system setting up and operations in the real world.

The system setting up of TrustEngine includes the setting up of its database and system components. The TrustEngine uses TrustDatabase for its data storage. The suitable type of database should be chosen and installed at first. The data storage mechanisms for trust relationships, instances of trust relationships, and trust parameters must be defined. In the case of a relational database, all data are stored in a set of tables. The TrustDatabase must be set up before TrustEngine can perform its functions of trust management.

The important system components have been described in the last section. Their customization and setting up are based on the real situations of business and system requirements. In the implementation of the unified framework of trust in the real world, a customized list of the above computing components will be developed and installed. It is also possible to need more computing components that are beyond the above mentioned system components. These additional components will belong to component packages of LocatingTrust, EvaluatingTrust, or ConsumingTrust.

TrustEngine looks after all the trust management tasks that could be separated from applications. At runtime, when there is a trust request from an application, a set of system operations of TrustEngine will be activated. A typical sequence of involved system operations is as follows:

- TC1: TrustEngine controller is the first computing component to be activated and it will assign a task to locating trust controller.
- LT1: Locating trust controller assigns a task to trust relationship locator.
- LT2: Trust relationship locator finds the required trust relationship and returns it to locating trust controller.
- LT3: Locating trust controller requires authentication controller to perform the task of authentication for the involved trustee.
- LT4: Authentication controller performs the task of authentication.
- LT5: Locating trust controller returns information of locating of trust to TrustEngine controller.
- TC2: TrustEngine controller requires trust evaluation controller to evaluate the trust relationship.
- TE1: Trust evaluation controller assigns evaluation tasks to the computing components of credential evaluation, reputation evaluation, stored data evaluation and environment evaluation.
- TE2: Credential evaluation checks credentials.
- TE3: Reputation evaluation performs the computing tasks of reputation evaluating.
- TE4: Stored data evaluation performs the evaluation of trust against stored data.
- TE5: Environment evaluation performs the evaluation of trust against environment variables.
- TE6: Trust evaluation controller integrates the results of TE2, TE3, TE4, and TE5 and returns final evaluating result to TrustEngine controller.
- TC3: TrustEngine controller assigns trust consuming controller to manage the consuming of the evaluated trust relationship.
- TU1: Trust consuming controller assigns consuming tasks to application consuming controller, and system consuming controller.
- TUA1: Application consuming controller assigns tasks to direct trust consuming controller, credential generator consuming and data storage consuming.
- TUA2: Direct Trust Consuming Controller informs the application of the initiator of the trust request for the consuming of trust.

- TUA3: Credential generator consuming generates credentials based on the result of trust evaluation. The credentials will be stored or delivered based on the specific requirements of a real system.
- TUA4: Data storage consuming formats the data and saves it with different data storage mechanisms such as local database, remote database, and profiles.
- TUS1: System consuming controller assigns tasks to TrustEngine consuming controller and auditing consuming controller.
- TUS2: TrustEngine consuming controller performs functions for trust consuming by TrustEngine and it saves data in TrustDatabase.
- TUS3: Auditing consuming controller performs functions of trust consuming for the auditing purpose.

The above typical sequence of system operations provides the general description of the behaviors of TrustEngine at runtime. It shows the flow of logic within TrustEngine and the interactions between TrustEngine and applications. The relationships and the interactions between system components are emphasized.

7. AN APPLICATION EXAMPLE

In order to illustrate our TrustEngine architecture proposed above, we make a scenario example based on possible requirements in the federated medical services. In federated distributed medical services, there are multiple trust relationships between entities such as patients, physicians, hospitals, insurance companies, pharmacies, etc and we believe that trust plays an important role. The modeling and evaluating of trust relationships are beyond the normal authentication and authorization. Trust relationships are context-based and must be evaluated dynamically. Trust relationships may be modified at any time. We

will employ TrustEngine architecture described in section 4 and system components of TrustEngine described in section 5 to develop the sub system for trust management.

In the target trust management system, there are many trust relationships and they could be very complicated. Here we only consider some of involved trust relationships for illustrating our TrustEngine architecture. In federated medical services, there is an enormous variety of applications that require making complex trust decisions that are dependent on runtime situations. The trust requirements are normally dynamic and flexible. Trust mechanism in federated medical services needs to be highly dynamic and independent from any particular application. Here we will choose three typical trust relationships in the federated medical services and use them as examples to discuss the evaluation and consuming of trust in a real system. We provide some discussions about the system setting up for trust management in federated medical services. Then we give two run time scenarios based on corresponding trust relationships. We hope that readers can get a general feeling of TrustEngine architecture and the framework for trust management.

7.1 Modeling Trust Relationships

In our previous work (Zhao et al., 2005a, 2005b), we have discussed how to model trust relationship in distributed information systems based on proposed formal definition of trust relationship and properties of trust relationships. There are several stages for modeling trust relationships in distributed information systems such as extracting trust requirements, identifying possible trust relationships from trust requirements, choosing the whole set of trust relationships from possible trust relationships and implementing and maintaining trust relationships. The trust relationships in federated medical services are very complicated. We will not consider the details of trust relationships in such a system. For our purpose, here we only model the following three trust relationships to illustrate the usage of TrustEngine architecture. The trust relationships are:

- $T_1 = <R_1, E_1, C_1, P_1>$. R_1 includes patients; E_1 includes doctors; C_1 includes medical practitioner licences; and P_1 includes that doctors have the ability to do general practice.
- $T_2 = <R_2, E_2, C_2, P_2>$. R_2 includes patients; E_2 includes doctors; C_2 includes cardiologist licenses; and P_2 includes that doctors have the ability to do heart checks or attend the heart surgeries as non-principal doctor.
- $T_3 = <R_3, E_3, C_3, P_3>$. R_3 includes patients; E_3 includes doctors; C_3 includes cardiologist licenses, reputation for more than 5 year cardiology practice, experience of successful heart surgery in the specified hospital and there is surgery room in specified date and hospital; P_3 includes that doctors have the ability to be principal doctor in the heart surgery at the specified hospital on a specified date.

These trust relationships are stored in TrustDatabase before they may be used by any other computing component in TrustEngine.

7.2 System Setting Up

The sub system for trust management of federated medical services will utilize TrustEngine architecture described in Section 4 to perform all computing tasks about trust. We use the federated medical services as an example to cover all the computing components in TrustEngine architecture. The computing components in packages TrustControl and LocatingTrust are always necessary in any system. Different authentication mechanisms can be employed using the interface of authentication controller. In the package of TrustEvaluating, the computing components will be customized according to specified require-ments. In federated medical services, it is possible to evaluate trust against credential, reputation, stored data and environment parameters and therefore all computing components in package TrustEvaluating should be installed. In federated medical services, all the three application consuming ways may be involved. The direct trust consuming controller, credential generator controller and consuming data storage controller are all necessary to be developed and installed in the system. TrustEngine consuming controller is installed for the result of trust evaluation to be used by TrustEngine. Auditing consuming controller is installed for the result of trust evaluation to be used by auditing system.

7.3 Run Time Scenarios

Here we provide two run time scenarios based on the corresponding trust relationships modeled in sub section 7.1. We assume that the whole system has been set up and all necessary computing components have been installed. In these scenarios, we will provide the sequence of operations at run time. We hope these scenarios are helpful for readers to understand the computing components and operations of TrustEngine.

Scenario 1: When a patient books a general medical practice through federated medical services, trust relationship T_1 in sub section 8.1 will be involved. The request of trust is initiated by booking application of federated medical services. At run time, system operations will be activated in the following orders: TC1, LT1, LT2, LT3, LT4, LT5, TC2, TE1, TE2, TE6, TC3, TU1, TUA1, TUA2, TUS1, TUS2, TUS3. These operations perform whole set of trust management tasks for the involved trust request. Particularly, TE2 is the operation to verify the validity of the medical practitioner license associated with the involved doctor. We assume that booking application will use the evaluated trust relationship immediately and TUA2 is the operation for the direct trust consuming. TUS1, TUS2, TUS3 are operations for system consuming based on specific system requirements.

Scenario 2: When a patient books a heart surgery through federated medical services, trust relationship T3 in section V-A will be involved. This trust relationship is complicated and it needs multiple mechanisms for the evaluation. There are multiple ways for the consuming of this trust relationship as well. We assume that the request of trust is initiated by the booking application of surgeries and trust management is controlled by information system of the specified hospital of the possible surgery. At run time, when the trust request is sent to the information system of specified hospital, system operations will be activated in the following orders: TC1, LT1, LT2, LT3, LT4, LT5, TC2, TE1, TE2, TE3, TE4, TE5, TE6, TC3, TU1, TUA1, TUA2, TUA3, TUA4, TUS1, TUS2, TUS3. For trust evaluation, TE2 verifies the cardiologist license; TE3 calculates and checks over all reputation of the doctor over recent 5 years; TE4 checks the experience of successful heart surgery in the specified hospital; TE5 checks there is surgery room or not in specified date and hospital. TE6 will integrate the results of TE2, TE3, TE4 and TE5 and return the overall result to TrustEngine controller. In this scenario, we assume that the evaluated trust will be used by the booking application of heart surgery. Based on the trust evaluation, some credentials (certificates) can be generated to provide the information about this evaluated trust and the credentials will be delivered for further usage in the system. The evaluated trust will be also stored in database for further usage of applications in the information system. TU1, TUA1, TUA2, TUA3, TUA4 are activated one by one. TUS1, TUS2, TUS3 are possible operations for system consuming.

8. RELATED WORK

The concept of trust has been used in a broad variety of contexts. There are different concep-

tions of trust. Trust is a general term broadly used in day to day life and its original concept is rooted in social sciences such as sociology, social psychology, law, and economics. In the computing world, trust has been initially used in trusted systems (TCSEC, 1985) and trusted computing (Landauer, Redmond, & Benzel, 1989). S. Marsh gave a formalization of trust (Marsh, 1994). The term trust has been used in reputation systems and some researchers view trust as reputation. Trust has also been a key concept in Microsoft's domain trust, web service trust language (WS-Trust), and trust management systems.

The fundamental meaning of trust is normally related to the existence of some kind of relationship between two entities, and confident positive expectations regarding the other's conduct or behavior. J. D. Lewis and A. Weigert (Lewis & Weigert, 1985) point out that trust is indispensable in social relationships. J. K. Rempel and R. Souster (Rempel & Souster, 1986) claim that trust is one of the most important and necessary aspects of any close relationship and trust has three fundamental elements, namely predictability, dependability, and faith. Many researchers have given different definitions of trust. M. Deutsch (Deutsch, 1958) provided one of the earliest definitions of trust as follows: "an individual may be said to have trust in the occurrence of an event if he expects its occurrence and his expectations lead to behavior which he perceives to have greater negative consequences if the expectation is not confirmed than positive motivational consequences if it is confirmed". In M. Deutsch's definition, trust involves the notion of motivational relevance as well as the notion of predictability. There have been several different research streams on trust between humans. P. Worchel (Worchel, 1979) classifies them into three main categories, namely individual trust, societal trust, and relationship trust. The individual trust (Rempel, Holmes, & Zanna, 1985; Rotter, 1971) is the approach of personality theorists that focuses on the characteristics of individual personality. Trust as a belief, expectancy, or feeling, is rooted in the personality based on early psychological development and past experiences. Societal trust (Lewis & Weigert, 1985; Earle & Cvetkovich, 1995) is the approach of sociologists and economists that focuses on the development of trust between individuals and institutions.

As a general societal view of trust, an individual has to trust an institution (such as an organization) or a societal structure (such as a judicial system). Based on T. C. Earle and G. T. Cvetkovich (Earle & Cvetkovich, 1995), social trust is the process by which individuals assign to other persons, groups, agencies, or institutions, the responsibility to work on certain tasks. Relationship trust (Butler, 1991; Schlenker, Helm, & Tedeschi, 1973) is the approach of social psychologists that focuses on the factors that create or destroy trust in individuals involved in a personal or work relationship. Relationship trust is viewed as an expectation of the other party in a relationship. Butler (Butler, 1991) states "trust in a specific person is more relevant in terms of predicting outcomes than is the global attitude of trust in generalized others". B. R. Schlenker et al (Schlenker et al., 1973) define trust as "the reliance upon information received from another person about uncertain environmental states and their accompanying outcomes in a risky situation".

Some researchers have tried to provide a general definition of trust that can cover all of the aspects of individual trust, societal trust, and relationship trust. D. Gambetta (Gambetta, 1990) defines trust as: "trust (or, symmetrically, distrust) is a particular level of the subjective probability with which an agent assesses that another agent or group of agents will perform a particular action, before he can monitor such action (or independently of his capacity ever to be able to monitor it) and in a context in which it affects his own action". D. Gambetta's definition gathers together the thoughts from a broad variety of research areas. The subjective nature of the probability means that the individual's personality characteristics hold an important role in trust.

Both individuals and institutions can be viewed as agents, and a relationship between agents is implied in the definition.

In the computing world, the trust is initially used in the context of Trusted Computing Base (TCB) that is the totality of protection mechanisms within a computer system, including both the trusted hardware and trusted software (TCSEC, 1985; Landauer et al., 1989). The "trusted" refers to the status that the system, hardware, or software will behave in specific ways. In this context, security and consistency are the attributes of trust.

S. Marsh (Marsh, 1994) presents formalism for trust as a computational concept. The formalism targets many aspects of trust in sociology, social psychology, and distributed artificial intelligence. Marsh's work provides a further step in the direction of a proper understanding and definition of human trust. Marsh's formalism provides the social sciences with a valuable tool for a precise discussion of trust. It provides a basis for multi-agent systems to embed trust within agents. In Marsh's formalism, trust is a subjective measure that can be used as a reasoning tool in embodied agents. The formalism allows a precise reasoning about trust while being relatively simple. The formalism provides agents the capability of using trust as a decision making tool for the evaluation of interactions. The formalism is extensible in its implementations.

The trust management problem was first identified as a distinct and important component of security in distributed information systems by M. Blaze, J. Feigenbaum, and J. Lacy in their proposed PolicyMaker (Blaze et al., 1996). M. Blaze et al claimed that "trust management, introduced in the PolicyMaker, is a unified approach to specifying and interpreting security policies, credentials, and relationships, that allows direct authorization of security-critical actions" (Blaze et al., 1999). Before the term trust management was introduced, Pretty Good Privacy (PGP) (pgp6d5, 1999) and X.509 public-key certificates (Housley, Polk, Ford, & Solo, 2002; Adams, Farrell, Kause, &

Mononen, 2005) had already included the implicit notion of trust management. Trust management focuses on building a trust management layer with a new philosophy for codifying, analyzing, and managing, trust decisions in distributed information systems. The trust management covers both "why" trust is granted and "how" trust is enforced. Trust management is an important issue in security analysis and design, particularly when centrally managed security is not possible. Multiple trust management systems (Blaze et al., 1996, 1999; Chu et al., 1997) have been developed to address the issue of trust management. These trust management systems help applications answer the question whether an operation can conform to the required security policies or not. These trust management systems separate generic mechanisms of trust management from application-specific policies which are defined by each application. Normally, security credentials are employed in these trust management systems to describe a specific delegation of trust among public keys. These credentials provide evidence for authorization of required actions. In most trust management systems, trust is established in a particular context. Trust management layer makes software designers and application developers consider trust management explicitly and put the design of security policies, credentials, and trust relationships, in a unified framework.

PGP (Atkins, Stallings, & Zimmermann, 1996; Callas, Donnerhacke, Finney, & Thayer, 1998) was created by P. Zimmermann as the software for secure e-mail and file encryption on the Internet. PGP targets private personal communications, and empowers people to take their privacy into their own hands (Zimmermann, 2008). PGP uses a public key cryptography system (Atkins et al., 1996; Callas et al., 1998; Callas, 2006) to enable people who have never met earlier to transmit messages securely over the Internet, to guard against unauthorized reading, and to add digital signatures on messages to guarantee their authenticity.

A public key infrastructure (PKI) (Weise, 2001) is composed of security and operation policies, security services, and communication protocols, that are needed for ongoing management of keys and associated certificates in a distributed system. A PKI provides a foundation on which other security components for applications, operating systems, or networks, are built. A PKI enables principals to be authenticated to verifiers without having to exchange any secret information in advance. Certificate Authority (CA) is a trusted authority that issues, renews, and revokes certificates. A PKI employs one or more CAs to achieve the secure generation, distribution, and management, of public keys and associated public key certificates.

PolicyMaker and KeyNote are trust management systems developed by AT&T Research (Blaze et al., 1996, 1999; Blaze, Feigenbaum, Ioannidis, & Keromytis, 1999b). The PolicyMaker is the first one to be explicitly claimed as a trust management system. Being independent of any particular application or service, PolicyMaker (Blaze et al., 1996) is designed as a general tool for the development of services with features of privacy and authenticity. KeyNote (Blaze, Feigenbaum, Ioannidis, & Keromytis, 1999a; Blaze et al., 1999) is the successor of PolicyMaker and is more extensible and expressive. Both PolicyMaker and KeyNote can be embedded into applications as relatively an independent module, or run as a "daemon" service. PolicyMaker serves applications as a query engine.

REFEREE (Chu et al., 1997) is the acronym of Rule-controlled Environment for Evaluation of Rules and Everything Else. REFEREE is designed as a trust management system for web applications. In the web environment, both web clients and web servers have critical trust issues. On the web, there are some sensitive and high value web transactions that require a strict proof of security; meanwhile there are some applications or web resources which can be accepted based on weaker forms of evidence. For example, a recommendation from a close friend may convince someone to trust that a piece of software is virus-free. As a trust management system, REFEREE follows the design principles of PolicyMaker (Blaze et al., 1996) and employs PICS label (Resnick, 1996) credential to state some properties of an Internet resource. Trust decisions are recommended by the compliance checker based on the actions requested, credentials provided, and the policies satisfied.

IBM Trust Establishment (TE) (IBM, 2001; Herzberg, Mass, Mihaeli, Naor, & Ravid, 2000) is a trust management system for e-business where the involved parties are not known in advance, and some trust can be established based on public key certificates that provide references obtained from third parties. TE system supports the establishment of dynamic ad-hoc relationships based on "web of trust", that is, accepting recommendations from community/networks rather than requiring a predefined hierarchy with one or more trust roots such as PKI. As an extension of the role-based access control systems, TE system provides a mechanism that allows a business to define a policy for mapping accessed users to roles based on certificates received from the user and/or collected automatically by the system.

Trust negotiation, sometimes referred to as automated trust negotiation as well, is a promising approach that enables the establishment of trust between entities, without enough prior knowledge of each other, through an iterative exchange of digital credentials. Trust negotiation normally occurs in open systems, such as the Internet, for the purpose of sensitive interactions across different security domains. There has been much research addressing the underlying theory and required policy languages for trust negotiations (Winsborough, Seamons, & Jones, 2000; Seamons, Winslett, & al, 2002; Yu, Winslett, & Seamons, 2003; Yu & Winslett, 2003; Bertino, Ferrari, & Squicciarini, 2004; Skogsrud, Benatallah, & Casati, 2004a; Winsborough & Li, 2004). Trust negotiations have also been studied in a broad range of contexts such as web services (Skogsrud, Benatallah, &

Casati, 2003), semantic web services (Olmedilla, Lara, Polleres, & Lausen, 2005), digital library web services (Skogsrud, Benatallah, & Casati, 2004b), peer-to-peer systems (Ye, Makedon, & Ford, 2004), and healthcare information systems (Vawdrey, Sundelin, Seamons, & Knutson, 2003). Researchers have developed a prototype system, called TrustBuilder (Winslett et al., 2002; Seamons et al., 2003; Smith, Seamons, & Jones, 2004), for negotiating trust across organizational boundaries. The architecture of TrustBuilder incorporates trust negotiation into standard network technologies such as HTTP, SSL/TLS, and IPSec.

9. CONCLUDING REMARKS

In this chapter, we describe our approach to unified trust management framework. We devise a generic trust management system referred to as TrustEngine to express the framework. The unified framework for trust management is based on our research results of the formal model of trust relationship, the unified taxonomy framework of trust, and the methodology for analysis and modeling of trust relationships. It targets a goal that the developers of trust management systems can have a solid high level architecture to evolve system functions for trust management tasks by simply implementing some business logic. The development of a trust management system in the real world can be automated to substantially high level based on the proposed framework.

The framework puts multiple trust mechanisms including credentials, reputation, stored data, and environment parameters under the same umbrella, so they may cooperate with each other to satisfy some complex trust requirements. The framework supports multiple ways of trust consumption. The framework has the ability to embrace existing trust standards and computing functions/utilities/systems for trust management tasks.

The proposed TrustEngine provides a standard high level architecture for trust management systems with a series of generic computing components for trust management tasks. In the trust management architecture, trust request, trust evaluation, and trust consuming are handled in a comprehensive and consistent manner. The details of generic computing components in the trust management architecture are provided. A generic description of system setting up and system operations of TrustEngine is provided. An application example is provided with practical details for the implementation of proposed unified trust management framework.

The proposed framework for trust management provides a unified framework for a range of trust mechanisms and multiple ways of trust consumption. The framework has the ability to embrace established standards and has a high extensibility.

The proposed trust management framework is still at the developing stage. In the real world, there are different kinds of distributed information systems with a broad range of trust requirements. There may be complicated situations with specific characteristics of business requirements and emerging technologies in these information systems. It may be necessary to extend the current unified trust management framework to embrace emerging business requirements and technologies. When multiple trust relationships are defined in the security policy of an open system, policy conflicts can arise. Conflicts can also arise due to differences in interests among trustors and trustees in systems. Further research work is needed to represent and resolve such conflicts in trust relationships in distributed information systems and there may be necessary to devise new computing components that will be extensions of the current trust management architecture.

REFERENCES

Aberer, K., & Despotovic, Z. (2001). Managing trust in a peer-2-peer information system. In *Proceedings of the CIKM'01: Tenth international conference on information and knowledge management* (pp. 310-317). New York: ACM Press.

Adams, C., Farrell, S., Kause, T., & Mononen, T. (2005). *Internet x.509 public key infrastructure certificate management protocol* (RFC 4210). Retrieved from http://www.ietf.org/rfc/rfc4210.txt

An introduction to cryptography, in pgp 6.5 manual (Tech. Rep.). (1999). Network Associates.

Atkins, D., Stallings, W., & Zimmermann, P. (1996). *Pgp message exchange formats* (RFC 1991). Retrieved from http://www.ietf.org/rfc/rfc1991.txt

Bertino, E., Ferrari, E., & Squicciarini, A. (2004). Trust negotiations: concepts, systems, and languages. *Computing in Science & Engineering, 6*(4), 27–34. doi:10.1109/MCSE.2004.22

Blaze, M., Feigenbaum, J., Ioannidis, J., & Keromytis, A. (1999a). *The keynote trust-Management system version 2*. Retrieved from http://tools.ietf.org/html/rfc2704

Blaze, M., Feigenbaum, J., Ioannidis, J., & Keromytis, A. (1999b). The role of trust management in distributed systems security. In *Secure internet programming: Security issues for mobile and distributed objects* (pp. 185-210). Berlin, Germany: Springer Verlag.

Blaze, M., Feigenbaum, J., & Keromytis, A. D. (1999). Keynote: Trust management for public-key infrastructures. *Lecture Notes in Computer Science, 1550*, 59–63. doi:10.1007/3-540-49135-X_9

Blaze, M., Feigenbaum, J., & Lacy, J. (1996). Decentralized trust management. In *Proceedings of the IEEE symposium on security and privacy* (pp. 164-173).

Butler, J. K. J. (1991). Toward understanding and measuring conditions of trust: Evolution of a conditions of trust inventory. *Journal of Management, 17*(3), 643–663. doi:10.1177/014920639101700307

Callas, J. (2006). *An introduction to cryptography* (Tech. Rep.). PGP Corporation. Retrieved from http://www.pgp.com/downloads/whitepapers/

Callas, J., Donnerhacke, L., Finney, H., & Thayer, R. (1998). *Openpgp message format* (RFC 2404_. Retrieved from http://www.ietf.org/rfc/rfc2440. txt

Chu, Y.-H., Feigenbaum, J., LaMacchia, B., Resnick, P., & Strauss, M. (1997). Referee: Trust management for web applications. *Computer Networks and ISDN Systems, 29*(8-13), 953-964.

*conference on autonomous agents and multiagent system*s (pp. 467-474).

Damiani, E., Vimercati, D. C. d., Paraboschi, S., Samarati, P., & Violante, F. (2002). A Reputation-based approach for choosing reliable resources in peer-to-peer networks. In *Proceedings of the Ccs '02: 9th ACM conference on computer and communications security* (pp. 207-216). New York: ACM Press. (

Deutsch, M. (1958). Trust and suspicion. *The Journal of Conflict Resolution, 2*(4), 265–279. doi:10.1177/002200275800200401

Earle, T. C., & Cvetkovich, G. T. (1995). *Social trust: Toward a cosmopolitan society.* Westport, CT: PRAEGER.

Gambetta, D. (1990). Can we trust trust? In *In trust: making and breaking cooperative relations* (pp. 213-237). Oxford, UK: Basil Blackwell.

Herzberg, A., Mass, Y., Mihaeli, J., Naor, D., & Ravid, Y. (2000). Access control meets public Key infrastructure, or: assigning roles to strangers. In *Proceedings of IEEE symposium on security and privacy* (pp. 2-14).

Housley, R., Polk, W., Ford, W., & Solo, D. (2002). *Internet x.509 public key infrastructure Certificate and certificate revocation list (crl) profile* (RFC 3280). Retrieved from http://tools. ietf.org/html/rfc3280

IBM. (2001). *Trust establishment.* Retrieved from http://www.haifa.il.ibm.com/projects/software/e-Business/TrustManager/index.html

Kinateder, M., Baschny, E., & Rothermel, K. (2005). Towards a generic trust model - comparison

Landauer, J., Redmond, T., & Benzel, T. (1989). Formal policies for trusted processes. In

Lee, S., Sherwood, R., & Bhattacharjee, B. (2003). Cooperative peer groups in NICE. In

Lewis, J. D., & Weigert, A. (1985). Trust as a social reality. *Social Forces, 63*(4), 967–985. doi:10.2307/2578601

Marsh, S. (1994). *Formalising trust as a computational concept.* Unpublished doctoral dissertation, University of Stirling.

(■■■). of various trust update algorithms. *Lecture Notes in Computer Science, 3477*, 177–192.

Olmedilla, D., Lara, R., Polleres, A., & Lausen, H. (2005). Trust negotiation for semantic web

Personality and Social Psychology, 49(1), 95-112.

Proceedings of computer security foundations workshop II (pp. 31-40).

Proceedings of twenty-second annual joint conference of the ieee computer and communications societies (Vol. 2, pp. 1272-1282).

Pujol, J. M., Sanguesa, R., =& Delgado, J. (2002). Extracting reputation in multi agent systems by means of social network topology. In *Proceedings of AAMAS '02: The first international joint*

Rempel, J. K., Holmes, J. G., & Zanna, M. P. (1985). Trust in close relationships. *Journal of*

Rempel, J. K., & Souster, R. (1986). How do i trust thee? *Psychology Today*, 28–34.

Resnick, P. (1996). PICS: Internet access controls without censorship. *Communications of the ACM*, *39*(10), 87–93. doi:10.1145/236156.236175

Retrieved from ftp://ftp.pgpi.org/pub/pgp/6.5/docs/english/IntroToCrypto.pdf

Rotter, J. B. (1971). Generalized expectancies for interpersonal trust. *The American Psychologist*, *26*(5), 443–452. doi:10.1037/h0031464

Schillo, M., Rovatsos, M., & Funk, P. (2000). Using trust for detecting deceitful agents in Artificial societies. *Applied Artificial Intelligence Journal*, *14*(8), 825–848. doi:10.1080/08839510050127579

Schlenker, B. R., Helm, B., & Tedeschi, J. T. (1973). The effects of personality and situational variables on behavioral trust. *Journal of Personality and Social Psychology*, *25*(3), 419–427. doi:10.1037/h0034088

Seamons, K., Chan, T., Child, E., Halcrow, M., Hess, A., Holt, J., et al. (2003). Trustbuilder: negotiating trust in dynamic coalitions. In *Proceedings of darpa information survivability conference and exposition* (Vol. 2, pp. 49-51).

Seamons, K., Winslett, M., et al. (2002). Requirements for policy languages for trust negotiation. In *Proceedings of 3rd international workshop policies for distributed systems and networks)* (pp. 68-79).

services. (•••)... *Lecture Notes in Computer Science*, *3387*, 81–95.

Skogsrud, H., Benatallah, B., & Casati, F. (2003). Model-driven trust negotiation for web services. *IEEE Internet Computing*, *7*(6), 45–52. doi:10.1109/MIC.2003.1250583

Skogsrud, H., Benatallah, B., & Casati, F. (2004a). Trust-serv: model-driven lifecycle Management of trust negotiation policies for web services. In *Proceedings of the WWW '04: 13th international conference on World Wide Web* (pp. 53-62). New York: ACM Press.

Skogsrud, H., Benatallah, B., & Casati, F. (2004b). A trust negotiation system for digital library web services. *International Journal on Digital Libraries*, *4*(3), 185–207. doi:10.1007/s00799-004-0083-y

Smith, B., Seamons, K., & Jones, M. (2004). Responding to policies at runtime in trustbuilder. In *Proceedings of fifth ieee international workshop on policies for distributed systems and networks* (pp. 149-158).

Suryanarayana, G., Erenkrantz, J., Hendrickson, S., & Taylor, R. (2004). Pace: an architectural style for trust management in decentralized applications. In *Proceedings of fourth working IEEE/IFIP conference on software architecture* (pp. 221-230).

TCSEC. (1985). *Trusted computer system evaluation criteria* (Tech. Rep.). USA National Computer Security Council.

Vawdrey, D., Sundelin, T., Seamons, K., & Knutson, C. (2003). Trust negotiation for Authentication and authorization in healthcare information systems. In *Proceedings of 25th annual international conference of the IEEE engineering in medicine and biology society* (Vol. 2, pp. 1406-1409).

Weise, J. (2001). *Public key infrastructure overview* (Tech. Rep.). Sun Microsystems, Inc. Retrieved from http://www.sun.com/blueprints/0801/publickey.pdf

Winsborough, W., & Li, N. (2004). Safety in automated trust negotiation. In *Proceedings of IEEE symposium on security and privacy* (pp. 147-160).

Winsborough, W., Seamons, K., & Jones, V. (2000). Automated trust negotiation. In *Proceedings of DARPA information survivability conference and exposition* (Vol. 1, pp. 88-102

Winslett, M., Yu, T., Seamons, K., Hess, A., Jacobson, J., & Jarvis, R. (2002). Negotiating trust in the web. *IEEE Internet Computing, 6*(6), 30–37. doi:10.1109/MIC.2002.1067734

Worchel, P. (1979). Trust and distrust. In W. G. Austin & S. Worchel (Eds.), *The social psychology of intergroup relation.* CA: Wadsworth.

Ye, S., Makedon, F., & Ford, J. (2004). Collaborative automated trust negotiation in peer-topeer systems. In *Proceedings of fourth international conference on peer-to-peer computing* (pp. 108-115).

Yu, T., & Winslett, M. (2003). A unified scheme for resource protection in automated trust negotiation. In *Proceedings of symposium on security and privacy* (pp. 110-122).

Yu, T., Winslett, M., & Seamons, K. E. (2003). Supporting structured credentials and sensitive policies through interoperable strategies for automated trust negotiation. *ACM Transactions on Information and System Security, 6*(1), 1–42. doi:10.1145/605434.605435

Zhao, W., Varadharajan, V., & Bryan, G. (2004). Modelling trust relationships in distributed environments. *Lecture Notes in Computer Science, 3184*, 40–49.

Zhao, W., Varadharajan, V., & Bryan, G. (2005a). Analysis and modelling of trust in distributed information systems. *Lecture Notes in Computer Science, 3803*, 106–119. doi:10.1007/11593980_8

Zhao, W., Varadharajan, V., & Bryan, G. (2005b). Type and scope of trust relationships in Collaborative interactions in distributed environments. In *Proceedings of 7th international conference on enterprise information systems* (Vol. 3, pp. 331-336).

Zhao, W., Varadharajan, V., & Bryan, G. (2006). General methodology for analysis and modeling of trust relationships in distributed computing. *Journal of Computers, 1*, 42–53.

Zhao, W., Varadharajan, V., & Bryan, G. (2007). A unified taxonomy framework of trust. In *Trust in E-Service: Technologies, Practices and Challenges* (pp. 29-50).

Zimmermann, P. (2008). *Why do you need pgp?* Retrieved from http://www.pgpi.org/doc/whypgp/en/

Chapter 7

Trust–Aware Recommender Systems for Open and Mobile Virtual Communities

N. Sahli
Dhofar University, Sultanate of Oman

G. Lenzini
Telematica Instituut/Novay, The Netherlands

ABSTRACT

This chapter surveys and discusses relevant works in the intersection among trust, recommendations systems, virtual communities, and agent-based systems. The target of the chapter is showing how, thanks to the use of trust-based solutions and artificial intelligent solutions like that understanding agents-based systems, the traditional recommender systems can improve the quality of their predictions. Moreover, when implemented as open multi-agent systems, trust-based recommender systems can efficiently support users of mobile virtual communities in searching for places, information, and items of interest.

VIRTUAL COMMUNITIES

A virtual community, e-community, or online community is "a group of people that primarily interact via communication media such as newsletters, telephone, email or instant messages rather than face to face, for social, professional, educational or other purposes" (cf. Wikipedia). According to Preece (2000), who has suggested a definition that is broad enough to cover a wide range of communities but precise enough to fit into social science definitions, an on-line community consists of the following elements:

- Socially interacting people, performing special roles or satisfying their needs.
- A purpose, which is the reason behind the community.
- Policies to govern people interaction.
- Computer Systems that support social interaction.

Other authors have additionally distinguished four different types of communities: Competing Communities, Cooperative Communities, Goal-oriented Communities, and Ad Hoc Communities (Rana et al., 2005). El Morr and Kawash (2007) have proposed a more general classification based on three factors: Degree of virtualisation (physical/virtual),

DOI: 10.4018/978-1-60566-414-9.ch007

Degree of mobility (still/mobile), and Degree of cooperation (notification/collaboration). Following this last classification, this chapter focuses in cooperative and mobile virtual communities.

This chapter focuses also in open communities, which means that members can freely join and leave at any time. The members of an open community can represent different stakeholders with different aims and objectives. Examples of open communities are the Grid (Foster et al., 2001), the Semantic Web (Berners-Lee et al., 2001), the Virtual Organizations (Norman et al., 2004), the Open Agent Architecture (Cheyer & Martin, 2001), e-commerce environments (He et al., 2003), and peer-to-peer networks like for example, Gnutella[1]. According to Preece (2000), the success of open communities depends on their degree of sociability and usability. Many factors affect the degree of sociability and usability; the following list comments the most known:

- **Policies, Privacy, and Trust:** These three elements are necessary to ensure a good reputation for a community, which is a major criterion in attracting new members and convincing existing members to stay in the community.
- **Anonymity:** To limit anonymity of members may increase the sense of responsibility among them and help to establish a notion of reputation and trust in the community (Kawash et al., 2007).
- **Critical Mass:** The number of members is an important issue for the sociability of the community. The size of a community should be significant so that members are more likely to see their requests fulfilled; it is also a prominent factor for attracting new members and retaining existing ones.
- **Presence and Maintenance:** The continual presence is an important feature in all online services: a non-interrupted online presence of members is a symptom of

wellness of the community. It may be also a criterion to assess the usability.
- **Simplicity:** This factor mainly suggests easy to use interfaces. Indeed, navigating the software that implements the community and using its features should be as simple as possible in order to guarantee better usability for the community.

Another factor that has an impact on the sociability of a community is the number of lurkers, the community's passive members (Elinor, 1990). The ratio of lurkers in on-line communities can range from 40% to 80% (Nonnecke & Preece, 2000). Although a small number of lurkers do not imply a high sociability, a large number of lurkers may compromise the success of the community.

Sharing Rating and Recommendations

One common application for virtual communities is providing and sharing ratings. A rating, in general, is an evaluation or an assessment of something in terms of quality. Ratings are common in e-commerce to evaluate on-line buyers and sellers. In Amazon (www.amazon.com), for example, buyers can leave their ratings after a transaction has taken place; the ratings express an evaluation of the quality of the services as the buyers have experienced.

In addition to provide a feedback to the community of users, ratings are also processed by recommender systems to suggest users with items that are likely of her/his interest. Depending on how recommendations are computed, recommender systems are generally classified into three categories (Balabanovic & Shoham, 1997):

- **Content-based filtering systems:** Recommended items are similar to the ones the user has preferred in the past. One of the limitations of the content-based filtering approach is that the features describing items to be recommended are to be explicitly associated to these items. Thus, either the content must be in a form that can be parsed automatically by a computer (e.g., texts but not images) or the features must be manually assigned to items (e.g., by tagging). Besides, a user has to rate a large number of items before a content-based recommender system can really provide him with reliable recommendations. Another major problem of this approach is serendipity: the system is only able to recommend items whose content was previously encountered. Therefore, a user who has no experience with Greek cuisine would never receive a recommendation for even the best Greek restaurant in his city.

- **Collaborative filtering systems:** Recommendations about which items a user might like are composed using items that people with similar tastes and preferences liked in the past. Even if this approach overcomes some of the limitations of the previous one (e.g., items can be recommended regardless of their content), it suffers from bootstrapping problems. The most known problems are known as "the new user problem" (if a user gives few ratings, the system cannot appropriately learn his preferences and thus cannot make reliable recommendations), "the early rater problem" (if nobody has rated an item, the item cannot be recommended), and "the sparsity problem" (if each user has rated very few items, users cannot be matched).
- **Hybrid systems:** Recommendations are obtained through a combination of content-based and collaborative methods. This combination can be achieved in different ways; by implementing collaborative and content-based methods separately and combining their predictions; by incorporating some content-based characteristics into a collaborative approach and vice versa.

Hybrid systems can also contain a general unifying model that incorporates both content-based and collaborative characteristics. The three mentioned approaches are realised through two main techniques, called heuristic-based and model-based. The interested reader will find additional information in the survey (Adomavicius & Tuzhilin, 2005).

Nowadays recommender systems must cope with an increasing demand of complexity; for instance, a recommendation application for restaurant should take into account the contextual information (e.g., has the restaurant been recommended for a romantic dinner or for a business lunch?). Adomavicius and Tuzhilin (2005) suggest that recommender systems can provide better recommendation is they are extended according to the following criteria:

- *A more comprehensive understanding of users and items*: to extend the simple keyword-based techniques with advanced profiling techniques based on data mining rules, sequences, and signatures can be used to build user profiles and to describe items.
- *Multi-dimensional recommendations*: to extend the making of recommendations with contextual information. The utility of a certain item or product to a user may strongly depend on time, place, and situational factors.
- *Multi-criteria ratings*: to extend the single-criterion ratings with multi-criteria ratings (e.g., restaurant rated according to food, decor, and service).
- *Non-intrusiveness*: instead of requiring explicit feedback from the user, recommender systems may use nonintrusive techniques.

Advanced recommender systems already incorporate some of the previous characteristics. For example, the web site beauté-test.com (a recommender system for cosmetics) uses multi criteria ratings and quite detailed user profiles. Further extended features, mentioned in Adomavicius and Tuzhilin (2005), are explainability, trustworthiness, scalability, and privacy.

TRUST ASPECT IN OPEN VIRTUAL COMMUNITIES

A wide of variety of literature now exists on trust, ranging from specific applications to general models (Artz & Gil, 2007). However, the meaning of trust as used by each researcher differs across the span of existing work. These differences are mainly due to (a) the different type of communities and (b) the type of trustee (Huynh, 2006). The focus of this chapter is on open virtual communities; therefore, we present only definitions that fit with the open virtual community context.

Even restricting the focus on open virtual communities, there is little consensus in the literature on the definition of trust between members. Two main views of trust have been identified in the literature, namely, the cognitive view and the probabilistic view.

The cognitive view was introduced by Falcone and Castelfranchi (2001). According to this paradigm, and following a natural view of trust from socio-psychological work, a member A that wants to evaluate its trust in another member B, has to model the mental states of member B. This task is too complicated in open communities and such an approach is thus not applicable.

According to the probabilistic view (Yu & Singh 2002), a member A does not consider the intentions of member B directly. Instead, A's experiences are used to predict the future behaviour B. McKnight and Chervany (1996) give a broad definition that fits here: "Trust is the extent to which one party is willing to depend on something or somebody in a given situation with a feeling of relative security, even though nega-

tive consequences are possible". This definition is quite generic and it does not take into account the attributes of trust that may interest the trustor. According to Becerra et al. (2007), a member A evaluates whether a member B can be trusted based on four attributes: Integrity (how ethical member B is in general), Motivation (how motivated member B is to complete a task), Predictability (how member A predicts member B to behave), and Competence (how much member B is skilled for the task). In the literature, different definitions focus on a selection of these attributes. For example, Grandison and Sloman (2000) have referred to the competence to act: "Trust is the firm belief in the competence of an entity to act dependably, securely, and reliably within a specified context". Olmedilla et al. (2005) have preferred to refer to actions (and not competence): "Trust of a party A to a party B for a service X is the measurable belief of A in that B behaves dependably for a specified period within a specified context (in relation to service X)".

In a human society, one can trust another based on two main sources: (1) private information obtained from direct interaction (direct trust), and (2) public opinions about the other (reputation). By analogy, trust in virtual communities can be built in the same manner. Therefore, direct trust reflects the subjective opinion of the judging member while reputation is a collection of opinions about a member from other members within a community. Reputation is usually considered an objective quality as it represents a collective evaluation of a group of members. Direct trust is personalised and subjective and it reflects an individual opinion.

The reputation of a member in a virtual community can be evaluated thanks to reputation systems. According to Wikipedia, "a reputation system is a type of collaborative filtering algorithm which attempts to determine ratings for a collection of entities, given a collection of opinions that those entities hold about each other". Reputation systems are similar to recommendation systems, but they have the purpose recommending community members one another rather than recommending some external set of objects (such as books, movies, or music).

Reputation-Based Trust

Reputation, as previously mentioned, is an assessment about the quality of a member of a community according to the experience of the community. In reputation-based trust (Shmatikov & Talcott, 2005), reputation serves as the basis of trust, although it is not the only source. The term reputation-based trust refers to the process of establishing the trustworthiness of a trustee considering the history of interactions with or of observations about an entity, either directly, or as reported by others, or both. Various reputation-based systems have been implemented in different open communities (e.g., in peer-to-peer systems). Two main approaches are used, namely, centralised or decentralised (Wang & Vassileva, 2007; Huynh, 2006).

Centralised Approach. Observations about communities' members are reported and then stored in a central database. The reputation system (usually the central database itself) uses these data to calculate the reputation of each member. This approach is used in the reputation systems of eBay (www.ebay.com) and of Amazon, for example. Existing on-line trust and reputation systems are prevalently centralised. Even though these systems are not complex, they may not be compatible with the design philosophy of open communities. Centralised approaches are not suitable for open virtual communities for the following three main reasons:

- It assumes that the system is accepted and trusted by all the individuals that join, while in an open community there is no central authority for all members;
- No personalised reputation, which means that the reputation of a particular member

is built upon the opinions of the whole community instead of a group of individuals which are selected by the member who is requesting this trust information;

- Members' preferences and profiles are not taken into account. Moreover, most of centralised reputation engines offer distorted ratings. For example, Resnick and Zeckhauser (2002) have found that only 0.6% of all ratings provided by buyers and only 1.6% of all ratings provided by sellers on eBay were negative, and claimed that it is too low to reflect reality. According to the authors, possible explanations of this phenomenon are that a positive rating simply represents an exchange of courtesies; positive ratings are given in the hope of getting a positive rating in return, or that negative ratings are avoided because of fear of retaliation from the other party.

An alternative solution consists on a decentralised approach where the main challenge is how to establish trust without the benefit of trusted third parties or authorities.

Decentralised approach. Members are in charge of storing their own observations locally. If a member, A, wants to find out about the reputation of a member, B, it looks for other members that have interacted with B (called witnesses) and asks them for their observations about B. The searching process is a distributed mechanism through A's neighbors which form the witnesses graph of A. In this approach, reputation is calculated in a distributed manner, which provides a level of freedom to members in choosing the method of calculating reputation according to their beliefs and preferences. Besides and since each member can choose its own witnesses, it provides him more confidence on the resulting reputation value compared to the centralised approach. Consequently, the decentralised approach is more convenient for open communities. Recent researches have adopted this approach (Miller et al., 2004; Olsson, 2006; Sabater & Sierra, 2002; Teacy et al., 2005; Tveit, 2001; Jøsang et al., 2006). Another variation of the distributed approach, suggests that a member *A* asks its "friends" for recommendations (Abdul-Rahman & Hailes 2000). These friends and recommenders have not necessarily interacted directly with *B*. The problem with this variation is that *A* may not find recommenders on *B* especially in large communities.

Software agent systems seem to be a well-suited platform for implementing the decentralised paradigm. (Zacharia & Maes, 2000) adopted a decentralised approach while using software agents.

Agent-Based Systems

Maes (1994) defines autonomous agents as computational systems that inhabit some complex dynamic environment and that sense and act autonomously in this environment; by doing so, they realise a set of goals or tasks for which they are designed. According to this definition, an agent is *Autonomous* (acts on its own), *Reactive* (responds timely to changes in its environment), *Proactive* (initiates actions that affect its environment), and *Communicative* (exchanges information with users, other agents, or both). These four properties are common to all agents and it is mandatory to design agents which are in accordance with the agent paradigm. Besides, an agent can have some optional properties; it can be *Continuous* (has a relatively long lifespan), *Mobile* (migrates from one site to another), or *Adaptive* (capable of learning).

Multi-Agent Systems. Software agents can build communities in a special domain area. Such systems are named multi-agent systems (often addressed as MAS). According to Ferber (1999), the term "multi-agent systems" is applied to each system that is composed of the following elements:

- An environment, that is, a space which generally has a volume.
- A set of passive objects.
- An assembly of agents, the specific active objects of the system.
- An assembly of relations that link objects (and thus agents) to each other.
- An assembly of operations that makes it possible for the agents to perceive, to produce, to consume, to transform, and to manipulate passive objects.
- Operators with the task of representing the application of these operations and the reaction of the world to this attempt at modifications (called "the laws of the universe").

A multi-agent system is a system composed of multiple interacting agents that work together to solve problems that are beyond the individual capabilities or knowledge of each agent (Jennings et al., 1998).

Organisational paradigms of multi-agent systems. The organisation of a multi-agent system is the collection of roles, relationships, and authority structures which govern its behaviour. All multi-agent systems possess some or all of these characteristics and therefore all have some form of organisation, although it may be implicit and informal. Just as with human organisations, the agent organisations guide how the members of the population interact with one another, not necessarily on a moment-by-moment basis, but over the potentially long-term course of a particular goal or a set of goals. A wide range of organisational paradigms exists in the literature. These include hierarchies, holarchies, coalitions, teams, congregations, societies, federations, markets, and matrix organisations. A complete survey on these paradigms (their characteristics, formation, benefits, and drawbacks) is available in (Horling & Lesser, 2004).

Depending on the closeness of cooperation, the duration and commonality among agents, three main types of agent groups have been proposed in the MAS community (Wang & Vassileva, 2003): *teams*, *coalitions*, and *congregations*. The main issue in these proposed paradigms is the specification of an organisational structure for the collection of agents at design-time. However, as multi-agent systems are more often situated in open and dynamic environments, rigid roles and static organisational structures become a severe problem. The challenge is then to define a scalable self-organising mechanism that determines the most appropriate organisational structure for agents at run-time. This mechanism should be adaptable to environment changes. The notion of self-organisation is popular in many different research fields; it refers to the fact that a systems structure or organisation appears without explicit control or constraints from outside the system (Serugendo et al., 2005). Researchers claim that, in open and dynamic environments, multi-agent systems should be self-building (able to determine the most appropriate organisational structure for the system by themselves at run-time) and adaptive (able to change this structure as their environment changes) (Turner & Jennings, 2000). Various models of self-organising multi-agent systems have been built (So & Durfee, 1996; Turner & Jennings, 2000; Schillo et al., 2002; Mamei & Zambonelli, 2004; Serugendo et al., 2005). These models address specific applications and particular constraints.

Agent-Based Recommender Systems for Open Virtual Communities

Agent-based solutions have been applied already in recommender systems for open communities. The following list describes and comments some meaningful solutions from the literature:

Jurca and Faltings (2003) define a set of broker agents (called R-agents) which are responsible for buying and aggregating reputation reports from other agents and selling back these information

to them when they need it. Although the R-agents are distributed in the system, each of them collects and aggregates reputation reports centrally, which is not really suitable for the context of an open community as previously discussed.

In "Regret" (Sabater & Sierra, 2002), each agent rates its partners performance after every interaction and records its ratings in a local database. The trust evaluation process in this reputation model is thus completely decentralised. Besides, agents can share their opinions about one another based on a witness reputation component. This later depends on the social network built up by each agent. However, "Regret" does not specify how such social networks are to be built.

Yu and Singh (Yu & Singh, 2002) proposed a mechanism to locate witnesses based on individual agents knowledge and help (through each agents contacts) without relying on a centralised service. Agents cooperate by giving, pursuing, and evaluating referrals (i.e., a recommendation to contact another agent). Each agent in the system maintains a list of acquaintances (other agents that it knows) and their expertise. When an agent needs specific information, he sends a query to his acquaintances; if these are not able to answer the query, they recommend other agents that they believe are likely to have the desired information. Even if this mechanism is only based on agent's expertise, and thus does not completely fit with our definition of trust, it represents a relevant attempt of applying open multi-agent systems in virtual communities.

TRAVOS (Teacy et al., 2005) is a trust model that is built upon probability theory and based on observations of past interaction between agents. It uses a binary rating to model the probability of having a successful interaction with a given agent. If the confidence of these trust values is low, an agent can seek witness information about the past performance of the target agents. After interacting with the target agent itself, the evaluator compares the received witness report with its own observations in order to weight the impact of the witness opinions on its future decisions. Nevertheless, the simplified representation of interaction ratings in TRAVOS is rather limited.

Mobile Virtual Communities

Most of the systems discussed so far are not suitable for mobile environments, which are known to require huge traffic between remote users. However, according to Exit Games (2006), mobility is in certain aspects better suited for social communities. Indeed, mobility brings evident advantages in such context. The most known are reported in the following list:

- **Ubiquitous access:** Members have an anytime-anyplace connection to their virtual communities.
- **Instant execution:** 2.5G and 3G mobile networks offer packet-switched data transfer. Compatible mobile devices can therefore instantaneously send and receive diverse types of data.
- **Personalised device:** Besides the fact that its original purpose was to connect people with each other, a mobile integrates different means of personalisation (e.g. ring tones, wallpapers) which allows users to add a personal touch to their device.
- **Location based services:** Every user of mobile community-services can be localised with the help of different positioning methods of mobile networks. These positioning technologies offer new possibilities to find other community-members in real life, and also to locate and tag points of interest.

With upcoming technologies (e.g., IP multimedia subsystem, High Speed Downlink/Uplink Packet Access) which enable faster network access and better opportunities to combine the different phone facilities, the importance of mobile networking applications will exponentially grow in the near future. According to Exit Games (2006), "after very little impact of mobile TV and other streaming services, the field of mobile communities could become the key application driving data usage on the networks". During the last few years, several applications in different domains have been proposed to support mobile virtual communities. We report the most relevant efforts in the list that follows.

- **Education:** Different researchers such as (Cole & Stanton, 2003) have investigated how mobile communities can trigger further educational experience by making data available when students are on the move. Some works even take into account user profiles and contextual information while permitting both synchronous and asynchronous communication between students (Schubert & Koch, 2003).
- **Entertainment:** Following the success of the Apple iPod portable digital players, recent researches have focused on applications of mobile music/sound communities (Carter & Fisher, 2004). Games and iTV are other fields of entertainment where communities may play a role in the few coming years. In 2006, a workshop (CHI2006) was hold in Montreal to discuss future interactive television (iTV) scenarios characterised by pervasive communications in contexts of entertainment.
- **Lifestyle:** Location-based services have been probably the most attractive research activity for the past few years in mobile virtual communities. Among popular services, spatial messaging (also called digital graffiti, air graffiti, or splash messaging). It allows a user to publish a geo-referenced note so that any other user that attends the same place can get the message. Different usage scenarios can be found in different projects such as E-Graffiti (Burrell & Gay, 2002), GeoNotes (Persson et al., 2003),

ActiveCampus Explorer (William et al., 2004), and ContextWatcher (Koolwaaij et al., 2006). Most of these projects do not take into account trust aspects. Only ContextWatcher uses the notion of confirmed buddy for security and trust purposes. Lifestyle mobile virtual communities also include communities that organise the members' leisure time (Schubert & Hampe, 2005) or just keep in touch (Burak and Sharon 2004), and communities for tourism journeys (Xiong & Liu, 2004). Other scenarios could be possible. For example, we can imagine a "speeding radar" community where spots indicate the locations of speeding radars. Members can thus be notified as they are roaming. Many other lifestyle applications with different purposes can be implemented: Garage sale hunt, cheap gas hunt, and traffic congestion spots (Kawash et al., 2007).

- **Health:** Mobile virtual communities have been recently applied to health care and are expected to play a prominent role in e-monitoring and e-health care in general. The project of reference in this domain is named COSMOS (Arnold et al., 2004; Leimeister et al., 2003). COSMOS creates virtual communities of cancer patients and tries to add mobile support to these communities.

Trust-Based Approach in Recommender Systems

Designers of recommender systems have recently looked with increasing attention to trust aspects to improve the accuracy of recommendations and to overcome the known limitations of traditional recommender systems (e.g., cold-start, serendipity, and sparsity). Traditional collaborative filtering-based prediction techniques, for example, build their predictions by processing the ratings given by like-minded people. Like-mindedness is measured in terms of similarities of past choices. Prediction algorithms implement the idea that individuals that have shown similar taste in the past will also share similar tastes in the present. Thus, when a user selects an item, the rating of this item is calculated considering the rating given by a set of like-minded neighbors (e.g., the top k similar).

Recently, Lathia et al. (2008) have studied an alternative approach to neighborhood-based recommendations that is based on trusted recommenders. According to the trust-based strategy, users learn who and how much to trust one another. Trust is measured in terms of utility of the rating information that has been received along a period of time. Lathia et al. justify the use of trust saying that the collaborative approach of recommender systems is a particular instance of a trust based systems; therefore the reverse approach can also be used, and new collaborative filtering algorithms can be designed starting from trust-based approaches. This statement is corroborated by results: the use of trust has been shown to improve the accuracy of prediction.

Dell'Amico and Capra (2008) have proposed an algorithm (called SOPHIA) that uses trustworthiness to improve the accuracy and the robustness of the traditional (i.e., similarity based) collaborative filtering systems; additionally, they distinguish and use two different kinds of trust, namely, *taste similarity* ("I trust those who has shown similar taste") and *social ties* ("I trust my friends, the people I know"). While the former defines competence, the second identifies well-intentioned users. High quality recommenders are both competent and well intentioned. The resulting recommender system is more accurate and proved to be resistant to a large Sybil attacks (where a large number of pseudonymous entities are created and used with the scope of gaining a large influence and of biasing future predictions).

Focusing on open virtual communities, Lenzini et al (2008) have proposed a high level design for context-aware trust-based recommender systems that aims to improve the quality of recommendations. Users maintain two distinct weighed trust networks, one of rated items (called TRat) and one of trusted/untrusted members (called TRec). The two networks are used to improve the prediction of the rating of new items (either via the analysis of the qualities of the items themselves or some of their witnesses, or via past experiences, or via the recommendations originating from the network of trust), and to maintain the trust relation among users (via the reputation that recommenders have in giving useful recommendations). An additional feature of this approach is that recommenders can justify their recommendations (e.g., "I liked that place because it was romantic and cosy"). The analysis of justifications helps the selection of persuasive recommendations. Persuasiveness is distinct from well-intention (a well-intentioned recommenders may give unjustified recommendations) and is distinct from taste-similarity (a recommender whose tastes are unknown, or whose tastes are usually different from that of the user, can sometimes give convincing recommendations that the user can take into account). The measure of the persuasiveness of a recommendation is estimated after the member has played an *argumentation game* (McBurney, P., & Parsons, S., 2002) with the recommender. Therefore, the recommendations that are taken into account are those which better match the member way of reasoning and the situational context. This trust model is part of an agent-based architecture for decentralised virtual communities.

Trust-based recommendations are used by two existing commercial applications, Rummble (www.rummble.com) and Whrrl (www.whrrl.com). These applications are two location-based social search and discovery tools that use recommendations of friends to help users find location more easily. A user can observe the places where his/her friends are right now and the places where they have been. Places are rated according to a user's personalised rating that depends upon the user's trust profile and the ratings left by the people in his/her social network. The tools are designed to be fully mobile.

AN ARCHITECTURE FOR TRUST-BASED RECOMMENDER SYSTEM FOR OPEN AND MOBILE COMMUNITIES

This section describes an example of agent-based architecture for trust-based recommender system for open and mobile virtual communities. From this point of view, the present section combines the topics introduced so far into a design exercise. The architecture has been taken from (Sahli et al., 2008), the trust model from (Lenzini et al, 2008). The architecture (Figure 1) is decentralised, with the only exception of a central component called Bulletin Board, which is in charge of keeping up-to-date the list of present members (useful for members discovery) and the list of items to be evaluated. It is build around three main concepts: virtual agora, delegate agent, and embedded agent.

A *virtual agora* is a virtual open space and meeting infrastructure (e.g., a web site, a server) where active entities meet, interact, and share experiences about items of interest. Items are advertised in the virtual agora, and their names and characteristics are known. For instance, an item can represent a restaurant and its description. The virtual agora enjoys the following three characteristics:

- openness, entities from various sources can freely join or leave at any time;
- decentralisation, no central authority controls entities.
- persistence, entities (if desired) can be continuously available.

To aforementioned requirements can be fulfilled by implementing the virtual agora as an open multi-agent system (Barber and Kim, 2002),

Figure 1. Simplified architecture supporting mobile users

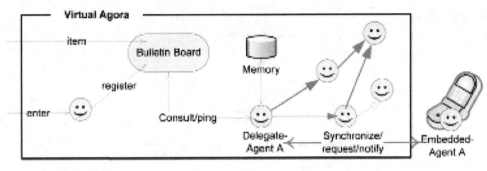

Virtual Agora

which represents a scalable and flexible system that matches the virtual community concept. Moreover, the two main features of open MULTI-AGENT SYSTEMS members (i.e., members can freely join and leave at any time and members are owned by different stakeholders with different aims and objectives) perfectly fit the description of delegate agents.

A *delegate agent* is a software agent that runs in the virtual agora. It models a member of the community. It interacts with other delegates and it builds and maintains the member's personal network of trust. In (Sahli et al., 2008) the authors consider two networks of trust, a register of rated items and a network of (un)trusted recommenders (namely the TRat and TRec described in the previous sections). In order to implement the delegate agents, the system needs the following capabilities:

- *Reasoning*: it should be able to evaluate trust values, build and update its knowledge and argue with other peers;
- *Autonomy*: it has to process the aforementioned tasks autonomously (without any manual assistance from its user);
- *Context-awareness*: it needs to capture the context of its user, which is needed to reason about the trust.

The internal architecture of delegate agents adopts a Belief-Desire-Intention (BDI) model (Rao & Georgeff, 1995). The BDI model offers an interesting framework to design deliberative agents that are able to act and interact autonomously and according to their mental states. Figure 2 illustrates the main components of the delegate agent's architecture. Rounded rectangles represent processes while rectangles represent the different data. In the "Memory" component, two different shapes are used to show whether the data is an input (e.g., Profile) or an output (e.g., Answer). In brief, the "Goal Generator" (corresponding to Desires in the BDI model) produces goals that the agent has to follow. A goal could be: to answer a user's (or peer) request, or to update its own network of trust. These goals are also influenced by the "User Profile", which in turn includes the user's context. In order to fulfil these Desires (or goals), the delegate agent has to formulate a set of Intentions, which will become actions. These Intentions are dictated and later executed by the "Recommender" and the "Argumentation Engine". Because of these actions, the knowledge (here, the two networks of trust TRat and TRec) of the delegate agent is updated, which constitutes the Beliefs of the agent. Based on these new Beliefs, more Intentions have to be processed (if the current goal is not yet satisfied) or a new goal is set (or updated). The same cycle continues as long as there are goals to be achieved.

Figure 2. Functional view of the Delegate-Agent's BDI architecture

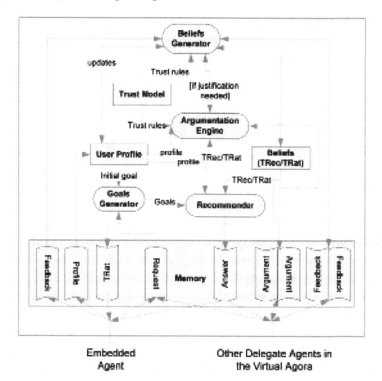

Extension to Mobile Users

The architecture described so far, can be easy extended to support mobile users. Since delegate agents have to request/argue about opinions to ensure high-quality recommendations, they obviously require more interaction. However, when users are mobile, exchanging these messages between peers (mobile users) would generate large and costly wireless communication traffic. It is thus necessary to avoid remote messages as much as possible and allow most of communication to be held locally (peers exchanging messages should be located at the same server). The virtual agora concept seems to be appropriate to fulfil this requirement since it constitutes a meeting infrastructure where all delegate agents can exchange local messages. But, how to make the link with mobile users? To achieve this goal, the

agent-based architecture is extended by assigning a second agent (in addition to the delegate agent) to each user (here mobile user). This agent is called *embedded agent* in Figure 2.

An *embedded agent*, it has few data and functionalities and it is a proxy between the user and the delegate agent. It resides in the mobile device of the user. It mainly (i) notifies delegate agent about the user's feedback, tags (e.g., ratings), changes of interests or preferences, etc., and (ii) requests recommendations on behalf of the user. While delegate agent is deliberative, embedded agent is more a reactive agent. Indeed, it does not support any reasoning; it is only making the bridge between the user and the delegate agent and reacting to incoming events. More details about the internal architecture of this agent are presented in (Sahli et al., 2008).

Example of Mobile Recommendations with Slow-Food Restaurants

This section describes a scenario where a mobile user, Bob, member of a slow food virtual community, likes to find a good food restaurant in places he is visiting. Bob likes sharing his experiences with other fans of slow food. During one of his travels in a certain city, he asks for reliable recommendation about a specific type of restaurant from people having the same preferences he has. The architecture implementing the virtual community and the recommender service is the architecture described in the previous section.

Bob signs up in a slow-food Virtual Agora and sends a Delegate-Agent (called MyDelegate) up there. The Embedded-Agent (EA-Bob) runs already in Bob's mobile phone. By signing up in the Virtual Agora (interfaced by a Web site to facilitate access for users), Bob had to fill in a form about his preferences concerning slow-food restaurants. For instance, he had to indicate which criteria are the most important according to him to rate a restaurant (price, quality of food, or service, etc.) or how he rates certain specific restaurants. This information is used by MyDelegate to argue about received recommendations (during the argumentation process) but also to build its initial list of rated restaurant and network of trusted recommenders. Since MyDelegate is new within slow-food Virtual Agora, it first forms trust relationships with agents by looking into similar profiles and preferences as Bob. Let us suppose that three agents (among others) Alice, Charlie and David are now part of the network of trusted recommenders of MyDelegate and that MyDelegate has an initial trust relationship with all of them. For sake of example, we use "stars" to measure trust; the initial trust value is "one star".

We suppose that, according to its description (announced in the Bulletin Board), the restaurant "The Four Wooden Spoons" seems interesting for Bob. The restaurant is appropriate for a date,

which fits Bob profile. MyDelegate asks its network of recommenders for advice and receives two conflicting recommendations about "The Four Wooden Spoons": Dave recommends it (e.g., "five stars") while Alice and Charlie do not (e.g., they have given "one star" each). These recommendations are not necessarily the result of direct experience; they could be inferred from the networks of the requested members. Since Dave is as trustworthy as the other two, without an argumentation mechanism MyDelegate would have decided to follow Alice and Charlie's advice (not to go to this restaurant). Instead, thanks to the argumentation mechanism, MyDelegate can make a more appropriate choice before notifying EA-Bob (and consequently Bob) with its final recommendation. To this end, it processes the following steps with each recommender. First, it checks the context associated to the received recommendation. This information comes with the initial recommendation (to avoid asking one more time the recommender) and may help MyDelegate understanding differences between opinions. This includes, for example, location and time (where and when the recommendation has been made), the social context (whether they went to the restaurant with friends, family or for a date). In our scenario, MyDelegate notices that the three recommenders have contexts that are similar to its own one.

A more refined argumentation process is then needed to understand the cause of the conflict between the recommenders. Therefore, MyDelegate starts an argumentation game with its recommenders by asking them to justify their opinions. Alice and Charlie claim that "The Four Wooden Spoons" has a bad quality of food while Dave affirms the opposite. Since it can not conclude from these contradictory reasons, MyDelegate asks them for proofs. Alice, which holds this rating from another recommender Henk, justifies its statement by the absence of vegetarian menus. This argument turns out to be unimportant for MyDelegate. Indeed, according to the The Four Wooden Spoon's specification there is a vegetarian menu, and according to Bob's profile, Bob is not vegetarian. Charlie justifies the same statement by the small amount of food. MyDelegate cannot attack this argument since it is out of its knowledge. The Charlie's recommendation is then kept. Dave, in the opposite, states that the food was tasty. This statement cannot be attacked as well, since it does not contradict the MyDelegate's knowledge. The Dave's recommendation is then also kept. The two recommendations are then candidates for being processed. If later a new agent is added to MyDelegate's network and which has an opinion about "The Four Wooden Spoons", the same procedure is launched by MyDelegate.

Let us suppose now that Bob is intending to have a date in restaurant "The Four Wooden Spoons". He then interacts with his mobile and asks for recommendation. EA-Bob forwards the request to MyDelegate. This latter processes the average rating of the memorised recommendations, here the rating "three stars" (i.e., the weighted average between "one star" from Charlie and "five stars" from Dave, both with neutral trustworthiness "one star"), and communicates this information to EA-Bob. Bob is finally notified on his mobile and decides to experience "The Four Wooden Spoons" since three "stars" is a quite positive rating. Once in "The Four Wooden Spoons", Bob appreciates his meal. He thus uses his mobile to positively rate the restaurant. EA-Bob forwards this rating to MyDelegate, which uses Bob's feedback to assess its recommenders. In this case, the feedback confirms that Dave was right and is likely to be trustful whereas Charlie is maybe not. Consequently, MyDelegate strengthens its relationship with Dave by giving a higher weight to the corresponding link and weakens its relationship with Charlie by giving a lower weight to the corresponding link. The experience of Bob is also registered; a previous ratings about "The Four Wooden Spoons" is substituted with the one entered by Bob.

CONCLUSION

The present chapter has presented an overview of the state of the art in trust-based recommender systems for open and mobile virtual communities. The chapter was motivated by the identification of those features that make decentralised recommender systems suitable for the open and mobile virtual community target. As an example, this chapter has described an agent-based solution especially designed for that target.

With only some exception (e.g., Quercia et al., 2007; Rummble.com and Whrrl.com) most of the solutions we have encountered were not suitable for mobile environments; they used witness reputation mechanisms, which require huge traffic between remote users. In the solution described in the chapter, mobile users are supported thanks to two agents, delegated and embedded, one running into the virtual community infrastructure, and the other running in the mobile device of the user, respectively.

Recently, some attention has been dedicated to personalisation of recommendation through trust relationships (e.g., Lathia et al, 2008; Dell'Amico & Capra, 2008), which well adapts a virtual community environment. The present chapter supports the idea of using trust to improve the usefulness (and thus the personalisation) of recommendations. For example, in the solution here described, the adoption of a BDI model gives agents more autonomy, which considerably frees users from managing their trust in other members. This ensures more reliable and trustworthy recommendations and preserves privacy. Taking into account several factors while evaluating trust in items or other members (e.g., namely profile and context similarities, justification of opinions, and personal experience) definitely improves the level of personalisation of recommendations. If it might be true that it is difficult to have a widespread reputation, in this case a member gets a much smaller set of opinions (in number) when asking for a recommendation. Nevertheless, these opinions are of higher quality since they are more personalised (trusted source, justified opinions, similar context, similar profile).

Context-awareness is also an important aspect in recommendation systems; it bounds a piece of information to the situational environment where it has been taken and, as such, it may improve accuracy in information retrieval and the usefulness in recommendation processing. Depending on the considered application, for example, "context" refers to *Domain* (domain in which it is matter to trust another agent), *Risk* (the cost of a possible negative outcome (Deriaz, 2007), *Time* (of the end-user), *Location* (geo-referenced location of the end-user), and *Social context of the end-user* (e.g., in a date, with friends, with family, etc.). But, how to capture context? Context can be automatically supported by applications like Context-Watcher (www.iyouit.eu), which aims at making it easy for an end-user to automatically record, store, and use context information (Koolwaaij et al., 2006). It automatically captures the aforementioned context's parameters. Despite, still few solutions focus on context-awareness, Adomavicius et al. (2005) have addressed context for personalisation and customisation of recommendations. Lenzini et al. (2008) have analysed both trust and context-awareness to improve the quality of recommendations; they also have proposed to evaluate the persuasiveness of recommendations by argumentation protocols.

The trust-based and context-aware approaches described in this chapter are complementary solutions, but only when used together with the classical solution may bring to innovative and advanced services. For example, the trust-based applications described so far can be integrated into the Duine Toolkit[2] (van Setten et al., 2002; van Setten et al., 2004). The Duine Toolkit is an open source software package that allows developers to create hybrid prediction engines for their own applications. It makes available a number of prediction techniques and it already includes some of the most common social filtering and content-based techniques. Moreover, it allows them to be combined dynamically.

Finally, another problem with mobile communities is that when a peer leaves the community, the referral pointers become obsolete and thus the knowledge of the quitter is lost. In the solution described in this chapter, each member shares its knowledge with the community. Thus, that member's knowledge remains available within members that have accepted it; the persistence of knowledge within distributed systems is then enhanced.

REFERENCES

Abdul-Rahman, A., & Hailes, S. (2000). Supporting trust in virtual communities. In *Proc. of the 33rd Hawaii International Conference on System Sciences, volume 6,* Maui, Hawaii (pp. 1-28). Washington, DC: IEEE Computer Society.

Adomavicius, G., Sankaranarayanan, R., Sen, S., & Tuzhilin, A. (2005). Incorporating Contextual Information in Recommender Systems using a Multidimensional Approach. *ACM Transactions on Information Systems, 23*(1), 103–145. doi:10.1145/1055709.1055714

Adomavicius, G., & Tuzhilin, A. (2005). Toward the next generation of recommender systems: A survey of the state-of-the-art and possible extensions. *IEEE Transactions on Knowledge and Data Engineering, 17*(6), 734–749. doi:10.1109/TKDE.2005.99

Arnold, Y., Daum, M., & Krcmar, H. (2004). Virtual communities in health care: Roles, requirements, and restrictions. In *Proc. of the IADIS Int. Conference, L*isbon, Portugal (pp. 370-377).

Artz, D., & Gil, Y. (2007). A survey of trust in computer science and the semantic web. *Web Semantics, 5*(2), 58–71.

Balabanovic, M., & Shoham, Y. (1997). Fab: content-based, collaborative recommendation. *Communications of the ACM, 40*(3), 66–72. doi:10.1145/245108.245124

Barber, K. S., & Kim, J. (2002). Soft security: Isolating unreliable agents from society. In *Proc. of the 5th Workshop on Deception, Fraud and Trust in Agent Societies, AAMAS 2002,* Bologna, Italy (pp. 8-17). New York: ACM.

Becerra, G., Heard, J., Kremer, R., & Denzinger, J. (2007). Trust attributes, methods, and uses. In *Proc. of the Workshop on Trust in Agent Societies, AAMAS-2007,* Honolulu, Hawaii, USA (pp. 1-6).

Berners-Lee, T., Hendler, J., & Lassila, O. (2001, May). The Semantic Web. *Scientific American,* 28–37.

Burak, A., & Sharon, T. (2004). Usage patterns of friend zone: mobile location-based community services. In *Proc. of the 3rd Int. Conf. on Mobile and ubiquitous multimedia MUM '04,* College Park, Maryland (pp. 93-100). New York: ACM.

Burrell, J., & Gay, G. K. (2002). E-graffiti: Evaluating real-world use of a context-aware system. *Interacting with Computers, 14*(4), 301–312. doi:10.1016/S0953-5438(02)00010-3

Carter, W., & Fisher, S. (2004). Mobile sound communities. In *Proc. of the 2004 ACM SIGCHI Int. Conference on Advances in computer entertainment technology,* Singapore (pp. 355-356). New York: ACM.

Cheyer, A., & Martin, D. (2001). The Open Agent Architecture. *Autonomous Agents and Multi-Agent Systems, 4*(1-2), 143–148. doi:10.1023/A:1010091302035

Cole, H., & Stanton, D. (2003). Designing mobile technologies to support co-present collaboration. *Personal and Ubiquitous Computing, 7*(6), 365–371. doi:10.1007/s00779-003-0249-4

Dell'Amico, M., & Capra, L. (2008). SOFIA: Social Filtering for Robust Recommendations. In *IFIP Int. Federation for Information Processing, 263, Trust Management II* (pp. 135-150). Boston, MA: Springer.

Deriaz, M. (2007). *Trusting Virtual Tags.* Université de Genéve, CUI.

El Morr, C., & Kawash, J. (2007). Mobile virtual communities: Current trends and future perspectives. *International Journal of Web Based Communities, 3*(4), 386–403. doi:10.1504/IJWBC.2007.015865

Elinor, O. (1990). *Governing the Commons: The Evolution of Institutions for Collective Action.* Cambridge, UK: Cambridge University Press.

Exit Games. (2006). *Mobile social software applications that drive social networking and maximize your revenues* [white paper]. Retrieved from http://www.exitgames.com

Falcone, R., & Castelfranchi, C. (2001). *Social Trust: a Cognitive Approach.* Amsterdam: Kluwer Academic Publishers.

Ferber, J. (1999). *Multi-Agent Systems: An Introduction to Distributed Artificial Intelligence.* Reading, MA: Addison-Wesley.

Foner, L. (1997). Yenta: A multi-agent, referral based matchmaking system. In *Proc. of the 1st Int. Conference on Autonomous Agents,* Marina del Rey, CA, USA (pp. 301-307). New York: ACM Press.

Foster, I., Kesselman, C., & Tuecke, S. (2001). The anatomy of the grid: Enabling scalable virtual organizations. *The International Journal of Supercomputer Applications, 15*(3), 200–222. doi:10.1177/109434200101500302

Grandison, T., & Sloman, M. (2000). A survey of trust in internet applications. *IEEE Communications Surveys and Tutorials, 4*(4), 2–16.

Griswold, W. G., Shanahan, P., Brown, S. W., Boyer, R., Ratto, M., Shapiro, R. B., & Truong, T. M. (2004). ActiveCampus: Experiments in Community-Oriented Ubiquitous Computing. *Computer*, *37*(10), 73–81. doi:10.1109/MC.2004.149

He, M., Jennings, N. R., & Leung, H.-F. (2003). On agent-mediated electronic commerce. *IEEE Transactions on Knowledge and Data Engineering*, *15*(4), 985–1003. doi:10.1109/TKDE.2003.1209014

Horling, B., & Lesser, V. (2004). A survey of multi-agent organizational paradigms. *The Knowledge Engineering Review*, *19*(4), 281–316. doi:10.1017/S0269888905000317

Huynh, T. D. (2006). *Trust and reputation in open multi-agent systems*. Unpublished doctoral dissertation, University of Southampton, USA.

Jadex. (2008). Retrieved from http://vsis-www.informatik.uni-hamburg.de/projects/jadex/

Jennings, N. R., Sycara, K., & Wooldridge, M. (1998). A roadmap of agent research and development. *Autonomous Agents and Multi-Agent Systems*, *1*(1), 7–38. doi:10.1023/A:1010090405266

Jøsang, A., Hayward, R., & Pope, S. (2006). Trust network analysis with subjective logic. In *Proc. of 29th Australasian Computer Science Conference*, Hobart, Tasmania, Australia (pp. 85-94).

Jurca, R., & Faltings, B. (2003). Towards incentive-compatible reputation management. *LNAI*, *2631*, 138–147.

Kawash, J., El Morr, C., & Itani, M. (2007). A novel collaboration model for mobile virtual communities. *International Journal of Web Based Communities*, *3*(4), 427–447. doi:10.1504/IJWBC.2007.015868

Koolwaaij, J., Tarlano, A., Luther, M., Nurmi, P., Mrohs, B., Battestini, A., & Vaidya, R. (2006). ContextWatcher - sharing context information in everyday life. In *Proc. of the Int. Conference on Web Technologies, Applications, and Services*, Calgary, Canada (pp. 39-60). ACTA Press.

Lathia, N., Hailes, S., & Capra, L. (2008). Trust-Based Collaborative Filtering. In *IFIP Int. Federation for Information Processing, 263, Trust Management II* (pp. 119-123). Boston, MA: Springer.

Leimeister, J. M., Daum, M., & Krcmar, H. (2003). Towards M-Communities: the Case of COSMOS Health Care. In *Proc. Hawaii International Conference on System Science*, Big Island, HI, USA (pp. 214). Washington, DC: IEEE Computer Society.

Lenzini, G., & Sahli, N. & Eertink. H. (2008). Agent Selecting Trustworthy Recommendations in Mobile Virtual Communities. In *Proc. of the Int. Workshop on Trust in Agent Societies, AAMAS 2008*, Estoril, Portugal.

Maes, P. (2004). Agents that reduce work and information overload. *Communications of the ACM*, *37*(7), 30–40. doi:10.1145/176789.176792

Mamei, M., & Zambonelli, F. (2004). Self-Organization in Multi Agent Systems: A Middleware Approach. *LNCS*, *2977*, 233–248.

McBurney, P., & Parsons, S. (2002). Games that agents play: A formal framework for dialogues between autonomous agents. *Journal of Logic Language and Information*, *11*(3), 315–334. doi:10.1023/A:1015586128739

McKnight, D. H., & Chervany, N. L. (1996). *The meanings of trust* (Technical report MISRC Working Paper Series 96-04). University of Minnesota, Management Information Systems Reseach Center.

McKnight, D. H., & Chervany, N. L. (2006). The meanings of trust. In R. Bachmann & A. Zaheer (Eds.), *Handbook of Trust Research* (pp 29-52). Cheltenham, UK: Edward Elgar Publishing.

Miller, B., Konstan, J., & Riedl, J. (2004). Toward a personal recommender system. *ACM Transactions on Information Systems, 22*(3), 437–476. doi:10.1145/1010614.1010618

Nonnecke, B., & Preece, J. (2000). Lurker demographics: counting the silent. In *Proc. of the Conference on Human Factors in Computing Systems* The Hague, The Netherlands (pp. 73-80). New York: ACM.

Norman, T. J., Preece, A., Chalmers, S., Jennings, N. R., Luck, M., & Dang, V. D. (2004). Agent-based Formation of Virtual Organisations. *Knowledge-Based Systems, 17*(2-4), 103–111. doi:10.1016/j.knosys.2004.03.005

Olmedilla, D., Rana, O. F., Matthews, B., & Nejdl, W. (2005). Security and trust issues in semantic grids. In *Proc. of Schloss Dagstuhl Seminar no. 05271: Semantic Grid: The Convergence of Technologies*, Dagstuhl, Germany.

Olsson, T. (2006). *Bootstrapping and Decentralizing Recommender Systems*. Unpublished doctoral dissertation, Uppsala University and SICS.

Persson, P., Espinoza, F., Fagerberg, P., Sandin, A., & Cöster, R. (2002). GeoNotes: a location-based information system for public spaces. In K. Höök, D. Benyon, & A. Munro (Eds.), *Readings in Social Navigation of Information Space* (pp. 151-173). Berlin, Germany: Springer.

Preece, J. (2000). *Online Communities: Designing Usability, Supporting Sociability*. New York: John Wiley and Sons.

Quercia, D., Hailes, S., & Capra, L. (2007). TRULLO - local trust bootstrapping for ubiquitous devices. In *Proc. of the 4th Annual Int. Conference on Mobile and Ubiquitous Systems: Computing, Networking and Services,* Philadelphia, PA (pp. 1-9).

Rana, O. F., Akram, A., & Lynden, S. J. (2005). Building Scalable Virtual Communities Infrastructure Requirements and Computational Costs. *Lectures Notes in Artificial Intelligence, 3413,* 68–83.

Rao, A. S., & Georgeff, M. (1995). Bdi agents: from theory to practice. In *Proc. of the 1st Int. Conference on Multi-Agent Systems (ICMAS95),* San Francisco, USA (pp. 312-319). Menlo Park, CA: AAAI Press.

Resnick, P., & Zeckhauser, R. (2002). Trust Among Strangers in Internet Transactions: Empirical Analysis of eBay's Reputation System. *Advances in Applied Microeconomics, 11,* 127–157. doi:10.1016/S0278-0984(02)11030-3

Sabater, J., & Sierra, C. (2002). Social regret, a reputation model based on social relations. *SIGecom Exchanges, 3*(1), 44–56. doi:10.1145/844331.844337

Sahli, N., Lenzini, G., & Eertink, H. (2008). Trustworthy agent-based recommender system in a mobile P2P environment. In *Proc. of the 7th Int. Workshop on Agents and Peer-to-Peer Computing, AP2PC08,* Estoril, Portugal (pp. 1-11).

Schillo, M., Fischer, K., Fley, B., Florian, M., Hillebrandt, F., & Spresny, D. (2002). Form - a sociologically founded framework for designing self-organization of multi-agent systems. In *Proc. of the Int. Workshop on Regulated Agent-Based Social Systems: Theories and Applications,* Bologna, Italy (LNCS 2934, pp. 156-175). Berlin, Germany: Springer-Verlag.

Schubert, P., & Hampe, J. F. (2005). Business models for mobile communities. In *Proc. of the 38th Annual Hawaii International Conference on System Sciences - HICSS'05,* Big Island, HI, USA (pp. 172-183). Washington, DC: IEEE Computer Society.

Schubert, P., & Koch, M. (2003). Collaboration platforms for virtual student communities. *In Proc. of the Hawaii International Conference on System Science*, Big Island, HI, USA. Washington, DC: IEEE Computer Society.

Serugendo, G. D. M., Gleizes, M. P., & Karageorgos, A. (2005). Self-organization in multi-agent systems. *The Knowledge Engineering Review, 20*(2), 165–189. doi:10.1017/S0269888905000494

Shmatikov, V., & Talcott, C. L. (2005). Reputation-based trust management. *Journal of Computer Security, 13*(1), 167–190.

So, Y., & Durfee, E. (1996). Designing tree-structured organizations for computational agents. *Computational & Mathematical Organization Theory, 2*(3), 219–246. doi:10.1007/BF00127275

Teacy, W., Patel, J., Jennings, N. R., & Luck, M. (2005) Coping with inaccurate reputation sources: Experimental analysis of a probabilistic trust model. In *Proc. of the 4th AAMAS*, Utrecht, The Netherlands (pp. 997-1004). New York: ACM press.

Turner, P. J., & Jennings, N. R. (2000). Improving the scalability of multi-agent systems. In *Proc. of the 1st Int. Workshop on Infrastructure for Scalable Multi-Agent Systems*, Barcelona, Spain (pp. 246-262). Berlin, Germany: Springer-Verlag.

Tveit, A. (2001). Peer-to-peer based recommendations for mobile commerce. In *Proc. of the 1st int. Workshop on Mobile commerce*, Rome, Italy (pp. 26-29). New York: ACM.

van Setten, M., Veenstra, M., & Nijholt, A. (2002). Prediction strategies: Combining prediction techniques to optimize personalization. In *Proc. of the Int. Workshop on Personalization in Future TV*, Malaga, Spain (pp. 23-32).

van Setten, M., Veenstra, M., Nijholt, A., & van Dijk, B. (2004). Case-based reasoning as a prediction strategy for hybrid recommender systems. In *Proc. of the Atlantic Web Intelligence Conference*, Cancun, Mexico (LNCS, 3034, pp. 13-22). Berlin, Germany: Springer-Verlag.

Wang, Y., & Vassileva, J. (2003). Trust and reputation model in peer-to-peer networks. In *Proc. of the 3rd International Conference on Peer-to-Peer Computing*, Linköping, Sweden (pp. 150-158). Washington, DC: IEEE Computer Society.

Wang, Y., & Vassileva, J. (2007). A review on trust and reputation for web service selection. In *Proc. of the 27th International Conference on Distributed Computing Systems Workshops*, Toronto, Canada (pp. 25-32). Washington, DC: IEEE Computer Society.

Xiong, L., & Liu, L. (2004). A reputation-based trust model for peer-to-peer ecommerce communities. *IEEE Transactions on Knowledge and Data Engineering, 7*(16).

Yu, B., & Singh, M. P. (2002). An evidential model of distributed reputation management. In *Proc. of 1st International Joint Conference on Autonomous Agents and Multi-Agent Systems AAMAS 2002*, Bologna, Italy (pp. 294-301). New York: ACM.

Zacharia, G., & Maes, P. (2000). Trust management through reputation mechanisms. *Applied Artificial Intelligence, 14*(9), 881–908. doi:10.1080/08839510050144868

ENDNOTES

[1] Gnutella is indeed the name for a protocol for distributed file sharing, but it is common to use the same name to refer to the network of Gnutella's users itself.

[2] Duine is available at http://sourceforge.net/projects/duine

Chapter 8
Securing Mobile–Agent Systems through Collaboration

Mohammed Hussain
Queen's University, Canada

David B. Skillicorn
Queen's University, Canada

ABSTRACT

Mobile agents are self-contained programs that migrate among computing devices to achieve tasks on behalf of users. Autonomous and mobile agents make it easier to develop complex distributed systems. Many applications can benefit greatly from employing mobile agents, especially e-commerce. For instance, mobile agents can travel from one e-shop to another, collecting offers based on customers' preferences. Mobile agents have been used to develop systems for telecommunication networks, monitoring, information retrieval, and parallel computing. Characteristics of mobile agents, however, introduce new security issues which require carefully designed solutions. On the one hand, malicious agents may violate privacy, attack integrity, and monopolize hosts' resources. On the other hand, malicious hosts may manipulate agents' memory, return wrong results from system calls, and deny access to necessary resources. This has motivated research focused on devising techniques to address the security of mobile-agent systems. This chapter surveys the techniques securing mobile-agent systems. The survey categorizes the techniques based on the degree of collaboration used to achieve security. This categorization resembles the difference between this chapter and other surveys in the literature where categorization is on the basis of entities/parts protected and underlying methodologies used for protection. This survey shows the importance of collaboration in enhancing security and discusses its implications and challenges.

INTRODUCTION

The concept of software agents originated in the artificial intelligence field as a paradigm for software

DOI: 10.4018/978-1-60566-414-9.ch008

design and development (Jennings & Wooldridge, 1998). Software agents have received attention in the distributed systems field, mainly because mobile agents add mobility to agency. A mobile-agent system (MAS) consists of a set of computing devices, called hosts, and autonomous programs called agents. Users of such a system encapsulate their tasks in agents. The agents then roam the hosts, hence the word mobile, finding and utilizing resources and information needed to accomplish their goals (Pham & Karmouch, 1998). The set of hosts visited by a mobile agent is its itinerary. Examples of mobile-agent frameworks include Telescript (White, 1994), JADE (Bellifemine, Caire, Poggi, & Rimassa, 2003), D'Agents (Gray, Cybenko, Kotz, Peterson & Rus, 2002), Aglet (Lange & Oshima, 1998), Concordia (Castillo, Kawaguchi, Paciorek & Wong, 1998), Voyager (Recursion Software, 2006), and Spider (Huang & Skillicorn, 2001).

Mobile agents combine software agency from artificial intelligence and software mobility from distributed systems. Advantages are inherited from both areas. Although mobile agents have no major application justifying their usage so far, their benefits have been suggested by many studies (Das, Shuster, Wu & Levit, 2005; Ghanea-Hercock, Collis & Ndumu, 1999; Guttman, Moukas & Maes, 1998; Maes, Guttman & Moukas, 1999). Mobile agents can:

- Reduce network traffic significantly by moving agents to where data resides rather than moving data to users.
- Perform their tasks when their owner is offline, a valuable feature when network connections cannot be sustained during an entire task execution.
- Facilitate parallel computing by utilizing groups of hosts.
- Execute on heterogeneous environments and adapt to changes.

E-commerce, parallel computing, information retrieval, and monitoring are a few applications for which mobile agents can be of a great help. Mobile agents can search for related products based on a consumer needs, compare offers from different merchants, and choose products that best fit the consumer criteria. In (Guttman et al., 1998) the automation of different stages of consumer buying behavior using mobile agents is studied. Telecommunication networks can utilize mobile agents to reconfigure networks and machines (sending an agent instead of sending a technician). Load balancing is another candidate task for mobile agents in telecommunication networks. Mobile agents are employed for a distributed and heterogeneous information retrieval system in (Das et al., 2005). Monitoring applications, especially distributed intrusion-detection systems, can also benefit from using mobile agents.

Industrial applications employing mobile agents, however, have not yet become mainstream. Lack of standards for mobile-agent platforms and challenging security problems are the main barriers to widespread adoption of this technology (Borselius, 2002; Vigna, 2004; Zachary, 2003). Malicious agents may consume hosts' resources, read private data, modify files, or use a host as a base to send spam. On the other hand, hosts have full control over mobile agents. Malicious hosts may deprive agents of resources, read or modify private data, masquerade as another host, supply illegal input, or re-execute the agent to reverse engineer it (Zachary, 2003). This has motivated research focused on devising techniques to address the security of MAS. These techniques vary in: the parts of systems being protected, the level of protection, and the cost of protection.

This chapter surveys the field of mobile-agent security. Techniques in this field are categorized on the basis of utilizing collaboration. The rationale behind this categorization is to emphasize the importance of collaborative security in the context of MAS. The benefits and costs associated with collaboration are also discussed. Previous surveys (Bellavista, Corradi, Federici, Montanari & Tibaldi, 2004; Borselius, 2002; Claessens, Preneel & Vandewalle, 2003; Jansen & Karygiannis, 2000; Pleisch & Schiper, 2004) focus on comparing the techniques based on entities protected and underlying methodologies used for protection.

What do we mean by Collaboration?

Let T a security technique for MAS, m a mobile agent, A the owner sending m, H an ordered list of hosts visited by m, $E(m, h_j)$ the execution of agent m at host h_j. The degree of the collaboration in T in terms of security depends on the following conditions:

1. The security of $E(m, h_j)$ relies on the interaction of h_j with a non-empty subset of $\{ h_x : 0 < x < j \}$.
2. The security of $E(m, h_j)$ relies on the interaction of m or h_j with other agents.
3. The security of $E(m, h_j)$ relies on the interaction of m or h_j with A or a trusted third party.
4. The security of $E(m, h_j)$ increases with the size of H.

Interaction refers to a wide variety of operations, *e.g.*, sharing information and performing multi-party computations. T is said to be collaborative, if T satisfies two or more conditions. T is said to be partially-collaborative, if T satisfies one condition. Otherwise T is said to be non-collaborative.

Chapter Organization

The remaining sections of the chapter are organized as follows. Next, we discuss the background information including security threats facing MAS, the associated security requirements, and the evaluation criteria of the security techniques. Then, a critical survey of security solutions for MAS is provided. The survey is in three sections. The first section presents techniques taking a non-collaborative approach for security. Partially-collaborative techniques are studied in the second section. Third section shows the collaborative techniques and elaborates on the implications and challenges of the collaboration. The survey also points out strengths and weaknesses of the techniques and presents open problems for further research. Finally, the chapter is summarized and concluded.

BACKGROUND

Mobile agent security has two aspects: host protection and mobile agent protection (McDonald, 2006). The first aspect includes protecting a host's memory, files, state, and resources. The second aspect includes preventing spying and illegal tampering with mobile-agent instructions, data, state, and communications. The following paragraphs provide an insight into security threats facing MAS and security requirements addressing these threats.

Security Threats Facing MAS

There are three entities in MAS: hosts, mobile agents, and environments. A mobile agent consists of three parts: code, state, and data. The agent's code specifies the agent's behavior. The agent's state keeps track of the variables' values, functions' call stack, program counter, and other information about the agent's current execution status. The agent's data stores the intermediate results obtained by executing the agent at different hosts. Agents arriving at a host are executed by the MAS environment at that host. The security of MAS, therefore, has two aspects: protecting hosts and protecting mobile agents (McDonald, 2006). The first aspect includes protecting a host's memory, files, and services. The second aspect includes preventing spying and illegal tampering with mobile-agent code, state, data, and communications. The following are the security threats that one entity in MAS may launch against others.

- *Masquerading.* Claiming the identity of another entity.
- *Denial of service.* Degrading the quality attributes of a service (e.g., responsiveness, usability).

Figure 1. Attacks of malicious entities in MAS

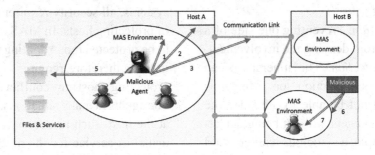

- *Spying.* Gaining illicit read access to another entity's information.
- *Integrity attack.* Gaining illicit write access to another entity's information.
- *Eavesdropping.* Listening to the communications of an entity.
- *Repudiation.* Denying the involvement in a transaction with another entity.

Figure 1 illustrates the different entities in MAS and the security threats that each entity poses on others. Malicious Agent can launch:

1. Spying or integrity attacks against the hosting MAS environment.
2. Masquerading as another agent to gain extra privileges, or repudiation of services.
3. Eavesdropping on the host's/other agents' communications.
4. Spying or integrity attacks against other agents within the hosting MAS environment.
5. Spying, integrity attacks, or denial of service against the host's files and services.

Malicious Host C can launch:

6. Spying or integrity attacks against its MAS environment.
7. Spying, integrity attacks, denial of service, or repudiation on agents within its MAS environment.

Security Requirements for MAS

As in any computer-based system, the security requirements of MAS must ensure *confidentiality, integrity, availability,* and *accountability* (Jansen & Karygiannis, 2000; McDonald, 2006). Confidentiality requires that any piece of data can be only read by a legitimate entity. Data should be created and updated only by legitimate entities to maintain data integrity. A system is available if its resources are accessible when needed. Accountability necessitates that entities should be accountable for their actions. Unfortunately, meeting such goals is harder in MAS than in traditional systems. The security requirements of a typical system are:

- *Authentication.* Verifying the claimed identity of an entity.
- *Authorization.* Deciding whether an authenticated entity has the right to access a resource.
- *Access control.* Extending authorization by allowing the decision of granting access to be based not only on the user and the resource, but also on other factors. Example factors are: the number of times that the resource had been accessed, other resources accessed by the same user, and programs currently running.
- *Logging.* Recording the system events to keep track of who did what and when.

- *Intrusion detection.* Detecting illicit behavior and attacks.
- *Non-repudiation.* Preventing one side of a transaction from denying the involvement.
- *Itinerary protection.* The itinerary of an agent requires protection too. Malicious hosts should not be able to influence the itinerary of an agent without being detected. For example, a malicious retailer could change the itinerary of a shopping agent to prevent it from visiting competitors.
- *Forward integrity.* If the ith host in a mobile agent itinerary is malicious, then a security technique that guarantees the protection of the partial results of the first to the i-1st host is said to achieve forward integrity.
- *Publicly verifiable forward integrity.* The ability of a host to determine whether forward integrity holds for a visiting mobile agent. Such a feature saves the owner from waiting for a mobile agent holding tampered results.
- *Forward privacy.* Some service providers and retailers may require anonymity; therefore, security techniques must be able to ensure that any host cannot infer from an agent the identity of the previous hosts.

To achieve confidentiality and integrity in MAS, both mobile agents and hosts must not gain illicit access to each other's memory or files. Implementing authentication and authorization requirements help preventing such illicit access. Implementing access-control requirements ensures availability. Logging and intrusion detection requirements aim to establish accountability.

Why is it hard to Secure MAS?

Ensuring the security of both mobile agents and their hosts is a difficult task. Techniques that achieve security for both must not incur significant performance overheads; otherwise, the overheads diminish the benefits gained from using

the mobile agents in the first place. In traditional systems, all security requirements have the goal of protecting hosts. In MAS, mobile agents need to be protected too. Adopting these requirements in MAS, therefore, requires careful handling since protecting a host may conflict with protecting mobile agents in many situations. Security measures at the host, such as access control, may lead to denial of service for the mobile agent. Furthermore, verifying agents' code to protect the host's integrity contradicts preserving the confidentiality of that code.

Evaluation Criteria

The next three sections provide a summary and a comparison of the techniques in surveyed in this chapter. The comparison is based on the criteria presented in Table 1. The first four criteria measure the complexity of the technique. Detection *vs.* prevention is based on the host/agent perspective. A technique that protects hosts and agents has two values for this criterion, from hosts' and agents' perspectives, respectively. Coverage refers to the security requirements achieved. Features describe other characteristics provided by the technique, e.g., ease of integration with other techniques.

MAS SECURITY WITHOUT COLLABORATION

Code Signatures and State Appraisal

Code signatures allow a host to verify the claimed identity of an agent, thus achieving authentication. The agent is executed if the host trusts the agent producer and or owner. Such techniques also verify the integrity of code. Public-key cryptography is needed for code signing. If code is modified on the way to the host, the signature verification will fail. When signature verification fails, either the code is not from the claimed producer, or the code has been modified before reaching the host. If verifica-

Table 1. Criteria used for comparison between security techniques

Criteria	Description
Time requirements	Extra time needed for security
Space requirements	Extra space needed for security
Bandwidth requirements	Extra bandwidth needed for security
Physical requirements	Extra hardware needed for security
Coverage	What is the security requirements covered?
Detection *vs.* prevention	Is the technique detective, preventive?
Features	Platform independence, ease of integration, fine granularity, fault tolerance

tion is passed, the authenticity and integrity of the code are ensured. Java and ActiveX support code signatures to determine authenticity and to verify the integrity of mobile code (Gong & Schemers, 1998; Hopwood, 1997). The Java virtual machine runs applets from trusted sources with full privileges, while untrusted applets run with very restricted privileges. In Microsoft products, users decide whether to run an ActiveX plugin. Permitting the plugin to execute, implies granting the plugin the same privileges as the user running it. Many mobile-agent frameworks, especially those based on Java, have adopted code signatures as a mechanism for host protection. Examples of such frameworks include Telescript (Tardo & Valente, 1996), Agent-Tcl which is currently known as D'Agent, Aglets, and Voyager.

The state-appraisal approach (Berkovits, Guttman & Swarup, 1998) helps hosts to detect mobile agents with abnormal states. In this approach, an agent's producer and owner add state-appraisal functions to the agent. These functions allow hosts to determine the privileges essential to perform a required computation. These functions request the needed privileges after examining the agent's state. Examining the agent's state may reveal illegal tampering by previous hosts. The following describes the steps of the state-appraisal approach.

1.   The producer equips the agent with a function specifying the maximum permissions based on the agent's state. The agent is then signed and shipped to the owner.

2.   The agent's owner attaches another state-appraisal function based on agent's state. The owner signs and dispatches the agent to designated hosts.

3.   Every host evaluates both state-appraisal functions. Both functions match the state to a set of acceptable states. Each function returns a set of permissions associated with the matching state. If no matching state is found, no permission is requested.

Signing code prevents an agent's owner from repudiating sending the mobile agent. Signing code does not incur significant time or space penalties. Being platform-independent and easy to integrate with other security mechanisms are additional advantages of these techniques. Code signatures are simple and effective; however, checking agent's authenticity and integrity is not enough. The presence of a signature does not imply secure execution. Mobile agents from trusted producers, when given full privileges, may still harm the host. Legitimate actions according to the policy of one host may be malicious to another. Moreover, a host may, in practice, need to run agents from unknown producers. Authorization and accountability are not addressed. A disadvantage of code signatures is the requirement to have a certificate authority, binding keys to parties.

State appraisal functions enable the specification of permissions based on an agent's state, which can be utilized to implement authorization.

Type Checking and Proof Carrying Code

The process of verifying that all variables have types and all operations are carried out on variables with the right types is called type checking. Type checking is employed to address type safety. Ensuring safety is a valuable feature for strengthening code security. Type checking looks for stack over/underflows, mismatch between actual and expected types of objects, program counters not within the corresponding method code fragment, uninitialized objects, and illegal accesses of object fields. Type checking is done by the Java bytecode verifier to prevent applets from accessing private data, jumping to the Java Virtual Machine's (JVM) private methods, and performing illegal type conversions (Leroy, 2001). To perform type checking in Java, source code is compiled to bytecode. For each method the JVM designates an activation record, containing a stack for the temporary results and a register for the local variables and parameters. The verifier simulates the execution of the method's instructions, but it is concerned about types rather than values. The verifier, therefore, stores the types of variables, parameters, and temporary results in the same way the activation records of the JVM store the values. Then the dataflow of each method is analyzed assuming all other methods are well-typed. The analysis is based on matching the effects of executing intrusions to a set of rules. The verifier executes each bytecode instruction and checks the corresponding rule. For example, consider the rule: *iadd(int.int.S,R)(int.S,R)*. The rule says that integer addition pops two integers from stack S and pushes an integer to S. The register R is unmodified by integer addition. Applying the rule with one integer in S results in a stack underflow,

whereas having one integer and one double result in a type mismatch.

A type-preserving compiler for Java is described in (League, Shao & Trifonov, 2003). The authors present a strongly-typed intermediate language supporting type-safety checks without restricting optimizations. Verification based on pattern structures (Huang, Jay & Skillicorn, 2006) parameterizes bytecode verifiers with security policies. The verifier is designed using the Bondi language, which is a variant of Objective Camel. Policies are treated as first-order values, alleviating the necessity of writing new programs to verify new policies. The approach is illustrated for Java bytecode, but the portability for other target languages is straightforward.

SafeTSA (Amme, Dalton, Von Ronne & Franz, 2001) presents an alternative code representation to Java bytecode. The representation is based on static single assignment (SSA) and type separation. SSA replaces assignments to variables with instructions modeling dataflow, while type separation provides different types with separate registers. SafeTSA produces a more compact code representation and minimizes the verification step at hosts.

TAL (Morrisett, Walker, Crary & Glew, 1999) is a strongly-typed assembly language, allowing assembly code to be type checked. A compiler is proposed to translate programs written in the polymorphic λ-calculus to TAL. Integers and pointers are treated as different abstractions. Arithmetic operations are applied to integers only, while dereferencing is available for pointers. Such characteristics make well-typed programs in TAL preserve useful safety and security properties. For instance, code cannot fake pointers to objects. To verify TAL code, the original program is not needed. TAL also permits many optimizing operations to be performed on code.

Proof-carrying code (PCC) (Necula, 1998) annotates mobile code with a proof of compliance with respect to a safety policy supplied by a group of interested hosts. The hosts can verify the proof and safely execute the code. There are three main steps in this approach. First, hosts and code producer agree on a safety policy that a mobile code must obey. Second, the code producer writes the code, generates a proof of compliance, and ships both code and proof to the hosts. Third, hosts use the policy and the shipped code to verify the validity of the proof. If the proof passes the validation, hosts execute the code without the need to have any further runtime checking. A safety policy declares the authorized operations, preconditions, invariants, and postconditions that the code must satisfy. First-order predicate logic is employed to formalize safety policies. Given a formalized policy and a piece of code, a verification condition (safety predicate) is generated in a form of a first-order predicate. If mobile code is altered during transmission in a way that threatens the policy, then the validation step fails.

The use of a certifying compiler facilitates PCC without the need of writing the code in assembly language. In (Necula & Lee, 1998), a certifying compiler for a subset of C is presented. After compiling a program using a C compiler, a certifier takes as input the generated assembly code and type rules representing the safety policy. The certifier then generates a safety predicate, proves the predicate, and verifies the proof's validity. For practical use of PCC, a standard for formalizing safety and security requirements is essential. The proof size, furthermore, should be small enough not to cause substantial bandwidth overhead. Model-carrying code (MCC), an approach similar to PCC, is described in (Sekar, Venkatakrishnan, Basu, Bhatkar & DuVarney, 2003). The code in MCC is accompanied by a model (an intermediate representation) showing the security-related behavior. Models are used by hosts to determine code safety.

The time and space required by the techniques in this subsection vary. Type checking needs less space than PCC, but needs more time. The more rules a type checker applies, the more time is spent in verification. The more safety require-ments a code producer addresses in PCC, the longer the generated proof. The techniques are developed mainly to handle safety requirement. These requirements share the same goals as many security requirements. Memory safety is well addressed by type checking and PCC. A limitation of verification techniques is the dependency on languages. Type checking is only suitable for strongly-typed languages. PCC transforms safety policies into typing rules and requires compilers to certify code; therefore, code produced by PCC depends on the compiler. The techniques are preventive. Type checking is used in many Java-based mobile-agent frameworks. PCC has been also implemented and tested. Problems for further research in this field include: the incorporation of high-level security requirements and the standardization of methods for specifying safety and security requirements in PCC.

Sandboxing and Safe Interpreters

A sandbox is an isolated virtual place in memory, where an untrusted program can run safely. A sandbox prevents a residing program from accessing any resource outside the designated memory space, except what is provided by the bounding sandbox. A program running in a sandbox, for example, cannot access files or open sockets. In JDK 1, Java employs a sandbox model in which downloaded applets run within a very restrictive environment. Signed applets are allowed to run as trusted applets in JDK 1.1. The Java 2 platform (also known as JDK 1.2) introduced the usage of security policies to ease the implementation of access control with fine granularity. Different applets can run in different sandboxes, each with separate security policy specifying the permissions given to the applet (Gong, Mueller, Prafullchandra & Schemers, 1997). The idea of a sandbox has been incorporated and extended as a security mechanism in many mobile-code systems.

Safe-code interpreters are alternatives to sandboxes. Potentially unsafe instructions can be made available to local code, but not to downloaded code. Safe interpreters may allow downloaded code to use safer and restricted versions of the instructions. This approach is more flexible than the sandbox model. Safe-Tcl (Ousterhout, Levy & Welch, 1998) is a secure variant of the scripting language Tcl. Applications in Safe-Tcl uses interpreters with full privileges called master interpreters. When an application wishes to run untrusted code, a safe interpreter is created. The safe interpreter does not contain any unsafe instruction. The interpreter, however, has aliases to these instructions. These aliases request the master interpreter to execute the unsafe instruction in a controlled manner, thus preventing direct access of untrusted code to system resources. The D'Agent framework employs Safe-Tcl.

Rewriting Agent Code and Policy Enforcement

Code rewriting (Chander, Mitchell, & Shin, 2001; Czajkowski & Von Eicken, 1998; Schneider, 2000; Walker, 2000) helps enforce safety and security requirements. In (Chander et al., 2001), security checks are added to code to control resource usage. The approach wraps potentially unsafe Java classes and methods to prevent mobile agents from launching denial-of-service and information-leak attacks. Their approach is based on editing the constant pool of a Java class file. References to potentially unsafe Java classes and methods are replaced with references to the authors' safer versions. *Thread.setPriority*, for example, can be replaced with *SafeThread.setPriority* that disallows mobile-code threads from having priorities higher than the host ones.

Security automata are used in (Schneider, 2000; Walker, 2000) to specify security policies. A security automaton consists of a set of states and transitions such that a transition to a 'bad' state is considered a violation of the corresponding policy. Transforming these automata to instructions inserted into mobile code enforces security

policies and detects violations. Code is searched for security-related instructions, such as accessing files or establishing connections. Each one of these instructions is wrapped in a code block that checks whether the instruction will cause any of the related security automata to reach a bad state. If so, the block terminates the mobile code. The approach tackles security by ensuring safety properties (*i.e.*, the absence of illegal actions). On the other hand, liveness properties (*i.e.*, the presence of desired actions) cannot be specified using automata without being too restrictive.

JRes (Czajkowski & Von Eicken, 1998) is a Java-based interface for resource accounting. Hosts utilize JRes to record the usage of memory, network, and CPU by code. Accountability is achieved by rewriting bytecode to monitor each running thread. Limits can be set for each thread and thread group. Actions to be taken when a thread exceeds a limit can be also specified. For instance, a limit of 2MB can be set for the memory occupied by any thread of a particular program. Denial-of-service attacks can be easily avoided by JRes. Performance, however, is one limitation to this approach. Adding bytecode to every run method of each thread, and every constructor and finalizer of each class imposes significant performance overhead. Extending the JVM to support JRes instead of rewriting code classes can minimize such problem, though this affects portability.

Policy-based frameworks are used for specifying restrictions and rules securing software systems. These frameworks facilitate the specification and enforcement of security policies, which is more convenient than hard-coding policies in software. KAoS (Uszok et al., 2003) is a collection of policy-management tools compatible with Nomads, Cougar, and other Java-based MAS. KAoS enables reasoning about policies, grouping users and agents into domains, and enforcing policies on domains. KAoS also supports dynamic changing of policies. Cabri, Ferrari & Leonardi (2006) employ a Java authentication and authorization system to enforce security policies. The approach simplifies the management of security policies for mobile agents using roles.

Techniques presented in this subsection provide a flexible solution for expressing and enforcing various security requirements, including access control and logging. The techniques are platform independent, since they do not impose restrictions on languages used for designing and implementing MAS. They are also preventive. As in the case of digital signatures, these techniques are widely used in mobile-agent frameworks. The Java security manager, for example, provides Java programs with a security-policy enforcement mechanism. An advantage of policy-based frameworks is the support for fine-grained access control and mobile agent protection. One of the main active research topics here is the design of policy-based frameworks that are capable of expressing security policies, analyzing the policies for conflicts, and enforcing the policies efficiently.

The techniques suffer from performance overhead due to the time wasted monitoring well-behaved code. This overhead depends on the number of security checks added in code rewriting, the implementation of sandboxes and safe interpreters, and the number of security policies enforced by policy-based tools.

Itinerary Protection via Onion Routing

An itinerary-protection technique is presented by Westhoff, Schneider, Unger & Kaderali (1999). The approach utilizes the onion routing scheme (Reed, Syverson & Goldschlag, 1998) which is a protocol for anonymous communication based on public cryptography. An owner encrypts the ordered list of host identities and data used at each host. Each host can only decrypt its designated data and the identities of its immediate predecessor and successor. Since the identity of a host in an agent's itinerary is only available to that host's immediate predecessor and successor, skipping

hosts or adding new hosts is easily detected. The authors extend the scheme by allowing a host to add new identities to the itinerary after signing the new list of hosts. New hosts are visited, and the agent is returned to the host who inserted the new list. The agent then continues with the old itinerary. One limitation of this approach is that the unavailability of the next host means that agents must either wait or return to owners.

Itinerary protection facilitates the enforcement of an agent itinerary, while achieving anonymous communication. Itinerary privacy and integrity are guaranteed, which results in forward privacy. Collusion attacks on the agent's itinerary can be also detected. The limitations of this technique are the time and bandwidth overhead associated with the setup of the onion network and the subsequent communications, especially in the presence of many onion routers.

PRAC, KAG, and Append Only Containers

Several solutions have been proposed to protect agents' partial results (Karjoth, Asokan & Gülcü, 1999; Karnik & Tripathi, 2000; Yee, 1997). In the partial results authentication code (PRAC) approach (Yee, 1997); an agent carries a list of keys, one for each host. Every host encrypts its partial results and erases the corresponding key before sending the agent to the next host. When the agent returns home, the owner can verify the integrity of the partial results, since the owner has a copy of all keys. This approach is enhanced by using a one-way hash function to reduce the number of keys. Each host receives a key from the predecessor, uses it to encrypt the results, hashes the used key, and sends the hash to the next host to be used as the key. The agent needs to carry only one key (the first key). In the first two cases of PRAC, PRAC ensures forward integrity. In both cases, however, the results can be verified only by the agent's owner. Publicly-verifiable forward integrity can also be achieved by extending

PRAC. Instead of keys, hosts use signature and verification functions. Verification functions are made public, while signature functions are kept private. Signing the results with a signature can only be verified by the corresponding verification function. Whenever a host signs the results, it destroys the signature function. Malicious hosts cannot forge the previous results, whereas honest ones can verify integrity.

Security protocols described in (Karjoth et al., 1999) extend PRAC for enhanced protection. The protocols are abbreviated as KAG. The first protocol establishes a chain between hosts. This is achieved by requiring each host to hash the signed results of the previous host together with the identity of the next one. Then, the host encrypts its results with the owner's key for confidentiality and signs the encrypted results along with the generated hash. Strong forward integrity (*i.e.*, forward integrity with the ability to detect a host changing its results) is guaranteed as well. The protocol also supports public verifiable forward integrity. Truncation and insertion attacks are detected due to the chaining property. Such attacks, however, cannot be detected if the agent visits two conspiring hosts or same malicious host twice. If hosts sign then encrypt, instead of encrypting then signing, anonymity is accomplished at the expense of losing public verifiability.

Append-only containers are part of the Ajanta framework for security (Karnik & Tripathi, 2000). As the name suggests, these containers allow the addition of results while preventing deletion. They also provide a host with the choice of making the protected results readable to future hosts. To append results to a container, the host passes a signed and an unsigned version of its results to the agent. The unsigned results are kept for future hosts to use. Hosts requiring the results to be confidential may ask the agent to encrypt the unsigned results with the owner's key. The agent updates an initially random checksum by concatenating the checksum to the host's signed results and encrypting the resultant string with

the owner's public key. Verification is performed by decrypting the checksum iteratively. If the last checksum is not equal to the initial random value, then the results have been tampered with. In each iteration, the signed results are decrypted using the corresponding host key and compared to the hash of the unsigned results. If both match, the results from that host are valid. The verification process needs the private key; therefore, integrity cannot be publicly verifiable.

PRAC, KAG and append-only containers secure the partial results computed at each host of an agent itinerary. Security is based on detecting attacks on the integrity of results by validating a list of host signatures. The techniques offer result privacy, result forward integrity, and non-repudiation. Public verifiability is possible except for append-only containers, where the verification may only take place at the owner. Time and space needed for encryption depend mainly on the size of the results. As the number of hosts in the itinerary grows, the space needed becomes a limitation. This is due to the extra network bandwidth required to transmit the agent to the new hosts. One common limitation facing all these techniques is the failure to detect attacks where more than one host colludes in attacking the agent. Collusion attacks succeed in inserting and deleting results of honest hosts visited between the conspiring ones.

Computing with Encrypted Functions and Code Obfuscation

Computing with encrypted data allows a server to perform a computation on encrypted data from a user without decryption. This has inspired work on computing with encrypted functions (CEF) (Sander & Tschudin, 1998). In CEF, a host receives an encrypted code and executes it without decryption; hence code privacy is achieved. CEF is based on homomorphic encryption schemes (HES). Given a function F, an HES enables one to compute $F(x+y)$ and $F(xy)$ from $F(x)$ and $F(y)$ without knowing x or y. The authors describe a scheme for encrypting polynomial and rational functions.

Gedrojc, Cartrysse & Van Der Lubbe (2006) achieve CEF using ElGamal encryption. The approach is used in private bidding scenarios to protect data; therefore, we describe it in the next subsection. Error-correcting codes (ECC) are used in designing public-key algorithms. ECC are methods of constructing messages, where receivers can automatically detect and correct errors. A similar approach is utilized for function hiding in (Loureiro & Molva 1999). To encode a function F as F', F is written in a matrix format. F' is constructed from F using an ECC. F' is sent to the host to be evaluated on the host's input. Results are returned to the function's owner for decryption.

Code obfuscation is another approach to protecting code privacy. Obfuscation is the process of generating new code and data representations from the original ones. In (Hohl, 1998), three example algorithms for obfuscation are presented. The first decomposes variables into segments and reconstructs new variables by combining the segments arbitrarily. References to the variables in the code are updated accordingly. The second converts control-flow elements, *e.g.*, conditional and loop statements, into *goto* like statements based on variables. The third encrypts different data with different keys, where the keys are obtained from a trusted server. Since the algorithms transform a straightforward piece of code into a complicated one, code obfuscation incurs performance overhead at agent creation and execution.

Undetachable Signatures

Even if an owner encrypts the function responsible for signing messages, malicious hosts may still reuse the function to sign another message. An undetachable signature is a function that signs messages if and only if they are the output of a predetermined function. The idea of undetachable signatures is first introduced in (Sander & Tschu-

din, 1998). A simple scheme is provided which binds a signature function s to a task function F by taking F_{signed} as the composition of s after F, *i.e.*, $F_{signed} = s o F$. F_{signed} and F are sent to a host which runs both F and F_{signed} on her input. The output of f is signed without the need to send s to the host. The authors describe some decomposition attacks against their scheme and discuss prevention.

RSA is used to implement the previously-mentioned undetachable-signature scheme securely (Kotzanikolaou, Burmester & Chrissikopoulos, 2000). The signature function, s, is the one used in RSA. The owner sends F and F_{signed} to the host. F is constructed from the owner's identity and requirements, whereas F_{signed} is as described before. The host executes F and F_{signed} on her input x, which is the host's identity and bid. With such a scheme, the owner's requirements, host's bid, and the signature are all linked. The scheme is claimed to be as secure as RSA.

CEF, undetachable signatures, and code obfuscation rely on the owner to secure the agent. These techniques use cryptography and transformation algorithms to create a black-box version of code. The privacy, as well as the integrity, of agent code, state, and results is achieved. Forward integrity, however, is not addressed. The main limitation here is that the transformed agent is much larger because of the transformation. The time required for execution is also increased. Undetachable signatures provide non-repudiation for hosts only. It also controls the signing process by allowing the signature function to operate only on the output of a corresponding constraint function. Hosts, therefore, cannot force agents to sign transactions for their benefits. CEF and code obfuscation are preventive, while undetachable signatures is detective.

Software Fingerprinting

Software watermarking enables code producers to embed hidden tags in the code to prove ownership. Software fingerprinting uses watermarking to place the tags of different copies in different locations to track users responsible for copyright violations. Watermarking and fingerprinting is used in (Esparza, Fernandez, Soriano, Mucoz & Forné, 2003) to detect attacks against mobile agents. An owner embeds a tag in a mobile agent and sends it to perform a computation. During the computation, the tag is transferred to the results. When the agent returns, the owner searches the agent's results for the tag. Tag absence or distortion signals an attack. This technique, however, is susceptible to collusion attacks where hosts cooperate to search for the tag, which is in same location for all hosts. Fingerprinting solves this problem by placing the tag in different locations. Codes with the identifiable parent property from coding theory are utilized to produce and trace tags. Watermarking and fingerprinting require space to store the tags which limits the applicability of the approach.

Software fingerprinting is a detective technique focusing on state integrity attacks. Fingerprinting needs extra time and space to process and store the hidden tags. The technique detects collusion attacks.

Secure Hardware

A secure coprocessor (Yee, 1997) is a physically-shielded hardware unit equipped with a CPU and non-volatile memory. The coprocessor's state can be only accessed using its I/O interface. Mobile agents trusting the manufacturer of a secure coprocessor can migrate and run on hosts containing that coprocessor. The coprocessor provides protection for mobile agent as well as hosts. Another instance is the tamper-proof environment (TPE) presented in (Wilhelm, Staamann & Buttyán, 1998). A TPE consists of a CPU, RAM, and non-volatile memory. Each TPE has a private key available solely to that TPE, not even to the host itself. TPE utilizes the cryptographically-protected-objects protocol. The protocol requires agents to be encrypted with the TPE public key. This prevents anyone other than

the designated TPE from decrypting the agents. After execution, an agent may migrate back to the owner or to another TPE using the same procedure. Introducing secure hardware into hosts achieves solid protection for both hosts and mobile agents. The benefits in many situations, however, do not justify the associated physical cost resulted from the installation of the extra hardware.

Installing secure hardware provides agents with the ability to execute within a protected environment. Most of the security requirements, therefore, are met. This includes preventing attacks on an agent's code, state, and collected results. Hosts are also shielded from malicious agents. The physical cost of installing expensive hardware is a huge limitation.

MAS SECURITY THROUGH PARTIAL COLLABORATION

Partial-collaborative techniques are studied in this section. These techniques satisfy one of the conditions of collaboration. Monitoring state transitions satisfies condition 4. Other techniques satisfy condition 3.

Environmental Key Generation

The environmental key-generation approach (Riordan & Schneier, 1998) enables the encryption of code and data, so that the decryption is only performed in certain conditions. An agent, for instance, may decrypt the content based on information available at a network resource, on a host's IP address, or simply during a specific time interval. Three constructs are described: a simple construct, where an agent searches a fixed data channel for a decryption key; a time construct, where the agent uses the time value as the key; and a general construct, where the key is gained through the agent's interaction with a host. By hashing data, the simple construct can search a host's database without revealing data to the host. The time construct uses one-way hash functions to encrypt data. This method requires the cooperation of an honest server to provide a correct time value. The agent uses the time as the key for decryption. The time construct can be employed for decrypting data after or before a predetermined time value. Nesting the time construct allows decryption to be possible in a time interval. In the general construct case, the key is made from a possible output of the agent's code. Decryption takes place at a host if and only if executing the agent at that host generates the required output.

Environmental key generation is a preventive approach for protecting the integrity and privacy of both code and state. The protection is achieved by encrypting the confidential parts, which introduces space requirements for storing the encryption and time requirements for the interactive decryption scheme.

Monitoring State Transitions

Two types of agent-replay attacks are identified by Yee (2003): internal replay, where a host re-executes an agent; and external replay, where two or more hosts send an agent back and forth among themselves. In the absence of secure hardware, internal replays are hard to detect since a host can always rerun the agent. Monitoring one-way state transitions is used to detect external replays. Internal replays are identified as follows: one-way transitions of an agent's state are identified and a monotonic bit per one-way transition is created. Whenever one of these transitions is encountered, the corresponding bit is set. If the agent is replayed, one of these transitions will be revisited eventually, signaling a replay attack. By monitoring the state transitions, some state-modification attacks can be detected as well. For the approach to work, an honest host must exist between the malicious ones. The approach can be implemented on each host or on a trusted third party (TTP).

Monitoring state transitions detects state-integrity attacks. The technique do not require substantial time and space to operate. Both are publicly-verifiable and helpful in protecting a host from tampered agents. The technique can also detect external replay attacks. The technique targets attacks which result in illegal state transitions. Attacks which do not exhibit such characteristics will go undetected.

Proxy Signatures

Owners may delegate signing messages to their agents using proxy signatures. Security requirements regarding proxy signatures include non-repudiation, unforgeability, and prevention of signature misuse. A strong proxy signature guarantees non-repudiation for both owners and hosts (strong non-repudiation). An example scheme based on RSA is introduced by Lee, Kim & Kim (2001). Strong non-repudiation is achieved by adding the host's signature to the signed transaction. The scheme, however, gives agents the capability of signing any message, permitting agents to abuse signatures.

Bamasak & Zhang (2004) describe another scheme that prevents an agent from having the full knowledge of its owner's proxy key. The owner divides the proxy key into two shares; one for the agent and the other for a TTP. Signing any message requires both shares. The scheme prevents the agent from intentionally or accidentally misusing the proxy key.

Strong proxy signatures prevent agents and hosts from repudiating their responsibilities after signing a transaction. The confidentiality of the owner's private key is maintained. Verifying the signatures can be performed by anyone (public verifiability). The approach does not address forward integrity. Another limitation is the time needed for signing the transactions.

Reference States and Protective Assertions

A reference state (Hohl, 2000) is a state an agent reaches when executing at an honest host based on a specific input. To detect the attacks of a malicious host, an owner measures the difference between the state of its agent at that host and the corresponding reference state. The technique depends on three attributes: the moment at which the state is checked, which could be after each host or after the agent returns; environmental conditions utilized in checking (e.g., input, host resources); and the checking algorithm (e.g., rule-based, agent re-execution). Checking after each host results in performance overhead, while storing the state information after each host and delaying checking incurs bandwidth overhead. The more complex the checking algorithm, the more attacks detected, but with additional performance overhead. An example agent application is provided along with the associated overhead of implementing reference states protection.

Protective assertions (Kassab & Voas, 1998) detect state-modification attacks. Assertions are embedded in an agent's code to test the state and return test results to the owner. The technique is performed as follows. By means of fault injection, weak parts of an agent's code are identified. Protective assertions are inserted in these parts to test the state of both the agent and the execution environment. The agent is then compiled and dispatched. The owner implements a mapping function that decides whether given assertion results are acceptable or malicious. The authors present a tool that facilitates the specification and insertion of assertions into Java bytecode. The results of the protective assertions at each host are collected and sent back to the owner for analysis. The absence of such results signifies the removal of assertions by the host or that the agent has been killed. Bandwidth overhead is a limitation for this technique.

Reference states and protective assertions are detective techniques focusing on state integrity attacks. Some code-integrity attacks affect the state, and so can be detected as well. Reference states and protective assertions also consume bandwidth by transmitting state information. Both techniques help to protect future hosts.

Set Authentication Codes

Set authentication codes presented by Loureiro, Molva & Pannetrat (2001) allow hosts to update collected results without hindering integrity. This is a useful feature in commercial settings, like auctions, where hosts wish to increase their bids. The key idea is to deal with the partial results as a cyclic group rather than an ordered list and to define a set integrity function for that group. The approach requires each host to share a secret key with the owner. When a host receives an agent for the first time, it generates an integrity proof using the offer and the secret key. The collection of integrity proofs is passed to the set integrity function to produce an authentication code. To update its offer, a host uses its key and the new offer to generate a new integrity proof. The host submits the proof and the updated offer to the agent. The agent then updates the set authentication code using the integrity function. The verification process is performed at the owner by analyzing the cyclic group properties.

Set authentication codes are modified in (Gunupudi & Tate, 2004). Hosts no longer need to set up a symmetric key with the owner beforehand, but use keys generated when receiving the agent. The generated keys are encrypted with the owner public key and embedded in the agent.

MAS SECURITY THROUGH COLLABORATION

This section presents the collaborative security techniques and the conditions satisfied by each technique. Recall that these techniques satisfy two or more conditions of collaboration.

Path and History-Based Trust

Any host on an agent's path could render a trusted agent malicious. One approach to establishing trust is to verify the trustworthiness of an agent's previous hosts. Checking the authenticity of hosts on an agent's itinerary is proposed in (Ordille, 1996). All hosts add their signatures to the agent; and therefore, each host can authenticate all previous ones. This is useful when a host does not trust the authentication procedure of its predecessors.

Edjlali, Acharya & Chaudhary (1998) present a history-based access control method that uses mobile agent behavior at previous hosts to determine the access rights to be given to that agent at the current host. This increases the set of rights that can be given to a mobile agent without endangering the security of the host.

Path and history-based approaches, however, are costly when the number of hosts on the agent's path is large. Extra space is required to store the signatures and behavioral information, and more time is needed to verify them by future hosts. Preventing one host from discarding the information of a previous host is not addressed.

Collaboration. Each host passes its identity and a description of the agent behavior to the next host, conditions 1 and 4.

Co-Signing Host Results

Karjoth et al. (1999) protocols achieve protection of a host's results by including the identities of the predecessor and successor hosts in the signed results. The protocols however are vulnerable to collusion attacks, where two or more hosts collaborate to discard agent results of other hosts or add fake results.

Cheng & Wei (2002) extends the protocols of (Karjoth et al., 1999). The extension considers the results of any host as invalid, unless it is signed by that host and by its predecessor. Each host signs an initial version of the results and sends the agent to the predecessor. The predecessor verifies the initial signature, signs it and sends it back to that host. The host sings the results and sends the agent to the next host. The extension defends against collusion attacks where two malicious hosts conspire to attack an agent's results (two-colluder problem). This is because the first colluder will have to request its predecessor to sign its results twice, once before the attack and once after.

Another extension of Karjoth's et al. (1999) protocols appears in (Xu, Harn, Narasimhan & Luo, 2006). The extension is based on linking each host to its predecessor and its two successors. Here, each host signs an initial version of the results and sends the agent to the next host. The next host computes its initial version, the identity of the next host, and sends the agent back to the previous host. The previous host replaces its initial results with a confirmed one including the identities of the next two hosts, and sends the agent to the next host. The extension defends against collusion attacks, regardless of how many malicious hosts are colluding, as long as there are no adjacent malicious hosts.

The solutions of Cheng & Wei (2002) and Xu et al. (2006) are two examples where a non-collaborative technique (Karjoth et al., 1999) has been extended to utilize collaboration. Both extensions enhance security of the non-collaborative approach without adding significant cost.

Collaboration. Signing agent results at one host requires the collaboration of that host and the next one. Conditions 1 and 4 are satisfied by execution tracing. Extended execution tracing satisfy conditions 3 and 4.

Execution Tracing

In execution tracing (Vigna, 1998), an owner analyzes the traces generated by an agent's code at each host. A trace is a sequence of statement identifiers and their signatures. Two types of statements are described, white and black statements. White statements update state variables based on other variables, whereas black statements update variables based on a host input or resources. The technique requires each host to sign the trace generated by the black statements before sending an agent to the next host. The next host replies with a signed message to the current host. On suspicion, the owner may request the first host to submit the actual trace and the second host to submit the signed trace. The agent is re-executed to verify whether the signed trace matches the simulated one. If they match, the first host is considered honest and the owner repeats the steps for the second host and so on. Space and time overheads in signing and storing traces are disadvantages of this technique. The technique is in this section due to the requirement that each host must obtain a signature from the next host, which is one form of collaboration.

Execution tracing is extended by Tan & Moreau (2002) by introducing a TTP for the verification process. The TTP here are servers that accept mobile agents, simulate their executions, and compare the resulted traces to the traces received from hosts. The protocol starts by an owner sending an agent to the first host and to the first verification server. The agent is executed at the host and simulated at the server. Upon agent migration, the host sends the agent along with the trace to the server. The server verifies the agent's trace to detect attacks. If the agent has not been tampered with, the agent is sent to the second host and verification server. The approach eliminates the requirement of storing execution traces. In addition to detecting attacks immediately, servers prevent tampered agents from migrating to new hosts.

Execution tracing detects attacks on an agent's itinerary. The technique requires time for gathering traces, space for storing traces, and bandwidth for sending them to owners. Execution tracing can be extended to involve TTP for verifying traces. The extension does not require hosts to store the traces

anymore. TTP are chosen to reduce the bandwidth consumed when sending the traces. Since agents must migrate to a TTP before entering hosts, hosts are protected from malicious agents.

Collaboration. Each pair of consecutive hosts exchange signed messages of the agent from one side and a confirmation from the other side. Conditions 1 and 4.

Threshold-Based Signatures

In (Borselius, Mitchell & Wilson, 2001), the undetachable signature scheme of (Kotzanikolaou et al., 2000) is combined with a threshold signatures scheme, producing undetachable threshold signatures. A threshold signature permits different agents to carry different shares of a secret key. For an agent to sign a message in a k threshold setting, it must posse k of the total shares. The scheme prevents a corrupted agent or less than k corrupted agents to sign an illegal transaction.

Collaboration. k out of total number of agents must collaborate to sign a message/transaction on a user behalf. Conditions 2 and 4.

Agent Replication

Agent replication and voting, by Minsky, Van Renesse, Schneider & Stoller (1996), is a technique that divides the computation into stages, where each stage consists of several hosts running replicated agents. All agents in the same stage perform the same computation. At every host in $stage_i$, the agent is executed and a copy is sent to each host in $stage_{i+1}$. Each host in $stage_{i+1}$ carries out voting among the received agents and uses the agent with the majority votes as the basis for the computation. Since the majority can be obtained without examining all agents, a host needs not to wait for all agents' arrival to proceed. As long as the majority of the hosts in each stage are honest, the computation is reliable. Malicious hosts may collude by claiming to be in the final stage and affect the voting results. This problem is mitigated by using a threshold signature or an authentication scheme to prevent hosts from claiming a different stage level. Although the technique provides fault tolerance, it leads to performance overhead due to replication of the computations.

Collaboration. Voting on which agent and results to be passed from one stage to another is a form of collaboration. Conditions 2 and 4.

Agent Co-Operation

Co-operating agents (Roth, 1999) split the hosts to be visited into two disjoint sets. An owner sends two agents, one per set. The motivation behind this protocol is to minimize collusion between hosts. An agent's sensitive data are not accessible to its host without the co-operating agent's approval. This helps the owner to hold hosts responsible for their actions. Two applications are studied that utilize the approach: protecting itineraries of mobile agents, and securing electronic transactions. In the first application, each agent records the actual itinerary of the other agent and compares it to the initial one. Hosts preventing agents from visiting competitors or truncating partial results can be detected. In the second application, the offers of a host to an agent are sent to the other agent. Making copies of offers prevents malicious hosts from repudiation.

Agent replication and co-operating agents utilize fault-tolerance concepts to enhance the reliability of mobile agents. By comparing the agents from a previous stage, server replication discards agents that have been, potentially, tampered with. This mitigates the problem of many code, state, and result-integrity attacks. Sometimes, this holds even in case of collusion. Cooperating agents can be used to protect the itinerary as well as the result integrity. Collusion can be also detected if the conspiring hosts belong to different groups. Bandwidth and time needed for the two approaches may become prohibitive.

Collaboration. Copies of the same agent collaborate to detect attacks by malicious hosts. Conditions 2 and 4.

DISCUSSION

This section evaluates the techniques in a tabular format. For clarity of comparison, we maintain the categorization used to group the techniques in the survey sections, the previous three sections. Table 3, 4, and 5 evaluate the non-collaborative techniques, the partially-collaborative techniques,

Table 2. Abbreviations used in Table 3, 4, and 5

Abbreviation	Meaning	Abbreviation	Meaning
CI	Code integrity	II	Itinerary integrity
CP	Code privacy	IP	Itinerary privacy
SI	State integrity	RI	Results integrity
SP	State privacy	RP	Results privacy
FI	Forward integrity	CD	Collusion detection
NR	Non-repudiation	FP	Forward privacy
FT	Fault tolerant	PV	Public verifiability
AC	Access control	AU	Authentication
LE	Logging events	ID	Intrusion detection
EI	Ease of integration	HAP	Host / agent protection
FG	Fine granularity	DoS	Denial of service

Table 3. Evaluation of non-collaborative techniques

Technique	Complexity	Coverage	Detective/ preventive	Features
Code signatures	time, space	AU, CI, CP, SI, SP	preventive, detective	
State appraisal	space	SI, AC, PV	preventive,detective	HAP
Type checking and PCC	time	AC	preventive	
Sandboxing and safe interpreters	time	AC	preventive	FG
Rewriting agent code and policy enforcement	time	AC, ID	preventive	FG
Itinerary protection	time, space	SI, SP, II, IP, FP, CD	preventive	
PRAC	time, space	RI, RP, FI, PV, NR	detective	
KAG	time, space	RI, RP, FI, PV, NR	detective	
Append only containers	time, space	RI, RP, FI, NR	detective	
CEF and Code obfuscation	time, space	CI, CP, SI, SP, RI, RP	preventive	
Undetachable signatures	time	NR	preventive	
Software fingerprinting	time	CI, SI, CD	detective	
Secure hardware	physical	CI, CP, SI, SP, RP, RI, FI	preventive, preventive	HAP

Table 4. Evaluation of partial-collaborative techniques

Technique	Complexity	Coverage	Detective/ preventive	Features
Environmental key generation	time, space	CI, CP, SI, SP	preventive	
Monitoring state transitions	time	SI, PV	preventive detective	HAP
Strong proxy signatures	time	PV, NR	preventive preventive	HAP
Reference states	bandwidth	CI, SI, DoS	detective	HAP
Protective assertions	bandwidth	CI, SI, DoS	preventive detective	HAP
Set authentication code	time, space	RI, RP, FI, PV, NR	detective	

Table 5. Evaluation of collaborative techniques

Technique	Complexity	Coverage	Detective/ Preventive	Features
Path and history-based trust	space, bandwidth	AC	preventive	
Co-signing host results	time, space	CD, RI, RP, FI, PV, NR	detective	
Agent replication	time, bandwidth	CI, SI, RI, CD	preventive detective	HAP, FT
Co-operating agents	time, bandwidth	RI, II, CD	preventive detective	HAP, FT
Threshold-based signatures	time, bandwidth	NR	preventive	
Execution tracing	time, space, bandwidth	SI, II, CI, LE	detective	
Extended execution tracing	time, space, bandwidth	SI, II, CI, PV, LE	preventive detective	HAP

and the collaborative techniques respectively. Abbreviations used in the comparison tables are listed in Table 2. Then, the open problems are outlined. Finally, some important collaboration-related issues are discussed.

Current and future research in the area of securing MAS includes the integration of these techniques to cover more security requirements in a single framework. For example, one can integrate a technique protecting partial results, such as PRAC, with a technique detecting state attacks, such as state appraisal. Non-cryptographic means are needed to minimize space and time requirements. For instance, error-correcting codes from coding theory have been used to implement an alternative to computing with encrypted functions. In addition, the use of TTPs is attracting research. Many of the existing techniques adopt or have been extended to include TTP. Policy frameworks, moreover, are potential candidates in this field since they provide protection for hosts as well as agents. Furthermore, these frameworks allow the separation of security policies from agent code, which is a valuable feature. Collusion attacks, where many malicious hosts conspire to attack an agent, are a major subject which requires careful attention. Although they are addressed by many techniques, almost all of them fail to completely mitigate this problem for free-roaming agents.

Motivation and Benefits of Collaboration

Due to the nature of mobile agents, securing MAS is a challenging task. In MAS, there are mobile agents roaming among hosts. Executing a mobile agent at a host generates a piece of information. Sharing such information with other agents and hosts is useful in the context of security. Moreover, allowing hosts/agents to cooperate enhances security (e.g., co-signing results). This has motivated the use of collaboration to secure MAS.

It is worth mentioning that the majority of the techniques are non-collaborative. Collaboration

of entities to achieve security, however, has a bigger potential. There are many benefits gained when collaboration is used to ensure the security of MAS. The benefits can be grouped in three aspects. Collaborative security:

1. *Solves new problems.* Collaboration helps implementing security requirements unachieved by non-collaborative techniques. For example, the problem of collusion attacks to discard agent results is solved by co-signing the results.

2. *Enhance previous solutions.* Collaboration helps solving problems already solved, but more efficiently. For instance, monitoring state transitions is more efficient than state appraisal.

3. *Adds more features.* Collaboration adds extra features to a security technique. Fault tolerance is achieved by agent replication.

There are several occasions where partial-collaboration or collaboration yielded solutions to problems never solved before. Co-signing an agent detects collusion attacks against agent's results. Co-operating agents and agent replication detect collusion attacks against agents' code and state. Non-collaborative techniques fail to secure agents against such attacks. Threshold-based signatures combined with undetachable signatures prevent corrupted mobile agents from signing transactions. Non-collaborative techniques do not prevent such signing. Protective assertions and reference states detect denial of service and other attacks against agents in real time.

Collaboration could be used to solve problems more efficiently. For example, history-based trust allows agents from less trusted sources to be trusted based on their behavior at previous hosts. This is useful for situations where a host does not know the agent producer, yet wants to allow the agent to execute. The more sound behavior the agent exhibits at previous hosts, the more trusted it becomes at future hosts. This technique is more efficient than rewriting the agent's code or prohibiting the agent from most of its requested resources. Another example is monitoring state. This technique is more efficient than state appraisal, since state appraisal require executing appraisal functions rather than just monitoring state transitions.

Collaboration can add benefits like fault tolerance. This feature is present in the co-operating agents and agent replication techniques. None of the non-collaborative techniques support this useful feature. Another benefit is the protection of both agents and hosts. Most of non-collaborative techniques do not have this feature.

Few techniques utilize collaboration, but as shown above, collaboration is a promising strategy in securing MAS. There are many opportunities to find suitable techniques to be extended for collaborative security.

Costs and Challenges of Collaboration

These benefits of collaboration are, however, accompanied with several costs and challenges. The costs and challenges can be summarized in these three points:

1. *Complexity overhead.* When different entities collaborate, bandwidth, space and time complexity increases due to added communications.
2. *Privacy concerns.* Collaboration implies sharing information which may be confidential to some entities. This raises privacy concerns over collaborative security techniques.
3. *Trust management.* Before entities collaborate they must decide whether they trust each other or not. One cost of collaboration is defining and managing trust.

Collaboration leads in many cases to extra complexity in terms of time, space, and band-

width. Co-operating agents and agent replication techniques are the most affected by this cost due to the replication of computations required by the techniques. Execution and extended execution tracing require the transfer the tracing information from hosts to verifiers, which incurs a significant complexity costs. Protective assertions and reference states requires the agent's owner to be online throughout the life time of the agent. This requirement contradicts with the expectation that mobile agents can be used without keeping the connections with their owners alive. Introducing a TTP solves this problem, but adds the complexity of having TTPs.

In history-based trust, the actions of a mobile agent at one host are disclosed to future hosts. This violates the privacy of the agent's owner. Collaboration requires collaborators to reveal their identities. That is another violation of privacy. The privacy concerns also exist in non-collaborative techniques too. For example, rewriting code means violating code integrity.

Whenever an entity wants to collaborate with another, it must ensure the trustworthy of the other entity. Managing who and how to trust is a challenge that collaborative techniques must deal with. Again, this problem is not exclusive to collaboration. Code signatures and state appraisal are based on trusting the entity producing the code signature. Managing the trust in collaboration should be similar to the case of no collaboration.

Should we use Collaboration?

By looking at the benefits and costs of collaboration, we find examples where collaboration greatly enhanced security with minimum costs. An example is co-signing agent results. Similarly, collaboration could incur costs that raise questions about the feasibility of collaboration. For instance, the space, time, and bandwidth consumed by execution tracing and extended execution tracing may become infeasible for some applications.

To answer the raised question, we note the following. The costs of collaboration are justifiable for security critical applications. Moreover, the potential of reducing the costs and risks of collaboration appears is more likely than solving hard security problems with non-collaborative techniques. Collaboration has been used in other fields, where the costs and risks of collaboration have been widely studied. We can make use of such studies. Therefore, we believe it is a good investment to study and use collaboration in securing MAS.

CONCLUSION

The field of securing MAS has been extensively researched, but it is far from complete. This is due to the difficulty introduced by the mobility and self-containment of mobile agents. On the one hand, malicious agents may violate privacy, attack integrity, and monopolize hosts' resources. On the other hand, malicious hosts may manipulate agents' memory, return wrong results from system calls, and deny access to necessary resources.

In this chapter, the techniques securing MAS are categorized, studied, and compared. The degree of collaboration used to achieve security is the basis of the categorization. This way of categorizing the techniques sets this survey apart from other surveys in the literature, where categorization is on the basis of the entities protected and the underlying methodologies used for protection. The survey sheds the light on the benefits and challenges of using collaboration to achieve better security.

The survey is in three sections. The first section presents techniques taking a non-collaborative approach for security. Partially-collaborative techniques are studied in the second section. Third section shows the collaborative techniques and elaborates on the implications and challenges of the collaboration. The survey also points out strengths and weaknesses of the techniques and presents open problems for further research.

It is worth mentioning that the majority of the techniques are non-collaborative. Collaborative techniques, generally, are easier to implement and deploy. They are also suitable for protecting the agent as well as hosts. The main disadvantage of collaboration is the bandwidth complexity associated with the interaction of different entities in MAS. Techniques that minimize the extra bandwidth consumed due to collaboration are needed to justify the feasibility. We believe that more research is needed to utilize collaboration in designing security techniques.

REFERENCES

Amme, W., Dalton, N., Von Ronne, J., & Franz, M. (2001). SafeTSA: A type safe and referentially secure mobile-code representation based on static single assignment form. In *Proceedings of the ACM Conference on Programming Language Design and Implementation* (pp. 137-147). New York: ACM Press.

Bamasak, O., & Zhang, N. (2004). A secure method for signature delegation to mobile agents. In *Proceedings of the ACM Symposium on Applied computing* (pp. 813-818). New York: ACM Press.

Bellavista, P., Corradi, A., Federici, C., Montanari, R., & Tibaldi, D. (2004). Security for mobile agents: Issues and challenges. In I. Mahgoub & M. Ilyas (Eds.), *Handbook of Mobile Computing* (pp. 941-959). Boca Raton, FL: CRC Press.

Bellifemine, F., Caire, G., Poggi, A., & Rimassa, G. (2003). *JADE: A white paper.* Retrieved Jan 2008, from http://jade.tilab.com/papers/2003/WhitePaperJADEEXP.pdf

Berkovits, S., Guttman, J. D., & Swarup, V. (1998). Authentication for mobile agents. In G. Vigna (Ed.), *Mobile Agents and Security* (pp. 114-136). Berlin, Germany: Springer-Verlag.

Borselius, N. (2002). Mobile agent security. *Electronics and Communication Engineering Journal*, *14*(5), 211–218. doi:10.1049/ecej:20020504

Borselius, N., Mitchell, C. J., & Wilson, A. (2001). Undetachable threshold signatures. In B. Honary (Ed.), *Proceedings of the 8th IMA International Conference on Cryptography and Coding* (pp. 239-244). Berlin, Germany; Springer-Verlag.

Cabri, G., Ferrari, L., & Leonardi, L. (2006). Applying security policies through agent roles: A JAAS based approach. *Science of Computer Programming*, *59*(1-2), 127–146. doi:10.1016/j.scico.2005.07.008

Castillo, A., Kawaguchi, M., Paciorek, N., & Wong, D. (1998). Concordia as enabling technology for cooperative information gathering. In *Proceedings of the Japanese Society for Artificial Intelligence Conference*. Retrieved May 2007, from http://www.merl.com/projects/concordia/WWW/JSAI98.htm

Chander, A., Mitchell, J. C., & Shin, I. (2001). Mobile code security by Java bytecode instrumentation. In *Proceedings of the DARPA Information Survivability Conference and Exposition* (pp. 27-40). Washington, DC: IEEE Computer Society.

Cheng, J. S. L., & Wei, V. K. (2002). Defenses against the truncation of computation results of free-roaming agents. In *Proceedings of the 4th International Conference on Information and Communications Security* (pp. 1-12). Berlin, Germany: Springer-Verlag.

Claessens, J., Preneel, B., & Vandewalle, J. (2003). How can mobile agents do secure electronic transactions on untrusted hosts? A survey of the security issues and the current solutions. *ACM Transactions on Internet Technology*, *3*(1), 28–48. doi:10.1145/643477.643479

Czajkowski, G., & Von Eicken, T. (1998). JRes: A resource accounting interface for Java. In *Proceedings of the 13th ACM Conference on Object-Oriented Programming, Systems, Languages, and Applications* (pp. 21-35). New York: ACM Press.

Das, S., Shuster, K., Wu, C., & Levit, I. (2005). Mobile agents for distributed and heterogeneous information retrieval. *Information Retrieval*, *8*(3), 383–416. doi:10.1007/s10791-005-6992-6

Edjlali, G., Acharya, A., & Chaudhary, V. (1998). History-based access control for mobile code. In *Proceedings of the the 5th ACM Conference on Computer and Communications Security* (pp. 38-48). New York: ACM Press.

Esparza, O., Fernandez, M., Soriano, M., Mucoz, J. L., & Forné, J. (2003). Mobile agent watermarking and fingerprinting: Tracing malicious hosts. In V. Marík, W. Retschitzegger, & O. Stepánková (Eds.), *Proceedings of the International Conference Database and Expert Systems Applications* (pp. 927-936). Berlin, Germany: Springer-Verlag.

Gedrojc, B., Cartrysse, K., & Van Der Lubbe, J. C. (2006). Private bidding for mobile agents. In M. Malek, E. Fernández-Medina, & J. Hernando (Eds.), *Proceedings of the International Conference on Security and Cryptography* (pp. 277-282). Setubal, Portugal: INSTICC Press.

Ghanea-Hercock, R., Collis, J. C., & Ndumu, D. T. (1999). Co-operating mobile agents for distributed parallel processing. In *Proceedings of the Third Annual Conference on Autonomous Agents* (pp. 398-399). New York: ACM Press.

Gong, L., Mueller, M., Prafullchandra, H., & Schemers, R. (1997). Going beyond the sandbox: An overview of the new security architecture in the Java development kit 1.2. In *Proceedings of the 1st Usenix Symposium on Internet Technologies and Systems* (pp. 103-112). Berkley, CA: USENIX.

Gong, L., & Schemers, R. (1998). Signing, sealing, and guarding java objects. In G. Vigna (Ed.), *Mobile Agents and Security* (pp. 206-216). Berlin, Germany: Springer-Verlag.

Gray, R. S., Cybenko, G., Kotz, D., Peterson, R. A., & Rus, D. (2002). D'Agents: Applications and performance of a mobile-agent system. *Software, Practice & Experience, 32*(6), 543–573. doi:10.1002/spe.449

Gunupudi, V., & Tate, S. R. (2004). Performance evaluation of data integrity mechanisms for mobile agents. In *Proceedings of the International Conference on Information Technology: Coding and Computing* (pp. 62-69). Washington, DC: IEEE Computer Society.

Guttman, R. H., Moukas, A., & Maes, P. (1998). Agents as mediators in electronic commerce. *Electronic Markets, 8*(1). doi:10.1080/10196789800000007

Hohl, F. (1998). Time limited blackbox security: Protecting mobile agents from malicious hosts. In G. Vigna (Eds.), *Mobile Agents and Security* (pp. 92-113). Berlin, Germany; Springer-Verlag.

Hohl, F. (2000). A framework to protect mobile agents by using reference states. In *Proceedings of the 20th International Conference on Distributed Computing Systems* (pp. 410-417). Washington, DC: IEEE Computer Society.

Hopwood, D. (1997). *Comparison between Java and ActiveX Security*. Retrieved June 2007, from http://www.users.zetnet.co.uk/hopwood/papers/compsec97.html

Huang, F., & Skillicorn, D. (2001). The Spider model of agents. In *Proceedings of the Third International Workshop on Mobile Agents for Telecommunication Applications* (pp. 209-218). Berlin, Germany: Springer-Verlag.

Huang, F. Y., Jay, C. B., & Skillicorn, D. B. (2006). Adaptiveness in well-typed Java bytecode verification. In *Proceedings of the 2006 Conference of the Center for Advanced Studies on Collaborative Research* (pp. 248-262). New York: ACM Press.

Jansen, W., & Karygiannis, T. (2000). *NIST special publication 800-19 - mobile agent security*. Gaithersburg, MD: NIST, Computer Security Division.

Jennings, N. R., & Wooldridge, M. J. (1998). Applications of intelligent agents. In N. R. Jennings & M. J. Wooldridge (Eds.), *Agent Technology: Foundations, Applications, and Markets* (pp. 3-28). Berlin, Germany: Springer-Verlag.

Karjoth, G., Asokan, N., & Gülcü, C. (1999). Protecting the computation results of free-roaming agents. In K. Rothermel & F. Hohl (Ed.), In *Proceedings of the Workshop on Mobile Agents* (pp. 195-207). Berlin, Germany: Springer-Verlag.

Karnik, N. M., & Tripathi, A. R. (2000). A security architecture for mobile agents in Ajanta. In *Proceedings of the 20th International Conference on Distributed Computing Systems* (pp. 402-409). Washington, DC: IEEE Computer Society.

Kassab, L., & Voas, J. M. (1998). Agent trustworthiness. In *Proceedings of the Workshop on Distributed Object Security and 4th Workshop on Mobile Object Systems Secure Internet Mobile Computations* (pp. 300). Berlin, Germany: Springer-Verlag.

Kotzanikolaou, P., Burmester, M., & Chrissikopoulos, V. (2000). Secure transactions with mobile agents in hostile environments. In E. Dawson, A. Clark, & C. Boyd (Eds.), *Proceedings of the 5th Australasian Conference on Information Security and Privacy* (pp. 289-297). Berlin, Germany: Springer-Verlag.

Lange, D. B., & Oshima, M. (1998). Mobile agents with Java: The Aglet API. *World Wide Web (Bussum), 1*(3), 111–121. doi:10.1023/A:1019267832048

League, C., Shao, Z., & Trifonov, V. (2003). Precision in practice: A type-preserving Java compiler. In *Proceedings of the International Conference on Compiler Construction* (pp. 106-120). Berlin, Germany: Springer-Verlag.

Lee, B., Kim, H., & Kim, K. (2001). Secure mobile agent using strong non-designated proxy signature. In *Proceedings of the Australasian Conference on Information Security and Privacy* (pp. 474-486). Berlin, Germany: Springer-Verlag.

Leroy, X. (2001). Java bytecode verification: An overview. In G. Berry, H. Comon, & A. Finkel (Eds.), *Proceedings of Computer Aided Verification* (pp. 265-285). Berlin, Germany: Springer-Verlag.

Loureiro, S., & Molva, R. (1999). Function hiding based on error correcting codes. In M. Blum & C. H. Lee (Eds.), *Proceedings of the International Workshop on Cryptographic Techniques and E-Commerce* (pp. 92-98). Hong Kong: City University of Hong-Kong.

Loureiro, S., Molva, R., & Pannetrat, A. (2001). Secure data collection with updates. *Electronic Commerce Research, 1*(1-2), 119–130. doi:10.1023/A:1011527713457

Maes, P., Guttman, R. H., & Moukas, A. G. (1999). Agents that buy and sell. *Communications of the ACM, 42*(3), 81–91. doi:10.1145/295685.295716

McDonald, J. T. (2006). *Enhanced security for mobile agent systems*. Florida State University, Tallahassee, FL. Retrieved August 2007, from http://www.cs.fsu.edu/research/dissertations/JTM.pdf

Minsky, Y., van Renesse, R., Schneider, F. B., & Stoller, S. D. (1996). Cryptographic support for fault-tolerant distributed computing. In *Proceedings of the ACM European Workshop on Systems Support for Worldwide Applications* (pp. 109-114). New York: ACM Press.

Morrisett, G., Walker, D., Crary, K., & Glew, N. (1999). From system F to typed assembly language. *ACM Transactions on Programming Languages and Systems, 21*(3), 527–568. doi:10.1145/319301.319345

Necula, G. C. (1997). Proof-carrying code. In *Proceedings of the 24th ACM symposium on Principles of programming language* (pp. 106-119). New York: ACM Press.

Necula, G. C., & Lee, P. (1998). The design and implementation of a certifying compiler. In *Proceedings of the ACM Conference on Programming Language Design and Implementation* (pp. 333-344). New York: ACM Press.

Ordille, J. J. *(1996). When agents roam, who can you trust? In Proceedings of the First Conference on Emerging Technologies and Applications in Communications* (pp. 188-191). Washington, DC: IEEE Computer Society.

Ousterhout, J. K., Levy, J. Y., & Welch, B. B. (1998). The Safe-Tcl security model. In G. Vigna (Eds.), *Mobile Agents and Security* (pp. 217-234). Berlin, Germany: Springer-Verlag.

Pham, V., & Karmouch, A. (1998). Mobile software agents: An overview. *IEEE Communications Magazine, 36*(7), 26–37. doi:10.1109/35.689628

Pleisch, S., & Schiper, A. (2004). Approaches to fault-tolerant and transactional mobile agent execution: an algorithmic view. *ACM Computing Surveys, 36*(3), 219–262. doi:10.1145/1035570.1035571

Recursion Software. (2006). *VOYAGER Edge User's guide*. Retrieved June 2007, from http://www.recursionsw.com/Products/voyager.html

Reed, M. G., Syverson, P. F., & Goldschlag, D. M. (1998). Anonymous connections and onion routing. *IEEE Journal on Selected Areas in Communications, 16*(4), 482–494. doi:10.1109/49.668972

Riordan, J., & Schneier, B. (1998). Environmental key generation towards clueless agents. In G. Vigna (Ed.), *Mobile Agents and Security* (pp. 15-24). Berlin, Germany: Springer-Verlag.

Roth, V. (1999). Mutual protection of co-operating agents. In J. Vitek & C. D. Jensen (Eds.), *Secure Internet Programming: Security Issues for Mobile and Distributed Objects* (pp. 275-285). Berlin, Germany: Springer-Verlag.

Sander, T., & Tschudin, C. F. (1998). Protecting mobile agents against malicious hosts. In G. Vigna (Ed.), *Mobile Agents and Security* (pp. 44-60). Berlin, Germany: Springer-Verlag.

Schneider, F. B. (2000). Enforceable security policies. *ACM Transactions on Information and System Security*, 3(1), 30–50. doi:10.1145/353323.353382

Sekar, R., Venkatakrishnan, V., Basu, S., Bhatkar, S., & DuVarney, D. C. (2003). Model-carrying code: A practical approach for safe execution of untrusted applications. In *Proceedings of the 19th ACM Symposium on Operating Systems Principles* (pp. 15-28). New York: ACM Press.

Tan, H., & Moreau, L. (2002). Extending execution tracing for mobile code security. *Proceedings of the International Workshop on Security of Mobile MultiAgent Systems* (pp. 51-59), German AI Research Center (DFKI) Research Report: RR-02-03.

Tardo, J., & Valente, L. (1996). Mobile agent security and telescript. In *Proceedings of the 41st IEEE International Computer Conference* (pp. 58-63). Washington, DC: IEEE Computer Society.

Uszok, A., Bradshaw, J., Jeffers, R., Suri, N., Hayes, P., Breedy, M., et al. (2003). KAoS policy and domain services: toward a description-logic approach to policy representation, deconfliction, and enforcement. In *Proceedings of the International Workshop on Policies for Distributed Systems and Networks* (pp. 93-96). Washington, DC: IEEE Computer Society.

Vigna, G. (1998). Cryptographic traces for mobile agents. In G. Vigna, (Ed.), *Mobile Agents and Security* (pp. 137-153). Berlin, Germany: Springer-Verlag.

Vigna, G. (2004). Mobile agents: Ten reasons for failure. In *Proceedings of the Mobile Data Management* (pp. 298-299). Washington, DC: IEEE Computer Society.

Walker, D. (2000). A type system for expressive security policies. In *Proceedings of the 27th ACM Symposium on Principles of Programming Languages* (pp. 254-267). New York: ACM Press.

Westhoff, D., Schneider, M., Unger, C., & Kaderali, F. (1999). Protecting a mobile agent's route against Collusions. In *Proceedings of the 6th Annual International Workshop on Selected Areas in Cryptography* (pp. 215-225). Berlin, Germany: Springer-Verlag.

White, J. (1994). *Mobile agents white paper*. Retrieved May 2007, from http://www.cs.cmu.edu/~rwh/courses/mobile/Telescript/White-Telescript.ps

Wilhelm, U. G., Staamann, S., & Buttyán, L. (1998). On the problem of trust in mobile agent systems. In *Proceedings of the Network and Distributed System Security Symposium* (pp. 114-124). Reston, VA: The Internet Society.

Xu, D., Harn, L., Narasimhan, M., & Luo, J. (2006). An improved free-roaming mobile agent security protocol against colluded truncation attacks. In *Proceedings of the 30th Annual International Computer Software and Applications Conference* (pp. 309-314). Washington, DC: IEEE Computer Society.

Yee, B. (1997). *A sanctuary for mobile agents* (Tech. Rep. No. CS97-537). San Diego, CA: University of California at San Diego, Department of Computer Science and Engineering.

Yee, B. (2003). Monotonicity and partial results protection for mobile agents. In *Proceedings of the 23rd International Conference on Distributed Computing Systems* (pp. 582-591). Washington, DC: IEEE Computer Society.

Zachary, J. (2003). Protecting mobile code in the wild. *IEEE Internet Computing, 7*(2), 78–82. doi:10.1109/MIC.2003.1189192

Chapter 9
How Trust and Reputation–Based Collaboration Impact Wireless Sensor Network Security

Noria Foukia
University of Otago, New Zealand

Nathan Lewis
University of Otago, New Zealand

ABSTRACT

Like wired network security, wireless sensor network (WSN) security encompasses the typical network security requirements which are: confidentiality, integrity, authentication, non-repudiation and availability. At the same time, security for WSNs differs from traditional security designed for classical wired networks in many points because of the new constraints imposed by WSN technology. Many aspects are due to the limited resources (memory space, CPU ...) and infrastructure-less property of WSNs. Therefore traditional security mechanisms cannot be applied directly and WSNs are more prone to existing and new threats than traditional networks. Typical threats are the physical capture of sensor nodes, the service disruption due to the unreliable wireless communication. Parameters specific to WSN characteristics may help to reduce the effect of threats. Examples of existing measures are efficient WSN power management strategies that can dynamically adjust the node cycles (sleeping or awake mode) based on the current network workload or the use of redundant information to locally detect lying nodes. In addition to adjusting existing WSN characteristics that impact security, establishing trust and collaboration is essential in WSNs for many reasons such as the high distribution of sensor nodes or the goal-oriented nature of many sensing applications. This chapter emphasizes the need of collaboration between sensor nodes and shows that establishing trust between nodes and using reputation reported by collaborating nodes can help mitigate security issues.

DOI: 10.4018/978-1-60566-414-9.ch009

INTRODUCTION

Wireless Sensor Networks (WSNs) are getting popular due to the many advantages that they provide for a lot of application domains (military, healthcare, emergency and disaster ...). Mainly, WSNs are easy and fast to deploy in hostile environments and will not depend on pre-existing infrastructure (infrastructure-less nature of WSN). These properties considerably reduce the deployment cost of WSNs. Other characteristics make WSN technology attractive but at the same time more vulnerable than traditional wired network technology.

Security for WSN differs from traditional security designed for classical wired network in many points due to new constraints imposed by WSN technology. Therefore new solutions need to be implemented to provide WSN security or existing security solutions need to be adapted (Ng. H.S., Sim. M.L., & Tan. C.M., 2006: Karlof. C., & Wagner. D., 2003).

This chapter reviews threats targeted to WSNs. It briefly describes the components of a WSN and provides details on constraints imposed by WSN technology and their impact in WSN security.

Then, the chapter will focus on trust and reputation-based collaboration for WSN and its relation to security. The chapter finishes with a section about privacy issues in WSN before concluding.

DESCRIPTION OF A TYPICAL WIRELESS SENSOR NETWORK INFRASTRUCTURE

A Wireless Sensor Network (WSN) consists of spatially distributed autonomous nodes called sensors that monitor physical or environmental conditions, such as temperature or pressure at different locations (Römer. K., & Mattern. F., December 2004). They are used in a variety of applications, such as climate sensing and control in office buildings. A WSN is often composed of many (from a dozen to thousands) tiny sensors that are dispatched in an ad hoc way throughout a physical environment (house, battlefield) or inside the phenomenon to sense (human body). Each sensor is powered by a battery and collects data, such as temperature, pressure, heart rate, or other environmental data. Collected data is relayed to neighbor nodes and via the neighbor nodes to a destination node called the base station (BS) or sink (Karlof. C., & Wagner. D., 2003). At the BS, the data coming from several nodes is aggregated before being processed in order to provide the desired output corresponding to the phenomenon being sensed.

Components of a Sensor Node

A typical sensor node is composed of (Akyildiz. F., Su. W., Sankarasubramaniam. Y., & Cayirci. E., 2002):

- A sensing unit (or sensor) which is deployed either inside the phenomenon to be sensed or very close to it. This unit measures physical information about the event that it senses, such as pressure, light, heat, sound, etc.
- A microcontroller with a simple processing unit that is limited in terms of computations and memory. Therefore, sensor nodes often locally carry out simple computations and transmit partially processed data to special nodes called fusion nodes. A fusion node collects and combines data from several nodes and gathers that information with its own collected data before sending it to another node or to the BS.
- A transceiver that combines transmitting and receiving capabilities of the sensor node. The transceiver can also stop transmitting/receiving and switch to a sleeping mode.

- A source of energy or power unit, usually a battery.
- A sensor node may have additional components such as a clock.

Components of a WSN

A typical WSN is composed of:

- A set of sensor nodes.
- A base station (BS) or sink: This is a specific node of the WSN that has larger resources (computation and memory), more energy and greater communication capability than a singular sensor node. A BS is usually acting as an interface between the WSN and the end-user. It often provides a management capability for the WSN.
- Wireless communication between the sensor nodes in the same radio range and between the sensor nodes and the BS.
- Wired communication often between the BS and the end-user via a wired network.

Characteristics of A WSN

There are many characteristics that make WSN technology attractive to a wide range of applications but at the same time they introduce several resource and technological constraints. The main characteristics are listed below:

- **Limited resources:** Sensors have limited computational/processing power. These resources are used to run the sensors, process the gathered information and communicate the data to other nodes. Sensor nodes are also limited in terms of memory and storage capability.
- **Limited power supply:** In order to be operational a sensor needs energy supplied by a battery. In many case the limitation in terms of energy is the biggest constraint of a WSN. The sensor power is mainly used

for communication and a small part is left to sensing data and computation (data processing). Moreover, in many applications, changing or recharging the battery after deployment is normally not feasible for different reasons (economical or environmental). Several types of sensor nodes are designed with event-driven operating system (OS) such as TinyOS[1]; the OS reacts to external sensed events happening in order to trigger a task. This may save energy since the battery is not used when no event is sensed.

- **Limited radio range:** Sensor nodes are situated at short radio distance to each other and the data transmission from a sensor node to the BS is typically a multi-hop transmission. Short range multi-hop transmission also contributes to save energy, avoiding the effect of polynomial growth of energy consumption according to the radio range because less power is required to transmit over shorter distances.
- **Attractive Cost:** In order to make them more attractive, WSNs are designed with low cost which is mainly due to their limitations in terms of resource (memory and computation), communication and energy that we already mentioned. Often, they are designed in such a way because they may be lost. For instance, when a large number of nodes are remotely dispatched in hostile environments (earthquake or battlefield areas), they will stay unattended and may be lost or caught by an attacker. Moreover, they cannot be accessed to charge the battery when empty, which leads to the same result. Obviously, the potential loss of nodes has an effect on the WSN security because security capabilities, such as tamper-proof hardware are too expensive. Other factors that reduce the cost of sensor nodes are their small size and the infrastructure-less nature of WSNs. Small size

sensors are designed with less complex hardware which makes them cheaper and the absence of a fixed infrastructure considerably reduces the deployment cost of WSNs.

- **Changing network topology:** Due to nodes mobility, the nodes states (awake or sleep mode), the deployment of new sensor nodes, the WSN topology changes constantly in a dynamic way. Mobility is mainly due to the movement of the sensor nodes but the BS can also move. For instance, sensor nodes can be dispatched from an aircraft transporting the BS in battlefield areas.

Security for Sensor Network

Like wired networks, WSN security encompasses the typical network security requirements which are: confidentiality, integrity, authentication, non-repudiation and availability[2].

- Confidentiality ensures that information is not passed to unauthorized entities (nodes, persons); in WSNs this means that sensor nodes should not disclose data that they read from the sensed phenomenon or data that they transfer through the wireless medium (Carman. D. W., Krus. P. S., & Matt. B. J., 2000).
- Integrity guarantees that a message is transferred without being altered or corrupted during the transfer; in WSNs threats targeted on integrity may be due to actual attacks altering the content of a sensor reading. Lack of integrity can also come from sensing channel inconsistencies.
- Authentication ensures that an entity (sender) is the entity it claims to be; in WSNs this means that a receiver node (BS or another node) needs to ensure that the data is originating from a correct trusted node and not from a malicious node.

- Non-repudiation ensures that a sender cannot deny having sent the data.
- Availability ensures that the system is operational and the services and information are accessible at any required moment; in WSNs examples of lack of availability are a sensor node captured by an attacker or a Denial of Service (DoS)[3].

Some sensor applications have imperative security requirements. For instance, integrity and availability are crucial for many critical real-time applications like those in the healthcare sector. Some security requirements are not required for some type of applications. For instance, confidentiality may not be necessary for applications measuring environmental conditions such as temperature or atmospheric pressure.

Several characteristics listed in the previous section represent an obstacle to designing WSN security that differs from security in traditional wired network. Many aspects are due to the limited resources (memory space, CPU …) and infrastructure-less property of WSNs. Almost all the aforementioned characteristics of a WSN may have an impact on security and on the necessity to adapt traditional solutions. This is particularly desirable because in a lot of application domains, sensor networks constitute a mission critical component requiring high security protection. Examples of mission critical applications are battlefield reconnaissance and earthquake surveillance.

WSN Characteristics that Impact Security

- Power limitation: Typical sensor nodes are powered by battery. When remotely deployed in an environment such as a battlefield or any other hostile environments, they cannot be easily accessed to charge or replace the battery. The current load of the battery power affects security for many reasons: Added processing of security functions (encryption algorithms), communication overhead due to larger messages exchange (ciphered data), new added messages (initialization data, encryption keys), and extra power for data storage (encryption keys). Therefore, maximizing the battery life time is a very important design feature that impacts the WSN security.

- Computation limitation has an effect on the code size that can be implemented and added to secure the sensor nodes. That means that greedy operations such as strong public key cryptography like RSA[4] algorithm usually used for classical wired networks cannot be implemented in the same way and must be replaced by lightweight implementations of public key cryptography. Even lightweight implementations of public key cryptography algorithms are particularly prohibitive since as previously said, the computation is also limited by the power limitation. Instead, symmetric encryption algorithms are preferred to cipher sensor nodes' communication, since they do not have as demanding computation as public key algorithms.

- Storage limitation: Sensor nodes have limited storage capability. Therefore, storing too many encryption keys is also prohibitive. At the opposite, limiting the key storage by sharing a minimum number of keys between nodes may be dangerous since if one key is compromised many nodes will be compromised. The code implemented and stored for providing the security primitives must also be small due to this storage limitation (Walters. J.P., Liang. Z., Shi. W., & Chaudhary. V., 2006).

- Cost: The design of cheap hardware makes sensor nodes prone to failures and easy to compromise. Expensive capabilities like tamper-proof hardware are not affordable and sensor nodes are often not designed with such capabilities.

- Proximity with the environment: One of the characteristics specific to sensor nodes is their strong immersion in the physical environment. Nothing prevents an intruder from introducing false data into the environment to compromise a node.

- Distribution and scalability: Highly distributed sensor nodes may pose scalability issues. Even when deployed in small areas WSNs can be composed of a large number of nodes depending on the application and the sensor cost. Scalability and distribution properties may impact the design choices of WSN security; for instance, pair wise distribution of keys should be limited to a small number of sensor nodes since it is not scalable as the number of nodes increase in the WSN (Avancha. S., Undercoffer. J., Joshi. A., & Pinkston. J., May 2004).

Because WSNs pose the above-mentioned challenges, traditional security mechanisms cannot be applied directly (Walters. J.P., Liang. Z., Shi. W., & Chaudhary. V., 2006: Noman. A.N.M., & Islam. Md. H., 2007) and WSNs are more prone to existing and new threats than traditional networks. The next section provides a list of more common threats on WSNs (Avancha. S., Undercoffer. J., Joshi. A., & Pinkston. J., May 2004: Perrig. A., Stankovic. J., & Wagner. D., June 2004).

Threats to WSNs

Physical Threats

Often deployed in inaccessible areas, nodes operate unattended and can be captured and replaced or tampered[5] with by attackers, that may force a non-legitimate node to act as an authenticated node of the network. The attacker can then replay or falsify routing information and prevent any communication in the WSN. Physical capture of nodes is considered as the main threat to WSN and is often the preamble of other threats and security weaknesses that we will describe below.

Weak and Non-Perfect Symmetric Key Distribution Protocols

In WSN, key distribution (Chan. H., Perrig. A., & Song. D., n.d.) is the process of distributing secret keys between communicating nodes in order to provide communication confidentiality and nodes' authentication. The simplest solution is to share a unique key between all the sensor nodes of the network before deployment. This is obviously the worse case since the compromise of the unique key will compromise all the WSN traffic.

Each node can also share a unique symmetric key with the BS that will be used to distribute a pair wise key to a pair of neighboring nodes that want to exchange data. As an example, in a system like the Security Protocols for Sensor Networks (SPINS) (Perrig. A., Szewczyk. R., Wen. V., Culler. D., & Tygar. D., July 2001), each sensor node shares a unique master key with the BS. However, the BS acts as a single point of failure and this solution requires that the BS is well protected against key stealing by an attacker. It also presupposes that the BS is trusted by all sensor nodes of the WSN. If the BS is compromised, sensor nodes cannot trust it anymore and all the security of the WSN is compromised.

Another solution consists of pre-distributing a symmetric key between each pair of nodes. This implies that before deployment, each node will share a key with each individual node that may be a potential neighbor[6]. This is necessary because of the dynamic changing network topology, nodes do not know a priori their neighbor nodes. In terms of key distribution, this impacts the scalability since the number of keys distributed to each node is proportional to the total number of nodes in the network.

Several other schemes (Chan. H., Perrig. A., & Song. D., May 2003) are derived from a first random key pre-distribution scheme proposed by Eschenauer and Gligor in (Eschenauer. L., & Gligor. V.D., November 2002). In this scheme, a large pool of keys is selected from the entire key space and each node is attributed a random subset of keys (called key ring) from the initial key pool before being deployed. Two neighbor nodes may communicate if they find a common key in the random subset of keys that they received before deployment. Two nodes will share at least one common key with probability p. The value of p depends on the size of the initial key pool. The problem with such probabilistic scheme is that there is a risk that the WSN may not be fully connected resulting in node isolation or network partitioning (Chan. H., Perrig. A., & Song. D., May 2003; Chan. H., Perrig. A., & Song. D., n.d.). Another risk is if an attacker can capture a sufficient number of nodes and access their key ring. From that the attacker can try to reconstruct the complete key pool[7].

Unreliable Wireless Communication

In a WSN, nodes communicate directly with other nodes in the same radio range only via wireless medium. The wireless medium presents some issues that may impact the WSN security:

- The transmission length is limited by the radio range of the wireless connection.
- Collision and transmission errors induce packet losses.
- The broadcast nature of wireless medium means that each transmission is heard by all potential listeners/receivers of the channel. This leads to security and privacy issues when eavesdroppers listen to the channel and can overhear sensed data. This also means that the wireless communication can easily be disrupted by jamming[8] signals or noise that will prevent legitimate

signal transmission to occur, potentially leading to a DoS.

- Due to obstacles in the environment, sensor nodes may have hidden neighbors that cannot be reached by wireless signal.
- Adding cryptographic primitive to provide secrecy of communication will increase the packet size. This communication overhead has a negative impact on the WSN communication performance.

Service Disruption

As we mentioned above, because of its broadcast nature, the wireless communication can easily be disrupted by jamming signals or noise[9] that will prevent legitimate signal transmission to occur and may induce a DoS. Moreover, in WSN technology the Medium Access Control[10] (MAC) layer should provide energy saving by efficiently switching unused nodes to sleeping mode. It should also handle collision detection and collision avoidance which occur when two nodes transmit at the same time through the same channel. An attacker can easily deny the service by constantly waking up sleeping nodes, which will waste energy. An attacker can also induce signal collisions by transmitting when another node is transmitting.

Mobility

Mobility is also a parameter that may affect the reliability of WSN communication.

- Mobility induces route changes and packet losses.
- Mobility can also induce node isolation leading to network partitions (also sleeping nodes).
- Mobility has an effect on battery consumption (Pham. H., & Jha. S., October 2004) since mobile nodes drain supplementary battery power. Moving nodes can also increase the chance of collisions in the

wireless medium. Therefore power management is required in mobile WSN.

Vulnerable Routing and Forwarding Protocols

Routing consists of selecting the correct route for a message to be delivered to a destination. Routing is of paramount importance to allow the forwarding of packets through a reliable path from a source node to a destination node. Current WSN routing protocols suffers from a lot of vulnerabilities which, for the majority, are summarized below and the details are well explained in papers such as (Karlof. C., & Wagner. D., 2003).

- **Alteration of routing information:** This creates routing inconsistencies, may disconnect one part of the WSN (isolation) and even lead to a DoS. Routing information can be spoofed, modified or replayed.
- **Selective forwarding:** in such an attack, malicious nodes seem to behave like normal nodes but selectively refuse to forward certain messages and drop them (often sensitive packets with routing information) (Yu. B., & Xiao. B., April 2006).
- **Sinkhole attack:** This attack consists of making a node (malicious node or a node under attack) particularly attractive from the point of view of the route quality (Ngai. E.C.H., Liu. J., & Lyu. M.R., June 2006). Depending on the routing algorithm, quality can be expressed in terms of the shortest path to the BS, the route with the lowest latency, the route with the highest reliability … A classical example is an intruder using a laptop that can provide a high quality route (higher computation and communication power) to the BS in a single hop. By spoofing surrounding nodes, it can send fake routing messages that will select the high quality route. Likely, all neighbor nodes will forward the data to the BS through the

malicious node. This is also made possible because a powerful attacker (via a laptop) can build and broadcast hello messages to announce itself to all the sensor nodes of the WSN, convincing them that it is a direct neighbor (in the same radio range).

By spoofing acknowledgments at the link layer, an adversary can convince a node that a disabled node is still alive and that the link to this node is quite reliable. It can then perform selective forwarding by manipulating nodes to forward packets to a weak link which will induce the loss of packets.

- **Wormhole attack:** In this case, colluding nodes tunnel packets from one location of the WSN (the malicious source end-point of the tunnel) to another location (the malicious destination end-point of the tunnel) making the illusion that the two malicious nodes of the tunnel are very close to each other. Wormholes are usually used to attract forwarding traffic from other legal nodes through the tunnel. Once the traffic is attracted via the tunnel, the colluding nodes can also perform selective forwarding (Khalil. I., Bagchi. S., & Shroff. N.B., 2005).
- **Sybil attack:** A single malicious node can present multiple identities to the WSN. Sybil attack can be used to defeat data fragmentation and replication necessary for distributed storage in WSN (James. N., Shi. E., Song. D., & Perrig. A., April 2004) by creating the illusion that the data has been stored at different locations (nodes), whereas the same malicious node using several identities gets the data. A Sybil attack can also affect the routing algorithms (Karlof. C., & Wagner. D., 2003) by forcing apparently multiple disjoint paths (preventing path diversity) to go through the same malicious node that uses several identities.

Parameters that May Help to Reduce the Effect of Threats

As stated in the introduction section of this chapter, traditional security implementations need to be adapted to the constraints imposed by WSNs. Notably, lightweight implementations of cryptographic functions are desirable in order to ensure confidentiality, integrity, authentication and non-repudiation. Other measures specific to WSN characteristics may help to reduce the effect of threats. A few examples are provided below:

- **Power management:** Power limitation can be mitigated by collaboration between layers so that upper layers are informed by lower layers in order to survive power limitation induced by lower layers such as the MAC layer. As example, Wood et al. propose in (Wood. A.D., Stankovic. J.A., & Son. S.H., 2003) a jamming detection system where the MAC layer detecting jamming nodes informs the application layer which can then apply power management strategies in order to help the node outlast the jamming.
- **Clustering and group management:** WSN can be organized as a set of clusters where nodes are grouped based on different attributes such as their location, the type of data being sensed ... Typically, sensor nodes grouped in a cluster share their data, which is aggregated by a selected sensor node of the cluster called the cluster head. Clustering can help to deal with the distributed nature of sensor nodes that makes data aggregation difficult. Grouping and managing nodes as a cluster is required in WSN since it can overcome the computation and power limitation of individual sensor nodes because data aggregation can be performed based on group membership and aggregated data is sent in a single data stream to the BS. One of the most

famous clustering mechanisms for WSN is called Low-Energy Adaptive Clustering Hierarchy (LEACH) (Heinzelman. W.R, Chandrakasan. A., & Balakrishnan. H., January 2000). In LEACH, cluster heads are elected for a fixed period of time called a round. At each round, a new node is elected as a cluster head in a probabilistic way based on how many times it has been a cluster head before.

It is necessary that the nodes contained in each cluster exchange data only with the authenticated trusted nodes contained in the cluster. Often the WSN is organized as a set of clusters, each one with its cluster head. It is also necessary that cluster heads only exchange data with other trusted clusters heads.

- **Use of redundancy:** When an event occurs it can be sensed by many surrounding sensor nodes leading to redundant information sent to a destination node (cluster head, sink or BS). Redundant information transmitted to the BS results in a waste of energy. However, redundant information can be locally exploited as a means to detect lying nodes reporting false data.

COLLABORATION, TRUST AND REPUTATION FOR SECURITY

Collaboration is essential in WSNs for many reasons such as the high distribution of sensor nodes or the goal-oriented nature of many sensing applications. This section emphasizes the need of collaboration between sensor nodes and shows that establishing trust between nodes and using reputation reported by collaborating nodes can help mitigate security issues.

As we saw, preserving security (authenticity, confidentiality, integrity …) of the sensitive data collected and processed by sensor nodes is essential. However, cryptographic methods required to ensure data security are quite expensive and not suitable for WSNs. Mainly, the usage of asymmetric cryptographic functions is prohibitive. Constraints that we already mentioned, such as low cost design without tamper-resistant hardware, expose the sensor nodes to physical capture and reprogramming by an attacker: cryptographic keys can be stolen and the node security compromised. Once keys have been stolen, a node cannot be distinguished from a legitimate node using solely cryptographic functions. Facing such attacks, trust will maintain a certain level of security allowing skeptical nodes to make secure decisions, discard or circumvent the un-trusted nodes and select the trustworthy nodes that encourage collaboration, thus compensating the lack of security.

Why We Need Collaboration in WSN and its Relation to Trust

The following items describe the effects of collaboration on different features of the WSNs that have direct or indirect effects on security. The need to establish a trust relation between collaborating is sometimes emphasized.

- **Collaboration helps to improve WSN efficiency:** Sensor network operations highly depend on distributed cooperation among network nodes. By nature, for a lot of applications called sense-response applications[11], sensor nodes are supposed to collect (sense) local information from their environment (Clouqueur. T., Saluja. K.K., and Ramanathan. P., March 2004) and collaborate towards a joint goal in order to give a global result of the phenomenon being sensed, often because outputs provided by individual nodes do not suffice to report the phenomenon. Tracking applications are typical examples. The collaborative processing of data done inside the network rather than processing the data at the BS or sinks greatly improves WSN efficiency.

The goal-oriented nature of WSN can only work if there is a certain level of trust between nodes.

- **Collaboration and redundancy help to detect inconsistencies:** Redundancy is due to the fact that an event can be detected by more than one node in its neighborhood. This is typical to sense-response applications and this has the benefit of preventing holes from being created in the covered area. The major drawback is that every node in the same neighborhood of the event will report the same event to the BS, which is a waste in communication energy. Moreover, many occurrences of the same event sent to the BS increase the risk of collisions. In reality, more often nodes collaborate to decide which node will send the event to the BS (Le. H.C., Guyennet. H., & Zerhouni. N.. March 2007).

Another advantage of combining node collaboration with event redundancy is that it helps to detect faulty nodes reporting suspicious or wrong events because they are inconsistent with the surrounding nodes.

- **Collaboration helps to maintain the WSN survivability:** Sensor limitations make collaboration imperious. Another constraint of WSNs comes from the limited power source of the components, requiring collaboration to be power efficient.

Many sensor applications need more than one sensor to accomplish the task together. Obviously, the benefit of using sensing units is to allow them to collaboratively perform small sensing tasks and summarize them in order to report the result to a destination node (BS or sink). These small tasks will save each sensor energy, allowing the survivability[12] of the whole WSN. But malicious nodes can be introduced, using the natural cooperation between nodes to attack the WSN. Therefore, trust must be guaranteed between collaborating nodes.

- **Collaboration helps to maintain a dynamic topology via self-organization:** Usually, the WSN does not have a fixed topology. The infrastructure-less nature of a WSN requires that nodes self-organize in order to maintain an ephemeral topology and to avoid losing routes. In the context of WSNs, a good definition of self-organization is provided by Collier and Taylor in (Collier. T.C., & Taylor. C., July 2004) as: "A self-organizing system [...] one where a collection of units coordinate with each other to form a system that adapts to achieve a goal more efficiently."

As explained previously in this chapter, because sensor nodes may fail, sleep or move, the radio signal may be lost due to environmental conditions, then the topology is dynamically changing and locally (a least at the scale of a node's radio range) nodes need to maintain the connectivity with their neighborhood. The global goal is that local connectivity between neighbor nodes will maintain the global multi-hop routing necessary to forward packets in WSNs.

Self-organization is also a property that is exploited in WSN to deal with the MAC problem, preventing two nodes from transmitting through the same channel at the same time by controlling the way multiple sensors share a common wireless channel. A system such as S-MAC (Ye. W., Heidemann. J., & Estrin. D., 2002) designs an access control protocol where neighbor nodes collaborate and self-organize to coordinate and reduce their listening mode in order to save energy. Another example of self-organizing protocol is Self-organizing Medium Access Control for Sensor networks (SMACS) (Sohrabi. K., Gao. J., Ailawadhi. V., & Pottie. G.J., 2000). SMACS allows the building of a flat WSN infrastructure (as opposed to a hierarchical clustered one). It is a distributed protocol where sensor nodes discover their neighbor nodes without the need of a local or global master nodes (cluster head)

- **Collaboration is required for key distribution (Chan. H., Perrig. A., & Song. D. (May 2003)):** In many situations, sensor nodes are dispatched in hostile or a priori unknown environments and are randomly distributed without a fixed infrastructure. This means that nodes do not know their neighborhood. This implies that neighbor nodes must find a way to collaborate in a trusted way in order to dynamically share encryption keys in an efficient and secure way. As example, (Chadha. A., Liu. Y., Das S. (September 2005)) proposes a Group Key Distribution model via Local Collaboration.

- **Collaboration improves the data centric nature of WSNs (Estrin. D., Govindan. R., Heidemann. J., & Kumar. S., August 1999; Qi. H., Kuruganti. P.T., & Xu. Y., 2002):** An application is said to be data centric because data is not collected based on sensor nodes' identifiers (IDs) but the application asks for the data to be collected based on attributes matching the data. When the attributes specified by the application match specific data, the collected data is often cached in collaborating neighbor nodes. Such collaboration plays a role in making the WSN more robust since if a node dies or fails, the application can still recover the data.

Collaboration for Packet Aggregation and Data Fusion

Aggregation consists of the collection of many sensor readings surrounding an aggregation point which is a selected sensor node of the WSN. The aggregated point will delay arriving messages from its surrounding neighbors until it receives a sufficient number of messages. Then it aggregates

the messages before sending them to the next hop (another sensor node or the BS).

In data fusion (Khan. A., October 2004), a node collects and combines data from several nodes and gathers that information with its own collected data before sending it to another node or the BS. Based on deduction or induction methods, the fusion node will infer intermediary results before sending to the BS. This in-network fusion has the advantage of providing more accurate and useful information from intermediary fusion nodes rather than a large stream of raw information provided by simple sensors. This also saves the WSN energy by reducing the total amount of traffic from the sensor nodes to the BS.

In the case of data fusion, fusion nodes are often considered as trusted. However, a malicious fusion node can send erroneous fusion reports to the BS. In this case, the BS may not easily suspect the malicious node since single nodes do not directly report to the BS and this data is hidden (summarized) in the fusion report sent by the fusion node to the BS. In order to prevent fake reports sent to the BS, Du et al. propose in (Du. W., Deng. J., Han. Y.S., &Varshney. P.K., December 2003) a scheme where the fusion node has to collaborate with designated witness nodes (m nodes) that will also perform the same data fusion from single nodes. Witness nodes do not send reports to the BS but compute a Message Authentication Code on the same raw data sent by single nodes that is added as a proof to the fusion report sent to the BS. Then, when at least n-1 of the m witness nodes agree with the fusion report, the BS accepts the fusion report.

- **Synchronization:** Time synchronization consists of attributing a common time (or clock) to all nodes of the WSN. It is quite difficult to achieve for large-scale distributed WSNs due to scalability issues that induce clock errors (or clock inconsistencies). Existing techniques of time synchronization are based on local collaboration between nodes exchanging packets with timing information (Servetto. S.D., May 2006). Time synchronization is a critical issue to the survivability of a WSN for instance, when time is used to retrieve an authenticated key from a chain of distributed keys.

- **Collaboration is necessary for packet routing and data forwarding:** Nodes must collaborate to define and maintain the path to the BS because if nodes are out of the range of each other, intermediary nodes need to be solicited in order to perform the routing function and forward packets. These intermediary nodes must discover or maintain a route to the destination. The collaborative route maintenance is particularly required in the presence of mobile sensor nodes that cause frequent route changes.

Moreover, collaboration between nodes at multi-hop can help to detect selective forwarding attacks since a packet dropped by an intermediate node won't reach the next hop in the multi-hop path. This node can detect an abnormal packet loss and report it back to the sending node using another safer path.

- **Collaboration helps preventing jamming:** Existing anti-jamming techniques such as spread spectrum techniques (Wood. A.D., Stankovic. J.A., & Son. S.H., 2003) are quite expensive for applications based on low cost sensors. Others solutions such as the one proposed by Wood et al. in (Wood. A.D., Stankovic. J.A., & Son. S.H., 2003) use nodes around a jammed node or region to isolate and circumvent this region. The proposed mechanism is also due to collaborating nodes that inform the neighborhood about the jammed nodes. In this work, two phases are based on collaboration between nodes:

1. The jamming detection phase where a node informs its neighbors before it is totally jammed.
2. The mapping group creation: neighbor nodes closer and around the jammed node receive a jamming notification and form a mapping group that isolates the jamming area. Then, nodes will simply route around the jamming area.

Conversely, when the node is not jammed anymore, it notifies it neighbors of the mapping group in order to update the mapping group information and trigger the withdrawal of the mapping members from the group.

- **Collaboration helps to detect mobility:** In (Pham. H., & Jha. S., October 2004) the authors design an energy efficient mobility-aware MAC protocol where each node detects that its neighbor nodes are moving according to the signal levels of periodical SYNC[13] messages received from its neighbors.

If there is a change in a signal received from a neighbor, it presumes that the neighbor or itself is moving.

- **Collaboration helps to mitigate attacks:** Sensor nodes can easily be physically accessed by attackers when deployed in remote areas. They can then be switched off or malicious nodes may be introduced and the WSN tricked into accepting them as legitimate. Consequently, reliability will not be maintained: Information may not be available where and when required, data may fail to reach its destination or malicious information may be introduced. Attackers can also directly collect the information from a node that has been isolated. Collaboration between nodes can help mitigating these attacks in different ways. For instance:

1. When a node is switched off, neighbor nodes can detect that this node

disappeared from their radio range and designate another node to relay the data. This presupposes mechanisms to regenerate the lost information and resend it via the new designated node.

2. When a malicious node is introduced, neighbor nodes must detect it and circumvent it. The example of collaborative detection of selective forwarding has already been given above.

The Concepts of Trust and Reputation for WSNs

Trust for WSNs

Many definitions of trust and trust models have been given for networked systems (Artz. D., & Gil. Y., March 2007; Zhu. H., Feng. B., & Deng. R.H, 2003) based on different interpretations. Trust is (Boukerch. A, Xu. L., & EL-Khatib. K., September 2007; Srinivasany. A., Teitelbaumy. J., Liangz. H., Wuyand. J., & Cardei. M., 2007) an important factor of human societies and can affect individuals' behavior. Trust is a notion that individuals need to refer to when there is a certain level of risk or a lack of certainty in their everyday lives. In the context of WSNs, when sensor nodes are deployed in unknown remote areas, there is a lot of uncertainty concerning the environment that cannot be predicted. Therefore, trust is a way to compensate for this lack of certainty.

Simply explained, from node A's point of view, the trust that a sensor node A grants a sensor node B is the degree of expectation/estimation that node B will act according to a way which is suitable to node A. For instance, A may consider that B has a suitable behavior if B is correctly routing the data, choosing the less exhausted node in terms of consumed energy, or if B itself does not switch to sleeping mode too often without any reason (saving battery, node under attack ...). Consequently, if A believes that B will act according to a trusted way (McKnight. D.H., Choudhury. V., & Kacmar.

C., 2002), it will be more willing to depend on B when performing future actions, for instance to route the data to the BS via B. Conversely if A believes that B's behavior is not trustworthy since B is always sleeping, it will rather select another node to route the data to the BS. A will adjust its trust in B based on what it knows about B's past behavior (history).

Some existing trust models are not adequate for WSNs since they consume high quantities of resources such as memory and energy or because nodes are not designed with the same constraints as sensor nodes. For instance, WSNs present some differences with Mobile Ad hoc NETworks (MANETs) such as:

- Participating MANET nodes are close to human users rather than close to or immersed in the remote environment that is to be sensed.

- MANET nodes are more heterogeneous nodes (the human-oriented nature of MANET nodes confers them different capabilities) which may involve more selfish or opportunistic behaviors than with sensor nodes, since nodes are less likely to work together for a common goal. For instance, a MANET node may be re-programmed by its owner so that it does not forward packets originating from other nodes in order to save resources.

- Re-programming sensor nodes is not possible in remote inaccessible areas. Energy constraints in MANETs are not as tight as in WSNs. Therefore, designing an energy-efficient trust model for WSNs is more challenging and trust models developed for MANETs cannot be applied per se to WSNs (Srinivasany. A., Teitelbaumy. J., Liangz. H., Wuyand. J., & Cardei. M., 2007).

Another example of trust parameter that may not applicable to WSNs in the same way as it is used in traditional network trust models is the history information (history of a node behavior) because of the switching mode of the sensors (sleep/awake) that limits constant or long-term node interactions, or because of the limited memory of nodes.

Reputation for WSNs

Reputation is another notion that can affect trust. In human societies, it is based on knowledge that others can provide about an individual and in case of uncertainty, reputation can help to establish trust in an unknown individual. Similarly, in the context of WSNs it may help nodes to adjust the trust granted to other nodes when, for instance, they cannot make a direct judgment (nodes out of the radio range, moving neighbor nodes, node newly appearing in the radio range ...). Node *A* will adjust its trust in *B* based on what it knows about *B*'s reputation. Combined with trust, reputation mechanisms can help to detect and eliminate both defective and malicious nodes that are misbehaving.

Trust-based and reputation-based collaboration are used for excluding malicious or defective sensor nodes of a WSN and for improving the WSN operation. Examples of existing recent works based on trust and reputation are provided in the two following sub-sections, often combining both the notion of trust and the notion of reputation.

Examples of Trust-Based Collaboration

Detecting Misbehaving Nodes

As explained earlier in this chapter, a misbehaving node can try to minimize its participation in the routing or the forwarding activity. It can do it voluntarily in order to save some resource or un-voluntarily if the node is defective. Designing a trust model that forces collaboration and cooperation can help dealing with misbehaving nodes. Classical WSN models, based on reputation information provided by trusted nodes propose that the misbehaving node be localized by its neighborhood, circumvented and excluded from any future collaboration. By being refused any cooperation with other neighbor nodes, the misbehaving node is encouraged to stop any opportunist operation and to start taking part in the route selection or in the packets forwarding.

Key Management and Authentication

When dealing with aging sensor nodes, we cannot guarantee that keys are not compromised. In (Dutertre. B., Cheung. S. & Levy. J., April 2004), the authors argue that sensors that are deployed at the same time can trust each other for a small time period after their deployment because it takes some time before an adversary may compromise the node and try to get the key.

Other schemes such as (Lewis. N., & Foukia. N., November 2007; Chan. H., & Perrig. A., 2005), propose a key establishment mechanisms based on a pre-established trust that two nodes *A* and *B* have in a common node *C*. The trusted node *C* is used to establish pair wise keys between *A* and *B*.

Earlier schemes such as the one used by SPINS (Perrig. A., Szewczyk. R., Wen. V., Culler. D., & Tygar. D., July 2001) rely on trust and on a symmetric key that each node shares with the BS acting as a key distribution center (KDC) for distributing keys. This means that each pair of nodes willing to communicate has to communicate with the trusted BS to establish the key between the two nodes. This concentrates the communication around the BS and drains more energy from the nodes closest to the BS that have to forward the traffic for key establishment (Chan. H., & Perrig. A., 2005).

Trust for Multi-Hop Routing Protocols

Usually, static sensor nodes can only perceive behavior of nodes in their radio range (neighbors).

Outside the radio range, the distrust increases. Multi-hop routing protocols can require the selection of an entire trusted path from a source node to the BS before the data is forwarded. This means that a node A in the path computes local trust values with its direct neighbors (based on first hand observation) and collaborates with its neighbor nodes that provide their own opinion based on their own observation (second hand information for node A).

Examples of Reputation-Based Collaboration

Location Discovery

Among recent works, the authors of (Srinivasany. A., Teitelbaumy., & Wu. J., 2006) propose a reputation-based scheme for accurate location discovery of sensor nodes in a WSN. In this work, specific nodes called beacon[14] nodes (or beacons) monitor their neighborhood in order to eliminate misbehaving beacons by computing a reputation value based on the accuracy of the location information. The beacons can determine their location and provide this information to sensor nodes that are unable to know their current location. The beacons collaborate with their respective neighbor sensor nodes by providing their current location and the table of reputation values of their beacon neighbors. Sensor nodes use this table to decide whether or not to use a beacon's localization information or to discard the location information provided by a lying beacon. The decision is done by a majority vote performed on the different reputation values provided by the different neighbor beacons in their tables.

Data Aggregation at Cluster Heads

When aggregating data, cluster heads or aggregation points need to establish the accuracy of the data reported by the group of cluster nodes. Reputation mechanisms can help detecting lying cluster nodes reporting false data to the cluster head.

At the same time, voting mechanisms based on reputation (Perez. C.R., December 2007) can be used to elect a new cluster head if the existing head has been compromised, preventing the compromised head from becoming a single point of failure.

Recently, Perez proposed in his master thesis (Perez. C.R., December 2007) a reputations system for data aggregation named Resilient Data Aggregation in Sensor Network (RDAS). Node A interacting with node B for a certain period of time records cooperative and non-cooperative sensed events (first-hand information). It also receives from its set of neighbors N the records of cooperative and non-cooperative events (second-hand information) that they observe with the same node B. The second-hand information is added to the first-hand information to compute the global reputation value. However, the importance of the second-hand information is mitigated by a function that gives greater weight to reporting nodes that node A trusts with a high value and at the same time guarantees that the second-hand information does not outweigh the first-hand information (refer to (Perez. C.R., December 2007) for the detail about the function which is used).

Route Selection

In (Lewis. N., & Foukia. N., May 2008), Lewis and Foukia propose a routing approach where nodes in a WSN rely on trusted neighbors and neighbors' reputation to dynamically select the best route to the destination. In a simple WSN, data is routed from the nodes to the BS and global maintenance messages are flooded from a BS to the nodes. When a node sends a request for information to the BS a route must be maintained to allow the reply to be sent back. In more complex situations a node may wish to send a message to a specific node, perhaps for data aggregation. The route selection is based on the trust and cost of a route. Simply explained, a sensor node A computes the trust and the cost of a route through one of its neighbors B to the BS by combining the direct trust $T_{NA \to B}$ (trust that node A grants to node B) and the direct cost $C_{NA \to B}$ (cost to transmit directly to B) that it has for node B with the indirect trust of the route from B to the BS ($TR_{B \to BS}$) and indirect cost of the route from B to the BS ($CRB \to BS$) that node B has broadcast.

Moreover, reputation is combined with trust in the following ways (Lewis. N., & Foukia. N., October 2008):

1. Each node records a trust value for each of its neighbors. These trust values can be transmitted to neighbors, where the receiving node uses them to calculate reputation.
2. Trust values are transmitted to all neighbors when they have changed beyond a certain threshold.
3. Reputations are used to adjust a node's own trust for its neighbors.

A node transmits a trust value to all of its neighbors. When a node receives such a transmission, it ignores trust values relating to any node it is not familiar with and records the trust value as a reputation associated with the corresponding known neighbor. When a node A has collected the required number of reputation values for a given neighbor B, it aggregates the information. First it finds the median (m) of the collected reputation values. It then discards reputations that are beyond a threshold (th) from the median. Any neighbor C of A contributing a reputation towards common neighbor B that is beyond the threshold from the median may be punished (its opinion differs too widely from the majority of the contributors). All neighbors contributing reputations that are within the threshold from the median will be rewarded. The remaining reputations are then weighted before being averaged. Each reputation is weighted by the trust that node A has for the contributing node as well as the age of the information (the time

since the reputation information was received). When node A is calculating the reputation for node B, the weighted reputation contribution from node C is as follows:

$$R_{WC \circledR B} = TN_{A \circledR C} \times R_{C \circledR B} \times AG_{C \circledR B}$$

where $TN_{A \to C}$ is the trust value that A grants C, $R_{C \to B}$ is the reputation value that C grants B and was transmitted to node A and $AG_{C \to B}$ is the age of the reputation information $R_{C \to B}$ that has been collected by node A.

The final weighted average of all reputations for node B, from contributing nodes is given by:

$$\frac{\sum_{C \in Contributor} RW_{C \to B}}{\sum_{C \in Contributor} (TN_{A \to C} \times AG_{C \to B})}$$

The average reputation for B is then used to adjust the trust value ($TN_{A \to B}$) that is already associated with node B as neighbor of A.

PRIVACY

What is Privacy?

Privacy is an evolving concept which mainly deals with socio-cultural and legal aspects. The concept of privacy evolves with the needs of society and user requirements (Want. R., December 2007).

In 1890, Warren and Brandeis articulated privacy as the individual's right to be left alone (Warren. S., & Brandeis. L., 1890). He pointed out that privacy is essential to protect the personality and the individual's independence, dignity and integrity. His concept of privacy infringement considered as a tort has been added to the U.S. common law.

More recently, according to Westin (Westin. A., 1967), information privacy is defined as "…

the claims of individuals, groups or institutions to determine for themselves when, how and to what extent information about them is communicated to the others."

Many definitions of privacy exist. In 1990, the Calcutt Committee[15] in the UK stated that they haven't found a wholly satisfactory definition of privacy. Of all the human rights, privacy is perhaps the most difficult to define (Michael. J., 1994) and the term privacy has been considered as problematic due to its interpretation and the lack of consensus about its scope, interpretation and delineation.

Based on the definition given by Westin (Westin. A., 1967), in the context of WSN technology, we define privacy as the user privilege to decide:

- who holds her private information or uses her private objects,
- who can access it and for which purpose and
- how this information or objects are handled (in order to avoid unauthorized changes or unauthorized transfers).

Privacy Issues in WSNs

Features such as small size, low cost and wireless communication makes WSN technology exceptionally attractive for many applications. Deployment of thousands of sensors at close proximity to the physical phenomenon being sensed leads to fine-grained data collection and monitoring of raw data by individual sensor nodes, and better tracking of the phenomenon in a ubiquitous way. These features that make WSN technology attractive for a lot of applications also raise real privacy concerns (Hanna. L., & Hailes. S.) because of the following reasons:

- Sensitive data can be collected, events can be correlated and analyzed.

Data can be accessed at different steps of the WSN operation: when nodes are sensing and collecting data, transmitting sensed data, storing data for some time, and aggregating data.

An attacker can get direct access to data stored within a sensor by physically accessing the sensor. He can also remotely and anonymously access sensitive data via the network by eavesdropping. The adversary may know how to derive sensitive information by sending apparently innocuous data queries to sensor nodes and waiting for the answer. He can also access simultaneously multiple sensor nodes and correlate information collected from these nodes to derive sensitive information.

- Technology is becoming more pervasive[16] and ubiquitous due to the small size of devices (sensors measure a few millimeters or are even smaller) and also due to their location in everyday environments (a sensor may be hidden and can track individuals' behaviors).

Sensor nodes are also getting cheaper which makes them more affordable even for clandestine surveillance.

The concept of pervasive computing refers to the visionary way introduced by Weiser in his seminal paper (Weiser. M., September 1991) of using information and communication technologies in our daily lives such that not just the computers, but the walls, tables, white boards, etc., will belong to our computing environment. For this purpose, electronic devices are miniaturized and embedded in common objects or will be worn in our bodies making computing ubiquitous and transparent in the world around us. For example, many existing healthcare or homecare applications have been attracted by WSN technology to sense human activities in patients' daily environments in a pervasive way (Stankovic. J. A., Cao. Q., Doan. T., Fang. L., He. Z., Kiran. R., Lin. S., Son. S., Stoleru. R., & Wood. A., June 2005). More wearable and unobtrusive sensors will be included in patients' clinical and home environments and will collect vast amounts of data that will serve medial or pharmaceutical research and studies. Among this data, personal data related to patient's heath or to their activities at home is quite sensitive and should belong to the patients' privacy. However, usually the sensor devices are under control of the healthcare providers that can easily transgress patients' privacy. Therefore, in such applications, guaranties must be provided to the patients that their privacy won't be transgressed and all the precautions must be taken to trace potential abuses by providers. For instance, healthcare providers should provide irrefutable records of the different accesses they performed on patients' personal data.

- Different organizations collecting sensed data can correlate their data which may be harmful for the consumer (Carbunar. B., Yu. Y., Shi. L., Pearce. M., & Vasudevan. V., 2007).

Data collected by sensor nodes may belong to a single WSN owner. However, it is not always the case and WSN deployment can depend on many different organizations (for instance, several funding institutions that deploy a WSN for research purposes). In the presence of multiple and different owners of the WSN infrastructure and accessors of its content, it is possible that misbehaviors and distrust may arise between them just because they may have different interests: For instance, an owner of a WSN wants to preserve the WSN survivability by controlling resource access whereas a client (a member of one of the involved organizations) authorized to access the WSN wants to hide his access profile. Therefore, a key element in such WSN is to guarantee collaborative trust.

- Different privacy protection laws are applied in different countries.

As example, in Europe the 95/46/EC[17] and 2002/58/EC[18] European Directives are applied whereas in USA, the Privacy Patriot Act[19] is applied. There is a difference in approach to data privacy protection between EU and its members, and U.S. laws. European Directives are more restrictive than American laws, which render these laws incompatible with each other.

The EU Data Protection Directives impose broader data privacy requirements on companies to protect their customers' personal data, whereas the U.S. Patriot Act imposes more law enforcement surveillance on companies by making them responsible for identifying customers of suspicious transactions.

Ensuring that sensed data is accessed only by trusted entities of the WSN is essential to preserve data privacy. Different approaches can be adopted and classical methods that have been adopted are listed below (He. W., Liu. X, Nguyen. H., Nahrstedt. K., & Abdelzaher. T., May 2007; Walters. J.P., Liang. Z., Shi. W., & Chaudhary. V., 2006):

- Access control based on privacy policies (Duri. S., Gruteser. M., Liu. X., Moskowitz. P., Perez. R., Singh. M., & Tang. J., 2002; Gruteser. M., Schelle. G., Jain. A., Han. R., & Grunwald. D., May 2003)

Usually, privacy protection approaches based on defining privacy policies are implemented at the BS layer after the data has been collected by individual sensor nodes and sent to the BS. These policies govern who can use private data gathered at the BS and for what purpose but does not guarantee that the readings of sensitive information by sensor nodes and the traffic sent to the BS stay private.

- Data obfuscation and traffic perturbation

Obfuscation (Duckham. M., & Kulik. L., May 2005) consists of deliberately degrading the quality of the data being sensed in order to protect data privacy. Some techniques add randomized data to sensed data in order to mask the private data. Similar techniques (Ozturk. C., Zhang. Y., & Trappe. W., October 2004) add random phantom traffic to routing traffic so that routing information, such as a data source, cannot be deduced by an attacker analyzing the traffic. Usually, it is combined with aggregation techniques.

- Anonymity

In the context of WSN technology, anonymity (Gruteser. M., & Hoh. B., April 2005) consists of preventing the collected data from being associated with any particular entity (user, agent…), whether by altering the data itself, or by combining it with other data.

CONCLUSION

Because of the unique challenges posed by WSNs, traditional security techniques cannot be applied as they are applied for other communication networks and new security techniques are required. The purpose of this chapter is not to give an exhaustive review of existing WSN security techniques. There are already many existing detailed reviews about WSN security in the literature. Rather, the authors endeavored to explain why constraints imposed by WSN technology impact security and explore how the effect of collaboration, trust and reputation can help to mitigate WSN constraints and reduce potential security threats targeting WSNs. This has been illustrated by the description of many examples taken from existing works of the WSN literature.

REFERENCES

Akyildiz, F., Su, W., Sankarasubramaniam, Y., & Cayirci, E. (2002, March). Wireless sensor networks: a survey. *Computer Networks*, *38*(4), 393–422. doi:10.1016/S1389-1286(01)00302-4

Artz, D., & Gil, Y. (2007, March). A survey of trust in computer science and the semantic web. *Journal of Web Semantics*, *5*(2). doi:10.1016/j. websem.2007.03.002

Avancha, S., Undercoffer, J., Joshi, A., & Pinkston, J. (May 2004, May). Security for wireless sensor networks. In C. S. Raghavendra, et al (Eds.), *Wireless Sensor Networks* (pp. 253-275).

Boukerch, A., & Xu, L., & EL-Khatib, K. (2007, September). Trust-based security for wireless ad hoc and sensor networks. *Computer Communications*, *30*(11-12), 2413–2427. doi:10.1016/j. comcom.2007.04.022

Carbunar, B., Yu, Y., Shi, L., Pearce, M., & Vasudevan, V. (2007). Query privacy in wireless sensor networks. In *Proceedings of the 4th Annual IEEE Communications Society Conference on Sensor, Mesh and Ad Hoc Communications and Networks (SECON 2007)*.

Carman, D. W., Krus, P. S., & Matt, B. J. (2000). *Constraints and approaches for distributed sensor network security* (Technical Report 00-010, NAI Labs). Glenwood, MD: Network Associates, Inc.

Chadha, A., Liu, Y., & Das, S. (2005). Group key distribution via local collaboration in wireless sensor networks. In *Proceedings of the Second Annual IEEE Communications Society Conference on Sensor and Ad Hoc Communications and Networks*, Santa Clara, California, USA. Chan, H., Perrig, A., & Song, D. (n.d.). *Key distribution techniques for sensor networks*. Retrieved from http://www-2. cs.cmu.edu/~haowen/randomkey.pdf

Chan, H., & Perrig, A. (2005). Pike: peer intermediaries for key establishment in sensor networks. In *Proceedings of IEEE Conference on Computer Communications (Infocom 2005),* Miami, Florida, USA.

Chan, H., Perrig, A., & Song, D. (2003, May). Random Key Predistribution Schemes for Sensor Networks. In *Proceedings of the IEEE Symposium on Security and Privacy,* Oakland, California, USA.

Clouqueur, T., Saluja, K. K., & Ramanathan, P. (2004, March). Fault tolerance in collaborative sensor networks for target detection. *IEEE Transactions on Computers Journal, 53*(3), 320–333. doi:10.1109/TC.2004.1261838

Collier, T. C., & Taylor, C. (2004, July). Self-organization in sensor networks. Academic Press, Inc. *Journal of Parallel and Distributed Computing, 64*(7), 866–873. doi:10.1016/j.jpdc.2003.12.004

Daintith, J., Illingworth, V., & Pyle, I. (2008, July). *A Dictionary of Computing.* Oxford, UK: Oxford University Press.

Du, W., Deng, J., Han, Y. S., & Varshney, P. K. (2003, December). A Witness-Based Approach for Data Fusion Assurance in Wireless Sensor Networks. In *Proceedings of GLOBECOM 2003,* San Francisco, USA.

Duckham, M., & Kulik, L. (May 2005). A formal model of obfuscation and negotiation for location privacy. In *Proceedings of the Pervasive 2005* (LNCS 3468, pp. 152-170). Berlin, Germany: Springer.

Duri, S., Gruteser, M., Liu, X., Moskowitz, P., Perez, R., Singh, M., & Tang, J. (2002). Framework for security and privacy in automotive telematics. In *Proceedings of the 2nd ACM International Worksphop on Mobile Commerce.*

Dutertre, B., Cheung, S., & Levy, J. (April 2004, April). *Lightweight key management in wireless sensor networks by leveraging initial trust* (SDL Technical Report SRI-SDL-04-02).

Eschenauer, L., & Gligor, V. D. (2002, November). A key-management scheme for distributed sensor networks. In *Proceedings of the 9th ACM Conference on Computer and Communication Security* (pp. 41-47).

Estrin, D., Govindan, R., Heidemann, J., & Kumar, S. (1999, August). Next century challenges: scalable coordination in sensor networks. In *Proceedings of the 5th annual ACM/IEEE International Conference on Mobile Computing and Networking,* Seattle, Washington, USA (pp. 263-270).

Gruteser, M., & Hoh, B. (2005, April). On the anonymity of periodic location samples. In *Proceedings of the Second International Conference on Security in Pervasive Computing (SPC 2005),* Boppard, Germany.

Gruteser, M., Schelle, G., Jain, A., Han, R., & Grunwald, D. (2003, May). Privacy-aware location sensor networks. In *Proceedings of the 9th Workshop on Hot Topics in Operating Systems (HOTOS 2003),* Hawaii, USA. Hanna, L., & Hailes, S. (n.d.). *Privacy and wireless sensor networks.* University College London. Retrieved from http://www.petsfinebalance.com/docrepo/privacy_and_WSN.PDF

He, W., Liu, X, Nguyen, H., Nahrstedt, K., & Abdelzaher, T. (2007, May). PDA: privacy-preserving data aggregation in wireless sensor networks. In *Proceedings of 26th Annual IEEE Conference on Computer Communications (Infocom 2007),* Anchorage, Alaska, USA.

Heinzelman, W. R., Chandrakasan, A., & Balakrishnan, H. (2000, January). Energy-efficient communication protocol for wireless microsensor networks. In *Proceedings of the Hawaii International Conference on System Sciences,* Maui, Hawaii, USA.

James, N., Shi, E., Song, D., & Perrig, A. (2004, April). The sybil attack in sensor networks: analysis and defenses. *In Proceedings of the Third International Symposium on Information Processing in Sensor Networks (IPSN 2004)* (pp. 259-268). New York: ACM.

Karlof, C., & Wagner, D. (2003, May 11). Secure routing in wireless sensor networks: attacks and countermeasures. In *Proceedings of the First IEEE Workshop on Sensor Network Protocols and Applications* (pp. 113-127).

Khalil, I., Bagchi, S., & Shroff, N. B. (2005). LITEWORP: A lightweight countermeasure for the wormhole attack in multihop wireless networks. In *Proceedings of the International Conference on Dependable Systems and Networks (DSN 2005)* (pp. 612-621).

Khan, A. (2004, October). *Data fusion in sensor networks.* Retrieved from http://www.cse.buffalo.edu/~qiao/cse620/fall04/Data_Fusion.ppt

Le, H. C., Guyennet, H., & Zerhouni, N. (2007, March). March). Redundant communication avoidance for event-driven wireless sensor network. *International Journal of Computer Science and Network Security, 7*(3), 193–200.

Lewis, N., & Foukia, N. (2007, November). Using trust in key distribution in wireless sensor Networks. In *Proceedings of the IEEE Workshop on Wireless Mesh and Sensor Networks,* Washington, USA.

Lewis, N., & Foukia, N. (2008, October). An Efficient Reputation-based Routing Mechanism for Wireless Sensor Networks: Testing the Impact of Mobility and Hostile Nodes. In *Proceedings of the Sixth Annual Conference on Privacy, Security and Trust (PST 2008)*, Fredericton, New Brunswick, Canada.

Lewis, N., & Foukia.,N. (2008, May). Key distribution and route selection in wireless sensor networks. In *Proceedings of AAMAS 2008 Workshop in Agent Technology for Sensor Networks (ATSN 2008)*, Estoril, Portugal.

McKnight, D. H., Choudhury, V., & Kacmar, C. (2002). Developing and validating trust measures for e-commerce: an integrating typology. *Information Systems Research Journal, 13*(3), 334–359. doi:10.1287/isre.13.3.334.81

Michael, J. (1994). *Privacy and human rights.* Paris: UNESCO.

Ng, H. S., Sim, M. L., & Tan, C. M. (2006). Security issues of wireless sensor networks in healthcare applications. *BT Technology Journal, 24*(2), 138–144. doi:10.1007/s10550-006-0051-8

Ngai, E. C. H., Liu, J., & Lyu, M. R. (2006, June). On the intruder detection for sinkhole Attack in wireless sensor networks. In *Proceedings of the IEEE International Conference on Communications, (ICC 2006) Vol. 8* (pp. 3383-3389).

Noman, A.N.M., & Islam, Md. H. (2007). *A generic framework for defining security environments of sensor applications.* Unpublished master's thesis, Department of Computer And System Science, Royal Institute of Technology (KTH), DSV, Stockholm University.

Ozturk, C., Zhang, Y., & Trappe, W. (2004, October). Source-location privacy in energy constrained sensor network routing. In *Proceedings of the 2nd ACM Workshop on Security of Ad hoc and Sensor Networks (SASN 2004)*, Washington, USA.

Perez, C. R. (2007, December). *Reputation-based resilient data aggregation in sensor network.* Unpublished master's thesis, Purdue University, USA. Retrieved from http://docs.lib.purdue.edu/ecetheses/11/.

Perrig, A., Stankovic, J., & Wagner, D. (2004, June). Security in wireless sensor networks. *Communications of the ACM, 47*(6), 53–57. doi:10.1145/990680.990707

Perrig, A., Szewczyk, R., Wen, V., Culler, D., & Tygar, D. (2001, July). SPINS: Security protocols for sensor networks. In *Proceedings of the Seventh Annual International Conference on Mobile Computing and Networks (ACM Mobicom)*, Rome, Italy.

Pham, H., & Jha, S. (2004, October). An adaptive mobility-aware MAC protocol for sensor networks (MS-MAC). In *Proceedings of the IEEE International Conference on Mobile Ad-hoc and Sensor Systems* (pp. 558-556).

Qi, H., Kuruganti, P. T., & Xu, Y. (2002). The development of localized algorithms in wireless sensor networks. *IEEE Sensors Journal, 2*(6), 286–293.

Römer, K., & Mattern, F. (2004, December). The design space of wireless sensor networks. *IEEE Wireless Communications, 11*(6), 54–61. doi:10.1109/MWC.2004.1368897

Servetto, S. D. (2006, May). From "sensor networks" to "sensor networks." In *Proceedings of the Third IEEE Workshop on Embedded Networked Sensors (EmNets 2006),* Cambridge, MA, USA.

Sohrabi, K., Gao, J., Ailawadhi, V., & Pottie, G. J. (2000). Protocols for self-organization of a wireless sensor network. *IEEE Personal Communications Journal, 7*(5), 16–27. doi:10.1109/98.878532

Srinivasany, A., Teitelbaumy, J., Liangz, H., Wuyand, J., & Cardei, M. (2007). Reputation and trust-based systems for ad hoc and sensor networks. In A. Boukerche (Ed.), *On Trust Establishment in Mobile Ad-Hoc Networks.* New York: Wiley & Sons.

Srinivasany, A., Teitelbaumy, J., & Wu, J. (2006). DRBTS: Distributed reputation-based beacon trust system. In *Proceedings of the 2nd IEEE International Symposium on Dependable, Autonomic and Secure Computing (DASC 2006)* (pp. 277-283).

Stankovic, J. A., Cao, Q., Doan, T., Fang, L., He, Z., Kiran, R., et al. (2005, June). Wireless sensor networks for in-home healthcare: potential and challenges. In *Proceedings of the High Confidence Medical Device Software and Systems Workshop (HCMDSS 2005),* Philadelphia, PA, USA (pp. 2-3).

Walters, J. P., Liang, Z., Shi, W., & Chaudhary, V. (2006). Wireless sensor network security: a survey. In Y. Xiao (Ed.), *Security in Distributed, Grid, and Pervasive Computing.* Boca Raton, FL: Auerbach Publications, CRC Press.

Want, R. (2007, December). You're not paranoid: they really are watching you! *IEEE Journal of Pervasive Computing, 6*(4), 2–4. doi:10.1109/MPRV.2007.90

Warren, S., & Brandeis, L. (1890). The right to privacy. *Harvard Law Review, 4*(1), 193–220. doi:10.2307/1321160

Weiser, M. (1991, September). The Computer for the twenty-first century. *Scientific American, 265*(3), 94–100.

Westin, A. (1967). *Privacy and Freedom.* New York: Atheneum.

Wood, A. D., Stankovic, J. A., & Son, S. H. (2003). JAM: a jammed-area mapping service for sensor networks. In *Proceedings of the 24th IEEE Real-Time Systems Symposium (RTSS 2003)* (pp. 286- 297).

Ye, W., Heidemann, J., & Estrin, D. (2002). An energy-efficient mac protocol for wireless sensor networks. In *Proceedings of the 21st International Annual Joint Conference of the IEEE Computer and Communications Societies (INFOCOM 2002),* New York, NY, USA.

Yu, B., & Xiao, B. (2006, April). Detecting selective forwarding attacks in wireless sensor networks. In *Proceedings of the Parallel and Distributed Processing Symposium (IPDPS 2006)*.

Zhu, H., Feng, B., & Deng, R. H. (2003). Computing of trust in distributed networks. In *Cryptology ePrint Archive: Report 2003/056*. Retrieved from http://eprint.iacr.org

ENDNOTES

[1] TinyOS is an open-source operating system designed for wireless embedded sensor networks. See TinyOS community forum at http://www.tinyos.net/.

[2] These requirements are taken from the definition of computer security referenced (Daintith, J., Illingworth. V., & Pyle., I., July 2008)

[3] A DoS makes a computer or network resource (in our case the WSN) unavailable to the end users by flooding the network with bogus traffics that exhaust sensor nodes.

[4] RSA stands for Rivest Shamir Adleman, the names of the three mathematicians who invented RSA in 1976 and published in 1977.

[5] An attacker that captures a node can extract sensitive date such as cryptographic keys or change the content of the node, for instance reprogram the node or insert its own malicious data (authentication keys, bogus routing information …).

[6] Neighbors are nodes in the same radio range.

[7] A more accurate risk metric actually computes the expected number of nodes to capture before any link can be eavesdrop with a certain probability q.

[8] A jamming signal is a radio propagation that is unwanted and disruptive.

[9] A signal of high energy can interfere with normal communication signal adding noise. An attacker can use powerful laptops with high energy to trigger noise.

[10] The MAC layer controls access to the physical transmission medium in a local network. In case of WSNs, it controls access to the wireless medium.

[11] In a sense-response application, sensor nodes monitor an area for events of interest and report the event to the BS. After receiving the event, the BS launches a prompt physical response. Examples of such applications are: natural disaster monitoring, fire detection …

[12] Survivability: The degree to which essential functions are still available even though some part of the system is down.

[13] SYNC stands for synchronization. SYNC packets are used at the MAC layer.

[14] A beacon is usually a specific device that helps for localization and navigation. Combined with sensor nodes, they can use radio signals with limited localization or direction information in order to inform surrounding sensors nodes about their location.

[15] The Calcutt Committee was appointed by the UK Government in 1989 to report on privacy and related matters.

[16] Pervasive computing refers to visionary new ways of applying Information and Communication Technologies (ICT) to our daily lives.

[17] Data Protection Directive (DPD).

[18] Directive dealing the processing of personal data and the protection of privacy in the electronic communications (DPEC).

[19] **U**niting and **S**trengthening **A**merica by **P**roviding **A**ppropriate **T**ools **R**equired to **I**ntercept and **O**bstruct **T**errorism Act of 2001" (Public Law 107-56).

Chapter 10
Trusted Computing for Collaboration

Joerg Abendroth
Technische Universität München, Germany

Holger Kinkelin
Technische Universität München, Germany

ABSTRACT

The term "trusted computing" refers to a technology developed by the Trusted Computing Group. It mainly addresses two questions: "Which software is executed on a remote computer?" and "How can secret keys and other security sensitive data be stored and used safely on a computer?". In this chapter the authors introduce the ideas of the trusted computing technology first and later explain how it can help us with establishing "trust" into a business partner (e.g., for B2B or B2C interactions). More precisely: the authors explain how to establish trust into the business partner's computing machinery. So in their chapter "trust" means, that one business partner can be sure, that the other business partner's computing system behaves in an expected and non malicious manner. The authors define "trust" as something that can be measured by cryptographic functions on one computer and be reported towards and evaluated by the business partner's computer, not as something that is derived from observations or built upon legal contracts.

INTRODUCTION

Collaboration in business environment requires trust. Often this trust is established by a legal framework, which is cumbersome and in case of computer interactions sometimes impossible. Trusted Computing aims to bridge this gap, but as the problem is hard, the solution is not a general one. One has to pay attention about the trust relationships and business models to benefit from the technology.

Other chapters in this book define trust as something that can be built up and achieved gradually over time and interactions. In this chapter trust is derived from cryptographic functions, integrity measurements of computer system components and credentials in signed certificates by known trusted parties.

DOI: 10.4018/978-1-60566-414-9.ch010

The rest of the chapter first speaks about the basis of Trusted Computing, the history and scope of standardization, the required hardware and finally concepts. Then a section about the trust relationships in business environment opens the discussion on "Using Trusted Computing for Business". Here the different collaboration types are shown and relevant business cases are outlined. Last thoughts on Trusted Computing for collaboration conclude the chapter.

About Trusted Computing

Ideas similar to Trusted Computing are almost as old as history in computing. E.g., in 1987 IBM developed the 4758 PCI Cryptographic Coprocessor, which was used in numerous research activities. Other research focused on securing the operating system itself.

Today operation systems are very complex, which makes them prone to errors. These errors often lead to exploits that can make critical calculations vulnerable for attacks. So it seems necessary to have a tamper-proof environment, e.g. a special chip, where critical calculations can be executed safely and secrets stored securely.

In 1999 the Trusted Computing Platform Alliance (TCPA), a first standardization organization to provide an interoperable standard for such a secure computing environment, was founded. The concepts of the TCPA where different to the current concepts of Trusted Computing standards and can best be characterized by including all components of a computing system. Today's standards provide separate building blocks and leave out elements that could provide the ability of remotely controlling a device. While this scope is consumer friendly it introduces pitfalls in the area of business models, which will be discussed in the Section "Using Trusted Computing for Business".

The Trusted Computing Group (TCG)

The Trusted Computing Group (TCG) is the standardization organization that defines open, vendor-neutral standards for Trusted Computing. The current so called "promoter members" are

- AMD
- Fujitsu Limited
- Hewlett-Packard
- IBM
- Infineon
- Intel Corporation
- Lenovo Holdings Limited
- Microsoft
- Seagate Technology
- Sun Microsystems, Inc.
- Wave Systems

There are further 131 companies that have a "contributor" or "adopter" membership, which points towards wide adoption of the technology and broad scope.

The TCG consists of several subgroups, namely:

- Authentication
- Hardcopy
- Infrastructure
- Mobile
- PC-Client
- Server
- (Trusted) Software Stack (TSS)
- Storage
- Trusted Network Connect (TNC)
- Trusted Platform Module (TPM)
- Virtualized Platform

In the following, some TCG subgroups will be introduced briefly. For an comprehensive introduction to the scope of all working groups the reader is kindly asked to visit the TCG website https://www.trustedcomputinggroup.org/groups/.

Trusted Platform Module and (Trusted) Software Stack Workgroup

The Trusted Platform Module Workgroup (TPM WG) standardizes the TPM chip, which must be considered as the main element of Trusted Computing. All trust is rooted in this chip and lifted up to the Trusted Software Stack, the operating system and applications using a chain of trust. The TPM WG defines the inner working and capabilities of the TPM chip; the Trusted Software Stack working group defines the application level interfaces.

The parts that are missing are the boot process (BIOS, Boot Loader, Low level parts of the OS), but these are straight forward and partly in scope of the virtualization working group.

Important publications include:

- Replacing Vulnerable Software with Secure Hardware
- Design Principles
- TCG Architecture Overview
- TCG Software Stack (TSS) Specification

Infrastructure Workgroup

Whenever cryptographic functions are used and trust is established using signed certificates (involving a PKI[1]), an infrastructure is required to support the functionality. The function of attestation (please cf. to the next subsection for an introduction) requires special infrastructure support. These are the elements of the infrastructure working group. From the business perspective it might be added that the TCG does not aim at operating the special infrastructure elements, but leaves this open for commercial exploitation.

Important publications include:

- Reference Architecture for Interoperability
- Architecture Part II: Integrity Management

PC-Client, Server and Mobile Workgroup

PC-Client, Server and Mobile Workgroup, are groups focused on a special platform. The TPM chip alone is not sufficient; it has to be integrated into the platform and in some cases further Trusted Computing technology needs to be added. While these working groups do not define the actual implementation of the mechanism in the OS, they agree on interoperable methods to allow e.g. remote parties to benefit from Trusted Computing support. For applications engineers, the Trusted Software Stack standards are of bigger interest, for companies interacting with client platforms it might be worth to check for the special Trusted Computing flavor on that specific platform.

Important publications include:

- TCG Architecture Overview
- TCG Generic Server Specification
- TCG Mobile Reference Architecture

Trusted Network Connect Workgroup

Trusted Network Connect (TNC) is the first workgroup that provides standards for a full business case. The standards example of the TNC application is as follows: A company laptop was exposed to manipulation and tries to connect to the company network (LAN or VPN). Using TNC, the configuration and integrity of the computer can be checked prior the computer gets company network access. Only if the TNC server is confident about the trustworthiness of the laptop, it grants network access to the laptop.

For achieving this, TNC provides mechanisms for the company IT department to examine the status of the laptop remotely. This examination is used to induce confidence into the configuration and the integrity of the laptop. For example, by using TNC it is possible to check that no malware is installed on the laptop, that the virus checker uses the latest signatures, and that the firewall is enabled.

Important publications include:

- TCG TNC Architecture for Interoperability
- Networking Industry and IT Support for Trusted Network Connect (TNC) and its IF-MAP Specification

Authentication Workgroup

The TPM has commands that require special authority, for which the user has to be authenticated. Currently a basic mechanism of nonce and textual secret is used. The authentication working group also defines mechanisms to utilize biometric devices or smart cards in trusted platforms.

Hardware

The Hardware behind the technology Trusted Computing consists of the TPM chip at its core and Trusted Computing aware versions of standard PC platform components like the BIOS or boot loader. While the TPM chip provides the security functions the rest of the platform has to use them and abide to the concept of the chain of trust. Only in case of a coherent chain of trust, platform attestation is meaningful and can be trusted and a remote party can convince herself that the configuration of the communication partner is trustworthy. Rephrased for the business setting: a business partner can mitigate risk by remotely verifying the trustworthiness of involved computer systems.

1) Chain of Trust

How does the chain of trust work? As the TPM chip is a passive element, each element in the boot chain has to cooperate to create a coherent chain of trust. First the CRTM (Core Root of Trust

Figure 1. The elements of trusted computing

Figure 1. The elements of trusted computing

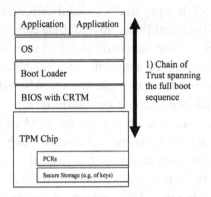

Measurement), a special part of the BIOS, stores a hash of the BIOS image in the TPM.

Next, the CRTM stores the hash of the Boot Loader which is the next element in the boot process and of the chain of trust in the TPM. Now CPU control is handed over to the Boot Loader which also stores a hash of the OS loader in the TPM before handing control to the OS loader. Finally the OS loader creates and stores integrity measurements of the Kernel and the Kernel modules.

For the chain of trust it is important that each element of the computer system computes and stores the hash of the next component it hands control to in the TPM. More specifically these hashes are stored in one of several, so called platform configuration registers (PCR) which cannot be set by an attacker to a specific value. So the attacker cannot hide a program once it was executed on the computer. This chain of trust provides the basis for remote attestation. In business environment this means not only the computer or server needs a TPM on the motherboard, but it also requires that BIOS, Boot Loader and OS need to be suitable for Trusted Computing.

2) TPM Chip

The Trusted Platform Module (TPM) provides the capabilities that are required for Trusted Computing to be a suitable anchor for trustworthiness. In principle a physically secured chip, such as a smart card could also provide these capabilities. However if one wants to be sure that a certain key is on a certain computer, then a removable smart card would not be the right solution. Also in terms of attack resistance of the interface between the platform and the smart card, the TPM chip is a better solution. No open connection, such as the port of a smart card reader, is needed, since the TPM chip is inseparably soldered to the main board of the computer. There have been approaches to even embed the TPM into the north-bridge of the computer, integrating it deep into the computer architecture.

3) TPM Keys and Certificates

Each TPM chip, possesses a RSA "master key", the so called Endorsement Key (EK) and a EK credential. The EK credential is a certificate of the EK, created by the TPM manufacturer, vouching for the standard compliancy of the TPM chip. Since the EK is unique, it can be regarded as the identity of the TPM chip and thus of the whole machine.

The EK is used for creating certificates for other keys generated in the TPM, again vouching for the trustworthiness of the newly generated key, i.e. that the key was generated in a valid TPM. This kind of EK signed keys is called Attested Integrity Key (AIK). AIKs can be seen as an alias of the EK. The AIK certificates can be validated using the EK credential. The EK credential again can be validated using the root certificate of the TPM vendor which can be obtained by the vendors PKI.

If privacy concerns are not important, using EK certified AIKs is sufficient. If privacy is crucial, a so called PCA (privacy CA) might create a certificate for an AIK which is not linkable anymore to a certain TPM. This certificate only guarantees that the AIK resides in a standard compliant TPM, but it does not reveal the identity of the according TPM.

The two main functionalities provided by the TPM chip are explained below:

4) Remote Attestation

The chain of trust guarantees that each component running on the platform leaves traces in the platform configuration registers (PCRs). The process of remotely reading the PCRs is called "remote attestation". Basically spoken, a dump of PCR values is sent from a computer to a remote party. In most cases this dump will be signed by the TPM with an AIK to guarantee that the values are untampered by malware and that the values originated from a valid TPM.

By verification of this signature, a remote party can be confident that the reported PCR dump is unmodified. In the next step, the remote party compares the reported PCR values to reference values of well known and trusted software. If the reported PCR values are identical to the expected reference value, the remote party can be sure that the platform runs trustworthy software and is in a trustworthy configuration.

Using remote attestation, business partners are able to verify the actions of each other, e.g. by verifying that certain (security) programs are running as precautions or by checking that the interaction program has not been altered.

For completeness reasons a note on attestation versus runtime attestation has to be given. Attestation always restricts to the configuration of a platform at a certain point in time. This means that any alterations that have been done past this point in time, e.g. by exploiting a software vulnerability, will remain undetected. For detecting these kinds of attacks, runtime attestation would be needed. Current research on runtime attestation is at an early state. Today the best approach is to utilize shielded execution environments to stop applications with software vulnerabilities to cause greater damage.

5) Secure Storage

The second feature of the TPM chip is secure storage. The TPM can store given data or keys in a secure way. It can also generate new RSA key pairs whose private key cannot leave the TPM. Only the public part of the key (encryption key) can be exported and used outside of the TPM or even the computer. This means that only one specific TPM holds the decryption key. The process of encrypting data (or a symmetric key) with a key that only a certain TPM can decrypt is called "binding". Thus remote parties can then be sure that a document encrypted with a certain key can only be decrypted on a specific computer. It is worth to note that binding of data to a TPM is a slow process and it is better to bind a symmetric key. This symmetric key can be used to encrypt the data outside of the TPM.

Sealing is a special form of binding. While binding enforces that only a specific TPM can decrypt the data, sealing tells the TPM to do this only if the PCR hold certain values. I.e. when the computer is in a certain trusted configuration. Sealing can be used to bind passwords to an application and to be sure that not key logger is installed underneath.

Currently the biggest business case of secure storage is hard disk encryption (e.g. Microsoft Bitlocker). The encryption key is generated and stored in the TPM. If the hard-disk gets stolen, its data cannot be decrypted in another computer. Additionally upon disposal of the computer it is enough to give the command to clear the TPM to make all data on the hard-disk unreadable.

Using Trusted Computing for Business

All innovations provide business opportunities, Trusted Computing included. Although today only the most evident opportunity: producing and selling of TPMs and TPM enabled computers has been leveraged. Some companies might think of introducing TPMs in their own products, but caution is necessary as TPMs are not the silver bullets of computer security.

Threat Scenarios

To understand the business cases it is important to understand what kind of trust the TPM provides and what trust relationship a certain business case requires. In the following threat scenarios are described and it will be identified if and how the TPM can provide additional trust. It does not need to be mentioned specifically that an attacker with access to inner TPM functions (i.e. maybe even hidden functions), can not be defeated.

1) Network

The attacker is in the network and is able to eavesdrop and replay messages, but has no physical access to the client. A typical scenario is a laptop that has stored sensitive information and wishes to communicate them over the network to another computer. As the attacker does not have physical access to the laptop, monitoring the network connection and altering messages is the only option.

In this case the TPM can not provide additional trust. Encrypting the network connection, e.g. by using TLS is sufficient.

2) Remote & Local

The attacker reads network traffic, steals the end device or manipulates the end device. The rightful user does not assist the attacker. In this attack the physical access to the device including the option to use boot media (e.g. CD to boot from) is the key parameter.

In this case the TPM can provide trust about the keys that are stored in the TPM. Hard disk encryption can stop an attacker even though he has full read/write access to the hard disk device. Applications such as VPN can store vital authen-

Figure 2. The different threat scenarios

tication keys in the TPM so that VPN access can not be stolen. Trusted Network Connect (TNC) can reveal manipulations on the installation, such as installation of a key logger. This is important if a device is only temporarily under control of the attacker and the laptop user does not know about the changes.

3) Buffer Overflow

If the local software has is prone to a buffer overflow vulnerability and the attacker exploits this, then two phases must be distinguished:

- The platform has booted and the PCRs are set. Then the attacker has exploited the buffer overflow. No reboot has taken place yet.
- In the second phase the attacker (or user) has rebooted the platform after the exploit.

In the first phase, only runtime attestation would provide additional trust. While in the second phase the boot process would record the alterations made after the exploit and thus the attack would be noticed using remote attestation. In general the choice of defense is secure coding and hardening of the platform up to the point of sandboxing like done in Java.

Trust and Business Environment

The previous section has shown that only scenarios where local attacks are feared, such as against the storage media, are the right scenarios for deploying trusted platforms. Scenarios where the OS will be manipulated or in the general case where the local user can setup the client in the way he wants can also benefit from TPM usage. Here the constraint is that the exploitation of a buffer overflow without a reboot or a user running code which is not known on the remote side, negates the benefit of the TPM chip.

In this section business scenarios will be discussed. In general scenarios are separated to Business to Customer[2] (B2C) or Business to Business (B2B). B2B collaborations often involve fewer constraints and build on initial trust, e.g. created through legal contracts. Most collaboration occurs in B2B interactions. Legal bindings and fear of penalties influence the behavior. In case of B2C the initial trust is different. Legal contracts can be crafted, but might be considered less binding. Quality of the service might depend on the end user device configuration and the relevant part of the contract has been ignored. Due to the number of B2C relationships technical enforcement seems to be better than legal binding.

A Business Relationship with TPM Involvement

As an example we consider a business case where a client uses a community portal. Providing some location information, the portal interacts with advertisement providers, displays the advertisements, receives revenue and pays a portion of it to the user. The user might even watch high quality commercial films for which he also gets paid. Because the amount of payment depends on the location and quality of viewing device, users have an incentive to cheat to gain more profit. In return advertisers will notice the cheats and in the long run use their contractual hooks to avoid false payments. Hence the company in the middle, the community portal, has a reason to increase the trustworthiness of the user's assertions at the B2C relationship. In the following it should also be considered whether TPM assisted trust can be beneficial.

Location of TPM Enabled Computer

Looking at the TPM involvement in the example given above, one could put a TPM on every of the platforms: Consumer, Portal Server and Advertisement Provider - this may not be necessary.

- TPM on the advertisement provider

The relationship between the portal and advertisement provider is B2B hence contractual enforcement through communication and punctual checks is a good option. Reviewing what negative actions the advertisement provider could do (e.g. displaying inappropriate ads, providing big adds that include two advertisements, etc.) it becomes clear that not the computer configuration, but other elements of enforcement are required.

- TPM on the web portal server

The advertisement provider might fear that the portal does not show the ads, fakes user requests or does not provide enough opportunities for advertisement. It is conceivable that a code review of the portal code and subsequent TPM enforcement, that exactly that reviewed code handles the ads would be an option. However contractual enforcement is more appropriate.

The customer might fear that he gets not sufficient opportunity (ads) to earn credit, but for this a code review and subsequent portal to client attestation seems to be too much effort. More likely is the reason that the customer wants to be sure that his private information is not misused

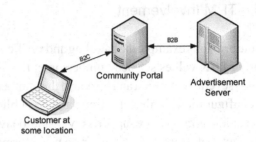

Figure 3. Example business relationships

by the portal. Then a kind of certification is needed, where the business practices setup and also computer configurations are reviewed and a certificate stating the trust level issued.

- TPM on the customer computer

The customer has a reason for cheating. The number of customers make the review and manual certification not feasible. The trusted computing technology provides a good way out. The portal can require the user to get the location information and viewing capabilities of this device from a trusted source. The TPM in his platform can vouch for trustworthiness of the source. Automated verification assists the portal and advertisement provider.

The verification process would require the client to use one of the accepted configurations. Accepted configurations can be centrally provided by a service assisting the web portal in the verification process. Today the number of configurations, such as the specific set of applications a user might have installed on his device, the patch level of these applications and finally boot loader configuration is so large, that a predefined database of valid PCR values is non-existent. A potential solution can be that the client provides his set of PCR values and configuration information upon registration, then the information will be manually verified and put into the verification database as a valid set of values.

Three Cases of Trust Relationships with TPM Involvement

In the previous example the handling and verification of PCR values seemed cumbersome; this is due to several facts. First and foremost the number of configurations is almost infinite and no public attestation infrastructure support is available today. The fact that users maintain their own platforms is largely the reason for the high number of configurations. In the enterprise environment the IT department maintains a small set of configurations and the users have only limited influence when patches are applied. In the controlled enterprise environment remote configuration verification becomes feasible.

As a general rule, whenever the remote party can influence the configuration of the TPM enabled device, Trusted Computing technology is beneficial. Then remote attestation can be used for configuration management, and to see changes due to attacks towards the local setup. Three cases of TPM deployments are seen in all of them the party who owns the platform is also the one wanting to verify integrity.

- A device manufacturer uses TPM for own products and is able to verify if firmware modifications or unauthorized updates have been done
- The IT department administrates the employees laptops and desktops ensuring platform integrity
- In the B2C or B2B case a dedicated virtual compartment is owned and controlled by the remote party.

In all cases the remote party can securely cooperate with the client and in all cases the TPM can be the trust anchor. The trust into the TPM can be lifted to trust on a fair behavior on the client side. This trust on fair behavior in return will enable several business cases that have been

Figure 4. Business case device manufacturer

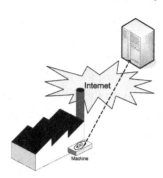

formerly impossible due to high risk of client side cheating.

1) Device Manufacturer

The collaboration of the device manufacturer with the buyer of the machine (Figure 4) is reduced on maintenance and firmware updates, for this it is business practice that the device manufacturer uses proprietary features and protects the sold machines in a special way. TPM technology supports the device manufacturer, it can be verified that the firmware has not been altered. Administration processes, such as which component configuration is valid at boot time can be verified by use of PCR values. Threats in these scenarios may come from the buyer of the machine that has an interest to upgrade features without payment, but also third parties that copy hardware and want to reuse efforts in firmware maintenance of the original hardware. A secure key storage helps the device manufacturer to address only real hardware with update operations.

2) IT Department and employees laptops

In this scenario (Figure 5), not the manufacturer of the laptop has the interest in the device configuration and integrity of the software, but the company, more specifically the IT department. A stolen laptop is a risk, but also laptops that have

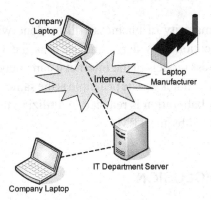

Figure 5. Business case IT department

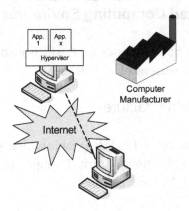

Figure 6. Business case virtualized compartment

been altered, e.g. a Trojan got installed, might open doors for industrial espionage. To cope with this, TPM technology, such as Trusted Network Connect (TNC), is an ideal tool. The IT department cooperates with the laptop manufacturer (and maybe also with the TPM manufacturer) to achieve confidence that the root of trust (i.e. TPM, Motherboard and BIOS) is trustworthy. Then the IT department takes ownership of the TPM and can utilize the attestation feature for configuration, verification and partly for device management.

In terms of collaboration, the remote party, the laptop user, and the IT department have a trust relationship that has to be verified. Basic authentication mechanisms are not sufficient, because the computer configuration may be altered during the period outside of the company network.

3) Virtual Compartment

In the secure collaboration case (Figure 6) where the second party (e.g. a laptop) has no special relationship with the entrusting party, matters become more complex. However this is the standard TPM case and standards for all aspects exist. First there needs to be support of the manufacturer of both the remote party and of the TPM manufacturer. Credentials that proof originality of TPM

and connection to the platform are required. The standards define the role of a Privacy CA that has knowledge of the TPM and platform manufacturers and can verify correctness of credentials. A user of the TPM can generate a special identity key (AIK) that is certified by the Privacy CA of being of origin in a trustworthy TPM. A remote party can verify the AIK certificate and then choose to trust that device. Once this root is laid to identify the TPM and Root of Trust (i.e. BIOS) then the PCR values can help the remote party to identify the configuration of the device. For practical reasons it is suggested to utilize results of the research projects such as OpenTC or IBM Secure Bootstrapping. Then it is possible to have a well known boot sequence up to a Hypervisor, which is reflected in the PCR values and can be verified by the remote party. Next the actual secure collaboration can begin, for example the remote party provides mobile code that runs on that well defined trusted environment, or the client on the remote device can be verified to be well behaving, by means of identifying the binary that is run (up to the patch level and compile version). Secure collaboration that is rooted in the hardware and cryptographic functions becomes possible and the real behavior can be seen, without any chance of disguising to later exploit the achieved reputation values.

More Business Cases in the Trusted Computing Environment

Further business cases exist, which are described here for reasons of completeness.

TPM Manufacturer

Manufacturing TPMs is a viable business case, as many applications of trusted computing technology require these chips.

Platform Vendor

Platform vendors, such as of laptops or mobiles can benefit from differentiation that is provided by TPM support. Although today that feature can be seen as a common one.

Privacy CA

The role of the Privacy CA is needed in cases where the TPM enabled device and remote party with an interest in secure collaboration do not have another direct trust relationship. A privacy CA will have good contacts (and verification methods) of TPM – and device manufacturers, so to be able to verify correctness of the devices. It will then decide how strong verification is needed and also how much of the real life identity a TPM user has to reveal to get a certified AIK credential. Then remote parties can select to trust the Privacy CA and derive from that trust, trust into remote parties for secure collaboration.

Trusted Infrastructure Provider

If a remote party does not want to maintain own data about configuration of devices and trust levels, it can chose to select a trust infrastructure provider, that converts the PCR values received through attestation to known trust levels needed for collaboration.

Application Provider

The majority of business will be done with the application providers. And such as the various business models in the Internet it can not be summarized quickly. The principle is the same: risk of the collaboration is reduced by utilizing the trust provided by the TPM.

CONCLUSION

In the beginning of this chapter the idea, history and some basics of Trusted Computing Technology have been introduced. Later on, we also showed how collaboration between entities can be build upon the trust rooted in TPMs. We also have shown how different collaborations can benefit by examples taken from real business scenarios.

REFERENCES

Balacheff, B., Chen, L., Pearson, S., Plaquin, D., & Proudler, G. (2002). *Trusted Computing Platforms: TCPA Technology in Context*. Upper Saddle River, NJ: Prentice Hall.

Challener, D., Yoder, K., Catherman, R., Safford, D., & Van Doorn, L. (2007). *A Practical Guide to Trusted Computing*. Armonk, NY: IBM Press.

Gajek, S., Sadeghi, A.-R., St¨uble, C., & Winandy, M. (n.d.). *Compartmented Security for Browsers - Or How to Thwart a Phisher with Trusted Computing, OpenTC deliverables*. Retrieved from http://www.opentc.net/

Hendricks, J., & Van Doorn, L. (2004). Secure Bootstrap is Not Enough: Shoring up the Trusted Computing Base. In *Proc. of the Eleventh SIGOPS European Workshop, ACM SIGOPS*, Leuven, Belgium.

Sailer, R., Zhang, X., Jaeger, T., & van Doorn, L. (2004, August). *Design and Implementation of a TCG-based Integrity Measurement Architecture.* Paper presented at the 13th Usenix Security Symposium, San Diego, CA.

Trusted Computing Group. (2008). *Replacing Vulnerable Software with Secure Hardware.* Retrieved August 2008, from https://www.trustedcomputinggroup.org/groups/tpm/The_Trusted_Platform_Module_Overview_March_2008.pdf

Trusted Computing Group. (2008). *TPM Working Group, Design Principles.* Retrieved August 2008, from https://www.trustedcomputinggroup.org/specs/TPM/mainP1DPrev103.zip

Trusted Computing Group. (2008). *TPM Working Group, TCG Architecture Overview.* Retrieved August 2008, from https://www.trustedcomputinggroup.org/groups/TCG_1_4_Architecture_Overview.pdf

Trusted Computing Group. (2008). *TSS Working Group, TCG Software Stack (TSS) Specification.* Retrieved August 2008, from https://www.trustedcomputinggroup.org/specs/TSS/TSS_1_2_Errata_A-final.pdf

Trusted Computing Group. (2008). *Infrastructure, Reference Architecture for Interoperability.* Retrieved August 2008, from https://www.trustedcomputinggroup.org/specs/IWG/IWG_Architecture_v1_0_r1.pdf

Trusted Computing Group. (2008). *Infrastructure, Architecture Part II - Integrity Management.* Retrieved August 2008, from https://www.trustedcomputinggroup.org/specs/IWG/IWG_ArchitecturePartII_v1.0.pdf

Trusted Computing Group. (2008). *Server Working Group, TCG Generic Server Specification.* Retrieved August 2008, from https://www.trustedcomputinggroup.org/specs/Server/TCG_Generic_Server_Specification_v1_0_rev0_8.pdf

Trusted Computing Group. (2008). *Mobile Working Group, TCG Mobile Reference Architecture.* Retrieved August 2008, from https://www.trustedcomputinggroup.org/specs/mobilephone/tcg-mobile-reference-architecture-1.0.pdf

Trusted Computing Group. (2008*). Trusted Network Connect, TCG TNC Architecture for Interoperability.* Retrieved August 2008, from https://www.trustedcomputinggroup.org/specs/TNC/TNC_Architecture_v1_3_r6.pdf

Trusted Computing Group. (2008). *Trusted Network Connect, Networking Industry and IT Support for Trusted Network Connect (TNC) and its IF-MAP Specification.* Retrieved August 2008, from https://www.trustedcomputinggroup.org/news/events/interop_2008/IFMAP_support_statements_april_21_final.pdf

ENDNOTES

1 Public Key Infrastructure
2 P2P (Peer-to-Peer) relationships are subsumed to B2C, as all relevant properties are the same.

Chapter 11
Trust–Privacy Tradeoffs in Distributed Computing

Rima Deghaili
American University of Beirut, Lebanon

Ali Chehab
American University of Beirut, Lebanon

Ayman Kayssi
American University of Beirut, Lebanon

ABSTRACT

In distributed computing environments, it is often needed to establish trust before entities interact together. This trust establishment process involves making each entity ask for some credentials from the other entity, which implies some privacy loss for both parties. The authors present a system for achieving the right privacy-trust tradeoff in distributed environments. Each entity aims to join a group in order to protect its privacy. Interaction between entities is then replaced by interaction between groups on behalf of their members. Data sent between groups is saved from dissemination by a self-destruction process. Simulations performed on the system implemented using the Aglets platform show that entities requesting a service need to give up more private information when their past experiences are not good, or when the requesting entity is of a paranoid nature. The privacy loss in all cases is quantified and controlled.

1. INTRODUCTION

Computing has evolved to increasingly complex and distributed environments. Billions of computational entities interact in ever-changing systems. In such dynamic environments, users are required to take multiple decisions without necessarily being able to rely on a fixed information infrastructure. In order to take accurate decisions, knowledge about other entities is required to establish trust relationships. Every transaction is then preceded by a negotiation phase where an entity asks for some credentials from the other entity which implies privacy loss. Since both trust and privacy are essential elements in a well-functioning environment, we present a system that properly addresses this conflict by achieving the right trade-off between trust and privacy. The rest of this chapter is organized as follows: Section 2 surveys previous work in the areas of trust and privacy. Section 3 presents the system model

DOI: 10.4018/978-1-60566-414-9.ch011

while Section 4 shows the simulations results and their evaluation. Finally, conclusions are given in Section 5.

2. PREVIOUS WORK

Among the different trust models, (Abdul-Rahman & Hailes, 1998) present a decentralized approach to trust management aiming at reducing ambiguity by using explicit trust statements and defining a recommendation protocol to exchange trust-related information.

Other trust models in are based on reputation (Abdul-Rahman, & Hailes, 2000 ;Mui, Mohtashemi & Halberstadt, 2002; Ramchurn, Jennings, Sierra & Godo, 2003). Agents are able to reason about trust and to have opinions based on other agents' recommendations as well as on previous experiences.

In (Damiani, Samarati, De Capitani di Vimercati, Paraboschi & Violante, 2002), the model is a self-regulating system where the peer-to-peer network is used to implement a reputation mechanism, while preserving anonymity. Reputation is computed using a distributed polling algorithm whereby resource requestors can find out about the reliability of another entity.

In (Tan 2003), a trust matrix model is used to build trust for conducting first trade transactions in electronic commerce. The model aims at finding a relation between anonymous procedural trust and personal trust based on past experience to model online trust between trading partners having never traded before.

The authors of (Jiang, Xia, Zhong & Zhang, 2004) present an autonomous trust management system for mobile agents where agents build trust relationships based on trust path searching or trust negotiation and exchange trust information to achieve global trust management without the need of a trust authority.

In (Gummadi & Yoon, 2004), security issues in peer-to-peer file sharing applications are con-

sidered. These include "peer selection" where peers having malicious tendencies are banned and "request resolution" where a peer has to choose the peer that exhausts its capabilities the least. The concept of reputation is introduced as a collective measure of all peers with a particular peer.

The TRUMMAR model (Derbas, Kayssi, Artail & Chehab, 2004) is based on reputation and aims to protect mobile agent systems from malicious hosts. TRUMMAR takes into account the concepts of reputation, first impression, loss of reputation with time, and host's sociability. The model was later enhanced as the PATROL model (Tajeddine, Kayssi, Chehab & Artail, 2006).

The authors (Wang & Vassileva, 2004) simulate a file sharing system in a peer-to-peer network where trust is defined using attributes such as reliability, honesty and competence of a trusted agent.

FIRE (Huynh, Jennings & Shadbolt, 2004) is a decentralized model for trust evaluation in open multi-agent systems where each agent should be responsible for storing trust information and evaluating trust itself. FIRE deals with open multi-agent systems in which agents are owned by many stakeholders and can enter and leave the system at any time.

The TRAVOS model (Patel, Teacy, Jennings & Luck, 2005) computes trust using probability theory and takes into account past interactions between agents.

The Trust-X model (Bertino & Squicciarini, 2004 and Bertino, 2004) for trust negotiation preserves privacy by using credential verification in order to establish trust between two parties. Disclosure policies protect sensitive credentials which contents are gradually disclosed to provide a higher degree of privacy protection.

Bharagava develops a method to minimize privacy loss. He uses entropy to mathematically model it. He also presents the PRETTY model (Bhargava, Lilien, Wang & Zhong, 2004-2006) that uses "privacy negotiators" to evaluate privacy loss involved in each credential disclosure.

Bhargava also proposes a scheme for privacy-preserving data dissemination where an entity associates with its sensitive data some metadata including its privacy preferences and policies. When a bundle is about to be compromised, it chooses apoptosis or data evaporation over risking a privacy disclosure. His method for trust-based privacy preservation in peer-to-peer data sharing networks uses a proxy for data acquirement. The requestor sends the query and gets its result through the proxy which makes it difficult for the eavesdroppers to explore the real interest of a node.

(Seigneur, 2005) argues that trust and privacy both depend on knowledge about an entity in opposite ways. He proposes to use pseudonymity as a level of indirection, which allows the establishment of trust without exposing the real-world identity.

In all the previous models, the trust and privacy models are not clearly quantified and rules are not well defined to determine how privacy is traded for trust. In addition, data apoptosis is only mentioned without details about how it may be implemented. We address both issues in this chapter.

3. TRUST-PRIVACY TRADEOFF SYSTEM

The environment we consider is a number of *groups* each of which consists of one or more *agents*. Each group has an administrator that interacts with other groups on behalf of its agents. An agent is an active communicating entity which plays one or several roles in a group. It joins a group in order to protect its privacy and to gain from the services offered by other group members without additional overhead.

The group administrator is trusted by all its members and can communicate with other group administrators. Joining a group to handle a role must be requested by the candidate agent or group and is not necessarily rewarded.

An agent a can join a group g to play a role r according to an acceptance evaluation function if and only if:

$F(a,g,r) = $ TRUE (role function)

$T(a,g) > \alpha$ (trust function)

$P(a,g) = 0$ (privacy function)

In other words, an agent can join a group if it offers attractive services for the group (in this case, the role function will return TRUE), and is willing to give up all its privacy in order to gain sufficient trust from the administrator and the group members to join the group. When an agent joins a group, it gains the trust experiences of the group in addition to protecting its privacy from other groups. This also enables the agent to access the services offered by the group with the least possible overhead. The agent joining a group will give the group administrator a list of the services it can provide. The group administrator will then publish these services as services offered by the group.

3.1. Trust Information

Trust is computed using several pieces of information about the previous experiences of an agent such as reputation scores, details about the past experiences results, and the identity of groups involved in these experiences. The reputation score is received by each agent after an interaction; it is issued by a group administrator and cannot be modified by the agent.

If an agent has been newly added to the environment, it will be subject to a testing period. During this period, the agent is sent non-essential data with known results until its reputation stabilizes. This is known as the first impression phase.

The information that is sent during the negotiation phase is divided into categories according to its importance, as shown in Table 1.

Table 1.*Information categories and corresponding importance*

Type	Importance
Time since last experience	Low
Reputation certificate (score)	Low
Time of joining the group	Medium
Certificate issuer (the issuer's group)	Medium
Past experience type	Medium
Group involved in past experience	Medium
Number of previous interactions	Medium
Information about identity	Important
Position of member in community (if administrator or not)	Important
Past experience result	Very Important

During the negotiation phase and the interaction, information is sent according to a specific XML format as represented in Figure 1.

The Sender-Id corresponds to the agent identifier when the agent sends the information to the group administrator. Then, the group administrator replaces it with the group identifier before sending it to the other group.

For each agent, we define a set of numbers representing the privacy loss involved in a transaction. Loss is represented as a number between 0 and 10 where 0 indicates that nothing has been revealed.

Each agent has two predefined thresholds α_1 and α_2. Each agent accepts to send information as long as its cumulative privacy loss is below α_1. It stops sending information if the privacy loss reaches α_2. If the privacy loss involved in a transaction is between these two thresholds, the agent makes a decision depending on the difference between the loss reached and its thresholds and the difference between the trust gain reached on the other side and its thresholds. These thresholds are agent dependant.

3.2. Interaction between Groups

Since trust should be established between parties before any interaction takes place, the process involves privacy loss. In our system, the process is incremental and proceeds as follows (Figure 2):

- An agent M_1 from group G_1 wants to interact with group G_2 (M_1 is requesting a service advertised by G_2).

Figure 1. XML Message Forma. XML Format

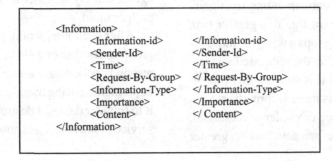

Figure 2. The System Flowchart

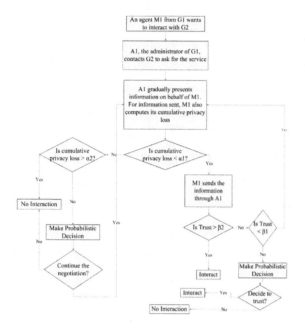

- M_1 sends an interaction request to G_2 through the group administrator A_1 of group G_1. A_1 contacts the administrator of G_2, A_2.
- The agent from G_2, M_2 that is actually offering the advertised service asks for information about M_1's past experiences through the administrators, and without knowing M_1's identity.
- A_1 starts to gradually present information on behalf of its agent, M_1. The more details are revealed, the more the loss is important. Before sending each piece of evidence to G_2, M_1 computes its cumulative privacy loss. If the cumulative privacy loss is less than α_1, M_1 sends the information.
- M_2 computes the corresponding trust gain. If the cumulative trust gain is greater than a threshold β_2, M_2 stops asking for more information and offers the requested service. If the trust gain is less than another threshold β_1, M_2 requests more information.
- For each new piece of evidence requested, if the cumulative privacy loss is greater

than α_2, M_1 decides to stop sending information and there will be no interaction between the two groups. If the cumulative privacy loss and the cumulative trust gain are between the two thresholds (α's and β's), the agents decide to interact or not depending on how close to the upper and lower thresholds the reached trust gain and privacy loss are.

- An agent requesting a service is thus willing to send information about its past experiences as long as its cumulative privacy loss is below the lower privacy threshold α_1. On the other hand, it refuses to send more information if the cumulative privacy loss becomes greater than the upper privacy threshold α_2.

On the other side, the agent offering the service keeps requesting information about past experiences from the other party as long as the cumulative trust gain is below the lower trust threshold β_1. It stops asking for information and establishes a trust relationship with the other party when the cumulative trust gain becomes higher than the upper trust threshold β_2. In this case, an interaction can take place between the two parties.

It is only when the privacy loss and the trust gain reached by the agents are between the two thresholds, that the agents should take a decision depending on context, how close to the upper and lower thresholds, the trust gain and privacy loss are.

In fact, the threshold values are different for different agents depending on the nature of the agent, namely whether it is "trusting", "normal" or "paranoid".

After each interaction, the data sent from one group to another one should be deleted. This corresponds to the data evaporation (apoptosis). This is implemented using mobile agents whose only role is to transfer data and destroy it after the requested service is provided, as shown in Section 4.

4. THE SYSTEM SIMULATION

The system was implemented and tested using the Aglets platform (Aglets. http://www.trl.ibm. com/aglets/ Accessed: June 2008). An aglet is a Java agent capable of autonomously moving from one host to another. It includes a complete Java mobile agent platform with a standalone server (Tahiti) and a library allowing the developer to build mobile agents and to embed the Aglets technology in their applications.

4.1. The Aglets Model

There are two ways to create an aglet: It can be instantiated from scratch (creation process) or it can be copied from an existing aglet (cloning process). A cloned aglet has the same properties of the original one. The creation of an aglet takes place in a context. The newly created aglet is assigned an identifier, inserted into the context, and initialized. As it has been successfully initialized, the aglet starts executing.

Aglets are defined as mobile agents; hence, they have the ability to move in two different ways: active and passive. The first is characterized by an aglet pushing itself from its current host to a remote host. This process is called "dispatching". If a remote host pulls an aglet away from its current host to it, this would be "retracting" and constitutes the passive type of aglet mobility. Dispatching an aglet from one context to another will remove it from its current context and insert it into the destination context, where it will restart execution. Retracting an aglet will remove it from its current context and insert it into the context from which the retraction was requested.

Multiple aglets may exchange information to accomplish a given task. This is known as aglets messaging. Messaging between aglets involves sending, receiving, and handling messages synchronously as well as asynchronously.

Finally, the destruction of aglets is also possible through the disposal process. This is necessary in order to be able to control the population of aglets in a context. The disposal of an aglet will halt its current execution and remove it from its current context.

4.2. The System Implementation

To implement the trust-privacy tradeoff system using the Aglets platform, a Tahiti server was created on different computers. The Tahiti server is used as a context to create aglet proxies and aglets. To represent a host (administrator or regular group member), we create a stationary aglet that is responsible for creating other mobile aglets moving between members and administrator or between administrators.

The stationary aglet representing a group member is able to create mobile aglets, to read and parse the XML-formatted information that is sent via mobile aglets, and to compute corresponding cumulative trust gain or privacy loss.

The stationary aglet representing a group administrator is able to determine which member should be contacted for the requested service, to create mobile aglets, to read XML attachments, attach XML information to other aglets and dispatch them.

The mobile aglets are of two types: one is responsible for moving in a group, between an administrator and the members, while the other is responsible for circulating between group administrators. These mobile aglets can be used to send the request for the service, the information from past experiences, the acceptance or the refusal of offering the service. They are also able to dispose of themselves thus assuring the data evaporation. None of the stationary aglets can kill these mobile aglets. During a negotiation and before disposing of itself, each mobile aglet creates a new mobile aglet that is responsible to do the next step in the negotiation, and then it kills itself. This way, when the aglet is destroyed, the information it is carrying will also be destroyed, which achieves privacy preserving through apoptosis.

When an agent receives a piece of information, the cumulative trust gain is modified as follows:

Trust Value = Previous Trust Value + CTG / N (1)

Note that CTG is the computed trust gain, calculated as 0.5×Reputation when reputation is sent, or Weight×Trust_Gain, otherwise. N is the number of pieces of information of the same importance sent previously.

Before sending further information, an agent computes the cumulative privacy loss as follows:

Privacy Loss = Previous Loss + CPL / N (2)

Note that CPL is the computed privacy loss, calculated as Weight×Privacy_Loss, and N is the number of pieces of information of the same importance sent previously.

In order to evaluate the effectiveness of this trust-privacy tradeoff system in distributed computing, we ran different simulations on a network of interacting entities. Different cases are considered where some agents tend to be trustful, others normal and yet others paranoid. Accordingly, α_1 was set to 1, 3, and 5; α_2 was set to 4, 6, and 9, respectively. On the other hand, the trust thresholds were β_1 set to 5, 3, and 1; and β_2 set to 9, 6, and 4 respectively.

4.3. Results

In the simulation results shown in Figure 3, we consider an agent M_1 with a good past, with its reputation scores above 3/5. The red dots on the graph mark the cases where two negotiating entities reach an agreement to interact. The thresholds α_1 and α_2 represent the privacy loss values of M_1, while β_1 and β_2 represent the trust gain thresholds for a trusting agent, a normal agent and a paranoid agent. When M_2 is of a trusting

nature, the equilibrium is reached with a privacy loss for M_1 of 1.14 (less than α_1) and a trust gain for M_2 of 4.03 (greater than β_2). When M_2 has normal behavior, the equilibrium is reached with a privacy loss for M_1 of 2.97 (less than α_1) and a trust gain for M_2 of 5.86 (less than β_2 but closer to β_2 than to β_1). When M_2 is of a paranoid nature, the equilibrium is reached with a privacy loss for M_1 of 4.15 (greater than α_1 but closer to α_1 than to α_2) and a trust gain for M_2 of 7.04 (less than β_2 but closer to β_2 than to β_1). We can then conclude that for an agent M_1 with a good past and a normal behavior, the negotiation always leads to an agreement to interact. However, this agreement is sometimes in the "uncertain" zone of the receiving agent M_2.

Similarly, and from simulating other cases, we notice that reaching an agreement is faster and involves less privacy loss when the requesting agent has a good past, or whenever it has a trusting or a normal behavior. This becomes more difficult and even sometimes impossible when the past experiences reflect a bad reputation or when the interacting agents are paranoid. In all cases, privacy loss is limited.

Figure 4 shows the cumulative trust gain reached by the receiving agent M_2 as a function of the pieces of evidence sent by the requesting agent M_1. Pieces of evidence can be of a low, medium, high or very high importance. We notice that when the requesting agent is a bad host, the information sent about its past experiences adds less to the cumulative trust gain of the receiving agent than for a good requesting agent. The successful end of negotiation is also reached earlier in a case of a requesting agent with a good past.

This system constitutes an improvement over the previous work since it introduces the capability of minimizing the privacy loss before interacting. In the previous models, the requesting agent used to give all available information about its past experiences, and hence completely lose privacy. Hence, we view the difference of privacy loss of the current model as actually a privacy gain over

Figure 3. Simulation Results

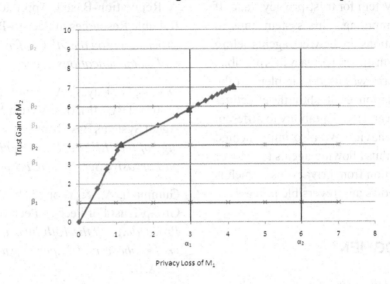

Figure 4. Cumulative Trust gain comparison

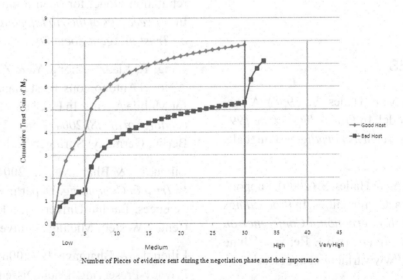

the previous models. The privacy gain is thus equal to **10 - privacy loss** since **10** is associated with the maximum privacy loss that an agent can have.

On the other hand, the current system is slower to converge. In fact, since the previous systems send all past information at once, the number of steps to reach a decision to interact or not is equal

to one. In our system, this number is equal to the number of messages sent from the agent requesting the services. However, we should mention that these messages are small in size in comparison to the bigger message sent previously containing all the information.

5. CONCLUSION

We presented a system for trust-privacy tradeoff in distributed computing. This system aims to establish trust relationships between agents before any interaction, with the least privacy loss possible. The Aglets platform was used to implement the system. The simulation results show the effectiveness of the system and its adaptability to different types of agent behavior. We also implemented data evaporation thus allowing agents to recover after each transaction from privacy loss which is usually considered as an irreversible process.

ACKNOWLEDGMENT

The authors would like to thank and acknowledge the support of the Lebanese National Council for Scientific Research and the AUB University Research Board.

REFERENCES

Abdul-Rahman, A., & Hailes, S. (1998). A Distributed Trust Model. In *Proceedings of the 1997 workshop on New security paradigms,* Langdale, Cumbria.

Abdul-Rahman, A., & Hailes, S. (2000). Supporting Trust in Virtual Communities. In *Proceedings of the 33rd Hawaii International Conference on System Sciences. Aglets.* (n.d.). Retrieved June 2008, from http://www.trl.ibm.com/aglets/

Bertino, E. (2004). *Trust Negotiation Concepts and Issues.* CS & ECE Departments, CERIAS, Purdue University.

Bertino, E., & Squicciarini, A. C. (2004). Privacy preserving Trust Negotiations. In *Proceedings of the 5th CACR,* Toronto.

Damiani, E., Samarati, P., De Capitani di Vimercati, S., Paraboschi, S., & Violante, F. (2002). A Reputation-Based Approach for Choosing Reliable Resources in Peer-to-Peer Networks. In *Proceedings on the 9th Conference on Computer and Communications Security.*

Derbas, G., Kayssi, A., Artail, H., & Chehab, A. (2004). TRUMMAR - A Trust Model for Mobile Agent Systems Based on Reputation. In *Proceedings of the IEEE/ACS International Conference on Pervasive Services (ICPS'04).*

Gummadi, A., & Yoon, J. P. (2004). Modeling Group Trust For Peer-to-Peer Access Control. In *Proceedings of the 15th International Workshop on Database and Expert Systems Applications (DEXA).*

Huynh, T. D., Jennings, N. R., & Shadbolt, N. R. (2004). Developing an integrated trust and reputation model for open multi-agent systems. In *Proceedings of the 7th International Workshop on Trust in Agent Societies.*

Jiang, Y., Xia, Z., Zhong, Y., & Zhang, S. (2004). A Novel Autonomous Trust Management Model for Mobile Agents. In H. Chen, et al. (Eds.), *Proceedings of the ISI 2004* (LNCS 3073, pp. 56-65). Berlin, Germany: Springer-Verlag.

Lilien, L., & Bhargava, B. (2004). *Introduction to Trust in Computing.* Department of Computer Sciences, Purdue University, CERIAS Security Center, Western Michigan University.

Lilien, L., & Bhargava, B. (2006). A Scheme for Privacy-Preserving Data Dissemination. *IEEE Transactions on Systems, Man, and Cybernetics. Part A, Systems and Humans, 36*(3). doi:10.1109/TSMCA.2006.871655

Lu, Y., Wang, W., Xu, D., & Bhargava, B. (2004). Trust-based privacy preservation for peer-to-peer data sharing. In *Proceedings of the Workshop on Secure Knowledge Management (SKM).*

Mui, L., Mohtashemi, M., & Halberstadt, A. (2002). A Computational Model of Trust and Reputation. In *Proceedings of the 35th Hawaii International Conference on System Sciences*.

Patel, J., Teacy, W. T. L., Jennings, N. R., & Luck, M. (2005) A Probabilistic Trust Model for Handling Inaccurate Reputation Sources. In *Proceedings of the 3rd International Conference on Trust Management*, Rocquencourt, France.

Ramchurn, S. D., Jennings, N. R., Sierra, C., & Godo, L. A. (2003). Computational Trust Model for Multi-Agent Interactions based on Confidence and Reputation. In *Proceedings of the Workshop on Trust, Privacy, Deception and Fraud in Agent Societies*. Melbourne, Australia: AAMAS.

Seigneur, J.-M. (2005). *Trust, Security and Privacy in Global Computing*. Unpublished doctoral dissertation, Trinity College Dublin.

Tajeddine, A., Kayssi, A., Chehab, A., & Artail, H. (2006). PATROL: a comprehensive reputation-based trust model. In *Autonomic and Trusted Computing* (LNCS 4158, pp. 205-216). Berlin, Germany: Springer.

Tan, Y. (2003). A Trust Matrix Model for Electronic Commerce. In *Proceedings of the Trust Management First International Conference, iTrust*.

Wang, Y., & Vassileva, J. (2004). Bayesian Network Trust Model in Peer-to-Peer Networks. In G. Moro, C. Sartori, & M. P. Singh (Eds.), *Proceedings of the AP2PC 2003* (LNAI 2872, pp. 23-34). Berlin, Germany: Springer-Verlag.

Xu, D., Lilien, L., & Bhargava, B. (2004). *Private and Trusted Interactions*. Department of Computer Sciences, Purdue University, CERIAS Security Center, CWSA.

Zhong, Y., & Bhargava, B. (2004) Using entropy to trade privacy for Trust. In *Proceedings of Security and Knowledge Mangement (SKM)*, Amherst, NY. Zhong, Y., Bhargava, B., & Lilien, L. (n.d.). *Trust and Privacy in Authorization*. Retrieved from http://www.cs.purdue.edu/homes/bb/bb_Pgh_PI_meetg.ppt

Zhong, Y., Lilien, L., & Bhargava, B. (2005). *P2D2: A Mechanism for Privacy-Preserving Data Dissemination*. Department of Computer Sciences, Purdue University, CERIAS Security Center, Western Michigan University.

Selected Readings

Chapter 12
A Proposition for Developing Trust and Relational Synergy in International e-Collaborative Groups

Bolanle A. Olaniran
Texas Tech University, USA

ABSTRACT

Trust and relational development represents a critical challenge in online collaboration groups. Often the problem is attributed to several factors including physical distances, time differences, cultures, and other contributing factors. The challenge in virtual teams centers on creating a successful cohort that functions as a team and develops a sense of trust and cohesion in the process of accomplishing respective group goals. However, the lack of trust in online groups hinders relational development. The author contends that while online collaboration can be clouded by problems with trust and relational synergy as a whole, the problem is exacerbated in international online or e-Collaborative groups. The development of trust is essential to relational synergy and warmth that fosters successful task and social goal accomplishment. After reviewing related and extant research in online communication, the author offers some practical suggestions for facilitating and sustaining trust and relational synergy in international online collaboration with information communication technologies (ICTs).

INTRODUCTION

Computer-mediated communication (CMC) mediums such as e-mail and distribution lists are major ways in which business is being conducted in modern organizations (Craig, 2001-2002; Finholt & Sproull, 1990; Yu, 2001). Text-based CMC via e-mail, list servers, newsgroups (asynchronous), and chat rooms (synchronous) provide ways for individuals to be connected to other individuals and groups, and to obtain information or help that would have been difficult or impossible to obtain otherwise. The dawn of the new millennium has seen increasing globalization wherein organizational communication and group interaction occurs through information communication technologies. Perhaps not surprising, estimates from Gartner Inc. suggest that the amount of time a particular employee will spend with others in different geographical location will increase by 40 percent before 2010 (Solomon, 2001).

BACKGROUND

At the same time, communication technology media are not without their criticism. For instance, online collaboration consists of meetings and interactions that exist through virtual space—that is, where participants interact, using communication technology media. A major criticism of online collaboration medium is the lack of nonverbal cues during interaction. The lack of nonverbal cues is believed to render the technology ineffective especially when compared with a face-to-face medium (Garton & Wellman, 1995; Olaniran, 2007a). While there is other communication technology (i.e., videoconferencing) that offers nonverbal cues via audio and video cues in virtual team collaboration, for the most part, virtual teams operate asynchronously to accommodate different time zones and to foster round the clock organizational applied resources and productivity. As organizations embark on online team collaboration and projects, they find themselves at a crossroad where accomplishing task goals are just as important as achieving relational goals in any given projects. Thus, organizations are challenged to attend to and balance both set of goals if they are to be effective. In an overview of extant literature that reveals findings from original research to explore strategies that users can develop or adapt to overcome the lack of nonverbal cues in the CMC media technology, the intent of this discussion is

to improve the potential of virtual communication for constructing relationships. Specifically, the focus is on adapting communication technology media to develop trust and relational synergy in international online collaboration groups.

MAIN FOCUS OF THE CHAPTER

International online collaboration (e-Collaborative) teams represent a way for including employees in organizational participation and decision making processes (Olaniran, 2007a). Although one study showed that employee participation is correlated with commitment and that committed employees are more likely to be intrinsically fulfilled and have positive relational synergy with other employees (Mathieu & Zajac, 1990), one must be aware that commitment to an organization as a whole and commitment to work teams are different ideas (Becker & Billings, 1993; Morrow, 1993).

From most organizational standpoints, the impetus to use virtual teams for group collaboration is often economically driven (i.e., cost cutting, speed, and efficiency); however, there are some key challenges that often hinder success. Challenges in e-Collaborative teams include misunderstandings and conflicts through fragmented communication and difficulties maintaining relational ties among group members. Armstrong and Cole (2002) found that while geographically dispersed groups become integrated over time, they nonetheless experience problems associated with proximity (see also, Crampton, 2002; Olaniran, 1996a; 2001a; Solomon, 2001). Armstrong and Cole (2002) found that national cultures and distances, in general, experience problems that extend beyond miles and time zones even in integrated groups. Thus, they argued that organizational problems sometimes are recreated and reinforced within distributed groups. Similarly, Crampton (2002) contends that working from dispersed locations reduces the situational, and more importantly, the personal information, that collaborators have about one another. Consequently, the lack of this information affects how group members process information and leads to the formation of *in-groups* and *out-groups* along with the associated behavior tendencies. While the lack of cultural competency can result in attribution errors, additional factors including motivation and other personality factors can also influence attribution processes that lead to errors (Armstrong & Cole, 2002; Olaniran, 2001b). In other words, the development of meaningful collaboration in international e-Collaborative group collaboration transcends cultural boundaries and calls for greater communication competence— that is, the ability to adapt to varieties of situations (Olaniran, 2004).

Olaniran (2004) argues that the challenge facing geographically dispersed international online collaboration teams is further intensified because team members' intra-cultural communication competence does not translate to cross-cultural competence. One reason is that dimensions of communication competence involve two factors, namely, *effectiveness* which is the ability to accomplish goals. The other is the notion of *appropriateness* which is the suitability of a given action in a particular setting (Roy, 2001; Spitzberg & Cupach, 1989). People from different cultures in general use varying beliefs, values, and norms as the foundation for their behavior (e.g., perception and interpretation) of other members' behaviors. As a result, Olaniran (2004) concludes that an appropriateness dimension is the most difficult to achieve in cross-cultural virtual teams especially those involving international collaborators. In essence, there is the need to adapt communication and behaviors in international online collaboration groups. Furthermore, social structure creates unique cultural difference that determines how individuals appropriate or use communication technologies in group interaction. For example, there is a suppression of e-mail use in virtual interactions in East Asian cultures (Lee, 2002). Also, certain cultures, for example the Dutch,

prefer more structure in online team collaborations than the U.S. does (Gezo, Oliverson, & Zick, 2000; Kiser, 1999).

Other problems in online international group collaborations include fragmented communication, confusion during teleconferences, failure to return phone calls or respond to inquiries, and members being left off distribution lists. Misunderstandings often intensify ongoing conflicts. Proximity interferes with communication that requires nonverbal cues for clarity (e.g., Armstrong & Cole, 2002; Solomon, 2001). In general, communication technology is believed to decrease social dimensions, group solidarity, and trust which is essential for members to communicate freely and openly (Bal & Foster, 2000; Carleta, Anderson, McEwan, 2000).

One of the challenges of virtual teams is the failure to post or respond to messages when members are geographically distant. For example, Lee (2002) reports that, the value of showing respect is more important than simply getting a job done (i.e., performance). This may explain why Koreans and Japanese employees shy away from e-mail use. Their perception is that e-mail may be perceived by supervisors to be rude, and therefore, they would rather use alternative communication media which may delay feedback but are considered to appropriately convey respect (Lee, 2002). However, given that Western cultures do not share the same perception of respect, such action would be inappropriately perceived, hence resulting in conflict. In essence, the role of culture and the complexity that it creates in international online collaboration projects must be explored as team members work on their respective tasks, while at the same time negotiating and building relationships with co-collaborators.

As might be expected, proximity and culture inevitably interfere with interactions among international online groups. People in collocated virtual groups have greater access to multiple communication media and thus, have the benefit of using multiple channels, which in turn permits a broader range of messages, cues, and at times, immediate feedback. Armstrong and Cole (2002) stressed this point when they reported that more e-mail messages were sent to collocated group members than to internationally located group members. Specifically, the authors indicated that remote sites fell off the radar screens and were ignored during both telephone and video conferences. Similarly, this condition was referred to as out of sight leading to out of mind neglect (Olaniran, 2004; 2007). In some instances, *time* creates distance, causing problems in finding a time that works for group members located in different time zones.

Notwithstanding, the temporary nature of most international online groups necessitates establishing common history, as well as developing relational synergy that leads to trust building. It has been established that when mediated group members in geographically dispersed groups have limited future interaction, they fail to seek adequate social and contextual information to support their perceptions (Crampton, 2002; Olaniran, 1994; Walther, 2002). As a result, members are unable to draw on experiences with each other in making attributions (Crampton, 2002; Olaniran, 2001b). Such faulty communication leads to overemphasis on task goals at the expense of relational goals in virtual groups. Unfortunately, when this is the case, things go wrong, hence, members are more likely to blame one another rather than focusing on the assessments of situational concerns (Olaniran, 2004).

Very few studies of virtual teams attempt to identify factors leading to communication effectiveness, and the studies that have been done are not conducive to meaningful comparison of the collocated (nearby) to international online groups. Thus it is difficult to compare team member commitment in the micro and macrocosmic settings (Becker, 1992; Matthieu & Zajac, 1990). A conclusion from the studies revealed that socialization from face-to-face encounters among members from formal and informal meetings is transferred to and reinforced in collocated virtual teams, such that team members' commitment to the organization and their work team are positively enhanced (Dodd-McCue & Wright, 1996; Powell, Galvin, & Piccoli, 2006). On the other hand, the shared dependence on communication technologies in international collaborative groups for communication interaction and activity coordination hinders socialization (Ahuja & Galvin, 2003; Chidabaram, 1996; Olaniran, 2004). Trust development and trust building are precluded because time and geographical distance often prevent the use of synchronous communication technologies in some settings. Powell et al. (2006) argue that controls and coordination with which team members are familiar in collocated teams are, at times, lacking in the dispersed virtual environment. The net result is that trust building and trust development prove to be very difficult. The *trust* perception represents a key difference between collocated and dispersed virtual teams, given the role of group structure on team member's commitment. Yet, team members and people in general, seem to trust people rather than technologies (Friedman, Kahn, & Howe, 2000).

Research highlighted and sometimes suggested that face-to-face interaction is necessary for team development in geographically dispersed online groups especially at the inception of the team leading when relationship building, commitment, and increased trust are so critical (Lee-Kelley, Crossman, & Cannings, 2004; Olaniran, 2004). So the very reason for e-communication (circumvention of travel) prevents trust building when it is needed to initiate trust toward relationship building. Thus, having face-to-face meetings may defeat the purpose of online meetings (Olaniran, 2007a, 2007b). Nevertheless, it is hard to argue with the evidence indicating that periodic face-to-face meetings in virtual teams can help increase solidarity, commitment, and relational synergy and development (Byrne & LeMay, 2006; Lee-Kelly et al., 2004; Nandhakumar & Baskerville, 2006; Olaniran, 2004; Powell et al., 2006).

At the same time, Nandhakumar and Baskerville's study (2006) reports the issue of cultural differences such as reinforcement of strong hierarchical norms in organizations that constrain communication interactions across hierarchical levels in spite of the strong effort to promote online collaboration teams' idea of communicating anytime and anywhere. For example, in the study, it was reported that the junior managers and subordinates felt they had to rely on the senior management when they participated in online collaboration teams because senior managers always like to take the lead in discussion against the desires of junior managers.

Similarly, the role of identification is important in work contexts (Jian & Jeffres, 2006). It is difficult for online team members to identify with individuals they cannot trust and the people they perceived as having ulterior motives or different agendas. Furthermore, it will be difficult for online group members to commit to the project or the organization as a whole, especially when they feel that they must constantly second-guess the motives of their fellow participants in virtual teams (Olaniran, 2004).

The choice of communication technologies can also be made in a way that suits the intent of managers and leaders in online collaboration groups. For example a manager may insist on the use of videoconferencing rather than e-mail or other text-based medium to force subordinate members to conform to organizational norms as dictated by the hierarchy. However, when such manipulation or deliberate selection of a communication medium takes place, it can lead to subordinates' interpretation of the move as an attempt to circumvent opinions and further undermine trust in online collaboration teams (e.g., Carlson & Zmud, 1999; El-Shinnawy & Markus, 1997). In other words, when the choice of collaborative technological media by top management fails to meet that of employee's expectation, the trust level will be drastically low. This argument found some justification from the study of different media in organization communication that reports that trust in top management is linked to the quality of information received from top management and supervisors, which in turn is directly linked to the satisfaction with organization and job performance (Byrne & LeMay, 2006). Therefore, one can argue that employees' expectations about norms of how information should be communicated within organization can explain trust and satisfaction with organizations and ensuing communication process in online group collaborations.

In summary, the discussion above brings into the foreground that when looking at the role of communication technologies in international online collaboration within organizations, it is very difficult to assume that communication technology fosters satisfying employee participation. The discussion above illustrates this position with international online collaborative groups. Arguments also establish that there are significant or considerable differences between collocated and international online or virtual teams. The discussion points out that the selection and use of communication technologies often reinforces existing organization norms which are transferred to online group contexts, thus hindering trust and relational development in online groups. This may be the case even when communication technologies allow for multiple social cues including nonverbal (i.e., rich media) such as videoconferencing. The question however, remains, how does one facilitate trust and relational development in international online collaboration teams? The next section of the paper attempts to offer some guidelines and recommendations that could help organizations establish and improve their international e-communication through building trust and relationships.

SOLUTIONS AND RECOMMENDATIONS

In order to facilitate and foster trust and relational development in international online groups, effective organizations with technical expertise to understand the unique characteristics of electronic communication must be established (Olaniran, 2007; Solomon, 2001). Organizations deploying communication technologies for online group collaborations must be able to create a sense of communal experience in order to allow interactions that lead to greater creativity, knowledge sharing, and personal development. They must learn to use the appropriate technology to communicate and collaborate in a manner in which team members feel connected to one another and the task. There are few ways to accomplish this goal.

First, organizations must make a conscious decision about helping members to build trust when interacting with communication technologies. Too often, top management is more concerned about economical and cost savings because of technology than the actual communication process and employees' satisfaction. Therefore, it is recommended that top management be genuine in its decision to select and use communication technology. Successful implementation of communication technologies need not help superiors extend their authority over the subordinates, especially if trust and relational development is a goal within the organization. It is quite important for top management to create an environment that encourages free flow information across the organization, especially in international online collaboration groups where trust is usually suspect. Top management can allow open communication by not creating the impression that they are monitoring subordinate interactions. This may require that top management is not present in some online meetings with the subordinates. Furthermore, management should also give subordinates the latitude to implement some of their ideas and decisions. Specifically, restriction about who gets to participate and how employees participate in online collaboration teams must be scrutinized in a way that enhances trust and members' relations to develop and blossom.

Second, the short term vs. ongoing virtual teams points to the importance of time in trust development. It seems that in theory, on-going virtual team members have greater incentive to build trust with fellow participants. However, this is not going to occur automatically; it takes some work. Olaniran (2004) stresses this point, when he argues that anticipation of future interaction (AFI)—which addresses the need for communicators to behave in certain manner when faced with future meeting potentials, is helpful in relational development. The anticipation of future interaction in deployment of communication technologies for online groups helps facilitate social and relational messages that are essential for trust building and consequently satisfaction (Heide & Meiner, 1992; Olaniran, 1994, 2001b; Walther 1994). Walther (1994) found that anticipation of future interaction predicts relational intimacy or trust more than any other variable. Thus, it is essential that conditions that encourage anticipation of future interaction is established in virtual group when trust is critical to goals or task performances and opportunity for FtF interaction is not available as it is in collocated teams (see Olaniran, 2004). Thus, online group members should be exposed to, and preferably trained in how to develop relationships leading to increased trust in international online collaboration teams where social cues are scant.

Third, there is a need for good leadership and group structure in international online collaboration groups. Olaniran (2004) argues that online groups especially international online groups and members must be aware that a well planned virtual project is still going to face unforeseen issues. Thus, good leadership structure is useful in addressing any unforeseen events (Lee-Kelley, 2002). With good leadership, information regarding potential challenges, attributable to cultural differences, can be identified and if possible collectively resolved within online groups and organization. Also, the leadership ought to establish protocols in how to address issues and expectations along with offering group members assistance. Efforts to avert individual or liberal interpretations of deadlines and time issues should be in place (Olaniran, 2004; Vroman & Kovacich, 2002). It is important that virtual team members communicate clearly and leave nothing to chance. Online communication of any kind is challenging, let alone when international cultural factors that create ambiguities are added; therefore, augmented levels of accountability, trust, and adaptability are needed in the groups, more so, than in the face-to-face interactions (Roebuck & Britt, 2002). Establishing close personal relationships may require virtual team leaders or facilitators to hold several preliminary sessions in which information exchanges are focused on getting to know other team members before actually working on a project. Also, in preliminary sessions, clarity of norms and addressing cultural biases and key assumptions that could obscure effective communication needs to be a priority of global organizations where cultural differences complicate communication activities (See Olaniran, 2004, 2007a).

The need to include review and feedback opportunities into team structure ensures that members receive periodic updates regarding performance. Along this line, group leaders are to establish criteria for appropriate behaviors in virtual teams. For instance, misunderstandings occur more easily due to lack of understanding of communication rules and protocols required by technology. Good structure on the part of leaders and the team as a whole boosts performances and assists in the development of trust building, which is an important component in virtual teams (Pauleen, 2001). At the same time, individuals who trust one another often put the interest of the group ahead of self and are more socially in tune with other participants. Therefore, trust promotes group members' ability to learn, work, and respect one another, which may be crucial for effective task, conflict management, and overall group satisfaction.

Along with the group structure, there is also the need to use small size groups in international online collaboration projects. Keeping an international online collaboration group size small allows for reduced lurking opportunity and predisposes the group to increased interactivity, which promotes open communication and eventual high relational development (Bell & Kozlowski, 2002). Small size also promotes interactivity that allows team members to engage in "deep dialogue," which encourages a high level of relational trust development as individuals express their feelings with one another in group dynamics (Holton, 2001; Solomon, 2001).

Fourth, satisfaction, which is an outcome variable in virtual teams is usually based on the assessment of aggregate individual perception of feelings (Bailey & Pearson, 1983; Olaniran 1995, 1996a); however, individuals base their perception on the assessment of relationships developed with others in a given encounter (i.e., communication media). When assessment of relationship development is negative, the ratings assigned to satisfaction with the meeting process and the evaluation of accompanying communication medium or media will be negative accordingly. Thus, satisfaction in online collaboration groups involves the degree to which a communication medium is perceived to be helpful in accomplishing both task and relational (social) goals. Olaniran (1996a) in his model of satisfaction identifies two predictors of satisfaction in ICTs which include Ease of use and Decision confidence. Ease of use (EOU) is the degree to which a medium is perceived to be free of effort, and decision confidence (DC) is the degree to which one believes that a solution reached over a medium will solve a given problem (Olaniran, 1996a). EOU in particular, was found to be the strongest contributor to satisfaction in CMC groups (Olaniran, 1996a).

The importance of EOU on satisfaction and relational communication in communication technologies and online collaboration is essential when considering the idea of "immediacy." Immediacy addresses the feelings (i.e., perception) or awareness of group members' accessibility during interactions by virtue of quick message response and the general perception that communicators are in tune with one another's feelings. Immediacy is a critical element in the development of socio-emotional and relational synergy in group interaction (Walther, 1994). The awareness is prompted by the speed of message feedback to individual messages. Different ICTs have different rates of feedback, and for the most part communication technologies aside from videoconferencing have slower rate of feedback relative to FTF. Furthermore, the rate of feedback in asynchronous communication media is further retarded when compared to synchronous communication media (Olaniran, 2001a; Smith & Vanecek, 1990). When an individual lacks the opportunity for immediate feedback to messages, effective clarification decreases. The tendency to over-attribute also occurs and consequently results in attribution error which would cause frustration with the system and the group processes (Olaniran, 1995, 1996a). At the same time, when frustration sets in, overall satisfaction will go down.

Given that silence and delayed feedback negatively impacts performance, and these effect are more pronounced in asynchronous than synchronous encounters, it would seem that the selection of synchronous ICTs can add to immediacy, perceived EOU, DC, and satisfaction (see also Olaniran, 1994, 2004; Vroman & Kovacich, 2002). Satisfaction can still be accomplished in asynchronous CMC, however, virtual participants would have to put in place norms that guide contributions and facilitate immediacy while enhancing DC. Overall, facilitating immediacy improves relational synergy development and consequently, the confidence in group decision.

A key point to bear in mind is that the mere passage of time during online collaborations will not automatically result in good relational communication and relational development. It seems that there is a strong foundation for the interaction of time and anticipation in the differences between asynchronous and synchronous online collaboration. The motivation to engage in information seeking behavior that fosters greater "positive regard" and "friendliness" is higher in synchronous than asynchronous CMC and deserves greater attention. According to Walther (1994), the anticipation of future interaction propels the individual's tendency to engage in relational communication that is socially soothing. It would seem that this effect would be more pronounced in synchronous CMC where such behavior is more likely and evident.

The measure of satisfaction, trust, and relational warmth with communication technologies appears to be done in comparison to other traditional mediums and with the idea that face-to-face represents a baseline from which other communication media are judged. This assessment fails to account for the fact that face-to-face medium is different and is also disadvantageous in its own ways and in certain contexts, even with the presence of nonverbal cues. Given that text based CMC messages lack nonverbal cues, it is essential that online collaboration teams develop mechanisms that allow for relational communication, synergy, and trust to develop gradually and systematically even if it is slower in comparison to other traditional communication media. The cue substitution technique is one way to bring about the gradual development of a lasting relational interaction in international online collaboration teams. With cue substitution, communicators develop different symbols for expressing relational messages in CMC that are otherwise not available due to the lack of nonverbal cues. The cue substitution technique also explains how messages in computer mediated communication can be used to convey social messages in ways similar to those in FtF (Cunha & Cunha, 2001). Furthermore, the cue manipulation technique in online interaction illustrates users' adaptive use of technology to improvise for the lacking cues in CMC.

The insufficient time, history, and inexperience in electronic groups affect more than productivity and is central to the development of relational dynamics over time. Therefore, it would seem that virtual teams require longer durations to adjust to each other and the dynamics of interaction in electronic meetings in order to develop relational bonds. Hence, project managers are encouraged to use and employ virtual teams in which members' interaction are long-term, ongoing, and provide opportunity for members to work on different projects. This is necessary for inducing the effects of anticipation of future interaction (e.g., likeness, cohesions, and other relational strategies) into a group. However, one must recognize that certain short-term virtual task groups are also inevitable. Thus, when the time is short for virtual teams, exchanging pictures can help give a head start to relational development for participants (Walther, Slovacek, & Tidwell, 2001). Pictures improve affection and social attractiveness in short-term groups with no interaction history. Given that longer term or group history in distributed work groups fosters interpersonally positive relations than shorter ones, it is beneficial for group leaders to manipulate anticipation of future interaction. A simple approach such as informing virtual team members of the possibility of future collaboration could help accomplish the relational benefits of anticipation of future interaction effects. For instance, group members would strive to get to know one another and doing so at a faster pace, they would avoid error attribution, they would work harder, and they would increase self-disclosure activities and personal questions that are essential for the development of trust and relational synergy. Other alternatives might be to incorporate multiple electronic media whenever possible to develop a sense of community.

Teleconferencing and videoconferencing, for instance, allows for voice and video cues that may help the relational development process. Therefore, technology-mediated groups should be augmented with other communication media that are more supportive of social interaction, especially for the introduction of new members and when relationships are being formed (Carleta et al., 2000). However, caution needs to be exercised with videoconferencing. First, different time zones render them problematic. Second, proximity has been found to negatively influence interactivity, such that remote sites were ignored during interactions (Armstrong & Cole, 2002). Third, the need to retain some level of ambiguity in CMC interaction in order to make members function effectively has been stressed (Bal & Foster, 2000; Cunha & Cunha, 2001; Walther, 1994) and should be preserved.

The ability to share feelings and perhaps self disclose at greater levels is critical in developing online trust and intimacy. Along this line, the need to move online communication and relationships to offline is worth further consideration (Carter, 2005). Notwithstanding, this recommendation has significant implications for organizations using computer-mediated communication technologies for international online collaborations. First, the tendency to reduce cost is one of the primary reasons why organizations engage in international online collaborations. This implies that collaboration has to be initiated online; but if at all possible, individuals should be encouraged to take interactions or collaborations offline using other traditional media and travel. Second, if extending online collaboration to offline is aimed at building and sustaining relational trust, then the self presentation in online must be based on or anchored by truth. Otherwise, the absence of truth and candor would hinder the same trust the idea is supposed to enhance. In other words, participants in international online collaboration cannot pretend to be someone different online than who they are offline. Significant care must be taken in the attempt to use offline interaction as a trust building platform especially in international online collaboration. Carter (2005) expresses the importance of truthfulness in both online and offline identities when she recounts her own experience in *Cybercity* (an online community) when attempting to meet an online friend in person. She stresses that "failure to do so [be truthful] would have destroyed our friendship [relationship and trust] (p. 163).

Furthermore, environmental shifts cannot be discounted. Well planned projects are likely to face unforeseen contingencies and events, which necessitate the need for good or strong leadership structure to stay on top of things (Lee-Kelley, 2002). International online groups cannot afford to omit the process of explicitly establishing norms, determining group goals, and setting clear expectations for team leaders and members. Online group leaders need to be able to recognize problems as they occur and take immediate corrective action similar to traditional communication media. When online team participants are located across time and culture, they usually have to interact asynchronously, it is difficult for leaders to execute managerial tasks. The suggestion is that leaders need to focus on structuring or facilitating activities (Bell & Kozlowski, 2002; Pauleen, 2001). Emphasis on structure in online collaboration provides an advantage that may help enhance not only performance but also the development of trust-building an important component in groups (Pauleen, 2001).

FUTURE DIRECTIONS

In summary, as international online collaboration continues to gain ground, so is the need to cultivate a sense of groupness and a common understanding that demonstrates common goal and collective accountability among participants. In essence, approaches that help e-collaborators to be aware of their interconnectedness as they actively interact with one another are called for. In order to help bring about trust, relational warmth, and organizational synergy, it is imperative that organizations, groups, and individuals alike develop a way that helps communicate and negotiate meaning while avoiding disparate cultural challenges that could derail communication competency. As such, future trends in online collaboration may need to focus on deploying communication technologies (hardware and software designs) that fosters such tendencies. For instance, a one-stop design that offers multiple communication channels both asynchronous and synchronous media is called for.

Furthermore, the option to place multiple communication channels at the hands of international collaborators could help mediate challenges with cultural issues by providing back channel feedback that could foster mutual understanding and at the discretion of the users. It would seem appropriate to begin to explore social software structure such as blog, wiki, picture sharing, videocasting, and videoconferencing altogether to create a sense of community. The approach would help users to choose or select how they plan to negotiate relationships with their co-participants while building trust and relational trust with one another. However the level of control would not be at the hand of a particular individual but rather at the preferences of the users. Similarly, social software structure could help collaborators to develop a sense of community that is neither his or hers, but rather, collectively theirs in the process of group collaboration and in accomplishing organizational goals.

The fact that messages differ and are interpreted differently depending on the socio-cultural contexts requires attention towards mobilization of knowledge that addresses cross-cultural competency. Thus, increased emphasis on language and cultural training is essential prior to embarking on international online collaborations. Also, the shifting and complex nature of workplace through globalization, technologies, and information based economy, requires the need to focus less on homogenized workforce and ideologies to a more balance and non-Eurocentric or Western ways of knowing. On the contrary, an approach that acknowledges cultural diversities of the workforce and recognizes their implications for international online collaborations is needed. It is argued that social software and individual awareness of each others' differences can allow individuals to address social and cultural needs idiosyncratically. For example, the use of blog among collaborators may help bloggers and their readers to gain deeper insight into a particular culture and without taking away from the task goals, while at the same time, helping people to develop relationships that is based on trust and respects accordingly.

It is important to recognize that not all human needs can be anticipated and designed into communication media. Designers can do their best to anticipate the needs and try to crisis-proof their technology systems. Notwithstanding, users (both novices and experts) need to have a sense of relief in knowing that when trouble arises, it will be addressed with expedience. The knowledge that a technical glitch or difficulty would be taken care of would give users the added comfort that inspires confidence and motivates participation.

As for researchers, there is the need to collect empirical data in attempt to determine how different cultural classifications influence interactions in general, and trust development and relational synergy in particular. While cross-cultural data are difficult to collect, however, consultants and organizational practitioners may be of help in this area because the information gathered can help various organizations while informing the academic community at the same time. Also, while addressing cultural effects in virtual groups, it would help if future research can separate the differences between organizational cultures and national cultures and their interaction effects on trust development in virtual groups. From

a research perspective, a mixed methodology, rather than those pitting quantitative analysis over rhetorical and qualitative methods, should be embraced to gain a fuller understanding of the communication and interaction processes as they relate to trust and relational development in these groups.

Finally, emphasis should be given to issues of access to technologies. It appears that systems designers and organizational leaders need to focus on designing and selecting communication media that are easily accessible to all users regardless of users' location and infrastructure. Communication technologies that give potential users options to accommodate various cultural preferences present in a virtual group would also go a long way to assist international online group members and their interactions.

CONCLUSION

Certainly trust is a major contributing factor to developing, maintaining, and solidifying relational synergy and intimacy in online interaction in general and more so in international online collaboration. This research reveals that relational trust and intimacy is not impossible in international online collaboration. However, it will take time and greater commitment on the part of participants, group members, and organizations using international online collaboration to coordinate activities and projects. Research on ideas to foster such relational development and trust in international online collaborations has been applied to real and hypothetical scenarios that merit attention by those interested in improving international and intercultural relations. The paper also addresses critical issues for future considerations by different stakeholders including designers, research and researchers, and the users respectively.

REFERENCES

Ahuja, M.K., & Galvin, J.E. (2003). Socialization in virtual groups. *Journal of Management, 29*(2), pp.161-185.

Armstrong, D. J., & Cole, P. (2002). Managing distances and differences in geographically distributed work groups. In P. Hinds & S. Kiesler (Eds.), *Distributed Work* (pp. 167- 186).

Bal, J., & Foster, P. (2000). Managing the virtual team and controlling effectiveness. *International Journal of Production Research, 38*(17), 4019-4032.

Becker, T.E. (1992). Foci and bases of commitment: Are they distinctions worth making? *Academy of Management Journal, 35*(1), 232-244.

Becker, T.E., & Billings, R.S. (1993). Profiles of commitment: An empirical test. *Journal of Organizational Behavior, 14*(2), 177-190.

Bell, B. S., & Kozlowski. S. W. (2002). A typology of virtual treatment: Implications for effective leadership. *Group & Organizational Management, 27*, 14-49.

Berger, C. R., & Bradac, J. J. (1982). *Language and social knowledge: Uncertainty in interpersonal relations*. London: E. Arnold Publishers.

Byrne, Z. S., & LeMay, E. (2006). Different media for organizational communication: Perceptions of quality and satisfaction. *Journal of Business and Psychology, 21*(2), 149-173.

Carleta, J., Anderson, A., & McEwan, R. (2000). The effects of multimedia communication technology on non-collocated teams: A case study. *Ergonomics, 43*(8), 1237-1251.

Carlson, J., & Zmud, R. (1999). Channel expansion theory and the experiential nature of media richness perceptions. *Academy of Management Journal,* (42), 153-170.

Carter, D. (2005). Living in virtual communities: An ethnography of human relationships in cyberspace. *Information communication & Society, 8*(2), 148-167.

Chidabaram, L. (1996). Relational development in computer-supported groups. *MIS Quarterly,* (20), 143-163.

Connolly, T., Jessup, L. M., & Valacich, J. S. (1990). Effects of anonymity and evaluative tone on idea generation in computer-mediated groups. *Management Science, 36*, 97-120.

Craig, D. V. (2001-2002). View from an electronic learning environment: Perceptions and patterns among students in an online graduate course. *Journal of Educational Technology Systems, 30*(2), 197-219.

Crampton, C. D. (2002). Attribution in distributed work groups. In P. Hinds & S. Kiesler (Eds.), *Distributed work* (pp. 191-212).

Cunha, P. & Cunha, M. J. V. (2001). Managing improvisation in cross cultural virtual teams. *International Journal of Cross Cultural Management, 1*, 187-208.

Dodd-McCue, D., & Wright, G.B. (1996). Men, women, and attitudinal commitment: The effects of workplace experiences and socialization. *Human Relations, 49*(8), 1065-1091.

El-Shinnawy, M. M., & Markus, M. L. (1997). The poverty of media richness theory: Explaining people's choice of electronic mail vs. voice mail. *International Journal of Human-Computer Studies, 46*, 443-167.

Finholt, T., & Sproull, L. S. (1990). Electronic groups at work. *Organization Science, 1*, 41-51.

Friedman, B., Kahn, P., & Howe, D. (2000). Trust online. *Communications of the ACM, 43*, 34-40.

Garton, L., & Wellman, B. (1995). Social impacts of Electronic mail in organizations: A review of the research literature. In B. R. Burleson (Ed.), *Communication Yearbook*, 18 (pp. 434-453). Thousand Oaks, CA: Sage.

Gezo, T., Oliverson, M., & Zick, M. (2000). Managing global projects with virtual teams. *Hydrocarbon Processing, 79*, 112c-112I.

Heide, J. B., & Miner, A. (1992). The shadow of the future: Effects of anticipated future interaction and frequency of contact on buyer-seller cooperation. *Academy of Management Journal, 35*, 265-291.

Holton, J. A. (2001). Building trust and collaboration in a virtual team. *Team Performance Management, 7*(3 & 4), 36-47.

Jian, G., & Jeffres, L. W. (2006). Understanding employees' willingness to contribute to shared electronic databases: A three dimensional framework. *Communication Research, 33*(4), 242-261.

Kiser, K. (1999). Working on world time. *Training, 36*(3), 28-34.

Lee, O. (2002). Cultural differences in email use of virtual teams a critical social theory perspective. *Cyberpsychology & Behavior, 5*(3), 227-232.

Lee-Kelley, L (2002). Situational Leadership: Managing the virtual project team. *The Journal of Management Development, 21*(6), 461-476.

Lee-Kelley, L., Crossman, A., & Cannings, A. (2004). A social interaction approach to managing the "invisibles" of virtual teams. *Industrial Management & Data Systems, 104*(8/9), 650-657.

Mathieu, J.E., & Zajac, D.M. (1990). A review and meta-analysis of the antecedents, correlates, and consequences of organizational commitment. *Psychological Bulletin, 108*(2), 171-94.

Morrow, P.C. (1993). *The theory and measurement of work commitment.* Greenwich, CT: JAI Press.

Nandhakumar, J., & Baskerville, R. (2006). Durability of online teamworking: Patterns of trust. *Information Technology & People, 19*(4), 371-389.

Olaniran, B. A. (1994). Group performance in computer-mediated and face-to-face communication media. *Management Communication Quarterly, 7*, 256-281.

Olaniran, B. A. (1995). Perceived communication outcomes in computer-mediated communication: An analysis of three systems among new users. *Information Processing & Management, 31*, 525-541.

Olaniran, B. A. (1996a). A model of satisfaction in computer-mediated and face-to-face communication. *Behavioural and Information Technology, 15*, 24-36.

Olaniran, B. A. (1996b). Group process satisfaction and decision quality in computer-mediated communication: An examination of contingent relations. In R. S. Carthcart, L. Samovar, & L. Henman (Eds.). *Small group communication: Theory & practice* (pp. 134-146). Dubuque, IA: Brown & Benchmark.

Olaniran, B. A. (2001a). Computer-mediated communication and conflict management process: A closer look at anticipation of future interaction. *World Futures, 57*, 285-313.

Olaniran, B. A. (2001b). The effects of computer-mediated communication on transculturalism. In V. Milhouse, M. Asante, & P. Nwosu (Eds.) *Transcultural realities* (pp. 83-105). Thousand Oaks, CA: Sage.

Olaniran, B. A. (2004). Computer-mediated communication in cross-cultural virtual groups. In G. M. Chen & W. J. Starosta (Eds.). *Dialogue among diversities* (pp. 142-166). Washington, DC: NCA.

Olaniran, B. A. (2007a). Challenges to implementing e-learning and lesser developed countries. In A. Edmundson (Ed.), *Globalized e-learning cultural challenges*. New York: Idea Group.

Olaniran, B. A. (2007b). Culture and communication challenges in virtual workspaces. In K. St-Amant (Ed.), *Linguistic and cultural online communication issues in the global age* (pp. 79-92)*. PA: Information science reference (IGI Global).

Pauleen, D. J. (2001). Facilitators' perspectives on using electronic communication channels to build and manage relationships with virtual tam members. *Proceedings of Society for Information Technology and Teacher Education Conference, 3*, 2913-2918.

Pauleen, D. J., & Yoong, P. (2001). Relationship building and the use of ICT in boundary-crossing virtual teams: A facilitator's perspective. *Journal of information Technology, 16*, 205-220.

Powell, A., Galvin, J., & Piccoli, G. (2006). Antecedents to team member commitment from near and far: A comparison between collocated and virtual teams. *Information Technology & People, 19*(4), 299-322.

Roebuck, D. B., & Britt, A. C. (2002). Virtual teaming has come to stay—guidelines and strategies for success. *Southern Business Review, 28*, 29-39.

Roy, M. H. (2001). Small group communication and performance: Do cognitive flexibility and context matter? *Management Decision, 39*(4), 323-330.

Smith, J. Y., & Vanecek, M. T. (1990). Dispersed group decision making using nonsimultaneous computer conferencing: A report of research. *Journal of Management Information Systems, 7*, 71-92.

Solomon, C. M. (2001). Managing virtual teams. *Workforce, 80*(6), 60-65.

Spitzberg, B. H. & Cupach, W. R. (1989). *Handbook of interpersonal competence research*. New York: Springer-Verlag.

Vroman, K. & Kovacich, J. (2002). Computer-mediated interdisciplinary teams: Theory and reality. *Journal of Interprofessional Care, 16*, 161-170.

Walther. J. B. (2002). Time effects in computer-mediated groups: Past, present, and future. In P. Hinds & S. Kiesler (Eds.), *Distributed sork* (pp. 235-257).

Walther, J. B. (1994). Anticipated ongoing interaction versus channel effects on relational communication in computer-mediated interaction. *Human Communication Research, 20*, 473-501.

Walther, J. B., Slovacek, C., & Tidwell, L. C. (2001). Is a picture worth a thousand words? Photographic images in long term and short term virtual teams. *Communication Research, 28*, 105-134.

Yu, F. (2001). The efficacy of electronic telecommunications in fostering interpersonal relationships. *Journal of Educational Computing Research, 26*(2), 177-189.

KEY TERMS

Collaboration: Involves interaction among individuals over electronic technology medium.

Computer-Mediated Communication (CMC): Computer-mediated communication involves communication interactions that exist over computer networks.

Culture: Consists of different value preferences that influence communication interaction and how people create meaning.

Cultural Communication Competence: Focuses on communicators' ability to interact with members of another culture in a way that is both effective and appropriate in terms of goal accomplishment.

Globalization: Involves economic and sociocultural ideas where organizations are able transcend national geographic and cultural boundaries through convergence of space and time in attempt to accomplish goals.

International Online Collaboration: Involves groups or team of individuals from different countries and national cultures operating in a virtual workspaces made possible by information communication technologies.

Online Interaction: Involves individuals or group engaging in communication process that is taking place over Internet or technology network environment.

Virtual Collaboration: Consists of communication interaction taking place in a virtual space with the aid of communication and information technologies.

Chapter 13
Trust–Based Usage Control in Collaborative Environment

Li Yang
University of Tennessee at Chattanooga, USA

Chang Phuong
University of Tennessee at Chattanooga, USA

Andy Novobilski
University of Tennessee at Chattanooga, USA

Raimund K. Ege
North Illinois University, USA

ABSTRACT

Most access control models have formal access control rules to govern the authorization of a request from a principal. In pervasive and collaborative environments, the behaviors of a principal are uncertain due to partial information. Moreover, the attributes of a principal, requested objects, and contexts of a request are mutable during the collaboration. A variety of such uncertainty and mutability pose challenges when resources sharing must happen in the collaborative environment. In order to address the above challenges, we propose a framework to integrate trust management into a usage control model in order to support decision making in an ever-changing collaborative environment. First, a trust value of a principal is evaluated based on both observed behaviors and peer recommendations. Second, the usage-based access control rules are checked to make decisions on resource exchanges. Our framework handles uncertainty and mutability by dynamically disenrolling untrusted principals and revoking granted on-going access if access control rules are no longer met. We have applied our trust-based usage control framework to an application of file sharing.

INTRODUCTION

Conventionally registered parties behind firewalls collaborate in well controlled environments. With new virtual communities emerging, parties communicate directly with one another to exchange information or execute transaction in a peer-to-peer (P2P) fashion. The dynamism of the P2P communities means that the principal that offers services will meet requests from unrelated or unknown principals. Peers need to collaborate and obtain services within environments that are unfamiliar or even hostile. Therefore, peers have to manage the risks involved in the collaboration when prior experience and knowledge about each other are incomplete. One way to address this uncertainty is to develop and establish trust among peers. Trust can be built by either a trusted third party (Atif, 2002) or by community-based feedback from past experiences (Resnick, Kuwabara, Zeckhauser, & Friedman, 2000) in a self-regulating system. Trust leads naturally to a decentralized approach to security management that can tolerate partial information.

In such a complex and collaborative world, a peer can protect and benefit itself only if it can respond to new peers and enforce access control by assigning proper privileges to new peers. Access control models (Bertino, 2001a; Jajodia, Samarati, Sapino, & Subrahmanian, 2001) determine authorization based on principals' permission on target objects. Usage of a digital object is temporal and transient in a virtual community, such as online reading, which is beyond an instantaneous access. The usage control (UCON) model (Park & Sandhu, 2004) is proposed to handle continuity of access decisions and mutability of subject and object attributes. Authorization decisions are made before an access and repeatedly checked during the access. The on-going access may be revoked if the security policies are not satisfied due to changes of the subject, object, or system attributes.

The general goal of our work is therefore to investigate the design of a novel approach to addressing both uncertain information and mutable attributes. If successful, this approach will offer significant benefits in emerging applications such as P2P. It will also benefit collaboration over the existing Internet when the identities and intentions of parties are uncertain. We integrate trust evaluation with usage control to handle uncertainty of entities and mutability of attributes. Underlying our framework is a formal computational model of trust and access control that will provide a formal basis to interface authentication with authorization.

Related Works

Most recent research on access control includes task-based authorization controls (Thomas & Sandhu, 1998), team-based access control (Georgiadis, Mavridis, Pangalos, & Thomas, 2001), role-based access control (Gerraiolo, 2001), temporal role-based access control (Bertino, 2001b), and X-GTRBAC (Bhatti, Ghafoor, Bertino, & Joshi, 2005). Recently, UCON (Park & Sandhu, 2004) handles the attribute mutability of a principal or an object when the system makes decision for a request. All of them assume that a principal or an object is defined and represented by its attributes. This means that the identity, role, or group of the subject can be identified through certain authentication mechanisms and that information about behaviors of a principal is certain. However, in a pervasive and collaborative environment, identity may not be identified. Moreover, identity itself can not convey priori information about the likely behavior of a principal. Behaviors of a principal may change between friendly and malicious when privileges are executed. A principal can not make access control decision only based on identity information because identity itself can not ensure friendly behaviors.

Reasoning and building trust for each peer allow peers to make decision when they are interacting with others in a peer-to-peer fashion. Li, Mitchell, and Winsborough (2002) and Yao (2003) use explicit incremental negotiation to establish mutual trust. An overview of trust management is discussed by Grandison, Sloman, and Sloman (2000). Trust management has many applications in e-commerce areas such as works from Atif (2002) and Resnick et al. (2000). Xiong and Liu (2004) handle trust evaluation, especially the community-related context factors and transaction context factor of e-commerce. Zouridaki, Mark, Hejmo, and Thomas (2005) and Yang, Kizza, Cemerlic, and Liu (2007) apply trust evaluation into routing protocols of mobile wireless ad hoc networks (MANETs).

Sandhu and Zhang (2005) apply peer-to-peer access control to trusted computing, enforcing trust and hardware encryption. The SECURE (Cahill, Gray, Seigneur, Jensen, Chen, Shand, et al., 2003) project proposed the seminal ideas to handle trust and secure collaboration in an uncertain environment. Their work can tolerate partial information and overcome initial suspicion to allow secure collaboration to take place by reasoning about trust and risk. Dimmock, Belokosztolszki, Eyers, Bacon, and Moody (2004) incorporate notions of trust into rule inference process of OASIS (Bacon, Moody, & Yao, 2002), a policy-driven access control system. Mutable attributes, obligations, context, and revocation of the authorization are not handled.

Both attribute mutability and uncertain behaviors of a principal are needed to be considered in collaborative resources sharing. In this work we integrate trust management into usage-based access control, which allows collaboration when attributes of a principal are mutable or information on a principal's behaviors is incomplete.

A FRAMEWORK TO INTEGRATION TRUST INTO USAGE CONTROL

Overview of UCON

The UCON model proposed by Park and Sandhu (2004) is a generalization of access control to cover authorization, obligation, conditions, continuity (ongoing controls), and mutability. Authorization handles decisions on user accesses to target resources. Obligations are the mandatory requirements for a subject before or during a usage exercise. Conditions are subject, object, environmental, or system requirements that have to be satisfied before granting of accesses. Subject and object attributes can be mutable. Mutable attributes can be changed because of accesses, whereas immutable attributes can be changed only by administrative actions.

Trust Evaluation

For every request, the owner of resources assigns a trust value within [0, 1] to the requester. The trust is evaluated based on history observations and peer recommendations from referees. The history-based observations are the previous interactions the owner had with the requester. The peer recommendations may include signed trust-assertions from other principals, or a list of referees whom the owner can contact for recommendations.

The owner first computes trust given a sequence of observations from interaction history, then combines the trust with *recommendations* to calculate the *total trust* to the requester. As show in Figure 1, the trust evaluation includes five steps: (1) An owner i calculates the trust value T_{ij} to a requester j based on its observed histories; (2) The owner i receives recommendation ($T_{rj} \dots T_{zj}$) from multiple peers (reporters) r to z; (3) The owner i does *deviation test* to evaluate trustworthiness of the reporters; (4) The owner i updates the trustworthiness of the reporter r to

Figure 1. Trust evaluation

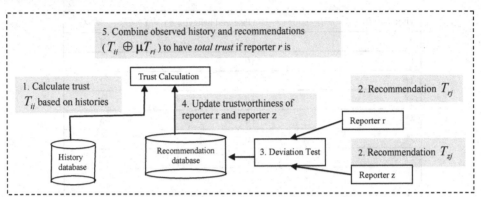

z, for instance, reporter r is trustworthy; and (5) The owner i merges the observation-based trust T_{ij} with reporter r's recommendation T_{rj}. Each step is detailed as follows.

Step 1: Calculate the Trust of Behaviors Based on Observations of Histories

The owner i models the behavior of requester j as an actor. Owner i thinks that the friendly behaviors of requester j follow a probability of T_{ij}, based on outcomes drawn independently from observations. Probability T_{ij} varies for every different requester j and every owner i. The parameters T_{ij} are unknown, and owner i models this uncertainty by assuming that T_{ij} is drawn from a distribution (the prior) that is updated by available new observations. This thinking is under the Bayesian framework. We use the distribution Beta(α,β) for the prior because it is a conjugate distribution. When a conjugate prior is multiplied with= the likelihood function, it gives a posterior probability having the same functional form as the prior, thus allowing the posterior to be used as a prior in further computations. Therefore, T_{ij} ~Beta(α,β) after updating. For a given requester j for owner i, we define a sequence of variables $T_{ij}^0, T_{ij}^1, T_{ij}^2, \ldots, T_{ij}^{k-1}$. T_{ij}^k characterizes the trust at sampling time points (0, 1, 2, ... k-1, k), where T_{ij}^0 ~Beta(α_0, β_0), T_{ij}^1~Beta(α_1, β_1), T_{ij}^2~Beta(α_2, β_2),..., T_{ij}^{k-1}~Beta($\alpha_{k-1}, \beta_{k-1}$), and T_{ij}^k~Beta(α_k, β_k).

Initially, the owner i has no knowledge about the requester j, therefore, shape parameters are set the same (we use 1 here) as $\alpha_0=\beta_0=1$ at time 0, which means that the trust value has uniform distribution over the interval [0, 1], that is, T_{ij}^0 ~$U[0, 1] = Beta(1, 1)$. When a new observation is made, α are β are updated. For example, N_k is the number of observed behaviors and G_k is the number of observed friendly behaviors at k-th moment. The prior is updated according to $\alpha_k = \alpha_{k-1} + G_k$ and $\beta_k = \beta_{k-1} + N_k - G_k$. In particular, if T_{ij}^{k-1} ~Beta($\alpha_{k-1}, \beta_{k-1}$), we have T_{ij}^k~$Beta(\alpha_{k-1}+g_k, \beta_{k-1} + n_k - g_k)$ given that $N_k = n_k$ and $G_k = g_k$. Therefore, T_{ij}^k is characterized by the parameters α_k and β_k defined recursively as follows:

$$\alpha_k = \alpha_{k-1} + g_k \text{ and } \beta_k = \beta_{k-1} + n_k + g_k.$$

We define the trust $\overline{t_k}$ from observation assigned to a requester at a moment k to be equal to the expectation value of the Beta(α,β) where

$$\overline{t_k} = E(T_{ij}^k) = \frac{\alpha_k}{\alpha_k + \beta_k} \qquad (1)$$

Table 1 is a detailed example how an owner i updates its trust assignment to the requester j based on the interaction owner i had with j in a given window based on the observed behavior. A window stands for a certain number of observation i has to j. α and β are the shape parameters for

Table 1. Trust calculation based on history observation

Time	Observed behavior # (N_k)	G_k	N_k-G_k
0	0	1	1
1st	10	9	1
2nd	10	8	2
3rd	10	7	3
4th	10	5	5
5th	10	3	7
1 to 5	50	33	19
$\bar{t}_5 = E(T_{ij}^5) = \dfrac{\sum\limits_{k=0}^{5} G_k}{\sum\limits_{k=0}^{5}(N_k - G_k)}$	---	.63	.37
3 to 5	---	15	15
$\bar{t}_5 = E(T_{ij}^5) = \dfrac{\sum\limits_{k=3}^{5} G_k}{\sum\limits_{k=3}^{5}(N_k - G_k)}$	---	.50	.50

probability density function of the Beta distribution that indicates whether a requester is good or malicious. For example, at first time point, 10 behaviors ($n_1 = 10$) are observed and 9 behaviors ($g_1=9$) are friendly. The parameters are updated as $\alpha = \alpha_0 + g_1$ and $\beta = \beta + n_1 - g_1$. If owner i has observed up to time 5, α and β are updated to 35 and 17, respectively.

There are two alternative ways to update trust values. One is to update trust values based on all the observations and recommendations. The other ways is to update trust values based on recent information only. The advantage of the latter is two folds: reduce the computation complexity and detect the changing of behaviors early. For instance, a requestor is misbehaving in a short time range, and then recent observation together with reports is more reflective to the behavior changing than the overall observation. Table 2 gives the legends in Step 1.

Step 2-3: Deviation Test of Recommendations

If owner i also receives the recommendation on requester j from its peers (e.g., reporter r), it needs to detect and avoid false reports. The owner i will do a deviation test to update the trustworthiness of the reporter, thus deciding whether the owner i will absorb the recommendation or discard the recommendation. The deviation test is:

$$|E(Beta(\alpha', \beta')) - E(Beta(\alpha, \beta))| \geq d$$

(2)

Where the first term $E(Beta(\alpha', \beta')) = T_{ij}$ is the recommendation from reporter r, and the second term $Beta(\alpha, \beta)$ is the trust based on owner i's observation, $E(Beta(\alpha, \beta))$ is the expectation of Beta distribution, and d is a positive constant as the threshold. If the owner i thinks maximum 10% deviation between the recommendation and its own observation is trustworthy, d is set to be 0.1.

Table 2. Legends in step 1

Symbol	Notation
i	Owner
j	Requester
r, z	Reporters
k	Index of moments
α	The shape parameter for probability density function of the Beta distribution $Beta(\alpha,\beta)$ that indicates whether a requester is good.
β	The shape parameter for probability density function of the Beta distribution $Beta(\alpha,\beta)$ that indicates whether a requester is malicious.
$Beta(\alpha,\beta)$	The distribution to model the behaviors of requester j
T_{ij}	The probability that owner i thinks the behaviors of requester j is honest. $T_{ij} \sim Beta(\alpha,\beta)$
N_k	The variable of observed behaviors at k-th moment.
n_k	n_k is the number of observed behaviors at k-th moment.
G_k	The variable of observed friendly behaviors at k-th moment.
g_k	g_k is the number of observed friendly behaviors at k-th moment.
α_k	The shape parameter for probability density function of the Beta distribution $Beta(\alpha_k,\beta_k)$ that indicates whether a requester is good at k-th moment. $\alpha_k = \alpha_{k-1} + g_k$
β_k	The shape parameter for probability density function of the Beta distribution $Beta(\alpha_k,\beta_k)$ that indicates whether a requester is malicious at k-th moment. $\beta_k = \beta_{k-1} + n_k + g_k$
$Beta(\alpha_k, \beta_k)$	The distribution to model the behaviors of requester j at k-th moment.
T_{ij}^k	The probability that owner i thinks the behaviors of requester j is honest at k-th moment. $T_{ij}^k \sim (\alpha_k, \beta_k)$
$E(T_{ij})$	The expectation of $Beta(\alpha_k, \beta_k)$. $E(T_{ij}) = \dfrac{\alpha_k}{\alpha_k + \beta_k}$
$\overline{t_k}$	The trust value that the owner i has to the requester j at k-th moment. $\overline{t_k} = E(T_{ij})$

Step 4: Trustworthiness of Reporters

Trustworthiness of recommendation uses a similar Bayesian approach. Owner i thinks trustworthiness of reporter r's recommendation following the probability W_{ir}. $Beta(\phi, \gamma)$ is used to model trustworthiness of reporter r's recommendation and $W_{ir} \sim Beta(\phi, \gamma)$. The parameter ϕ and γ are the shape parameters for probability density function of the Beta distribution $Beta(\phi, \gamma)$ that indicates whether a reporter is trustworthy or not. Initially, owner is ignorant about trustworthiness of reporter, therefore, $\phi_0 = \gamma_0 = 1$ and $Beta(\phi_0, \gamma_0) = Beta(1, 1)$. An update is performed when the results of deviation test are available. A deviation test is used to compare owner i's observation ($T_{ij} \sim Beta(\alpha, \beta)$) with reporter r's recommendation ($T_{ij} \sim Beta(\alpha', \beta')$), as shown in Formula (2). The result of deviation tests is recorded in s. Let $s=1$ if the deviation test is positive, otherwise $s=0$ at a moment k. The trustworthiness of recommendation if updated by $\gamma_k = \gamma_{k-1} + s$; $\delta_k = \delta_{k-1} + (1-s)$. If the recommendation of the reporter r passes the deviation test, the trustworthiness of reporter r is updated, and reporter r's recommendation is merged to owner's history-based trust. If the recommendation of the reporter r does not passes the deviation test, the trustworthiness of reporter r will also be updated, but its recommendation is ignored. We define the trustworthiness μ_k assigned to a reporter at a moment k to be equal to the expectation valued of $Beta(\gamma_k, \delta_k)$, where

$$\mu_k = E(W_{ir}) = \frac{\gamma_k}{\gamma_k + \delta_k}$$

(3)

The owner i considers reporter r is trustworthy if $\mu_k < m$, otherwise the reporter r is considered as untrustworthy if $\mu_k \geq m$, where m is the threshold of trustworthiness. If the owner i trusts a reporter if its ratings deviate no more than in 25% of the cases, the threshold m is set to be 0.75.

Step 5: Merge History-based Trust with Recommendations

Meanwhile, recommendations from reporter r bring in new information T_{ij} on the requester's behaviors. The owner combines the new data T_{ij} with its own observation T_{ij} on the condition that the reporter r is trustworthy. If reporter r is trustworthy, its recommendation is merged to owner's history-based trust by $T_{ij} \oplus \mu T_{rj}$ where μ is the trustworthiness that the owner has to the reporter, as shown in Formula (3). After merging the trust based on its own observation with recommendations of the reporter, the owner has the total trust of the requester j.

We define total trust of i towards j as:

$$tt = T_{ij} \oplus \mu T_{rj} = \begin{cases} E(T_{ij}) + \mu E(T_{rj}) & \text{if } E(T_{rj}) > n \\ E(T_{ij}) - \mu E(T_{rj}) & \text{if } E(T_{rj}) \leq n \end{cases}$$

(4)

The owner needs to decide if the recommendation T_{ij} from reporter is positive or negative before it merges the recommendation with its own trust. The recommendation is compared against the threshold n that indicates the tolerance to the misbehaviors. If the owner i tolerates a requester j that misbehaves no more than half of the time, it should set the trust threshold n to 0.5. If the recommendation T_{ij} is above the threshold n, the recommendation is positive, which will increase the total trust to the requester, denoted by $tt = T_{ij}$

$\oplus \mu T_{rj} = E(T_{ij}) + \mu E(T_{ij})$. If the recommendation is below the threshold n, the recommendation is negative, which decrease the total trust to the requester, denoted by $tt = T_{ij} \oplus \mu T_{rj} = E(T_{ij}) - \mu E(T_{ij})$. Finally, when an owner decides whether it will trust the behavior of the requester j, it compares the total trust against the threshold n. The owner considers if the requester's behaviors are friendly if $tt < n$ and malicious if $tt \geq n$. Table 3 gives the legends from Step 2 to Step 5.

Trust-Based UCON

A state is an assignment of values to variables which consist of principal attributes, object attributes, and system attributes. The state transition system can be represented by $(\sum, S, s_0, \delta, F)$ where $\sum$ is input alphabet, S is a set of system states, s_0 is the initial state, δ is the state transition function $\delta: S \times \sum \rightarrow S$, and F is the final state. We define a special system state to specify the status of a single request and access process. The system state S includes *initialState, preTrust, deniedEnroll, trusting, disEnrolled, preAccess, deniedAcces, accessing, revoked,* and *end.* The initialState means the principal has not sent request; preTrust means the principal is waiting for the authentication decision; deniedEnroll means the system denies the enrollment of the principal based on history or recommendations; trusting means the principal is allowed to collaborate and will send access requests; disenrolled means the system revokes the enrollment of a principal based on runtime information; preAccess means the principal is waiting for the authorization decision; deniedAccess means they system denies the authorization request based on access control rules; accessing means the principal is executing granted privilege; revokedAccess means the system denied the privileges of a principal based on runtime mutable attributes; and end means a principal terminates the access. Actions change the state of the system, which is the input alphabet. If the action is performed successfully the

Table 3. Legends in step 2-5

Symbol	Notation
Beta(α', β')	The distribution to model the friendly behaviors of request j by the reporter r.
T_{ij}	The probability that reporter r thinks the behaviors of requester j is honest. $T_{ij} \sim$ Beta(α', β')
Beta(γ, δ)	The distribution to model trustworthiness of reporter r by owner i.
γ	The shape parameter for probability density function of the Beta distribution $Beta(\gamma, \delta)$ that indicates whether a reporter is honest and trustworthy.
δ	The shape parameter for probability density function of the Beta distribution $Beta(\gamma, \delta)$ that indicates whether a reporter is dishonest and untrustworthy.
W_{ir}	The probability that owner i thinks the reporter r is trustworthy. $W_{ir} \sim Beta(\gamma, \delta)$
Beta(γ_k, δ_k)	The distribution to model trustworthiness of reporter r by owner i at k-th moment.
s	Result of deviation test. $s=1$ if the deviation test succeeds, and $s=0$ otherwise.
γ_k	The shape parameter for probability density function of the Beta distribution $Beta(\gamma_k, \delta_k)$ that indicates whether a reporter is honest and trustworthy at a moment k. $\gamma_k = \gamma_{k-1} + s$
δ_k	The shape parameter for probability density function of the Beta distribution $Beta(\gamma_k, \delta_k)$ that indicates whether a reporter is dishonest and untrustworthy at a moment k. $\delta_k = \delta_{k-1} + (1-s)$
$E(W_{ir})$	The expectation of $Beta(\gamma_k, \delta_k)$. $E(W_{ir}) = \dfrac{\gamma_k}{\gamma_k + \delta_k}$
μ	Trustworthiness that the owner has to the reporter. $\mu = E(Beta(\gamma, \delta))$
m	Threshold of trust to behaviors
n	Threshold of trustworthiness to reporters
tt	Total trust. $tt = T_{ij} \oplus \mu T_{rj}$

action is true; attributes of the principal, object, and system are assigned a new value. A series of actions are defined to change the status of a request. The transition from one state to another is triggered by an action, as shown in Figure 2. These actions include:

1. *requestEnroll(p)*: Generates a new request (*p*) when a principal tries to join the community.
2. *denyEnroll(p)*: Rejects a request (*p*) to enroll the community because the requester can not meet the minimum authentication or trust requirement.
3. *enroll(p)*: Enrolls a principal (*p*) to the community.
4. *revokeEnroll(p)*: Revokes the allowed enrollment (*p*).
5. *requestAccess(p, o, r)*: Generates a new access request (*p, o, r*).
6. *denyAccess(p, o, r)*: Rejects an access request (*p, o, r*).
7. *grantAccess(p, o, r)*: Grants an access request (*p, o, r*).
8. *revokeAccess(p, o, r)*: Revokes an on-going and granted access request (*p, o, r*).
9. *endAccess(p, o, r)*: Terminates an access request (*p, o, r*).
10. *onUpdate(p, o, r)*: Updates the access request (*p, o, r*) when mutable attributes or uncertain behaviors of a principal change.

Figure 2. Trust-based UCON model

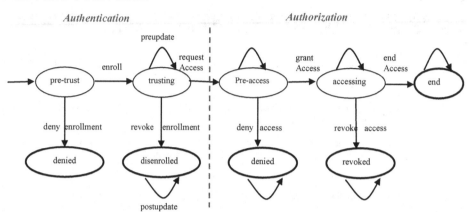

ARCHITECTURE OF TRUST-BASED USAGE CONTROL IN FILE SHARING

When a principal *p* requests to execute a right *r* on an object *o*, attribute of the principal, permission (right *r* and object *o*), and an optional list credentials are submitted to *secure context handler (SCH)* module. The credentials may include signed trust-assertions (recommendations) from other users or a certificate signed by certificate authority. The SCH looks up the relevant contexts for the requested action and queries the *trust calculator (TC)* module for a trust value about principal *p*. Trust calculator calculates the trust value for a requester based on both observed history and records in recommendation databases. A trust value is passed to *access control manager (ACM)* module for decision. The ACM looks up access control policies that entail several access control constraints. The *constraint service (CS)* module and the *dynamic manager (DAM)* module evaluates access control constraints, for example, time, location, and memberships.

Two categories of trigger events are possible to result in recalculation of trust value and reevaluation of access control policies. Recalculation and reevaluation may cause the revocation of current enrollment or on-going access. The *evidence handler (EH)* module is listening to the peer reports about the misbehaviors of a requester. The negative

report can include ignorance of obligation, dishonest behaviors, or the revocation of a requester's certificate. When the trust value of the request drops below a minimum threshold the on-going granted request will be revoked. The result of a trigger event is notified to SCH and execution of request is cancelled. The DAM module is listening to the attribute mutability of the principal, objects, or a context after the permission is granted. For example, the DAM module can be triggered by certain events (e.g., the subject left the group that entails the right). Once the DAM module receives an event, the corresponding access control polices are rechecked by ACM if necessary (e.g., to allow an ongoing usage to continue or revoke it).

Two trigger events may revoke the granted permissions. One is the TC and the other is the DAM. The first one tests whether the behaviors of the requester are too malicious to tolerate and the latter one checks whether the requester is violating the access control rules. Therefore, either one of two trigger events will revoke the in-progress permission.

The update in the TC or DAM may revoke the granted permission. The peers may report the dishonest behavior of the requester or the revocation of the requester's certificate so the trust value of the request is dropped below a scalar. This update will be notified to the *SCH* and cancel the execution of request. After the permission is granted, the DAM will be trigger by certain events such as change of the role. Once the DAM receives an event, the attribute values of the object and subject are retrieved and evaluated and corresponding policies are rechecked by the ACM if necessary (e.g., to allow an ongoing usage to continue or revoke it.)

PROTOTYPE SIMULATION

The architecture outlined in Figure 3 provides the framework for the simulation program of a usage-based access control model. This simulation works under the premise of several users, Tom, Mary, and Lisa, who may request access to files owned by each. Each of these users has been assigned a database to handle the framework described in Figure 3. For every request, a trust value is calculated given past history and current recommendations for the requesting principal. Another factor in consideration is a risk assessment of the action requested based on access control rules assigned to each available file. Each owner assesses the risks based on sensitivity of his/her file. Access to the file may be granted or denied based on trust evaluation, risk assessment, and access

control rules. If granted, the continuing usage of this access is contingent on maintaining the trust and risk values within the specified parameters of the rules governing this file. Access is terminated upon completion of the file usage.

Simulation Program

In the context of the simulation, each instantiated user serves as an owner, a requester, or a peer with assigned credentials, trust, and risk values. Additional peers are used and referenced with the purpose of providing recommendations, evidence alerts, and dynamic attribute alerts.

A data model is predefined and populated for use by each instantiated user. The simulation controls the initialization of each instantiated user and communication between instantiated users, configuration of requests, configuration of evidence and dynamic attribute alerts, and display simulation status, and allows for the viewing of the available files, the associated policies, and associated rules. A basic rules engine is implemented to allow simple rule execution.

The simulation program is made up of one single GUI shown in Figure 4 and consists of five sections that provide the means to setup various

Figure 3. Trust-based usage control architecture in file sharing

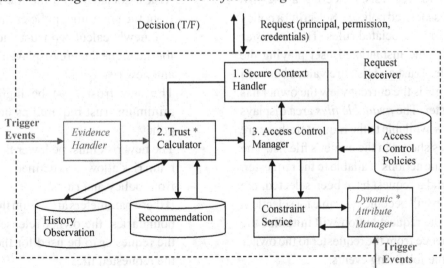

Figure 4. Simulation of trust-based usage control

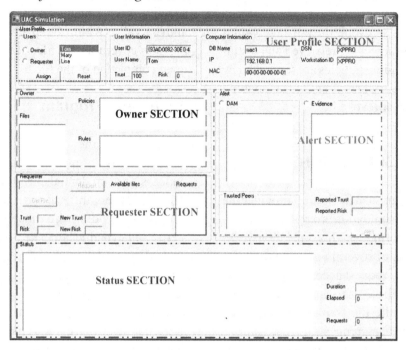

requests scenarios and alerts. The *user profile* section allows the assignment of the owner and requester. These assignments are required and must be performed to initialize any subsequent actions. The user profile also shows logical and physical credentials associated with the selected user. The *owner* section shows the instantiated user playing the owner role. It also shows the files the owner has exposed for requests. Selecting a file will display any associated policies. Selecting a policy will display any associated rules. The *requester* section shows the instantiated user playing the requester role. Trust and risk are values between 1 and 100. This is the current view the owner has of the requester. The *available files* area displays the list of files available to the requester; these are the same ones shown in the owner's file list. The *requests* are the actions available to the requester. Once a file and a request have been selected, the request button will become available for selection. Clicking on the request button will initialize the request sequence from the requester to the owner and trigger the following events:

- The requester will receive recommendations for trust and risk values from randomly generated numbers in the range of 30 to 100 and in the range of 1 to 70, respectively.
- The owner will respond to the request by calculating the trust values associated with the requester from history data and recommendations received from peer users.
- Risk associated with the file is calculated from the governing policies and rules.
- The newly calculated trust and risk values for the requester are displayed in new trust and new risk.
- The new trust must be higher than the minimum trust required as defined in the policy.
- The new risk must be lower than the maximum risk allowed as defined and calculated from policy and rules.
- If these parameters are within the acceptable boundaries, the owner releases a token to the requester to be used for the transfer of the requested file.

If the requester is granted access and receives a transfer token then the "get file" button will become available for selection. The alert section allows for two types of in-progress triggers that may halt the current file transfer initiated by the requester. These alerts simulate a trusted peer notification of malicious or negative behaviors. The alerts may be of *evidence* or DAM type. Either will prompt the owner to reevaluate the current trust and risk levels and perform a decision to either allow the transfer to continue or halt it. The status section displays the various messages from the UAC simulation GUI and instantiated users throughout the various states of the transactions. It also displays the number of requests attempted by the requester and the duration and time elapsed for each transfer.

Test Scenario

Several test scenarios are designed to test the ability of our simulation program including how to evaluate trust, evaluate requests against access control rule, and react to evidence alerts and change of mutable attributes. First, a request fails the authentication when the trust value of the request is lower than the minimum trust requirements. Second, a request passes the authentication but fails the authorization when a request does not meet the access control rules although its trust value is higher than the minimum trust requirements. Third, a request passes both authentication and authorization when the trust value of the request is higher than the minimum requirement and the request meets the access control rules. Forth, a request passes both the authentication and authorization; however, the on-going authorized request is revoked by negative evidence reports. Fifth, a request passes both authentication and authorization; however, the on-going authorized request is revoked by mutable attributes such as change of domain or membership, which is triggered by events received from the DAM. All of the above scenarios have passed tests, and we show the update of trust value in Scenario 1 and revocation of granted permission in Scenario 5.

Figure 5. Successful request

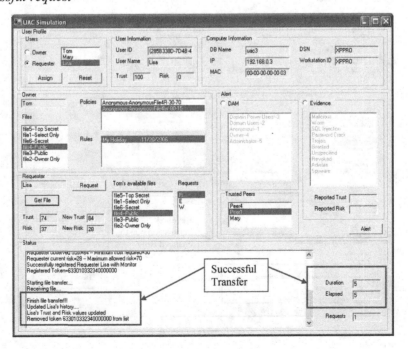

Figure 5 demonstrates a successful request that meets the minimum trust requirements and access control rules and passes authentication and authorization. The requester Lisa requests owner Tom for access to File4 for the purpose of reading the file. Tom's trust in Lisa based on Tom's observation histories is 74 out of 100; the higher Tom's trust in Lisa, the more likely Tom will allow Lisa to read the requested file. Tom will also take into account recommendation from peers (Mary, Peer 1, and Peer 4) with trustworthiness ratings of 65 or higher. Lisa's newly calculated Trust values triggered by her request are 84 and 28 respectively because the total trust value takes into account recommendations provided by Mary, Peer1, and Peer4.

File 4's classification is *public*. Owner Tom has three access control rules for his public file: (1) allow anonymous to read the file classified as public with minimum trust as 30; (2) allow anonymous to write the file classified as public with minimum trust as 80; (3) all the access happens during My Holiday on November 20, 2006.

After the successful transfer of File 4, Lisa's trust and risk are increased by 1 point making the final trust equal 85.

Figure 6 demonstrates the revocation of a granted permission by a DAM alert.

The requester Mary gained the permission to read File 3, but the request was terminated due to the alert generated by Peer 4. The alert reflects that Mary's role changed from a *domain power user* to a *domain user* who has no permission to read File 3. Therefore, owner Tom halts the transfer and terminates the connection. Transfer duration was 5. Actual elapsed value is 3 at the point the connection was terminated. The following is the sample output from Scenario 5.

Scenario Output

Owner=Tom
Requester=Mary

Peer4 reported trust value = 51
Peer4 reported risk value = 14

Figure 6. Revoked request triggered by DAM alerts

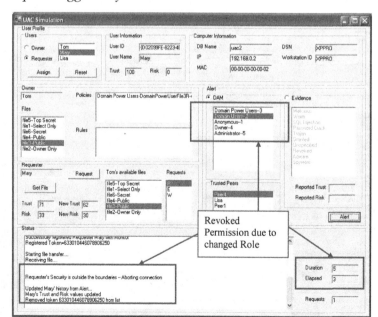

Lisa reported trust value = 78
Lisa reported risk value = 24
Peer1 reported trust value = 56
Peer1 reported risk value = 47

UserID=d02099fe-8223-4d40-9e08-97567a44e6f4
Requester Name=Mary
Requester IP=192.168.0.2
Requester observed trust=62 -- Minimum trust required=45
Requester current risk=30 -- Maximum allowed risk=79
Successfully registered Requester Mary with Monitor
Registered Token=633010446078906250

Starting file transfer....
Receiving file....
Requester's Security is outside the boundaries -- Aborting connection
Updated Mary' history from Alert...
Mary's Trust and Risk values updated
Removed token 633010446078906250 from list
Requester=Mary

CONCLUSION

We have proposed a framework to integrate trust management into usage-based access control. Our framework is designed to solve uncertainty and attributes mutability in a pervasive and collaborative environment. Our framework was simulated in the application of file sharing in order to demonstrate the feasibility. The authentication and authorization to an on-doing request is checked constantly during the request. The granted request will be terminated if the trust value is lowered due to negative peer reports or when access control rules are not met due to attributes mutability.

REFERENCES

Atif, Y. (2000). Building trust in e-commerce. *IEEE Internet Computing, 6*(1), 18-24.

Bacon, J., Moody, K., & Yao, W. (2002). A model of OASIS role-based access control and its support for active security. *ACM Transaction Information System Security, 5*(4), 492-540.

Bertino, E., Bonatti, P. A., & Ferrari, E. (2001). TRBAC: A temporal role-based access control model. *ACM Transactions on Information and System Security, 4*(3), 191-233.

Bertino, E., Catania, B., Ferrari, E., & Perlasca, P. (2001). A logical framework for reasoning about access control models. In *Proceedings of the Sixth ACM Symposium on Access Control Models and Technologies*, New York, (pp. 41-52). ACM Press.

Bhatti, R., Ghafoor, A., Bertino, E., & Joshi, J. B. D. (2005). X-GTRBAC: An XML-based policy specification framework and architecture for enterprise-wide access control. *ACM Transaction Information System Security, 8*(2), 187-227.

Cahill, V., Gray, E., Seigneur, J. M., Jensen, C.D., Chen, Y., Shand, B., et al. (2003). Using trust for secure collaboration in uncertain environments. *IEEE Pervasive Computing, 2*(3), 52-61.

Dimmock, N., Belokosztolszki, A., Eyers, D., Bacon, J., & Moody, K. (2004). Using trust and risk in role-based access control policies. In *Proceedings of the Ninth ACM Symposium on Access Control Models and Technologies*, New York, (pp. 156-162). ACM Press.

Ferraiolo, D. F., Sandhu, R., Gavrila, S., Kuhn, D. R., & Chandramouli, R. (2001). Proposed NIST standard for role-based access control. *ACM Transaction Information System Security, 4*(3), 224-274.

Georgiadis, C. K., Mavridis, I., Pangalos, G., & Thomas, R. K. (2001). Flexible team-based access control using contexts. In *Proceedings of the Sixth ACM Symposium on Access Control Models and Technologies* (pp. 21-27). ACM Press.

Grandison, T., Sloman, M.: Sloman (2000). A survey of trust in Internet applications. *IEEE Communications Surveys and Tutorials, 3*(4).

Jajodia, S., Samarati, P., Sapino, M. L., & Subrahmanian, V. S. (2001). Flexible support for multiple access control policies. *ACM Transaction Database System, 26*(2), 214-260.

Li, N., Mitchell, J. C., & Winsborough, W. H. (2002). Design of a role-based trust management framework. In *Proceedings of the IEEE Symposium on Security and Privacy*, Washington, D.C., (p. 114).

Papoulis, A. (1991). *Probability, random variables, and stochastic processes*. New York: McGraw-Hill.

Park, J., & Sandhu, R. S. (2004) The UCON usage control model. *ACM Transaction Information System Security, 7*(1), 128-174.

Resnick, P., Kuwabara, K., Zeckhauser, R., & Friedman, E. (2000) Reputation systems. *ACM Communications, 43*(12), 45-48.

Sandhu, R., & Zhang, X. (2005). Peer-to-peer access control architecture using trusted computing technology. In *Proceedings of the Tenth ACM Symposium on Access Control Models and Technologies*, New York, (pp. 147-158). ACM Press.

Thomas, R. K., & Sandhu, R. S. (1998). Task-based authorization controls (TBAC): A family of models for active and enterprise-oriented authorization management. In *Proceedings of the IFIP TC11 WG11.3 Eleventh International Conference on Database Security* (pp. 166-181). Chapman & Hall, Ltd.

Xiong, L., & Liu, L. (2004). Peertrust: Supporting reputation-based trust for peer-to-peer electronic communities. *IEEE Transaction Knowledge Data Engineering, 16*(7), 843-857.

Yang, L., Kizza, J. M., Cemerlic, A., & Liu, F. (2007). Fine-grained reputation-based routing in wireless ad hoc networks. In *Proceedings of IEEE Intelligence and Security Informatics Conference* (pp. 75-78). IEEE Computer Society Press.

Yao, W. T. M. (2003). Fidelis: A policy-driven trust management framework. In *Proceedings of the First International Conference on Trust Management* (LNCS 2692, p. 1071).

Zouridaki, C., Mark, B. L., Hejmo, M., & Thomas, R. K. (2005). A quantitative trust establishment framework for reliable data packet delivery in MANETS. In *Proceedings of the Third ACM Workshop on Security of Ad hoc and Sensor Networks*, New York, (pp. 1-10). ACM Press.

This work was previously published in International Journal of Information Security and Privacy, Vol. 2, Issue 2, edited by H. Nemati, pp. 31-45, copyright 2008 by IGI Publishing (an imprint of IGI Global).

Compilation of References

Abdul-Rahman, A., & Hailes, S. (1998). A Distributed Trust Model. In *Proceedings of the 1997 workshop on New security paradigms,* Langdale, Cumbria.

Abdul-Rahman, A., & Hailes, S. (2000). Supporting trust in virtual communities. In *Proc. of the 33rd Hawaii International Conference on System Sciences, volume 6,* Maui, Hawaii (pp. 1-28). Washington, DC: IEEE Computer Society.

Aberer, K., & Despotovic, Z. (2001). Managing trust in a peer-2-peer information system. In *Proceedings of the CIKM'01: Tenth international conference on information and knowledge management* (pp. 310-317). New York: ACM Press. (

Abraham, I., Dolev, D., Gonen, R., & Halpern, J. (2006). Distributed Computing Meets Game Theory: Robust Mechanisms for Rational Secret Sharing and Multiparty Computation. In *Proceedings of the 25th ACM Symposium on Principles of Distributed Computing* (pp. 53-62).

Acquisti, A. (2004). Privacy in Electronic Commerce and the Economics of Immediate Gratification. In *Proceedings of the ACM Electronic Commerce Conference* (pp. 21-29).

Adams, A. A., & Sasse, M. A. (1999). Users are not the enemy. *Communications of the ACM, 42*(23), 40–46. doi:10.1145/322796.322806

Adams, C., Farrell, S., Kause, T., & Mononen, T. (2005). *Internet x.509 public key infrastructure certificate management protocol* (RFC 4210). Retrieved from http://www.ietf.org/rfc/rfc4210.txt

Adomavicius, G., & Tuzhilin, A. (2005). Toward the next generation of recommender systems: A survey of the state-of-the-art and possible extensions. *IEEE Transactions on Knowledge and Data Engineering, 17*(6), 734–749. doi:10.1109/TKDE.2005.99

Adomavicius, G., Sankaranarayanan, R., Sen, S., & Tuzhilin, A. (2005). Incorporating Contextual Information in Recommender Systems using a Multidimensional Approach. *ACM Transactions on Information Systems, 23*(1), 103–145. doi:10.1145/1055709.1055714

Aggarwal, G., Mishra, N., & Pinkas, B. (2004). Secure Computation of the kth-Ranked Element. In *Proceedings of EUROCRYPT . Lecture Notes in Computer Science, 3027,* 40–55.

Ahuja, M.K., & Galvin, J.E. (2003). Socialization in virtual groups. *Journal of Management, 29*(2), pp.161-185.

Aitoro, J. R. (2008a, February 28). DHS gives itself a 'C' for cybersecurity. *Government Executive.* Retrieved from http://www.govexec.com/story_page.cfm?filepath=/dailyfed/0208/022808j1.htm

Aitoro, J. R. (2008b, March 2). OMB reports 60 percent increase in information security incidents. *Government Executive.* Retrieved from http://www.govexec.com/story_page.cfm?filepath=/dailyfed/0308/030208a1.htm

Akyildiz, F., Su, W., Sankarasubramaniam, Y., & Cayirci, E. (2002, March). Wireless sensor networks: a survey. *Computer Networks, 38*(4), 393–422. doi:10.1016/S1389-1286(01)00302-4

American Society for Industrial Security (ASIS)/Price-WaterhouseCoopers. (1999). *Trends in Proprietary Information Loss*. Alexandria, VA: ASIS.

Amme, W., Dalton, N., Von Ronne, J., & Franz, M. (2001). SafeTSA: A type safe and referentially secure mobile-code representation based on static single assignment form. In *Proceedings of the ACM Conference on Programming Language Design and Implementation* (pp. 137-147). New York: ACM Press.

An introduction to cryptography, in pgp 6.5 manual (Tech. Rep.). (1999). Network Associates.

Anderson, E. E., & Choobineh, J. (2008). Enterprise information security strategies. *Computers & Security*, 27(1-2), 22–29. doi:10.1016/j.cose.2008.03.002

Anderson, R. (1993). Why cryptosystems fail in. In *Proceedings of the 1st ACM Conference on Computer and Communications Security* (pp. 215-227). New York: ACM Press.

Androutsellis-Theotokis, S., & Spinellis, D. (2004). A survey of peer-to-peer content distribution technologies. *ACM Computing Surveys*, 36(4), 335–371. doi:10.1145/1041680.1041681

Armstrong, D. J., & Cole, P. (2002). Managing distances and differences in geographically distributed work groups. In P. Hinds & S. Kiesler (Eds.), *Distributed Work* (pp. 167- 186).

Arnold, Y., Daum, M., & Krcmar, H. (2004). Virtual communities in health care: Roles, requirements, and restrictions. In *Proc. of the IADIS Int. Conference, Li*sbon, Portugal (pp. 370-377).

Artz, D., & Gil, Y. (2007). A survey of trust in computer science and the semantic web. *Web Semantics*, 5(2), 58–71.

Artz, D., & Gil, Y. (2007, March). A survey of trust in computer science and the semantic web. *Journal of Web Semantics*, 5(2). doi:10.1016/j.websem.2007.03.002

Atallah, M., Bykova, M., Li, J., Frikken, K., & Topkara, M. (2004). Private Collaborative Forecasting and Benchmarking. In *Proceedings of the ACM Workshop on Privacy in an Electronic Society* (pp. 103-114).

Atif, Y. (2000). Building trust in e-commerce. *IEEE Internet Computing*, 6(1), 18-24.

Atkins, D., Stallings, W., & Zimmermann, P. (1996). *Pgp message exchange formats* (RFC 1991). Retrieved from http://www.ietf.org/rfc/rfc1991.txt

Avancha, S., Undercoffer, J., Joshi, A., & Pinkston, J. (May 2004, May). Security for wireless sensor networks. In C. S. Raghavendra, et al (Eds.), *Wireless Sensor Networks* (pp. 253-275).

Avoine, G. (2005). Adversarial Model for Radio Frequency Identification. *Cryptology ePrint Archive* (Report 2005/049).

Axelsson, S. (2000). *Intrusion detection systems: A survey and taxonomy* (Tech. Rep. 99-15). Sweden. Guteborg, Chalmers University of Technology, Department of Computer Engineering.

Bacon, J., Moody, K., & Yao, W. (2002). A model of OASIS role-based access control and its support for active security. *ACM Transaction Information System Security*, 5(4), 492-540.

Bakker, M., Leenders, R., Gabbay, S., Kratzer, J., & Engelen, J. (2006). Is trust really social capital? Knowledge sharing in product development projects. *The Learning Organization*, 13(6), 594–605. doi:10.1108/09696470610705479

Bal, J., & Foster, P. (2000). Managing the virtual team and controlling effectiveness. *International Journal of Production Research*, 38(17), 4019-4032.

Balabanovic, M., & Shoham, Y. (1997). Fab: content-based, collaborative recommendation. *Communications of the ACM*, 40(3), 66–72. doi:10.1145/245108.245124

Balacheff, B., Chen, L., Pearson, S., Plaquin, D., & Proudler, G. (2002). *Trusted Computing Platforms: TCPA Technology in Context*. Upper Saddle River, NJ: Prentice Hall.

Bamasak, O., & Zhang, N. (2004). A secure method for signature delegation to mobile agents. In *Proceedings of the ACM Symposium on Applied computing* (pp. 813-818). New York: ACM Press.

Barbaro, M., & Zeller, T., Jr. (2006, August). A Face Is Exposed for AOL Searcher No. 4417749. *The New York Times.*

Barber, K. S., & Kim, J. (2002). Soft security: Isolating unreliable agents from society. In *Proc. of the 5th Workshop on Deception, Fraud and Trust in Agent Societies, AAMAS 2002,* Bologna, Italy (pp. 8-17). New York: ACM.

Battré, D., Heine, F., & Kao, O. (2006). *Top rdf query evaluation in structured p2p networks.* Paper presented at 12th International Euro-Par Conference, Dresden, Germany.

Bauckhage, C., Alpcan, T., Agarwal, S., Metze, F., Wetzker, R., Ilic, M., & Albayrak, S. (2007). *An intelligent knowledge sharing system for web communities.* Paper presented at the IEEE International Conference on Systems, Man and Cybernetics, Montreal, Canada.

Becerra, G., Heard, J., Kremer, R., & Denzinger, J. (2007). Trust attributes, methods, and uses. In *Proc. of the Workshop on Trust in Agent Societies, AAMAS-2007,* Honolulu, Hawaii, USA (pp. 1-6).

Becker, T.E. (1992). Foci and bases of commitment: Are they distinctions worth making? *Academy of Management Journal, 35*(1), 232-244.

Becker, T.E., & Billings, R.S. (1993). Profiles of commitment: An empirical test. *Journal of Organizational Behavior, 14*(2), 177-190.

Bell, B. S., & Kozlowski. S. W. (2002). A typology of virtual treatment: Implications for effective leadership. *Group & Organizational Management, 27,* 14-49.

Bellavista, P., Corradi, A., Federici, C., Montanari, R., & Tibaldi, D. (2004). Security for mobile agents: Issues and challenges. In I. Mahgoub & M. Ilyas (Eds.), *Handbook of Mobile Computing* (pp. 941-959). Boca Raton, FL: CRC Press.

Bellifemine, F., Caire, G., Poggi, A., & Rimassa, G. (2003). *JADE: A white paper.* Retrieved Jan 2008, from http://jade.tilab.com/papers/2003/WhitePaperJADEEXP.pdf

Benaloh, J. (1987). *Verifiable Secret-Ballot Elections.* Unpublished doctoral dissertation, Yale University.

Bennett, K., Bradley, P., & Demiriz, A. (2000). *Constrained K-Means Clustering* (Microsoft Technical Report).

Ben-Or, M., Goldwasser, S., & Wigderson, A. (1988). Completeness theorems for non-cryptographic fault-tolerant distributed computation. In *Proceedings of the 20th ACM Symposium on Theory of Computing* (pp. 1- 10).

Bentley, J. (1975). Multidimensional Binary Search Trees used for Associative Searching. *Communications of the ACM, 18*(9), 509–517. doi:10.1145/361002.361007

Berger, C. R., & Bradac, J. J. (1982). *Language and social knowledge: Uncertainty in interpersonal relations.* London: E. Arnold Publishers.

Berkovits, S., Guttman, J. D., & Swarup, V. (1998). Authentication for mobile agents. In G. Vigna (Ed.), *Mobile Agents and Security* (pp. 114-136). Berlin, Germany: Springer-Verlag.

Berners-Lee, T., Hendler, J., & Lassila, O. (2001, May). The Semantic Web. *Scientific American,* 28–37.

Bertino, E. (2004). *Trust Negotiation Concepts and Issues.* CS & ECE Departments, CERIAS, Purdue University.

Bertino, E., & Squicciarini, A. C. (2004). Privacy preserving Trust Negotiations. In *Proceedings of the 5th CACR,* Toronto.

Bertino, E., Bonatti, P. A., & Ferrari, E. (2001). TRBAC: A temporal role-based access control model. *ACM Transactions on Information and System Security, 4*(3), 191-233.

Bertino, E., Catania, B., Ferrari, E., & Perlasca, P. (2001). A logical framework for reasoning about access control models. In *Proceedings of the Sixth ACM Symposium on Access Control Models and Technologies,* New York, (pp. 41-52). ACM Press.

Bertino, E., Ferrari, E., & Squicciarini, A. (2004). Trust negotiations: concepts, systems, and languages. *Computing in Science & Engineering, 6*(4), 27–34. doi:10.1109/MCSE.2004.22

Bethencourt, J., Franklin, J., & Vernon, M. (2005). Mapping Internet Sensors with Probe Response Attacks. In *Proceedings of the 14ᵗʰ USENIX Security Symposium* (pp. 193-208).

Bezzi, M., & Kounine, A. (2008). *Assessing Disclosure Risk in Anonymized Datasets.* Paper presented at Flocon '08.

Bhatti, R., Ghafoor, A., Bertino, E., & Joshi, J. B. D. (2005). X-GTRBAC: An XML-based policy specification framework and architecture for enterprise-wide access control. *ACM Transaction Information System Security, 8*(2), 187-227.

Blaze, M., Feigenbaum, J., & Keromytis, A. D. (1999). Keynote: Trust management for public-key infrastructures. *Lecture Notes in Computer Science, 1550,* 59–63. doi:10.1007/3-540-49135-X_9

Blaze, M., Feigenbaum, J., & Lacy, J. (1996). Decentralized trust management. In *Proceedings of the IEEE symposium on security and privacy* (pp. 164-173). -

Blaze, M., Feigenbaum, J., Ioannidis, J., & Keromytis, A. (1999a). *The keynote trust-Management system version 2.* Retrieved from http://tools.ietf.org/html/rfc2704

Blaze, M., Feigenbaum, J., Ioannidis, J., & Keromytis, A. (1999b). The role of trust management in distributed systems security. In *Secure internet programming: Security issues for mobile and distributed objects* (pp. 185-210). Berlin, Germany: Springer Verlag.

Bogetoft, P., Christensen, D., Damgard, I., Geisler, M., Jakobsen, T., Kroigaard, M., et al. (2008). *Multiparty Computation Goes Live.* Retrieved from http://eprint.iacr.org/2008/068

Boisot, M. (1995). Is your firm a creative destroyer? Competitive learning and knowledge flows in the technological strategies of firms. *Research Policy, 24,* 489–506. doi:10.1016/S0048-7333(94)00779-9

Bontis, N. (1999). Managing organizational knowledge by diagnosing intellectual capital: Framing and advancing the state of the field. *International Journal of Technology Management, 18*(5-8), 433–462. doi:10.1504/IJTM.1999.002780

Borselius, N. (2002). Mobile agent security. *Electronics and Communication Engineering Journal, 14*(5), 211–218. doi:10.1049/ecej:20020504

Borselius, N., Mitchell, C. J., & Wilson, A. (2001). Undetachable threshold signatures. In B. Honary (Ed.), *Proceedings of the 8th IMA International Conference on Cryptography and Coding* (pp. 239-244). Berlin, Germany; Springer-Verlag.

Boukerch, A., & Xu, L., & EL-Khatib, K. (2007, September). Trust-based security for wireless ad hoc and sensor networks. *Computer Communications, 30*(11-12), 2413–2427. doi:10.1016/j.comcom.2007.04.022

Brown, J. S., & Duguid, P. (2000). Balancing act: how to capture knowledge without killing it. *Harvard Business Review, 78,* 73–80.

Brueckner, S. (2000). *Return from the Ant: Synthetic Ecosystems for Manufacturing Control.* Unpublished doctoral dissertation, Humboldt-Universität: Berlin, Germany.

Burak, A., & Sharon, T. (2004). Usage patterns of friend zone: mobile location-based community services. In *Proc. of the 3ʳᵈ Int. Conf. on Mobile and ubiquitous multimedia MUM '04,* College Park, Maryland (pp. 93-100). New York: ACM.

Burrell, J., & Gay, G. K. (2002). E-graffiti: Evaluating real-world use of a context-aware system. *Interacting with Computers, 14*(4), 301–312. doi:10.1016/S0953-5438(02)00010-3

Butler, J. K. J. (1991). Toward understanding and measuring conditions of trust: Evolution of a conditions of trust inventory. *Journal of Management, 17*(3), 643–663. doi:10.1177/014920639101700307

Bye, R., Luther, K., Camtepe, S. A., Alpcan, T., Albayrak, S., & Yener, B. (2008a). *Decentralized Detector*

Generation in Cooperative Intrusion Detection Systems. Paper presented at 9th International Symposium on Stabilization, Safety, and Security of Distributed Systems, Paris, France.

Bye, R., Schmidt, S., Luther, K., & Albayrak, S. (2008b). *Application-level simulation for network security.* Paper presented at First International Conference on Simulation Tools and Techniques for Communications, Networks and Systems, Marseille, France.

Byrne, Z. S., & LeMay, E. (2006). Different media for organizational communication: Perceptions of quality and satisfaction. *Journal of Business and Psychology, 21*(2), 149-173.

Cabri, G., Ferrari, L., & Leonardi, L. (2006). Applying security policies through agent roles: A JAAS based approach. *Science of Computer Programming, 59*(1-2), 127–146. doi:10.1016/j.scico.2005.07.008

Cahill, V., Gray, E., Seigneur, J. M., Jensen, C.D., Chen, Y., Shand, B., et al. (2003). Using trust for secure collaboration in uncertain environments. *IEEE Pervasive Computing, 2*(3), 52-61.

Callas, J. (2006). *An introduction to cryptography* (Tech. Rep.). PGP Corporation. Retrieved from http://www.pgp.com/downloads/whitepapers/

Callas, J., Donnerhacke, L., Finney, H., & Thayer, R. (1998). *Openpgp message format* (RFC 2404_. Retrieved from http://www.ietf.org/rfc/rfc2440.txt

Caralli, R., & Wilson, W. (2004, July). *The Challenges of Security Management.* Carnegie Mellon University, Software Engineering Institute. Retrieved from http://www.cert.org/archive/pdf/ESMchallenges.pdf

Carbunar, B., Yu, Y., Shi, L., Pearce, M., & Vasudevan, V. (2007). Query privacy in wireless sensor networks. In *Proceedings of the 4th Annual IEEE Communications Society Conference on Sensor, Mesh and Ad Hoc Communications and Networks (SECON 2007).*

Carleta, J., Anderson, A., & McEwan, R. (2000). The effects of multimedia communication technology on non-collocated teams: A case study. *Ergonomics, 43*(8), 1237-1251.

Carlson, J., & Zmud, R. (1999). Channel expansion theory and the experiential nature of media richness perceptions. *Academy of Management Journal,* (42), 153-170.

Carman, D. W., Krus, P. S., & Matt, B. J. (2000). *Constraints and approaches for distributed sensor network security* (Technical Report 00-010, NAI Labs). Glenwood, MD: Network Associates, Inc.

Carter, D. (2005). Living in virtual communities: An ethnography of human relationships in cyberspace. *Information communication & Society, 8*(2), 148-167.

Carter, W., & Fisher, S. (2004). Mobile sound communities. In *Proc. of the 2004 ACM SIGCHI Int. Conference on Advances in computer entertainment technology,* Singapore (pp. 355-356). New York: ACM.

Castillo, A., Kawaguchi, M., Paciorek, N., & Wong, D. (1998). Concordia as enabling technology for cooperative information gathering. In *Proceedings of the Japanese Society for Artificial Intelligence Conference.* Retrieved May 2007, from http://www.merl.com/projects/concordia/WWW/JSAI98.htm

Castro, M., Druschel, P., Kermarrec, A. M., & Rowstron, A. I. T. (2002). Scribe: a large-scale and decentralized application-level multicast infrastructure. *IEEE Journal on Selected Areas in Communications, 20,* 1489–1499. doi:10.1109/JSAC.2002.803069

Census Bureau. (2004). *Compendium of Public Employment: 2002 Census of Governments, Volume 3, Public Employment.* U.S. Census Bureau.

Chadha, A., Liu, Y., & Das, S. (2005). Group key distribution via local collaboration in wireless sensor networks. In *Proceedings of the Second Annual IEEE Communications Society Conference on Sensor and Ad Hoc Communications and Networks,* Santa Clara, California, USA.

Chan, H., Perrig, A., & Song, D. (n.d.). *Key distribution techniques for sensor networks.* Retrieved from http://www-2.cs.cmu.edu/~haowen/randomkey.pdf

Challener, D., Yoder, K., Catherman, R., Safford, D., & Van Doorn, L. (2007). *A Practical Guide to Trusted Computing.* Armonk, NY: IBM Press.

Chan, H., & Perrig, A. (2005). Pike: peer intermediaries for key establishment in sensor networks. In *Proceedings of IEEE Conference on Computer Communications (Infocom 2005),* Miami, Florida, USA.

Chan, H., Perrig, A., & Song, D. (2003, May). Random Key Predistribution Schemes for Sensor Networks. In *Proceedings of the IEEE Symposium on Security and Privacy,* Oakland, California, USA.

Chander, A., Mitchell, J. C., & Shin, I. (2001). Mobile code security by Java bytecode instrumentation. In *Proceedings of the DARPA Information Survivability Conference and Exposition* (pp. 27-40). Washington, DC: IEEE Computer Society.

Cheng, J. S. L., & Wei, V. K. (2002). Defenses against the truncation of computation results of free-roaming agents. In *Proceedings of the 4th International Conference on Information and Communications Security* (pp. 1-12). Berlin, Germany: Springer-Verlag.

Cheyer, A., & Martin, D. (2001). The Open Agent Architecture. *Autonomous Agents and Multi-Agent Systems, 4*(1-2), 143–148. doi:10.1023/A:1010091302035

Chidabaram, L. (1996). Relational development in computer-supported groups. *MIS Quarterly,* (20), 143-163.

Chiles, T. H., & McMackin, J. F. (1996). Integrating variable risk preferences, trust, and transaction cost economics. *Academy of Management Review, 21,* 73–99. doi:10.2307/258630

Choi, B., & Lee, H. (2003). An empirical investigation of knowledge management styles and their effect on corporate performance. *Information & Management, 40,* 403–417. doi:10.1016/S0378-7206(02)00060-5

Chu, Y.-H., Feigenbaum, J., LaMacchia, B., Resnick, P., & Strauss, M. (1997). Referee: Trust management for web applications. *Computer Networks and ISDN Systems, 29*(8-13), 953-964.

CIDSS. (n.d.). *Common Intrusion Detection Signatures Standard (CIDSS).* Retrieved August 26, 2008, from http://xml.coverpages.org/appSecurity.html#cidss

Claessens, J., Preneel, B., & Vandewalle, J. (2003). How can mobile agents do secure electronic transactions on untrusted hosts? A survey of the security issues and the current solutions. *ACM Transactions on Internet Technology, 3*(1), 28–48. doi:10.1145/643477.643479

Clark, A., & Scarf, H. (1960). Optimal policies for a multi-echelon inventory problem. *Management Science, 6*(4), 475–490. doi:10.1287/mnsc.6.4.475

Clouqueur, T., Saluja, K. K., & Ramanathan, P. (2004, March). Fault tolerance in collaborative sensor networks for target detection. *IEEE Transactions on Computers Journal, 53*(3), 320–333. doi:10.1109/TC.2004.1261838

Cole, H., & Stanton, D. (2003). Designing mobile technologies to support co-present collaboration. *Personal and Ubiquitous Computing, 7*(6), 365–371. doi:10.1007/s00779-003-0249-4

Collier, T. C., & Taylor, C. (2004, July). Self-organization in sensor networks. Academic Press, Inc. *Journal of Parallel and Distributed Computing, 64*(7), 866–873. doi:10.1016/j.jpdc.2003.12.004

Collins, C. J., & Smith, K. G. (2006). Knowledge exchange and combination: The role of human resource practices in the performance of high-technology firms. *Academy of Management Journal, 49*(3), 544–560.

conference on autonomous agents and multiagent systems (pp. 467-474).

Connolly, T., Jessup, L. M., & Valacich, J. S. (1990). Effects of anonymity and evaluative tone on idea generation in computer-mediated groups. *Management Science, 36,* 97-120.

Coull, S., Collins, M., Wright, C. V., Monrose, F., & Reiter, M. (2007). On Web Browsing Privacy in Anonymized NetFlows. In *Proceedings of the 16th USENIX Security Symposium* (pp. 339-352).

Coull, S., Wright, C. V., Keromytis, A. D., Monrose, M., & Reiter, M. (2008). Taming the Devil: Techniques for Evaluating Anonymized Network Data. In *Proceedings of the 15th Network and Distributed Systems Security Symposium (NDSS '08)* (pp. 125-135).

Coull, S., Wright, C. V., Monrose, F., Collins, M., & Reiter, M. (2007). Playing Devil's Advocate: Inferring Sensitive Information from Anonymized Network Traces. In *Proceedings of the 14th Network and Distributed Systems Security Symposium (NDSS '07)* (pp. 35-47).

Craig, D. V. (2001-2002). View from an electronic learning environment: Perceptions and patterns among students in an online graduate course. *Journal of Educational Technology Systems, 30*(2), 197-219.

Crampton, C. D. (2002). Attribution in distributed work groups. In P. Hinds & S. Kiesler (Eds.), *Distributed work* (pp. 191-212).

Cunha, P. & Cunha, M. J. V. (2001). Managing improvisation in cross cultural virtual teams. *International Journal of Cross Cultural Management, 1*, 187-208.

Cuppens, F., & Miege, A. (2002). Alert correlation in a cooperative intrusion detection framework. In *Proceedings of the 2002 IEEE Symposium on Security and Privacy.*

Cvrcek, D., Kumpost, M., Matyas, V., & Danezis, G. (2006). A study on the value of location privacy. In *Proceedings of the ACM Workshop on Privacy in the Electronic Society* (pp. 109-118).

Czajkowski, G., & Von Eicken, T. (1998). JRes: A resource accounting interface for Java. In *Proceedings of the 13th ACM Conference on Object-Oriented Programming, Systems, Languages, and Applications* (pp. 21-35). New York: ACM Press.

Daintith, J., Illingworth, V., & Pyle, I. (2008, July). *A Dictionary of Computing.* Oxford, UK: Oxford University Press.

Damgard, I., & Jurik, M. (2001). A Generalisation, a Simplification and some Applications of Pailliers Probabilistic Public-Key System. In *Proceedings of International Conference on Theory and Practice of Public-Key Cryptography* (LNCS 1992, pp. 119-136).

Damiani, E., Samarati, P., De Capitani di Vimercati, S., Paraboschi, S., & Violante, F. (2002). A Reputation-Based Approach for Choosing Reliable Resources in Peer-to-Peer Networks. In *Proceedings on the 9th Conference on Computer and Communications Security.*

Damiani, E., Vimercati, D. C. d., Paraboschi, S., Samarati, P., & Violante, F. (2002). A Reputationbased approach for choosing reliable resources in peer-to-peer networks. In *Proceedings of the Ccs '02: 9th ACM conference on computer and communications security* (pp. 207-216). New York: ACM Press. (

Dantzig, G., & Thapa, M. (1997). *Linear Programming 1: Introduction.* Berlin, Germany: Springer-Verlag.

Danyliw, R., Meijer, J., & Demchenko, Y. (2007). *The Incident Object Description Exchange Format* [RFC 5070]. Retrieved August 26, 2008, from http://rfc.net/rfc5070.html

Das, S., Shuster, K., Wu, C., & Levit, I. (2005). Mobile agents for distributed and heterogeneous information retrieval. *Information Retrieval, 8*(3), 383–416. doi:10.1007/s10791-005-6992-6

Davenport, T. H., DeLong, D. W., & Beers, M. C. (1998). Successful knowledge management projects. *Sloan Management Review, 39*, 43–57.

Deba, H., Curry, D., & Feinstein, B. (2007). *The Intrusion Detection Message Exchange Format (IDMEF)* [RFC 4765]. Retrieved August 26, 2008, from http://rfc.net/rfc4765.html

Dell'Amico, M., & Capra, L. (2008). SOFIA: Social Filtering for Robust Recommendations. In *IFIP Int. Federation for Information Processing, 263, Trust Management II* (pp. 135-150). Boston, MA: Springer.

Derbas, G., Kayssi, A., Artail, H., & Chehab, A. (2004). TRUMMAR - A Trust Model for Mobile Agent Systems Based on Reputation. In *Proceedings of the IEEE/ACS International Conference on Pervasive Services (ICPS'04).*

Deriaz, M. (2007). *Trusting Virtual Tags.* Université de Genéve, CUI.

Deutsch, M. (1958). Trust and suspicion. *The Journal of Conflict Resolution, 2*(4), 265–279. doi:10.1177/002200275800200401

Di Crescenzo, G. (2000). Private Selective Payment Protocols. In *Proceedings of Financial Cryptography* (LNCS 1962, pp. 72-89).

Di Crescenzo, G. (2001). Privacy for the Stock Market. In *Proceedings of Financial Cryptography* (LNCS 2339, pp. 269-288).

Dilley, C. (2008). *Air Force Cyber Command: Defending Cyberspace, or Controlling It?* Center for Defense Information. Retrieved from http://www.cdi.org/friendlyversion/printversion.cfm?documentID=4357

Dimmock, N., Belokosztolszki, A., Eyers, D., Bacon, J., & Moody, K. (2004). Using trust and risk in role-based access control policies. In *Proceedings of the Ninth ACM Symposium on Access Control Models and Technologies*, New York, (pp. 156-162). ACM Press.

Dodd-McCue, D., & Wright, G.B. (1996). Men, women, and attitudinal commitment: The effects of workplace experiences and socialization. *Human Relations, 49*(8), 1065-1091.

Donovan, A., & Gil, Y. (2007). A survey of trust in computer science and the Semantic Web. *Journal of Web Semantics: Science . Services and Agents on the World Wide Web, 5*, 58–71. doi:10.1016/j.websem.2007.03.002

Du, W., Deng, J., Han, Y. S., & Varshney, P. K. (2003, December). A Witness-Based Approach for Data Fusion Assurance in Wireless Sensor Networks. In *Proceedings of GLOBECOM 2003*, San Francisco, USA.

Duckham, M., & Kulik, L. (May 2005). A formal model of obfuscation and negotiation for location privacy. In *Proceedings of the Pervasive 2005* (LNCS 3468, pp. 152-170). Berlin, Germany: Springer.

Duri, S., Gruteser, M., Liu, X., Moskowitz, P., Perez, R., Singh, M., & Tang, J. (2002). Framework for security and privacy in automotive telematics. In *Proceedings of the 2nd ACM International Workshpop on Mobile Commerce*.

Dutertre, B., Cheung, S., & Levy, J. (April 2004, April). *Lightweight key management in wireless sensor networks by leveraging initial trust* (SDL Technical Report SRI-SDL-04-02).

Earle, T. C., & Cvetkovich, G. T. (1995). *Social trust: Toward a cosmopolitan society.* Westport, CT: PRAEGER.

Economist. (2007, May 10). Estonia and Russia, a Cyber-Riot. *The Economist.*

Edjlali, G., Acharya, A., & Chaudhary, V. (1998). History-based access control for mobile code. In *Proceedings of the the 5th ACM Conference on Computer and Communications Security* (pp. 38-48). New York: ACM Press.

Edvinsson, L., & Malone, M. S. (1997). *Intellectual Capital: Realizing Your Company's True Value by Finding its Hidden Brainpower.* New York: Harper Business.

El Morr, C., & Kawash, J. (2007). Mobile virtual communities: Current trends and future perspectives. *International Journal of Web Based Communities, 3*(4), 386–403. doi:10.1504/IJWBC.2007.015865

Elinor, O. (1990). *Governing the Commons: The Evolution of Institutions for Collective Action.* Cambridge, UK: Cambridge University Press.

Eliopoulos, C., Ibarguen, K., Thompson, P., Draelos, T., Mcintyre, A., Neumann, W., & Schroeppel, R. (2007, June). *Cross-Domain Information Sharing: Final Report* (I3P Research Report no. 10). Retrieved from http://www.thei3p.org/docs/publications/cdisresearchrep10.pdf Personal Information: Privacy, California Civil Code §1798.29 and §1798.82. Retrieved from http://info.sen.ca.gov/pub/01-02/bill/sen/sb_1351-1400/sb_1386_bill_20020926_chaptered.html

El-Shinnawy, M. M., & Markus, M. L. (1997). The poverty of media richness theory: Explaining people's choice of electronic mail vs. voice mail. *International Journal of Human-Computer Studies, 46*, 443-167.

Erickson, G. S., & Rothberg, H. N. (2009). Intellectual Capital in Business-to-Business Markets. *Industrial Marketing Management, 38*(2), 159–165. doi:10.1016/j.indmarman.2008.12.001

Eschenauer, L., & Gligor, V. D. (2002, November). A key-management scheme for distributed sensor networks. In *Proceedings of the 9th ACM Conference on Computer and Communication Security* (pp. 41-47).

Esparza, O., Fernandez, M., Soriano, M., Mucoz, J. L., & Forné, J. (2003). Mobile agent watermarking and fingerprinting: Tracing malicious hosts. In V. Marík, W. Retschitzegger, & O. Stepánková (Eds.), *Proceedings of the International Conference Database and Expert Systems Applications* (pp. 927-936). Berlin, Germany: Springer-Verlag.

Estrin, D., Govindan, R., Heidemann, J., & Kumar, S. (1999, August). Next century challenges: scalable coordination in sensor networks. In *Proceedings of the 5ᵗʰ annual ACM/IEEE International Conference on Mobile Computing and Networking,* Seattle, Washington, USA (pp. 263-270).

Executive Order 12333 of Dec. 4, 1981, in 46 FR 59941, 3 CFR, 1981 Comp., p. 200.

Exit Games. (2006). *Mobile social software applications that drive social networking and maximize your revenues* [white paper]. Retrieved from http://www.exitgames.com

Falcone, R., & Castelfranchi, C. (2001). *Social Trust: a Cognitive Approach.* Amsterdam: Kluwer Academic Publishers.

FBI. (2008). FY 2009 Budget Request Summary: A Pathway to Achieving Critical End-State Capabilities for the Federal Bureau of Investigation. In *Department of Justice FY 2009 Congressional Budget Submission.* Retrieved from http://www.usdoj.gov/jmd/2009justification/pdf/fy09-fbi.pdf

Feinstein, B., & Matthews, B. (2007). *The Intrusion Detection Exchange Protocol (IDXP)* [RFC 4767]. Retrieved August 26, 2008, from http://rfc.net/rfc4767.html

Ferber, J. (1999). *Multi-Agent Systems: An Introduction to Distributed Artificial Intelligence.* Reading, MA: Addison-Wesley.

Ferraiolo, D. F., Sandhu, R., Gavrila, S., Kuhn, D. R., & Chandramouli, R. (2001). Proposed NIST standard for role-based access control. *ACM Transaction Information System Security, 4*(3), 224-274.

Fiat, A., & Saia, J. (2002). *Censorship resistant peer-to-peer content addressable networks.* Paper presented at Thirteenth Annual ACM-SIAM Symposium on Discrete Algorithms, San Francisco, USA.

Finholt, T., & Sproull, L. S. (1990). Electronic groups at work. *Organization Science, 1,* 41-51.

FISMA. (2002). *Title 44 USC Ch. 35, Federal Information Security Management Act of 2002.* Retrieved from http://csrc.nist.gov/drivers/documents/FISMA-final.pdf

Flegel, U., & Biskup, J. (2006). Requirements of Information Reductions for Cooperating Intrusion Detection Agents. In *Proceedings of the International Conference on Emerging Trends in Information and Communication Security* (pp. 466-480).

Foner, L. (1997). Yenta: A multi-agent, referral based matchmaking system. In *Proc. of the 1ˢᵗ Int. Conference on Autonomous Agents,* Marina del Rey, CA, USA (pp. 301-307). New York: ACM Press.

Foos, T., Schum, G., & Rothenberg, S. (2006). Tacit knowledge transfer and the knowledge disconnect. *Journal of Knowledge Management, 10*(1), 6–18. doi:10.1108/13673270610650067

Forelle, C. (2005, July 14). IBM tool dispatches employees efficiently. *Wall Street Journal,* pp. B3.

Forrest, S., Perelson, A. S., Allen, L., & Cherukuri, R. (1994). *Self-nonself Discrimination in a Computer.* Paper presented at 1994 IEEE Symposium on Research in Security and Privacy, Los Alamos, USA.

Foster, I., Kesselman, C., & Tuecke, S. (2001). The anatomy of the grid: Enabling scalable virtual organizations. *The International Journal of Supercomputer Applications, 15*(3), 200–222. doi:10.1177/109434200101500302

Fricke, S., Bsufka, K., Keiser, J., Schmidt, T., Sesseler, R., & Albayrak, S. (2001). Agent-based telematic services and telecom applications. *Communications of the ACM, 44,* 43–48. doi:10.1145/367211.367251

Friedman, B., Kahn, P., & Howe, D. (2000). Trust online. *Communications of the ACM, 43,* 34-40.

Frincke, D. A., Wespi, A., & Zamboni, D. (2007). From Intrusion Detection to Self Protection. *Computer Networks, 51*(5), 1233–1238. doi:10.1016/j.comnet.2006.10.004

Gajek, S., Sadeghi, A.-R., St"uble, C., & Winandy, M. (n.d.). *Compartmented Security for Browsers - Or How to Thwart a Phisher with Trusted Computing, OpenTC deliverables*. Retrieved from http://www.opentc.net/

Gambetta, D. (1990). Can we trust trust? In *In trust: making and breaking cooperative relations* (pp. 213-237). Oxford, UK: Basil Blackwell.

Gao, X., & Liu, W. (2005). Incentives for information sharing across branches in e-government. In *Proceedings of ICSSSM '05. 2005 International Conference on Services Systems and Services Management, 2005* (Vol. 2, pp. 1481-1483). Retrieved from http://ieeexplore.ieee. org/iel5/10017/32161/01500245.pdf

GAO. (2006). *Managing Sensitive Information: Departments of Energy and Defense Policies and Oversight Could Be Improved* (Report GAO-06-369). Retrieved from http://www.gao.gov/new.items/d06369.pdf

Garber, L. (2000). Denial-of-service attacks rip the Internet. *Computer, 33*(4), pp. 12-17. Retrieved from http://doi. ieeecomputersociety.org/10.1109/MC.2000.839316

Garton, L., & Wellman, B. (1995). Social impacts of Electronic mail in organizations: A review of the research literature. In B. R. Burleson (Ed.), *Communication Yearbook*, 18 (pp. 434-453). Thousand Oaks, CA: Sage.

Gaylord, C. (2008, August 13). *Anatomy of a cyberwar in Georgia, in Christian Science Monitor*. Boston, MA: The First Church of Christ.

Gedrojc, B., Cartrysse, K., & Van Der Lubbe, J. C. (2006). Private bidding for mobile agents. In M. Malek, E. Fernández-Medina, & J. Hernando (Eds.), *Proceedings of the International Conference on Security and Cryptography* (pp. 277-282). Setubal, Portugal: INSTICC Press.

Georgiadis, C. K., Mavridis, I., Pangalos, G., & Thomas, R. K. (2001). Flexible team-based access control using contexts. In *Proceedings of the Sixth ACM Symposium on Access Control Models and Technologies* (pp. 21-27). ACM Press.

Gezo, T., Oliverson, M., & Zick, M. (2000). Managing global projects with virtual teams. *Hydrocarbon Processing, 79*, 112c-112I.

Ghanea-Hercock, R., Collis, J. C., & Ndumu, D. T. (1999). Co-operating mobile agents for distributed parallel processing. In *Proceedings of the Third Annual Conference on Autonomous Agents* (pp. 398-399). New York: ACM Press.

Gibson, T. (2001). An Architecture for Flexible Multi-Security Domain Networks. In *Proceedings of the Network and Distributed Systems Security Symposium,* San Diego, CA. Retrieved from http://www.enhyper. com/content/gibson.pdf

Goldreich, O. (2004). *Foundations of Cryptography II: Basic Applications*. Cambridge, UK: Cambridge University Press.

Goldreich, O., Micali, S., & Wigderson, A. (1987). How to Play any Mental Game or A Completeness Theorem for Protocols with Honest Majority. In *Proceedings of the 19th ACM Symposium on Theory of Computing* (pp. 218-229).

Gong, L., & Schemers, R. (1998). Signing, sealing, and guarding java objects. In G. Vigna (Ed.), *Mobile Agents and Security* (pp. 206-216). Berlin, Germany: Springer-Verlag.

Gong, L., Mueller, M., Prafullchandra, H., & Schemers, R. (1997). Going beyond the sandbox: An overview of the new security architecture in the Java development kit 1.2. In *Proceedings of the 1st Usenix Symposium on Internet Technologies and Systems* (pp. 103-112). Berkley, CA: USENIX.

Gooch, D. J., Hubbard, S. D., Moore, M. W., & Hill, J. (2001). Firewalls — Evolve or Die. *BT Technology Journal, 19*(3), 89–98. doi:10.1023/A:1011994416892

Goranson, C. A., Fink, G. A., & Kuchar, O. A. (2007). *Data Network and Policy Modeling, Year-end Report, FY07* (PNNL-16927 FY07) [Unpublished]. Pacific Northwest National Laboratory, Richland, WA.

Grandison, T., & Sloman, M. (2000). A survey of trust in internet applications. *IEEE Communications Surveys and Tutorials, 4*(4), 2–16.

Grant, R. M. (1996). Toward a knowledge-based theory of the firm. *Strategic Management Journal, 17*(Winter), 109–122.

Gray, R. S., Cybenko, G., Kotz, D., Peterson, R. A., & Rus, D. (2002). D'Agents: Applications and performance of a mobile-agent system. *Software, Practice & Experience, 32*(6), 543–573. doi:10.1002/spe.449

Griswold, W. G., Shanahan, P., Brown, S. W., Boyer, R., Ratto, M., Shapiro, R. B., & Truong, T. M. (2004). ActiveCampus: Experiments in Community-Oriented Ubiquitous Computing. *Computer, 37*(10), 73–81. doi:10.1109/MC.2004.149

Gruteser, M., & Hoh, B. (2005, April). On the anonymity of periodic location samples. In *Proceedings of the Second International Conference on Security in Pervasive Computing (SPC 2005)*, Boppard, Germany.

Gruteser, M., Schelle, G., Jain, A., Han, R., & Grunwald, D. (2003, May). Privacy-aware location sensor networks. In *Proceedings of the 9ᵗʰ Workshop on Hot Topics in Operating Systems (HOTOS 2003)*, Hawaii, USA. Hanna, L., & Hailes, S. (n.d.). *Privacy and wireless sensor networks*. University College London. Retrieved from http://www.petsfinebalance.com/docrepo/privacy_and_WSN.PDF

Gummadi, A., & Yoon, J. P. (2004). Modeling Group Trust For Peer-to-Peer Access Control. In *Proceedings of the 15th International Workshop on Database and Expert Systems Applications (DEXA)*.

Gunupudi, V., & Tate, S. R. (2004). Performance evaluation of data integrity mechanisms for mobile agents. In *Proceedings of the International Conference on Information Technology: Coding and Computing* (pp. 62-69). Washington, DC: IEEE Computer Society.

Gupta, A. K., & Govindarajan, V. (2000a). Knowledge flows within multinational corporations. *Strategic Management Journal, 21*, 473–496. doi:10.1002/(SICI)1097-0266(200004)21:4<473::AID-SMJ84>3.0.CO;2-I

Gupta, A. K., & Govindarajan, V. (2000b). Knowledge management's social dimension: lessons from Nucor Steel. *Sloan Management Review, 42*, 71–80.

Guttman, R. H., Moukas, A., & Maes, P. (1998). Agents as mediators in electronic commerce. *Electronic Markets, 8*(1). doi:10.1080/10196789800000007

Haack, J. N., Fink, G. A., Maiden, W. M., McKinnon, A. D., & Fulp, E. W. (2009), "Mixed-Initiative Cyber Security: Putting humans in the right loop." In *Proceedings of the 2009 Workshop on Mixed-Initiative Multiagent Systems* (MIMS '09), 2009. PNNL-SA-64635

Hafner, K. (2006, August 23). Researchers Yearn to Use AOL Logs, but They Hesitate. *New York Times*.

Halpern, J., & Teague, V. (2004). Rational Secret Sharing and Multiparty Computation: Extended Abstract. *Proceedings of the 36th ACM Symposium on Theory of Computing* (pp. 623-632).

Hansen, M. T., & von Oetinger, B. (2001). Introducing t-shaped managers: Knowledge management's next generation. *Harvard Business Review, 79*, 107–116.

Hansman, S., & Hunt, R. (2005). A taxonomy of network and computer attacks. *Computers & Security, 24*, 31–43. doi:10.1016/j.cose.2004.06.011

He, M., Jennings, N. R., & Leung, H.-F. (2003). On agent-mediated electronic commerce. *IEEE Transactions on Knowledge and Data Engineering, 15*(4), 985–1003. doi:10.1109/TKDE.2003.1209014

He, W., Liu, X, Nguyen, H., Nahrstedt, K., & Abdelzaher, T. (2007, May). PDA: privacy-preserving data aggregation in wireless sensor networks. In *Proceedings of 26ᵗʰ Annual IEEE Conference on Computer Communications (Infocom 2007)*, Anchorage, Alaska, USA.

Heide, J. B., & Miner, A. (1992). The shadow of the future: Effects of anticipated future interaction and frequency of contact on buyer-seller cooperation. *Academy of Management Journal, 35*, 265-291.

Heine, F., Hovestadt, M., & Kao, O. (2005). *Processing complex rdf queries over p2p networks*. Paper presented at the 2005 ACM workshop on Information retrieval in peer-to-peer networks, New York, USA.

Heinzelman, W. R., Chandrakasan, A., & Balakrishnan, H. (2000, January). Energy-efficient communication protocol for wireless microsensor networks. In *Proceedings of the Hawaii International Conference on System Sciences*, Maui, Hawaii, USA.

Hendricks, J., & Van Doorn, L. (2004). Secure Bootstrap is Not Enough: Shoring up the Trusted Computing Base. In *Proc. of the Eleventh SIGOPS European Workshop, ACM SIGOPS,* Leuven, Belgium.

Herzberg, A., Mass, Y., Mihaeli, J., Naor, D., & Ravid, Y. (2000). Access control meets public Key infrastructure, or: assigning roles to strangers. In *Proceedings of IEEE symposium on security and privacy* (pp. 2-14).

Herzog, J. O. (2007). Why is there an increasing global demand for business intelligence? *Journal of Competitive Intelligence and Management, 4*(2), 55–70.

Hohl, F. (1998). Time limited blackbox security: Protecting mobile agents from malicious hosts. In G. Vigna (Eds.), *Mobile Agents and Security* (pp. 92-113). Berlin, Germany; Springer-Verlag.

Hohl, F. (2000). A framework to protect mobile agents by using reference states. In *Proceedings of the 20th International Conference on Distributed Computing Systems* (pp. 410-417). Washington, DC: IEEE Computer Society.

Holland, J. H., et al. (1999). What Is a Learning Classifier System? In *Proceedings of Learning Classifier Systems '99*. Heidelberg, Germany: Springer-Verlag.

Holton, J. A. (2001). Building trust and collaboration in a virtual team. *Team Performance Management, 7*(3 & 4), 36-47.

Hopwood, D. (1997). *Comparison between Java and ActiveX Security*. Retrieved June 2007, from http://www.users.zetnet.co.uk/hopwood/papers/compsec97.html

Horling, B., & Lesser, V. (2004). A survey of multi-agent organizational paradigms. *The Knowledge Engineering Review, 19*(4), 281–316. doi:10.1017/S0269888905000317

Housley, R., Polk, W., Ford, W., & Solo, D. (2002). *Internet x.509 public key infrastructure Certificate and certificate revocation list (crl) profile* (RFC 3280). Retrieved from http://tools.ietf.org/html/rfc3280

Huang, F. Y., Jay, C. B., & Skillicorn, D. B. (2006). Adaptiveness in well-typed Java bytecode verification. In *Proceedings of the 2006 Conference of the Center for Advanced Studies on Collaborative Research* (pp. 248-262). New York: ACM Press.

Huang, F., & Skillicorn, D. (2001). The Spider model of agents. In *Proceedings of the Third International Workshop on Mobile Agents for Telecommunication Applications* (pp. 209-218). Berlin, Germany: Springer-Verlag.

Huynh, T. D. (2006). *Trust and reputation in open multi-agent systems*. Unpublished doctoral dissertation, University of Southampton, USA.

Huynh, T. D., Jennings, N. R., & Shadbolt, N. R. (2004). Developing an integrated trust and reputation model for open multi-agent systems. In *Proceedings of the 7th International Workshop on Trust in Agent Societies*.

IBM. (2001). *Trust establishment*. Retrieved from http://www.haifa.il.ibm.com/projects/software/e-Business/TrustManager/index.html

IBM. (2006). I*BM Anonymous Resolution Version 4.1 Technical Information*. Retrieved from http://ibm.com/db2/eas/

Iyer, S., & Thuraisingham, B. (2007). Design and Simulation of Trust Management Techniques for a Coalition Data Sharing Environment. In *Proceedings of the 11ᵗʰ IEEE International Workshop on Future Trends of Distrubuted Computing Systems (FTDCS '07)*. Retrieved from http://ieeexplore.ieee.org/iel5/4144597/4144598/04144616.pdf

Jadex. (2008). Retrieved from http://vsis-www.informatik.uni-hamburg.de/projects/ jadex/

Jajodia, S., Samarati, P., Sapino, M. L., & Subrahmanian, V. S. (2001). Flexible support for multiple access control policies. *ACM Transaction Database System, 26*(2), 214-260.

James, N., Shi, E., Song, D., & Perrig, A. (2004, April). The sybil attack in sensor networks: analysis and defenses. *In Proceedings of the Third International Symposium on Information Processing in Sensor Networks (IPSN 2004)* (pp. 259-268). New York: ACM.

Janakiraman, R., Waldvogel, M., & Zhang, Q. (2003). *Indra: A peer-to-peer approach to network intrusion detection and prevention.* Paper presented at the Twelfth International Workshop on Enabling Technologies, Washington, DC, USA.

Jansen, W., & Karygiannis, T. (2000). *NIST special publication 800-19 - mobile agent security.* Gaithersburg, MD: NIST, Computer Security Division.

Jennings, N. R., & Wooldridge, M. J. (1998). Applications of intelligent agents. In N. R. Jennings & M. J. Wooldridge (Eds.), *Agent Technology: Foundations, Applications, and Markets* (pp. 3-28). Berlin, Germany: Springer-Verlag.

Jennings, N. R., Sycara, K., & Wooldridge, M. (1998). A roadmap of agent research and development. *Autonomous Agents and Multi-Agent Systems, 1*(1), 7–38. doi:10.1023/A:1010090405266

Jeong-Wook, K. (2007). Experiments and Countermeasures of Security Vulnerabilities on Next Generation Network. In *Proceedings of the Future Generation Communication and Networking (fgcn 2007)*.

Jian, G., & Jeffres, L. W. (2006). Understanding employees' willingness to contribute to shared electronic databases: A three dimensional framework. *Communication Research, 33*(4), 242-261.

Jiang, Y., Xia, Z., Zhong, Y., & Zhang, S. (2004). A Novel Autonomous Trust Management Model for Mobile Agents. In H. Chen, et al. (Eds.), *Proceedings of the ISI 2004* (LNCS 3073, pp. 56-65). Berlin, Germany: Springer-Verlag.

Jøsang, A., Hayward, R., & Pope, S. (2006). Trust network analysis with subjective logic. In *Proc. of 29th Australasian Computer Science Conference,* Hobart, Tasmania, Australia (pp. 85-94).

Jurca, R., & Faltings, B. (2003). Towards incentive-compatible reputation management. *LNAI, 2631,* 138–147.

Kamvar, S. D., Schlosser, M. T., & Garcia-Molina, H. (2003). *The eigentrust algorithm for reputation management in p2p networks.* Paper presented at 12th international conference on World Wide Web. New York, USA.

Kaplan, R. S., & Norton, D. P. (1992). The balanced scorecard: measures that drive performance. *Harvard Business Review,* (January-February): 71–79.

Karjoth, G., Asokan, N., & Gülcü, C. (1999). Protecting the computation results of free-roaming agents. In K. Rothermel & F. Hohl (Ed.), In *Proceedings of the Workshop on Mobile Agents* (pp. 195-207). Berlin, Germany: Springer-Verlag.

Karlof, C., & Wagner, D. (2003, May 11). Secure routing in wireless sensor networks: attacks and countermeasures. In *Proceedings of the First IEEE Workshop on Sensor Network Protocols and Applications* (pp. 113-127).

Karnik, N. M., & Tripathi, A. R. (2000). A security architecture for mobile agents in Ajanta. In *Proceedings of the 20th International Conference on Distributed Computing Systems* (pp. 402-409). Washington, DC: IEEE Computer Society.

Kassab, L., & Voas, J. M. (1998). Agent trustworthiness. In *Proceedings of the Workshop on Distributed Object Security and 4th Workshop on Mobile Object Systems Secure Internet Mobile Computations* (pp. 300). Berlin, Germany: Springer-Verlag.

Kawash, J., El Morr, C., & Itani, M. (2007). A novel collaboration model for mobile virtual communities. *International Journal of Web Based Communities, 3*(4), 427–447. doi:10.1504/IJWBC.2007.015868

Kean, T. H., Hamilton, L. H., Ben-Veniste, R., Kerrey, B., Fielding, F. F., Lehman, J. F., et al. (2004). *The 9-11 Commission Report: Final Report of the National Commission on Terrorist Attacks Upon the United States.* Washington, DC: U. S. Government Printing Office. Retrieved from http://govinfo.library.unt.edu/911/report/index.htm

Kerschbaum, F. (2007). Building a Privacy-Preserving Benchmarking Enterprise System. In *Proceedings of the IEEE EDOC Conference* (pp. 87-96).

Kerschbaum, F. (2007a). Distance-preserving pseudonymization for timestamps and spatial data. In *Proceedings of the ACM Workshop on Privacy in the Electronic Society* (pp. 68-71).

Kerschbaum, F. (2008). Practical Privacy-Preserving Benchmarking. In *Proceedings of the 23rd IFIP International Information Security Conference*.

Kerschbaum, F., & Terzidis, O. (2006). Filtering for Private Collaborative Benchmarking. In *Proceedings of the International Conference on Emerging Trends in Information and Communication Security* (LNCS 3995, pp. 409-422).

Kerschbaum, F., & Vayssiere, J. (2007). Privacy-preserving logical vector clocks using secure computation techniques. In *Proceedings of the 13th International Conference on Parallel and Distributed Systems*.

Khalil, I., Bagchi, S., & Shroff, N. B. (2005). LITEWORP: A lightweight countermeasure for the wormhole attack in multihop wireless networks. In *Proceedings of the International Conference on Dependable Systems and Networks (DSN 2005)* (pp. 612-621).

Khambatti, M., Ryu, K., & Dasgupta, P. (2004). Structuring Peer-to-Peer Networks Using Interest-Based Communities. In *Databases, information systems, and peer-to-peer computing* (LNCS 2944, pp. 48-63). Berlin, Germany: Springer.

Khan, A. (2004, October). *Data fusion in sensor networks*. Retrieved from http://www.cse.buffalo.edu/~qiao/cse620/fall04/Data_Fusion.ppt

Kinateder, M., Baschny, E., & Rothermel, K. (2005). Towards a generic trust model - comparison

King, J. (2008). *A Taxonomy, Model, and Method for Secure Network Log Anonymization*. Unpublished master's thesis, University of Illinois at Urbana-Champaign.

Kiser, K. (1999). Working on world time. *Training, 36*(3), 28-34.

Kohno, T., Broido, A., & Claffy, K. C. (2005). Remote Physical Device Fingerprinting. *IEEE Transactions on Dependable and Secure Computing, 2*(2), 93–108. doi:10.1109/TDSC.2005.26

Koolwaaij, J., Tarlano, A., Luther, M., Nurmi, P., Mrohs, B., Battestini, A., & Vaidya, R. (2006). ContextWatcher - sharing context information in everyday life. In *Proc. of the Int. Conference on Web Technologies, Applications, and Services,* Calgary, Canada (pp. 39-60). ACTA Press.

Kotzanikolaou, P., Burmester, M., & Chrissikopoulos, V. (2000). Secure transactions with mobile agents in hostile environments. In E. Dawson, A. Clark, & C. Boyd (Eds.), *Proceedings of the 5th Australasian Conference on Information Security and Privacy* (pp. 289-297). Berlin, Germany: Springer-Verlag.

Koukis, D., Antonatos, S., & Anagnostakis, K. (2006). On the Privacy Risks of Publishing Anonymized IP Network Traces. In *Proceedings of the 10th IFIP Open Conference on Communications and Multimedia Security* (pp. 22-32).

Koukis, D., Antonatos, S., Antoniades, D., Markatos, E., & Trimintzios, P. (2006). A Generic Anonymization Framework for Network Traffic. In *Proceedings of the IEEE International Conference on Communications (ICC '06)* (Vol. 5, pp. 2302-2309).

Kshetri, N. (2006). The simple economics of cybercrimes. *IEEE Security and Privacy, 4*(1), 33-39. Retrieved from http://doi.ieeecomputersociety.org/10.1109/MSP.206.27

Lakkaraju, K., & Slagell, A. (2008). Evaluating the Utility of Anonymized Network Traces for Intrusion Detection. In *Proceedings of the 4th Annual SecureComm Conference*.

Lamport, L. (1978). Time, clocks, and the ordering of events in a distributed system. *Communications of the ACM, 21*(7), 558–565. doi:10.1145/359545.359563

Landauer, J., Redmond, T., & Benzel, T. (1989). Formal policies for trusted processes. In

Lange, D. B., & Oshima, M. (1998). Mobile agents with Java: The Aglet API. *World Wide Web (Bussum)*, *1*(3), 111–121. doi:10.1023/A:1019267832048

Lathia, N., Hailes, S., & Capra, L. (2008). Trust-Based Collaborative Filtering. In *IFIP Int. Federation for Information Processing, 263, Trust Management II* (pp. 119-123). Boston, MA: Springer.

Le, H. C., Guyennet, H., & Zerhouni, N. (2007, March). March). Redundant communication avoidance for event-driven wireless sensor network. *International Journal of Computer Science and Network Security, 7*(3), 193–200.

League, C., Shao, Z., & Trifonov, V. (2003). Precision in practice: A type-preserving Java compiler. In *Proceedings of the International Conference on Compiler Construction* (pp. 106-120). Berlin, Germany: Springer-Verlag.

Lee, A., Tabriz, P., & Borisov, N. (2006). A privacy-preserving interdomain audit framework. In *Proceedings of the ACM Workshop on Privacy in the Electronic Society* (pp. 99-108).

Lee, B., Kim, H., & Kim, K. (2001). Secure mobile agent using strong non-designated proxy signature. In *Proceedings of the Australasian Conference on Information Security and Privacy* (pp. 474-486). Berlin, Germany: Springer-Verlag.

Lee, J., & Rao, H. R. (2007). Exploring the causes and effects of inter-agency information sharing systems adoption in the anti/counter-terrorism and disaster management domains. In *Proceedings of the 8th Annual international Conference on Digital Government Research: Bridging Disciplines & Domains,* Philadelphia, PA (pp. 155-163). New York: ACM. Retrieved from http://portal.acm.org/citation.cfm?doid=1248460.1248485

Lee, O. (2002). Cultural differences in email use of virtual teams a critical social theory perspective. *Cyberpsychology & Behavior, 5*(3), 227-232.

Lee, S., Sherwood, R., & Bhattacharjee, B. (2003). Cooperative peer groups in NICE. In

Lee-Kelley, L (2002). Situational Leadership: Managing the virtual project team. *The Journal of Management Development, 21*(6), 461-476.

Lee-Kelley, L., Crossman, A., & Cannings, A. (2004). A social interaction approach to managing the "invisibles" of virtual teams. *Industrial Management & Data Systems, 104*(8/9), 650-657.

Leimeister, J. M., Daum, M., & Krcmar, H. (2003). Towards M-Communities: the Case of COSMOS Health Care. In *Proc. Hawaii International Conference on System Science,* Big Island, HI, USA (pp. 214). Washington, DC: IEEE Computer Society.

Lenzini, G., & Sahli, N. & Eertink. H. (2008). Agent Selecting Trustworthy Recommendations in Mobile Virtual Communities. In *Proc. of the Int. Workshop on Trust in Agent Societies, AAMAS 2008*, Estoril, Portugal.

Leroy, X. (2001). Java bytecode verification: An overview. In G. Berry, H. Comon, & A. Finkel (Eds.), *Proceedings of Computer Aided Verification* (pp. 265-285). Berlin, Germany: Springer-Verlag.

Lesk, M. (2007). The New Front Line: Estonia under Cyberassault. *IEEE Security & Privacy, 5*(4), 76–79. doi:10.1109/MSP.2007.98

Lewis, J. D., & Weigert, A. (1985). Trust as a social reality. *Social Forces, 63*(4), 967–985. doi:10.2307/2578601

Lewis, N., & Foukia, N. (2007, November). Using trust in key distribution in wireless sensor Networks. In *Proceedings of the IEEE Workshop on Wireless Mesh and Sensor Networks,* Washington, USA.

Lewis, N., & Foukia, N. (2008, October). An Efficient Reputation-based Routing Mechanism for Wireless Sensor Networks: Testing the Impact of Mobility and Hostile Nodes. In *Proceedings of the Sixth Annual Conference on Privacy, Security and Trust (PST 2008)*, Fredericton, New Brunswick, Canada.

Lewis, N., & Foukia., N. (2008, May). Key distribution and route selection in wireless sensor networks. In *Proceedings of AAMAS 2008 Workshop in Agent Technology for Sensor Networks (ATSN 2008)*, Estoril, Portugal.

Li, J., & Atallah, M. (2006). Secure and Private Collaborative Linear Programming. In *Proceedings of the International Conference on Collaborative Computing* (pp. 19-26).

Li, N., Mitchell, J. C., & Winsborough, W. H. (2002). Design of a role-based trust management framework. In *Proceedings of the IEEE Symposium on Security and Privacy*, Washington, D.C., (p. 114).

Liebeskind, J. P. (1996). Knowledge, strategy, and the theory of the firm. *Strategic Management Journal, 17*, 93–107.

Lilien, L., & Bhargava, B. (2004). *Introduction to Trust in Computing.* Department of Computer Sciences, Purdue University, CERIAS Security Center, Western Michigan University.

Lilien, L., & Bhargava, B. (2006). A Scheme for Privacy-Preserving Data Dissemination. *IEEE Transactions on Systems, Man, and Cybernetics. Part A, Systems and Humans, 36*(3). doi:10.1109/TSMCA.2006.871655

Lin, H.-F. (2006). Impact of organizational support on organizational intention to facilitate knowledge sharing. *Knowledge Management Research & Practice, 4*, 26–35. doi:10.1057/palgrave.kmrp.8500083

Lincoln, P., Porras, P., & Shmatikov, V. (2004). Privacy-Preserving Sharing and Correlation of Security Alerts. In *Proceedings of the USENIX Security Symposium* (pp. 239-254).

Loeser, A., Naumann, F., Siberski, W., Nejdl, W., & Thaden, U. (2004). *Semantic overlay clusters within super-peer networks.* Paper presented at International Workshop On Databases, Information Systems and Peer-to-Peer Computing, New York City, USA.

Loureiro, S., & Molva, R. (1999). Function hiding based on error correcting codes. In M. Blum & C. H. Lee (Eds.), *Proceedings of the International Workshop on Cryptographic Techniques and E-Commerce* (pp. 92-98). Hong Kong: City University of Hong-Kong.

Loureiro, S., Molva, R., & Pannetrat, A. (2001). Secure data collection with updates. *Electronic Commerce Research, 1*(1-2), 119–130. doi:10.1023/A:1011527713457

Lu, Y., Wang, W., Xu, D., & Bhargava, B. (2004). Trust-based privacy preservation for peer-to-peer data sharing. In *Proceedings of the Workshop on Secure Knowledge Management (SKM).*

Luther, K., Bye, R., Alpcan, T., Albayrak, S., & Müller, A. (2007). *A Cooperative AIS Framework for Intrusion Detection.* Paper presented at IEEE International Conference on Communications, Glasgow, Scotland.

Lynch, N. (1996). *Distributed Algorithms.* San Francisco: Morgan Kaufmann.

MacQueen, J. (1967). Some Methods for classification and Analysis of Multivariate Observations. In *Proceedings of 5th Berkeley Symposium on Mathematical Statistics and Probability* (pp. 281-297).

Maes, P. (2004). Agents that reduce work and information overload. *Communications of the ACM, 37*(7), 30–40. doi:10.1145/176789.176792

Maes, P., Guttman, R. H., & Moukas, A. G. (1999). Agents that buy and sell. *Communications of the ACM, 42*(3), 81–91. doi:10.1145/295685.295716

Mamei, M., & Zambonelli, F. (2004). Self-Organization in Multi Agent Systems: A Middleware Approach. *LNCS, 2977*, 233–248.

Markoff, J. (2008, August 13). Before the Gunfire, Cyberattacks. *The New York Times.*

Marsh, S. (1994). *Formalising trust as a computational concept.* Unpublished doctoral dissertation, University of Stirling.

Marshall, R. S., Nguyen, T. V., & Bryant, S. E. (2005). A dynamic model of trust development and knowledge sharing in strategic alliances. *Journal of General Management, 31*, 41–57.

Mathieu, J.E., & Zajac, D.M. (1990). A review and meta-analysis of the antecedents, correlates, and consequences of organizational commitment. *Psychological Bulletin, 108*(2), 171-94.

Matson, E., Patiath, P., & Shavers, T. (2003). Strengthening your organization's internal knowledge market. *Organizational Dynamics, 32*(3), 275–285. doi:10.1016/S0090-2616(03)00030-5

Mattern, F. (1989). Virtual Time and Global States of Distributed Systems. In *Proceedings of the International Workshop on Parallel and Distributed Algorithms* (pp. 215-226).

McBurney, P., & Parsons, S. (2002). Games that agents play: A formal framework for dialogues between autonomous agents. *Journal of Logic Language and Information, 11*(3), 315–334. doi:10.1023/A:1015586128739

McDonald, J. T. (2006). *Enhanced security for mobile agent systems.* Florida State University, Tallahassee, FL. Retrieved August 2007, from http://www.cs.fsu.edu/research/dissertations/JTM.pdf

McHugh, J. (2000). Testing Intrusion Detection Systems: A Critique of the 1998 and 1999 DARPA Intrusion Detection System Evaluations as Performed by Lincoln Laboratory. *ACM Transactions on Information and System Security, 36*(4), 262–294. doi:10.1145/382912.382923

McKnight, D. H., & Chervany, N. L. (2006). The meanings of trust. In R. Bachmann & A. Zaheer (Eds.), *Handbook of Trust Research* (pp 29-52). Cheltenham, UK: Edward Elgar Publishing.

McKnight, D. H., Choudhury, V., & Kacmar, C. (2002). Developing and validating trust measures for e-commerce: an integrating typology. *Information Systems Research Journal, 13*(3), 334–359. doi:10.1287/isre.13.3.334.81

Michael, J. (1994). *Privacy and human rights.* Paris: UNESCO.

Miller, B., Konstan, J., & Riedl, J. (2004). Toward a personal recommender system. *ACM Transactions on Information Systems, 22*(3), 437–476. doi:10.1145/1010614.1010618

Mills, D. (1992). *Network Time Protocol (Version 3) -- Specification, Implementation and Analysis. IETF RFC 1305.* Retrieved from http://tools.ietf.org/rfc/rfc1305.txt

Minsky, Y., van Renesse, R., Schneider, F. B., & Stoller, S. D. (1996). Cryptographic support for fault-tolerant distributed computing. In *Proceedings of the ACM European Workshop on Systems Support for Worldwide Applications* (pp. 109-114). New York: ACM Press.

Morrisett, G., Walker, D., Crary, K., & Glew, N. (1999). From system F to typed assembly language. *ACM Transactions on Programming Languages and Systems, 21*(3), 527–568. doi:10.1145/319301.319345

Morrow, P.C. (1993). *The theory and measurement of work commitment.* Greenwich, CT: JAI Press.

Mui, L., Mohtashemi, M., & Halberstadt, A. (2002). A Computational Model of Trust and Reputation. In *Proceedings of the 35th Hawaii International Conference on System Sciences.*

Naccache, D., & Stern, J. (1998). A New Public-Key Cryptosystem Based on Higher Residues. In *Proceedings of the ACM Conference on Computer and Communications Security* (pp. 59-66).

Nahapiet, J., & Ghoshal, S. (1998). Social capital, intellectual capital, and the organizational advantage. *Academy of Management Review, 23*, 242–266. doi:10.2307/259373

Nandhakumar, J., & Baskerville, R. (2006). Durability of online teamworking: Patterns of trust. *Information Technology & People, 19*(4), 371-389.

Narayanan, A., & Shmatikov, V. (2006). How to Break Anonymity of the Netflix Prize Dataset (Technical Report cs/0610105). In *ACM Computing Research Repository.*

Necula, G. C. (1997). Proof-carrying code. In *Proceedings of the 24th ACM symposium on Principles of programming language* (pp. 106-119). New York: ACM Press.

Necula, G. C., & Lee, P. (1998). The design and implementation of a certifying compiler. In *Proceedings of the ACM Conference on Programming Language Design and Implementation* (pp. 333-344). New York: ACM Press.

Ng, H. S., Sim, M. L., & Tan, C. M. (2006). Security issues of wireless sensor networks in healthcare applications. *BT Technology Journal, 24*(2), 138–144. doi:10.1007/s10550-006-0051-8

Ngai, E. C. H., Liu, J., & Lyu, M. R. (2006, June). On the intruder detection for sinkhole Attack in wireless sensor networks. In *Proceedings of the IEEE International Conference on Communications, (ICC 2006) Vol. 8* (pp. 3383-3389).

Nielsen, B. B. (2005). The role of knowledge embeddedness in the creation of synergies in strategic alliances. *Journal of Business Research, 58,* 1194–1204. doi:10.1016/j.jbusres.2004.05.001

Nixon, L. (2006). The Stakkato Intrusions: What Happened and What Have We Learned? In *Proceedings of the Cluster Security Workshop (CCGrid '06)* (pp. 27).

Nojiri, D., Rowe, J., & Levitt, K. (2003). Cooperative Response Strategies for Large Scale Attack Mitigation. In *Proceedings of DARPA Information Survivability Conference and Exposition (DISCEX 2003)* (pp. 293-302). Washington, DC: IEEE Press.

Noman, A.N.M., & Islam, Md. H. (2007). *A generic framework for defining security environments of sensor applications.* Unpublished master's thesis, Department of Computer And System Science, Royal Institute of Technology (KTH), DSV, Stockholm University.

Nonaka, I., & Takeuchi, H. (1995). *The Knowledge-Creating Company.* New York: Oxford University Press.

Nonnecke, B., & Preece, J. (2000). Lurker demographics: counting the silent. In *Proc. of the Conference on Human Factors in Computing Systems* The Hague, The Netherlands (pp. 73-80). New York: ACM.

Norman, T. J., Preece, A., Chalmers, S., Jennings, N. R., Luck, M., & Dang, V. D. (2004). Agent-based Formation of Virtual Organisations. *Knowledge-Based Systems, 17*(2-4), 103–111. doi:10.1016/j.knosys.2004.03.005

O'Neil, L. R. (2005). *PNNL Risk Assessment Sensitivity Determination (RASD) tool.* Paper presented at DOE Cyber Security Group conference 2005, Denver, CO.

Okamoto, T., & Uchiyama, S. (1998). A new public-key cryptosystem as secure as factoring. In *Proceedings of EUROCRYPT* (LNCS, 1403, pp. 308-318).

Olaniran, B. A. (1994). Group performance in computer-mediated and face-to-face communication media. *Management Communication Quarterly, 7,* 256-281.

Olaniran, B. A. (1995). Perceived communication outcomes in computer-mediated communication: An analysis of three systems among new users. *Information Processing & Management, 31,* 525-541.

Olaniran, B. A. (1996a). A model of satisfaction in computer-mediated and face-to-face communication. *Behavioural and Information Technology, 15,* 24-36.

Olaniran, B. A. (1996b). Group process satisfaction and decision quality in computer-mediated communication: An examination of contingent relations. In R. S. Carthcart, L. Samovar, & L. Henman (Eds.). *Small group communication: Theory & practice* (pp. 134-146). Dubuque, IA: Brown & Benchmark.

Olaniran, B. A. (2001a). Computer-mediated communication and conflict management process: A closer look at anticipation of future interaction. *World Futures, 57,* 285-313.

Olaniran, B. A. (2001b). The effects of computer-mediated communication on transculturalism. In V. Milhouse, M. Asante, & P. Nwosu (Eds.) *Transcultural realities* (pp. 83-105). Thousand Oaks, CA: Sage.

Olaniran, B. A. (2004). Computer-mediated communication in cross-cultural virtual groups. In G. M. Chen & W. J. Starosta (Eds.). *Dialogue among diversities* (pp. 142-166). Washington, DC: NCA.

Olaniran, B. A. (2007a). Challenges to implementing e-learning and lesser developed countries. In A. Edmundson (Ed.), *Globalized e-learning cultural challenges.* New York: Idea Group.

Olaniran, B. A. (2007b). Culture and communication challenges in virtual workspaces. In K. St-Amant (Ed.), *Linguistic and cultural online communication issues in the global age* (pp. 79-92). PA: Information science reference (IGI Global).

Olmedilla, D., Lara, R., Polleres, A., & Lausen, H. (2005). Trust negotiation for semantic web

Olmedilla, D., Rana, O. F., Matthews, B., & Nejdl, W. (2005). Security and trust issues in semantic grids. In *Proc. of Schloss Dagstuhl Seminar no. 05271: Semantic Grid: The Convergence of Technologies*, Dagstuhl, Germany.

Olsson, T. (2006). *Bootstrapping and Decentralizing Recommender Systems*. Unpublished doctoral dissertation, Uppsala University and SICS.

Ordille, J. J. *(1996). When agents roam, who can you trust? In Proceedings of the First Conference on Emerging Technologies and Applications in Communications* (pp. 188-191). Washington, DC: IEEE Computer Society.

Ousterhout, J. K., Levy, J. Y., & Welch, B. B. (1998). The Safe-Tcl security model. In G. Vigna (Eds.), *Mobile Agents and Security* (pp. 217-234). Berlin, Germany: Springer-Verlag.

Ozturk, C., Zhang, Y., & Trappe, W. (2004, October). Source-location privacy in energy constrained sensor network routing. In *Proceedings of the 2nd ACM Workshop on Security of Ad hoc and Sensor Networks (SASN 2004)*, Washington, USA.

Padmanabhan, H., & Whang, S. (1997). Information distortion in a supply chain. *Management Science, 43*(4), 546–558. doi:10.1287/mnsc.43.4.546

Paillier, P. (1999). Public-Key Cryptosystems Based on Composite Degree Residuosity Classes. In *Proceedings of EUROCRYPT* (LNCS 1592, pp. 223-238).

Pang, R., & Paxson, V. (2003). A High-level Programming Environment for Packet Trace Anonymization and Transformation. In *Proceedings of the ACM SIGCOMM Conference* (pp. 339-351).

Pang, R., Allman, M., Paxson, V., & Lee, J. (2006). The Devil and Packet Trace Anonymization. *Computer Communication Review, 36*(1), 29–38. doi:10.1145/1111322.1111330

Papadopoulos, C., Lindell, R., Mehringer, J., Hussain, A., & Govindan, R. (2003). Cossack: coordinated suppression of simultaneous attacks. In *Proceedings of the 2003 DARPA Information Survivability Conference and Exposition*. Retrieved from http://ieeexplore.ieee.org/iel5/8503/26875/01194868.pdf

Papoulis, A. (1991). *Probability, random variables, and stochastic processes*. New York: McGraw-Hill.

Parekh, J., Wang, K., & Stolfo, S. (2006). Privacy-preserving payload-based correlation for accurate malicious traffic detection. In *Proceedings of the SIGCOMM workshop on Large-scale attack defense* (pp. 99-106).

Park, J., & Sandhu, R. S. (2004) The UCON usage control model. *ACM Transaction Information System Security, 7*(1), 128-174.

Parunak, H. V. D. (1997). Go to the Ant: Engineering Principles from Natural Multi-Agent Systems. *Annals of Operations Research, 75*, 69–101. doi:10.1023/A:1018980001403

Patel, J., Teacy, W. T. L., Jennings, N. R., & Luck, M. (2005) A Probabilistic Trust Model for Handling Inaccurate Reputation Sources. In *Proceedings of the 3rd International Conference on Trust Management*, Rocquencourt, France.

Pauleen, D. J. (2001). Facilitators' perspectives on using electronic communication channels to build and manage relationships with virtual tam members. *Proceedings of Society for Information Technology and Teacher Education Conference, 3*, 2913-2918.

Pauleen, D. J., & Yoong, P. (2001). Relationship building and the use of ICT in boundary-crossing virtual teams: A facilitator's perspective. *Journal of information Technology, 16*, 205-220.

Perez, C. R. (2007, December). *Reputation-based resilient data aggregation in sensor network*. Unpublished master's thesis, Purdue University, USA. Retrieved from http://docs.lib.purdue.edu/ecetheses/11/.

Perrig, A., Stankovic, J., & Wagner, D. (2004, June). Security in wireless sensor networks. *Communications of the ACM, 47*(6), 53–57. doi:10.1145/990680.990707

Perrig, A., Szewczyk, R., Wen, V., Culler, D., & Tygar, D. (2001, July). SPINS: Security protocols for sensor networks. In *Proceedings of the Seventh Annual Interna-*

tional Conference on Mobile Computing and Networks (ACM Mobicom), Rome, Italy.

Personality and Social Psychology, 49(1), 95-112.

Persson, P., Espinoza, F., Fagerberg, P., Sandin, A., & Cöster, R. (2002). GeoNotes: a location-based information system for public spaces. In K. Höök, D. Benyon, & A. Munro (Eds.), *Readings in Social Navigation of Information Space* (pp. 151-173). Berlin, Germany: Springer.

Petraeus, D. H. (2006). Learning Counterinsurgency: Observations from Soldiering in Iraq. *Military Review*. Retrieved from http://usacac.army.mil/CAC/milreview/English/JanFeb06/Petraeus1.pdf

Pham, H., & Jha, S. (2004, October). An adaptive mobility-aware MAC protocol for sensor networks (MS-MAC). In *Proceedings of the IEEE International Conference on Mobile Ad-hoc and Sensor Systems* (pp. 558-556).

Pham, V., & Karmouch, A. (1998). Mobile software agents: An overview. *IEEE Communications Magazine, 36*(7), 26–37. doi:10.1109/35.689628

Pleisch, S., & Schiper, A. (2004). Approaches to fault-tolerant and transactional mobile agent execution: an algorithmic view. *ACM Computing Surveys, 36*(3), 219–262. doi:10.1145/1035570.1035571

Polanyi, M. (1967). *The Tacit Dimension*. New York: Anchor Day Books.

Powell, A., Galvin, J., & Piccoli, G. (2006). Antecedents to team member commitment from near and far: A comparison between collocated and virtual teams. *Information Technology & People, 19*(4), 299-322.

Preece, J. (2000). *Online Communities: Designing Usability, Supporting Sociability*. New York: John Wiley and Sons.

Prusak, L., & Cohen, D. (2001). How to invest in social capital. *Harvard Business Review, 79*, 86–93.

Pujol, J. M., Sanguesa, R., =& Delgado, J. (2002). Extracting reputation in multi agent systems by means of social network topology. In *Proceedings of AAMAS '02: The first international joint*

Purser, S. A. (2004). Improving the ROI of the security management process. *Computers & Security, 23*(7), 542–546. doi:10.1016/j.cose.2004.09.004

Qi, H., Kuruganti, P. T., & Xu, Y. (2002). The development of localized algorithms in wireless sensor networks. *IEEE Sensors Journal, 2*(6), 286–293.

Quercia, D., Hailes, S., & Capra, L. (2007). TRULLO - local trust bootstrapping for ubiquitous devices. In *Proc. of the 4th Annual Int. Conference on Mobile and Ubiquitous Systems: Computing, Networking and Services*, Philadelphia, PA (pp. 1-9).

Radhakrishnan, R., Jamil, M., Mehfuz, S., & Moinuddin, M. (2007). Security issues in IPv6. In *Proceedings of the ICNS. Third International Conference on Networking and Services*.

Ramaswamy, R., & Wolf, T. (2007). High-Speed Prefix-Preserving IP Address Anonymization for Passive Measurement Systems. *IEEE/ACM Transactions on Networking, 15*(1), 26-39.

Ramchurn, S. D., Jennings, N. R., Sierra, C., & Godo, L. A. (2003). Computational Trust Model for Multi-Agent Interactions based on Confidence and Reputation. In *Proceedings of the Workshop on Trust, Privacy, Deception and Fraud in Agent Societies*. Melbourne, Australia: AAMAS.

Rana, O. F., Akram, A., & Lynden, S. J. (2005). Building Scalable Virtual Communities Infrastructure Requirements and Computational Costs. *Lectures Notes in Artificial Intelligence, 3413*, 68–83.

Rao, A. S., & Georgeff, M. (1995). Bdi agents: from theory to practice. In *Proc. of the 1st Int. Conference on Multi-Agent Systems (ICMAS95)*, San Francisco, USA (pp. 312-319). Menlo Park, CA: AAAI Press.

Ratnasamy, S., Francis, P., Handley, M., Karp, R., & Schenker, S. (2001). *A scalable content-addressable network*. Paper presented at 2001 SIGCOMM conference on Applications, Technologies, Architectures and Protocols for computer communications, San Diego, USA.

Recursion Software. (2006). *VOYAGER Edge User's guide*. Retrieved June 2007, from http://www.recursionsw.com/Products/voyager.html

Reed, M. G., Syverson, P. F., & Goldschlag, D. M. (1998). Anonymous connections and onion routing. *IEEE Journal on Selected Areas in Communications, 16*(4), 482–494. doi:10.1109/49.668972

Reiter, M., & Gong, L. (1993). Preventing Denial and Forgery of Causal Relationships in Distributed Systems. In *Proceedings of the IEEE Symposium on Security and Privacy* (pp. 30-40).

Rempel, J. K., & Souster, R. (1986). How do i trust thee? *Psychology Today*, 28–34.

Rempel, J. K., Holmes, J. G., & Zanna, M. P. (1985). Trust in close relationships. *Journal of*

Resnick, P. (1996). PICS: Internet access controls without censorship. *Communications of the ACM, 39*(10), 87–93. doi:10.1145/236156.236175

Resnick, P., & Zeckhauser, R. (2002). Trust Among Strangers in Internet Transactions: Empirical Analysis of eBay's Reputation System. *Advances in Applied Microeconomics, 11*, 127–157. doi:10.1016/S0278-0984(02)11030-3

Resnick, P., Kuwabara, K., Zeckhauser, R., & Friedman, E. (2000) Reputation systems. *ACM Communications, 43*(12), 45-48.

Retrieved from ftp://ftp.pgpi.org/pub/pgp/6.5/docs/english/IntroToCrypto.pdf

Ribero, B., Chen, W., Miklau, G., & Towsley, D. (2008). Analyzing Privacy in Enterprise Packet Trace Anonymization. In *Proceedings of the 15ᵗʰ Network and Distributed Systems Security Symposium (NDSS '08).*

Riordan, J., & Schneier, B. (1998). Environmental key generation towards clueless agents. In G. Vigna (Ed.), *Mobile Agents and Security* (pp. 15-24). Berlin, Germany: Springer-Verlag.

Rizzo, L. (1997). Dummynet: a simple approach to the evaluation of network protocols. *ACM Computer Communication Review, 27*(1), 31–41. doi:10.1145/251007.251012

Robinson, T. (2005). Data security in the age of compliance. *NetWorker, 9*(3), 24–30. doi:10.1145/1086762.1086764

Roebuck, D. B., & Britt, A. C. (2002). Virtual teaming has come to stay—guidelines and strategies for success. *Southern Business Review, 28*, 29-39.

Römer, K., & Mattern, F. (2004, December). The design space of wireless sensor networks. *IEEE Wireless Communications, 11*(6), 54–61. doi:10.1109/MWC.2004.1368897

Rose, M. (2007). *The Blocks Extensible Exchange Protocol Core* [RFC 3080]. Retrieved August 26, 2008, from http://rfc.net/rfc3080.html

Roth, V. (1999). Mutual protection of co-operating agents. In J. Vitek & C. D. Jensen (Eds.), *Secure Internet Programming: Security Issues for Mobile and Distributed Objects* (pp. 275-285). Berlin, Germany: Springer-Verlag.

Rothberg, H. N., & Erickson, G. S. (2002). Competitive capital: A fourth pillar of intellectual capital? In N. Bontis (Ed.), *World Congress on Intellectual Capital Readings* (pp. 94-103). Woburn, MA: Butterworth-Heinemann.

Rothberg, H. N., & Erickson, G. S. (2005). *From Knowledge to Intelligence: Creating Competitive Advantage in the Next Economy*. Woburn, MA: Elsevier Butterworth-Heinemann.

Rotter, J. B. (1971). Generalized expectancies for interpersonal trust. *The American Psychologist, 26*(5), 443–452. doi:10.1037/h0031464

Rowstron, A. I. T., & Druschel, P. (2001). *Pastry: Scalable, decentralized object location and routing for large-scale peer-to-peer systems*. Paper presented at IFIP/ACM International Conference on Distributed Systems Platforms (Middleware), Heidelberg, Germany.

Roy, M. H. (2001). Small group communication and performance: Do cognitive flexibility and context matter? *Management Decision, 39*(4), 323-330.

Sabater, J., & Sierra, C. (2002). Social regret, a reputation model based on social relations. *SIGecom Exchanges, 3*(1), 44–56. doi:10.1145/844331.844337

Sahli, N., Lenzini, G., & Eertink, H. (2008). Trustworthy agent-based recommender system in a mobile P2P environment. In *Proc. of the 7th Int. Workshop on Agents and Peer-to-Peer Computing, AP2PC08,* Estoril, Portugal (pp. 1-11).

Sailer, R., Zhang, X., Jaeger, T., & van Doorn, L. (2004, August). *Design and Implementation of a TCG-based Integrity Measurement Architecture.* Paper presented at the 13th Usenix Security Symposium, San Diego, CA.

Sander, T., & Tschudin, C. F. (1998). Protecting mobile agents against malicious hosts. In G. Vigna (Ed.), *Mobile Agents and Security* (pp. 44-60). Berlin, Germany: Springer-Verlag.

Sandhu, R., & Zhang, X. (2005). Peer-to-peer access control architecture using trusted computing technology. In *Proceedings of the Tenth ACM Symposium on Access Control Models and Technologies*, New York, (pp. 147-158). ACM Press.

Scher, M. (2006). On Doing 'Being Reasonable.' Retrieved from http://www.usenix.org/publications/login/2006-12/pdfs/scher.pdf

Schillo, M., Fischer, K., Fley, B., Florian, M., Hillebrandt, F., & Spresny, D. (2002). Form - a sociologically founded framework for designing self-organization of multi-agent systems. In *Proc. of the Int. Workshop on Regulated Agent-Based Social Systems: Theories and Applications,* Bologna, Italy (LNCS 2934, pp. 156-175). Berlin, Germany: Springer-Verlag.

Schillo, M., Rovatsos, M., & Funk, P. (2000). Using trust for detecting deceitful agents in Artificial societies. *Applied Artificial Intelligence Journal, 14*(8), 825–848. doi:10.1080/08839510050127579

Schlenker, B. R., Helm, B., & Tedeschi, J. T. (1973). The effects of personality and situational variables on behavioral trust. *Journal of Personality and Social Psychology, 25*(3), 419–427. doi:10.1037/h0034088

Schneider, F. B. (2000). Enforceable security policies. *ACM Transactions on Information and System Security, 3*(1), 30–50. doi:10.1145/353323.353382

Schneier, B. (1996). *Applied Cryptography* (2nd ed.). New York: John Wiley & Sons.

Schubert, P., & Hampe, J. F. (2005). Business models for mobile communities. In *Proc. of the 38th Annual Hawaii International Conference on System Sciences - HICSS'05,* Big Island, HI, USA (pp. 172-183). Washington, DC: IEEE Computer Society.

Schubert, P., & Koch, M. (2003). Collaboration platforms for virtual student communities. *In Proc. of the Hawaii International Conference on System Science,* Big Island, HI, USA. Washington, DC: IEEE Computer Society.

Seamons, K., Chan, T., Child, E., Halcrow, M., Hess, A., Holt, J., et al. (2003). Trustbuilder: negotiating trust in dynamic coalitions. In *Proceedings of darpa information survivability conference and exposition* (Vol. 2, pp. 49-51).

Seamons, K., Winslett, M., et al. (2002). Requirements for policy languages for trust negotiation. In *Proceedings of 3rd international workshop policies for distributed systems and networks)* (pp. 68-79).

Seigneur, J.-M. (2005). *Trust, Security and Privacy in Global Computing.* Unpublished doctoral dissertation, Trinity College Dublin.

Sekar, R., Venkatakrishnan, V., Basu, S., Bhatkar, S., & DuVarney, D. C. (2003). Model-carrying code: A practical approach for safe execution of untrusted applications. In *Proceedings of the 19th ACM Symposium on Operating Systems Principles* (pp. 15-28). New York: ACM Press.

Serugendo, G. D. M., Gleizes, M. P., & Karageorgos, A. (2005). Self-organization in multi-agent systems. *The Knowledge Engineering Review, 20*(2), 165–189. doi:10.1017/S0269888905000494

Servetto, S. D. (2006, May). From "sensor networks" to "sensor networks." In *Proceedings of the Third IEEE Workshop on Embedded Networked Sensors (EmNets 2006),* Cambridge, MA, USA.

Shmatikov, V., & Talcott, C. L. (2005). Reputation-based trust management. *Journal of Computer Security, 13*(1), 167–190.

Shoham, Y., & Tennenholtz, M. (2005). Non-Cooperative Computation: Boolean Functions with Correctness and Exclusivity. *Theoretical Computer Science*, *343*(1-2), 97–113. doi:10.1016/j.tcs.2005.05.009

Sicker, D., Ohm, P., & Grunwald, D. (2007). Legal Issues Surrounding Monitoring during Network Research. In *Proceedings of the Internet Measurement Conference (IMC'07)* (pp. 141-148).

Simatupang, T. M., & Sridharan, R. (2002). The Collaborative Supply Chain. *International Journal of Logistics Management*, *13*(1), 15–30. doi:10.1108/09574090210806333

Skelton, I. (2001). America's Frontier Wars: Lessons for Asymmetric Conflicts. *Military Review*, 24-27. Retrieved from http://usacac.army.mil/CAC2/MilitaryReview/Archives/COINReaderII.pdf

Skogsrud, H., Benatallah, B., & Casati, F. (2003). Model-driven trust negotiation for web services. *IEEE Internet Computing*, *7*(6), 45–52. doi:10.1109/MIC.2003.1250583

Skogsrud, H., Benatallah, B., & Casati, F. (2004a). Trust-serv: model-driven lifecycle Management of trust negotiation policies for web services. In *Proceedings of the WWW '04: 13th international conference on World Wide Web* (pp. 53-62). New York: ACM Press.

Skogsrud, H., Benatallah, B., & Casati, F. (2004b). A trust negotiation system for digital library web services. *International Journal on Digital Libraries*, *4*(3), 185–207. doi:10.1007/s00799-004-0083-y

Slagell, A., & Yurcik, W. (2005). Sharing Computer Network Logs for Security and Privacy: A Motivation for New Methodologies of Anonymization. In *Proceedings of the SECOVAL: The Workshop on the Value of Security through Collaboration*.

Slagell, A., Lakkaraju, K., & Luo, K. (2006). FLAIM: A Multi-level Anonymization Framework for Computer and Network Logs. In *Proceedings of the 20ᵗʰ USENIX Large Installation System Administration Conference (LISA '06)* (pp. 6).

Slagell, A., Li, Y., & Luo, K. (2005). Sharing Network Logs for Computer Forensics: A New Tool for the Anonymization of Netflow Records. In *Proceedings of the Computer Network Forensics Research Workshop*.

Smith, B., Seamons, K., & Jones, M. (2004). Responding to policies at runtime in trustbuilder. In *Proceedings of fifth ieee international workshop on policies for distributed systems and networks* (pp. 149-158).

Smith, J. Y., & Vanecek, M. T. (1990). Dispersed group decision making using nonsimultaneous computer conferencing: A report of research. *Journal of Management Information Systems*, *7*, 71-92.

Smith, S., & Tygar, D. (1994). Security and Privacy for Partial Order Time. In *Proceedings of the International Conference on Parallel and Distributed Computing Systems* (pp. 70-79).

Smith, T., Byrd, G. T., Xiaoyong, W., Hongiie, X., Thangavelu, K., Wang, R., & Shah, A. (2003). Dynamic PKI and secure tuplespaces for distributed coalitions. In *Proceedings DARPA Information Survivability Conference and Exposition*. Retrieved from http://ieeexplore.ieee.org/xpls/abs_all.jsp?arnumber=1194884

So, Y., & Durfee, E. (1996). Designing tree-structured organizations for computational agents. *Computational & Mathematical Organization Theory*, *2*(3), 219–246. doi:10.1007/BF00127275

Sohrabi, K., Gao, J., Ailawadhi, V., & Pottie, G. J. (2000). Protocols for self-organization of a wireless sensor network. *IEEE Personal Communications Journal*, *7*(5), 16–27. doi:10.1109/98.878532

Solomon, C. M. (2001). Managing virtual teams. *Workforce*, *80*(6), 60-65.

Specht, S. M., & Lee, R. B. (2004). Distributed Denial of Service: Taxonomies of Attacks, Tools and Countermeasures. In *Proc. 17th Int'l Conf. Parallel and Distributed Computing Systems (PDCS '04)*.

Spitzberg, B. H. & Cupach, W. R. (1989). *Handbook of interpersonal competence research*. New York: Springer-Verlag.

Srinivasany, A., Teitelbaumy, J., & Wu, J. (2006). DRBTS: Distributed reputation-based beacon trust system. In *Proceedings of the 2nd IEEE International Symposium on Dependable, Autonomic and Secure Computing (DASC 2006)* (pp. 277-283).

Srinivasany, A., Teitelbaumy, J., Liangz, H., Wuyand, J., & Cardei, M. (2007). Reputation and trust-based systems for ad hoc and sensor networks. In A. Boukerche (Ed.), *On Trust Establishment in Mobile Ad-Hoc Networks.* New York: Wiley & Sons.

Sripanidkulchai, K., Maggs, B. M., & Zhang, H. (2003). *Efficient content location using interest-based locality in peer-to-peer systems.* Paper presented at the 22nd Annual Joint Conference of the IEEE Computer and Communications Societies, San Francisco, USA.

Stankovic, J. A., Cao, Q., Doan, T., Fang, L., He, Z., Kiran, R., et al. (2005, June). Wireless sensor networks for in-home healthcare: potential and challenges. In *Proceedings of the High Confidence Medical Device Software and Systems Workshop (HCMDSS 2005),* Philadelphia, PA, USA (pp. 2-3).

Stoica, I., Morris, R., Karger, D., Kaashoek, M. F., & Balakrishnan, H. (2001). *Chord: A scalable peer-to-peer lookup service for internet applications.* Paper presented at 2001 SIGCOMM conference on Applications, Technologies, Architectures and Protocols for computer communications, San Diego, USA.

Suryanarayana, G., Erenkrantz, J., Hendrickson, S., & Taylor, R. (2004). Pace: an architectural style for trust management in decentralized applications. In *Proceedings of fourth working IEEE/IFIP conference on software architecture* (pp. 221-230).

Tajeddine, A., Kayssi, A., Chehab, A., & Artail, H. (2006). PATROL: a comprehensive reputation-based trust model. In *Autonomic and Trusted Computing* (LNCS 4158, pp. 205-216). Berlin, Germany: Springer.

Tam, H. P., Plowman, D., & Hancock, P. (2007). Intellectual Capital and Financial Returns of Companies. *Journal of Intellectual Capital, 9*(1), 76–95.

Tan, H., & Moreau, L. (2002). Extending execution tracing for mobile code security. *Proceedings of the International Workshop on Security of Mobile MultiAgent Systems* (pp. 51-59), German AI Research Center (DFKI) Research Report: RR-02-03.

Tan, Y. (2003). A Trust Matrix Model for Electronic Commerce. In *Proceedings of the Trust Management First International Conference, iTrust.*

Tardo, J., & Valente, L. (1996). Mobile agent security and telescript. In *Proceedings of the 41st IEEE International Computer Conference* (pp. 58-63). Washington, DC: IEEE Computer Society.

TCSEC. (1983). *Department of Defense Trusted Computer System Evaluation Criteria.* Department of Defense Computer Security Center.

TCSEC. (1985). *Trusted computer system evaluation criteria* (Tech. Rep.). USA National Computer Security Council.

Teacy, W., Patel, J., Jennings, N. R., & Luck, M. (2005) Coping with inaccurate reputation sources: Experimental analysis of a probabilistic trust model. In *Proc. of the 4th AAMAS,* Utrecht, The Netherlands (pp. 997-1004). New York: ACM press.

Teece, D. (1980). Economies of scope and the scope of the enterprise. *Journal of Economic Behavior & Organization, 1,* 223–248. doi:10.1016/0167-2681(80)90002-5

Thomas, R. K., & Sandhu, R. S. (1998). Task-based authorization controls (TBAC): A family of models for active and enterprise-oriented authorization management. In *Proceedings of the IFIP TC11 WG11.3 Eleventh International Conference on Database Security* (pp. 166-181). Chapman & Hall, Ltd.

Thomson, I. (2007). *Russia 'hired botnets for Estonia cyber-war.* Retrieved from http://www.itnews.com.au/News/53322,russia-hired-botnets-for-estonia-cyberwar.aspx

Toft, T. (2007). *Primitives and Applications for Multiparty Computation.* Unpublished doctoral dissertation, University of Aarhus.

Traynor, I. (2007, May 21). Russia accused of unleashing cyberwar to disable Estonia. *The Guardian*. Retrieved from http://www.guardian.co.uk/world/2007/may/17/topstories3.russia

Trusted Computing Group. (2008). *Infrastructure, Architecture Part II - Integrity Management*. Retrieved August 2008, from https://www.trustedcomputinggroup.org/specs/IWG/IWG_ArchitecturePartII_v1.0.pdf

Trusted Computing Group. (2008). *Mobile Working Group, TCG Mobile Reference Architecture*. Retrieved August 2008, from https://www.trustedcomputing-group.org/specs/mobilephone/tcg-mobile-reference-architecture-1.0.pdf

Trusted Computing Group. (2008). *Replacing Vulnerable Software with Secure Hardware*. Retrieved August 2008, from https://www.trustedcomputinggroup.org/groups/tpm/The_Trusted_Platform_Module_Overview_March_2008.pdf

Trusted Computing Group. (2008). *Server Working Group, TCG Generic Server Specification*. Retrieved August 2008, from https://www.trustedcomputinggroup.org/specs/Server/TCG_Generic_Server_Specification_v1_0_rev0_8.pdf

Trusted Computing Group. (2008). *TPM Working Group, Design Principles*. Retrieved August 2008, from https://www.trustedcomputinggroup.org/specs/TPM/mainP-1DPrev103.zip

Trusted Computing Group. (2008). *TPM Working Group, TCG Architecture Overview*. Retrieved August 2008, from https://www.trustedcomputinggroup.org/groups/TCG_1_4_Architecture_Overview.pdf

Trusted Computing Group. (2008). *Trusted Network Connect, Networking Industry and IT Support for Trusted Network Connect (TNC) and its IF-MAP Specification*. Retrieved August 2008, from https://www.trustedcomputinggroup.org/news/events/interop_2008/IFMAP_support_statements_april_21_final.pdf

Trusted Computing Group. (2008). *Trusted Network Connect, TCG TNC Architecture for Interoperability*. Retrieved August 2008, from https://www.trustedcom-putinggroup.org/specs/TNC/TNC_Architecture_v1_3_r6.pdf

Trusted Computing Group. (2008). *TSS Working Group, TCG Software Stack (TSS) Specification*. Retrieved August 2008, from https://www.trustedcomputinggroup.org/specs/TSS/TSS_1_2_Errata_A-final.pdf

Tsiakis, T., & Stephanides, G. (2005). The economic approach of information security. *Computers & Security*, 24(2), 105–108. doi:10.1016/j.cose.2005.02.001

Turner, D. (2008). *Symantec Internet Security Threat Report* (Tech.l Rep. Vol. XIII). Symantec Corporation.

Turner, P. J., & Jennings, N. R. (2000). Improving the scalability of multi-agent systems. In *Proc. of the 1st Int. Workshop on Infrastructure for Scalable Multi-Agent Systems*, Barcelona, Spain (pp. 246-262). Berlin, Germany: Springer-Verlag.

Tveit, A. (2001). Peer-to-peer based recommendations for mobile commerce. In *Proc. of the 1st int. Workshop on Mobile commerce*, Rome, Italy (pp. 26-29). New York: ACM.

United States Constitution. (n.d.). *Amendment IV,1791*. Retrieved from http://www.law.cornell.edu/constitution/constitution.table.html

US-CERT. (2008). Privacy Impact Assessment for Einstein 2. Retrieved from http://www.dhs.gov/xlibrary/assets/privacy/privacy_pia_einstein2.pdf

Uszok, A., Bradshaw, J., Jeffers, R., Suri, N., Hayes, P., Breedy, M., et al. (2003). KAoS policy and domain services: toward a description-logic approach to policy representation, deconfliction, and enforcement. In *Proceedings of the International Workshop on Policies for Distributed Systems and Networks* (pp. 93-96). Washington, DC: IEEE Computer Society.

Vainio, A. M. (2005). Exchange and combination of knowledge-based resources in network relationships. *European Journal of Marketing*, 39(9/10), 1078–1095. doi:10.1108/03090560510610734

van Setten, M., Veenstra, M., & Nijholt, A. (2002). Prediction strategies: Combining prediction techniques to optimize personalization. In *Proc. of the Int. Workshop on Personalization in Future TV,* Malaga, Spain (pp. 23-32).

van Setten, M., Veenstra, M., Nijholt, A., & van Dijk, B. (2004). Case-based reasoning as a prediction strategy for hybrid recommender systems. In *Proc. of the Atlantic Web Intelligence Conference,* Cancun, Mexico (LNCS, 3034, pp. 13-22). Berlin, Germany: Springer-Verlag.

Vawdrey, D., Sundelin, T., Seamons, K., & Knutson, C. (2003). Trust negotiation for Authentication and authorization in healthcare information systems. In *Proceedings of 25th annual international conference of the IEEE engineering in medicine and biology society* (Vol. 2, pp. 1406-1409).

Vigna, G. (1998). Cryptographic traces for mobile agents. In G. Vigna, (Ed.), *Mobile Agents and Security* (pp. 137-153). Berlin, Germany: Springer-Verlag.

Vigna, G. (2004). Mobile agents: Ten reasons for failure. In *Proceedings of the Mobile Data Management* (pp. 298-299). Washington, DC: IEEE Computer Society.

Vroman, K. & Kovacich, J. (2002). Computer-mediated interdisciplinary teams: Theory and reality. *Journal of Interprofessional Care, 16,* 161-170.

Wait, P. (2006, April 3). Feds fumble with FISMA performance: Some doubt that grades give a true picture. *Government Computer News.* Retrieved from http://www.gcn.com/print/25_7/40277-1.html

Walker, D. (2000). A type system for expressive security policies. In *Proceedings of the 27th ACM Symposium on Principles of Programming Languages* (pp. 254-267). New York: ACM Press.

Walker, R. (2007, May 21). Government taps the power of us. *Federal Computer Week.* Retrieved from http://www.fcw.com/print/13_16/news/102750-1.html

Walters, J. P., Liang, Z., Shi, W., & Chaudhary, V. (2006). Wireless sensor network security: a survey. In Y. Xiao (Ed.), *Security in Distributed, Grid, and Pervasive Computing.* Boca Raton, FL: Auerbach Publications, CRC Press.

Walther, J. B. (1994). Anticipated ongoing interaction versus channel effects on relational communication in computer-mediated interaction. *Human Communication Research, 20,* 473-501.

Walther, J. B., Slovacek, C., & Tidwell, L. C. (2001). Is a picture worth a thousand words? Photographic images in long term and short term virtual teams. *Communication Research, 28,* 105-134.

Walther. J. B. (2002). Time effects in computer-mediated groups: Past, present, and future. In P. Hinds & S. Kiesler (Eds.), *Distributed sork* (pp. 235-257).

Wang, Y., & Vassileva, J. (2003). Trust and reputation model in peer-to-peer networks. In *Proc. of the 3rd International Conference on Peer-to-Peer Computing,* Linköping, Sweden (pp. 150-158). Washington, DC: IEEE Computer Society.

Wang, Y., & Vassileva, J. (2004). Bayesian Network Trust Model in Peer-to-Peer Networks. In G. Moro, C. Sartori, & M. P. Singh (Eds.), *Proceedings of the AP2PC 2003* (LNAI 2872, pp. 23-34). Berlin, Germany: Springer-Verlag.

Wang, Y., & Vassileva, J. (2007). A review on trust and reputation for web service selection. In *Proc. of the 27th International Conference on Distributed Computing Systems Workshops,* Toronto, Canada (pp. 25-32). Washington, DC: IEEE Computer Society.

Want, R. (2007, December). You're not paranoid: they really are watching you! *IEEE Journal of Pervasive Computing, 6*(4), 2–4. doi:10.1109/MPRV.2007.90

Warren, S., & Brandeis, L. (1890). The right to privacy. *Harvard Law Review, 4*(1), 193–220. doi:10.2307/1321160

Waters, B., Balfanz, D., Durfee, G., & Smetters, D. (2004). Building an Encrypted and Searchable Audit Log. In *Proceedings of the Internet Society Network Distributed Systems Symposium.*

Weise, J. (2001). *Public key infrastructure overview* (Tech. Rep.). Sun Microsystems, Inc. Retrieved from http://www.sun.com/blueprints/0801/publickey.pdf

Weiser, M. (1991, September). The Computer for the twenty-first century. *Scientific American, 265*(3), 94–100.

Wenger, E. (1998). *Communities of Practice: Learning, Meaning, and Identify*. Cambridge, UK: Cambridge University Press.

Westhoff, D., Schneider, M., Unger, C., & Kaderali, F. (1999). Protecting a mobile agent's route against Collusions. In *Proceedings of the 6th Annual International Workshop on Selected Areas in Cryptography* (pp. 215-225). Berlin, Germany: Springer-Verlag.

Westin, A. (1967). *Privacy and Freedom*. New York: Atheneum.

White, J. (1994). *Mobile agents white paper*. Retrieved May 2007, from http://www.cs.cmu.edu/~rwh/courses/mobile/Telescript/White-Telescript.ps

Wilhelm, U. G., Staamann, S., & Buttyán, L. (1998). On the problem of trust in mobile agent systems. In *Proceedings of the Network and Distributed System Security Symposium* (pp. 114-124). Reston, VA: The Internet Society.

Winsborough, W., & Li, N. (2004). Safety in automated trust negotiation. In *Proceedings of IEEE symposium on security and privacy* (pp. 147-160).

Winsborough, W., Seamons, K., & Jones, V. (2000). Automated trust negotiation. In *Proceedings of DARPA information survivability conference and exposition* (Vol. 1, pp. 88-102

Winslett, M., Yu, T., Seamons, K., Hess, A., Jacobson, J., & Jarvis, R. (2002). Negotiating trust in the web. *IEEE Internet Computing, 6*(6), 30–37. doi:10.1109/MIC.2002.1067734

Wood, A. D., Stankovic, J. A., & Son, S. H. (2003). JAM: a jammed-area mapping service for sensor networks. In *Proceedings of the 24th IEEE Real-Time Systems Symposium (RTSS 2003)* (pp. 286- 297).

Worchel, P. (1979). Trust and distrust. In W. G. Austin & S. Worchel (Eds.), *The social psychology of intergroup relation*. CA: Wadsworth.

Xiong, L., & Liu, L. (2004). A reputation-based trust model for peer-to-peer ecommerce communities. *IEEE Transactions on Knowledge and Data Engineering, 7*(16).

Xiong, L., & Liu, L. (2004). Peertrust: Supporting reputation-based trust for peer-to-peer electronic communities. *IEEE Transaction Knowledge Data Engineering, 16*(7), 843-857.

Xu, D., Harn, L., Narasimhan, M., & Luo, J. (2006). An improved free-roaming mobile agent security protocol against colluded truncation attacks. In *Proceedings of the 30th Annual International Computer Software and Applications Conference* (pp. 309-314). Washington, DC: IEEE Computer Society.

Xu, D., Lilien, L., & Bhargava, B. (2004). *Private and Trusted Interactions*. Department of Computer Sciences, Purdue University, CERIAS Security Center, CWSA.

Yang, L., Kizza, J. M., Cemerlic, A., & Liu, F. (2007). Fine-grained reputation-based routing in wireless ad hoc networks. In *Proceedings of IEEE Intelligence and Security Informatics Conference* (pp. 75-78). IEEE Computer Society Press.

Yao, A. (1982). Protocols for Secure Computations. In *Proceedings of the IEEE Symposium on Foundations of Computer Science* (pp. 160-164).

Yao, W. T. M. (2003). Fidelis: A policy-driven trust management framework. In *Proceedings of the First International Conference on Trust Management* (LNCS 2692, p. 1071).

Ye, S., Makedon, F., & Ford, J. (2004). Collaborative automated trust negotiation in peer-topeer systems. In *Proceedings of fourth international conference on peer-to-peer computing* (pp. 108-115).

Ye, W., Heidemann, J., & Estrin, D. (2002). An energy-efficient mac protocol for wireless sensor networks. In *Proceedings of the 21st International Annual Joint Conference of the IEEE Computer and Communications Societies (INFOCOM 2002)*, New York, NY, USA.

Yee, B. (1997). *A sanctuary for mobile agents* (Tech. Rep. No. CS97-537). San Diego, CA: University of California at San Diego, Department of Computer Science and Engineering.

Yee, B. (2003). Monotonicity and partial results protection for mobile agents. In *Proceedings of the 23rd International Conference on Distributed Computing Systems* (pp. 582-591). Washington, DC: IEEE Computer Society.

Yee, K.-P. (2004). Aligning Security and Usability. *IEEE Security & Privacy*, 2(5), 48–55. doi:10.1109/MSP.2004.64

Yegneswaran, V., Barford, P., & Jha, S. (2004). *Global intrusion detection in the DOMINO overlay system.* Paper presented at Network and Distributed System Security Symposium (NDSS), San Diego, USA.

Yu, B., & Singh, M. P. (2002). An evidential model of distributed reputation management. In *Proc. of 1st International Joint Conference on Autonomous Agents and Multi-Agent Systems AAMAS 2002,* Bologna, Italy (pp. 294-301). New York: ACM.

Yu, B., & Xiao, B. (2006, April). Detecting selective forwarding attacks in wireless sensor networks. In *Proceedings of the Parallel and Distributed Processing Symposium (IPDPS 2006).*

Yu, F. (2001). The efficacy of electronic telecommunications in fostering interpersonal relationships. *Journal of Educational Computing Research, 26*(2), 177-189.

Yu, T., & Winslett, M. (2003). A unified scheme for resource protection in automated trust negotiation. In *Proceedings of symposium on security and privacy* (pp. 110-122).

Yu, T., Winslett, M., & Seamons, K. E. (2003). Supporting structured credentials and sensitive policies through interoperable strategies for automated trust negotiation. *ACM Transactions on Information and System Security, 6*(1), 1–42. doi:10.1145/605434.605435

Yurcik, W., Woolam, C., Hellings, G., Khan, L., & Thuraisingham, B. (2007). Scrub-tcpdump: A Multi-Level Packet Anonymizer Demonstrating Privacy/ Analysis Tradeoffs. In *Proceedings of the 3rd Workshop on the Value of Security through Collaboration (SECO-VAL '07)* (pp. 49-56).

Zacharia, G., & Maes, P. (2000). Trust management through reputation mechanisms. *Applied Artificial Intelligence, 14*(9), 881–908. doi:10.1080/08839510050144868

Zachary, J. (2003). Protecting mobile code in the wild. *IEEE Internet Computing, 7*(2), 78–82. doi:10.1109/MIC.2003.1189192

Zack, M. A. (1999a). Developing a knowledge strategy. *California Management Review, 41*(3), 125–145.

Zack, M. A. (1999b). Managing codified knowledge. *Sloan Management Review,* (Summer): 45–58.

Zander, U., & Kogut, B. (1995). Knowledge and the speed of transfer and imitation of organizational capabilities: An empirical test. *Organization Science, 6*(1), 76–92. doi:10.1287/orsc.6.1.76

Zhang, N. (2007). On the Communication Complexity of Privacy-Preserving Information Sharing Protocols. In *Proceedings of the Intelligence and Security Informatics, 2007 IEEE* (pp. 289-295). doi: 10.1109/ISI.2007.379487

Zhang, Q., & Li, X. (2006). An IP Address Anonymization Scheme with Multiple Access Levels. In I. Chong & K. Kawahara (Eds.), R*evised Selected Papers from the International Conference on Information Networking (ICOIN 2006): Advances in Data Communications and Wireless Networks* (pp. 793-802). Berlin, Germany: Springer.

Zhang, Q., Wang, J., & Li, X. (2007). On the Design of Fast Prefix-Preserving IP Address Anonymization Scheme. In *Proceedings of the International Conference on Information and Communications Security (ICICS '07)* (pp. 177-188).

Zhang, Y., Lee, W., & Huang, Y.-A. (2003). Intrusion detection techniques for mobile wireless networks. *Wireless Networks, 9,* 545–556. doi:10.1023/A:1024600519144

Zhao, W., Varadharajan, V., & Bryan, G. (2004). Modelling trust relationships in distributed environments. *Lecture Notes in Computer Science, 3184,* 40–49.

Zhao, W., Varadharajan, V., & Bryan, G. (2005a). Analysis and modelling of trust in distributed information systems. *Lecture Notes in Computer Science, 3803*, 106–119. doi:10.1007/11593980_8

Zhao, W., Varadharajan, V., & Bryan, G. (2005b). Type and scope of trust relationships in Collaborative interactions in distributed environments. In *Proceedings of 7th international conference on enterprise information systems* (Vol. 3, pp. 331-336).

Zhao, W., Varadharajan, V., & Bryan, G. (2006). General methodology for analysis and modeling of trust relationships in distributed computing. *Journal of Computers, 1*, 42–53.

Zhao, W., Varadharajan, V., & Bryan, G. (2007). A unified taxonomy framework of trust. In *Trust in E-Service: Technologies, Practices and Challenges* (pp. 29-50).

Zhong, Y., & Bhargava, B. (2004) Using entropy to trade privacy for Trust. In *Proceedings of Security and Knowledge Mangement (SKM)*, Amherst, NY. Zhong, Y., Bhargava, B., & Lilien, L. (n.d.). *Trust and Privacy in Authorization*. Retrieved from http://www.cs.purdue.edu/homes/bb/bb_Pgh_PI_meetg.ppt

Zhong, Y., Lilien, L., & Bhargava, B. (2005). *P2D2: A Mechanism for Privacy-Preserving Data Dissemination*. Department of Computer Sciences, Purdue University, CERIAS Security Center, Western Michigan University.

Zhu, H., Feng, B., & Deng, R. H. (2003). Computing of trust in distributed networks. In *Cryptology ePrint Archive: Report 2003/056*. Retrieved from http://eprint.iacr.org

Zimmermann, P. (2008). *Why do you need pgp?* Retrieved from http://www.pgpi.org/doc/whypgp/en/

Zouridaki, C., Mark, B. L., Hejmo, M., & Thomas, R. K. (2005). A quantitative trust establishment framework for reliable data packet delivery in MANETS. In *Proceedings of the Third ACM Workshop on Security of Ad hoc and Sensor Networks*, New York, (pp. 1-10). ACM Press.

About the Contributors

Jean-Marc Seigneur is Assistant Professor at the Université de Genève, Switzerland. His main research topic is computational trust and reputation management. He is also Chief Research Officer of Venyo, which is a leading company in online reputation services. He has co-authored more than 45 scientific publications and worked on many multi-million Euros R&D projects funded by the European Union.

Adam Slagell is a Sr. Security Engineer at the National Center for Supercomputing Applications (NCSA) at the University of Illinois where he leads the LAIM (Log Anonymization and Information Management) working group as the National Science Foundation (NSF) PI on a grant investigating effects of log anonymization on security, privacy and usability. He is also the security architect and policy developer for the Blue Waters petascale computing project to build the world's fastest supercomputer in 2011. Mr. Slagell has worked on a collaboration between the NCSA and the FBI, served as a co-chair of the SECOVAL workshop, and been a reviewer for IEEE journals and the NSF. His research interests and past projects include work in security visualization, applied cryptography, secure group communication, secure email list services, digital forensics, honeypots, risk analysis and intrusion detection.

* * *

Joerg Abendroth graduated in 2000 from the University of Applied Science owned by German Telekom. He continued studies at the Distributed Systems Group and also BRICS Denmark and received his PhD from the Trinity College Dublin in 2004. Since then he worked with Siemens AG and now Nokia Siemens Networks in the research department and is a visiting research at the Technical University Munich. He is delegate to the TCG and member of GI. His research interests include Trusted Computing, Identity Management, Access Control Models and Mechanisms, as well as other security topics.

Dr.-Ing. Sahin Albayrak is the chair of the professorship on Agent Technologies in Business Applications and Telecommunication (AOT) at Technische Universität Berlin. He is the founder and head of DAI-Labor, currently employing about 100 researchers and support staff. He is a member of "The Institute of Electrical and Electronics Engineers" (IEEE), "Association for Computing Machinery" (ACM), "Gesellschaft für Informatik" (German Computer Science Society, GI), and "American Association for Artificial Intelligence" (AAAI). Prof. Albayrak is one of the founding members of Deutsche Telekom Laboratories (T-Labs) and currently a member of its steering board. He was the initiator of many reputable research projects, e.g.: E@MC2, Sun-Trec, in which he has been supervising research networks at national and international levels. He is also a member of various industrial and political advisory committees, e.g.: Impulskreis "Vernetzte Welten".

Rainer Bye received the Diplom-Informatiker, comparable with int. master degree, in 2005 at Technische Universität Braunschweig. Currently he is working as a researcher and project leader at DAI-Labor at Technische Universität Berlin and pursuing his PhD. He worked on projects in Cooperative Intrusion Detection, Critical Infrastructure Security, Net-Centric Security and Network Security Simulation where "NeSSi²", the Network Security Simulator has been developed. His main area of research is "Collaborative Intrusion & Malware Detection" (CIMD), investigating the benefit of collaborative methods for Security. This also includes Peer-to-Peer Security, application of overlay networks for Security, Intrusion Detection, Network Simulation and Autonomous Security.

Seyit Ahmet Camtepe received the Ph.D. degree in Computer Science from Rensselaer Polytechnic Institute, Troy, NY, in 2007. He received the B.S. and M.S. degrees in Computer Engineering from Bogazici University, Istanbul, Turkey, in 1996 and 2001 respectively. During the years 1996 - 2002, he worked as a Network and Security Engineer in Pamukbank (currently Halkbank), Istanbul, Turkey. During his Ph.D. study, he worked on variety of security research projects including key management in wireless sensor networks, attack modeling and detection and social network analysis. He is currently doing his PostDoc and directing Competence Center Security in DAI-Labor at Technische Universität Berlin. His research interests include Autonomous Security, Economy of Information Security, Malicious Cryptography, Key Management, Distributed System Security, Attack Modeling-Detection-Prevention, AAA and VoIP Security.

Ali Chehab received his Bachelor degree in EE from the American University of Beirut (AUB) in 1987, the Master's degree in EE from Syracuse University, and the PhD degree in ECE from the University of North Carolina at Charlotte, in 2002. From 1989 to 1998, he was a lecturer in the ECE Department at AUB. He rejoined the ECE Department at AUB as an assistant professor in 2002 and became an associate professor in 2008. His research interests are VLSI Testing and Information Security and Trust.

Samuel Clements is a cyber security researcher at Pacific Northwest National Laboratory where he focuses on securing critical infrastructure communication systems. He holds a B.S. from Utah State University in Business Information Systems and an M.S. from Carnegie Mellon University in Information Security Policy and Management. Before joining PNNL he developed globally distributed IT training at CERT, maintained computer systems for the largest high school in Washington State, and was the IT department for a local Boys and Girls Club. He currently resides in Richland, WA with his wife and two children.

Rima Deghaili was born in Lebanon in 1984. She studied electrical and computer engineering and received the BE degree in 2006 from "Université Saint-Joseph". She pursued her master's degree at the American University of Beirut (AUB) and graduated in 2008. In September 2008, she joined Murex Systems where she currently works as an automation developer at the quality assurance department. Her research interests are in distributed computing and security systems including trust and privacy models.

G. Scott Erickson is Associate Professor and Chair, Department of Marketing/Law, in the School of Business at Ithaca College, Ithaca, NY. He holds a Ph.D. from Lehigh University, an MIM from Thunderbird and an MBA from SMU. He has published widely on intellectual capital, intellectual property, and competitive intelligence. His book with Helen Rothberg, From Knowledge to Intelligence: Creating Competitive Advantage in the Next Economy was published by Elsevier in 2005.

Glenn A. Fink, Ph. D. is a Senior Research Scientist at Pacific Northwest National Laboratory (PNNL) in Richland, Washington. Dr. Fink specializes in computer security, visualization, and Human-Centric Computing (centering computer systems' design and function around the needs and abilities of people). His research at PNNL is in adaptive computer security systems with a human-centric point of view. Previously Dr. Fink was a software engineer for the Naval Surface Warfare Center in Dahlgren, Virginia where he worked for 15 years on projects such as the Trident ballistic missile program, a unified ground-control station unmanned for aerial vehicles, and a virtual operations network for rapid-deployment coalition warfare. Dr. Fink served for 11 years as an Army Reserve officer in the Signal Corps where he attained the rank of Captain and commanded a communications company. Dr. Fink currently lives in the Tri-Cities area of Washington with his wife and two children.

Noria Foukia received a BS and MS Degrees in Pure and Applied Mathematics in 1995 and 1996, from the University of Science Lyon-I, France, and a MS Degree in Network and Distributed Systems from the University of Nice-Sophia Antipolis, France, in 1998. She joined the Teleinformatics and Operating Systems groups of the University of Geneva, Switzerland as Research Assistant, working on charging and accounting for the internet and on network security, and received her PhD Degree in 2004. She did a Post-Doc at the ISI/USC, USA from 2004 to 2005. She is currently a Lecturer at the University of Otago, New Zealand. Her research interests include network security, privacy, trust management, agent-based systems, sensor and pervasive networks.

Deborah Frincke is the Chief Scientist for Cyber Security Research at Pacific Northwest National Laboratory (PNNL) and Affilliate Professor at University of Washington's (UW) iSchool. Prior to joining PNNL, Dr. Frincke was a (Full) Professor at the University of Idaho, and co-founder of TriGeo Network Security. She is a charter organizer of the Department of Energy's cyber security grass roots community. Dr. Frincke's research emphasizes areas including infrastructure defense, security visualization, forensics, and computer security education. She is an active member of several editorial boards, including: Journal of Computer Security, the Elsevier International Journal of Computer Networks, International Journal of Information and Computer Security, and IEEE Security & Privacy Magazine. She is a steering committee member for RAID and SADFE.

Mohammed Hussain is a PhD candidate at the School of Computing at Queen's University, Canada. He received his B.Sc and M.Sc in computer sceinces from University of Sharjah, UAE in 2004 and Queen's University, Canada in 2006, respectively. His main interest is the area of software security and privacy-aware software.

Ayman Kayssi was born in Lebanon in 1967. He studied electrical engineering and received the BE degree, with distinction, in 1987 from the American University of Beirut (AUB), and the MSE and PhD degrees from the University of Michigan, Ann Arbor, in 1989 and 1993, respectively. In 1993, he joined the Department of Electrical and Computer Engineering (ECE) at AUB, where he is currently a full professor. He teaches courses in electronics and in networking, and has received AUB's Teaching Excellence Award in 2003. His research interests are in the areas of information security, and IC design and test, and has published more than 90 papers in the fields of VLSI, networking, security, and engineering education. He is a senior member of IEEE and a member of ACM.

Florian Kerschbaum is a senior researcher and project lead in the security & trust research program at SAP Research in Karlsruhe, Germany, and working towards his Ph.D. degree at the University of Dortmund, Germany. He hold a masterís degree from Purdue University, and a bachelorís degree from Berufsakademie Mannheim, Germany. Besides SAP he has worked for Siemens, a San Francisco startup, Intel and Digital Equipment in the job functions of project manager, software architect, and developer. He has published in scientific conferences and journals and patented on many security topics including network security, watermarking, biometrics, and applied cryptography.

Holger Kinkelin graduated in 2007 with a diploma degree in computer sciences from the University of Tübingen. Afterwards he joined the chair on "Computer Networks and Internet" as a scientific staff member and Ph.D. student. In the beginning of 2008 the chair moved to the Technische Universität München, where Holger is working now. His main research topics focus on trusted computing and network security. Holger contributes to an industry cooperation project together with Nokia Siemens Networks and to national and international projects dealing with autonomic networking.

Kiran Lakkaraju is pursuing a Ph.D. in the Department of Computer Science at the University of Illinois at Urbana-Champaign. He has three main areas of interest; Log Anonymization (particularly evaluating the trade-off between information loss and security); Network Security Visualization and the interweaving of human, visualization and machine learning techniques; and models of information dissemination in complex settings.

Gabriele Lenzini is a researcher at the Telematica Instituut/Noway (The Netherlands). He has been working in computer science research for about ten years (Univ. Pisa, ISTI-CNR, IIT-CNR in Italy and Univ. Twente in The Netherlands). His expertise is in formal models for trust, security, and privacy. Lenzini's research interest has focused on security protocol verification, privacy languages design, trustworthiness and security solutions for embedded systems. Recently, he directed his studies towards trust, security and privacy aspects in context-awareness, in reputation systems, and in virtual communities. Lenzini has publications in international conferences and journals. He hold two M.Sc., in information science and in informatics (Univ. Pisa), and a Ph.D. in computer science (Univ. of Twente).

Nathan Lewis is a research assistant of the university of Otago in New Zealand. He was working from 2006 to 2008 in a research project directed by Doctor Noria Foukia dealing with trust-based routing protocol for wireless sensor networks.

David McKinnon is a senior research scientist at the Pacific Northwest National Laboratory (Richland, WA). Dr. McKinnon has been a key contributor to several award-winning research projects and technology commercialization efforts at PNNL. His research interests are in the areas of distributed systems, especially distributed sensor systems, and network security. He is an active volunteer with the IEEE and IEEE Computer Society and an ACM member. Dr. McKinnon is also an adjunct computer science professor at Washington State University, where he has taught software engineering and computer and network security courses. He earned the B.S. and M.S. degrees in mathematics and computer science, respectively, from Brigham Young University and a Ph.D. in computer science from Washington State University.

Helen N. Rothberg is Professor of Strategy in the School of Management at Marist College, Poughkeepsie, NY. She holds a Ph.D. and M.Phil. from CUNY Graduate Center, and an MBA from Baruch College, CUNY. She has published in numerous academic and practitioner journals on knowledge management, competitive intelligence, and shadow teams. Her book with Scott Erickson, From Knowledge to Intelligence: Creating Competitive Advantage in the Next Economy was published by Elsevier in 2005.

Nabil Sahli obtained a diploma of Engineer in Networks and Communication from ENSIAS Morocco in 1999, a master and a PhD in Computer Science from Laval University (Quebec) in 2001 and 2006 respectively. He worked as a scientist researcher at Telematica Instituut (The Netherlands). He is now an assistant professor at Dhofar University in Oman (since 2008). In the last 5 years, he published more than 25 papers in international conferences and journals. His main interests are: multi-agent systems, agent-based geosimulation, agent-based planning, hazards simulation, e-government, trust and reputation, and virtual communities.

David Skillicorn is a Professor in the School of Computing at Queen's University in Canada. His research is in smart information management, both the problems of extracting and sharing useful knowledge from data, and the problems of accessing and computing with large datasets that are geographically distributed. He has published extensively in high-performance computing and data mining. At present his focus is on understanding complex datasets in applications such as biomedicine, geochemistry, network intrusion, fraud detection, and counterterrorism. He has an undergraduate degree from the University of Sydney and a Ph.D. from the University of Manitoba.

Vijay Varadharajan is the Microsoft Chair and Professor of Computing at Macquarie University, Sydney, Australia. He is also the Director of Information and Networked System Security Research. Previous to this, he was the Foundation Chair Professor and Head of School of School of Computing and IT at University of W. Sydney. Prior to this, he was responsible for Security Research at Corporate Hewlett-Packard Labs based at HP Labs Europe for many years. He has published more than 280 papers in International Journals and Conferences and has co-authored /edited 8 books. His current research interests are in distributed system security, network security, mobile agent security, trusted computing and secure peer to peer applications. He is on the Editorial Board of several journals including the IEEE Transactions in Dependable and Secure Computing, ACM Transactions on Information System Security and The International Journal of Information Security. He is a Fellow of IEE, BCS, IMA, ACS and IEAust.

Weiliang Zhao completed his PhD study in the School of Computing and Mathematics of University of Western Sydney, Sydney, Australia, in 2008. He received the Master of Honors for computing and information technology from University of Western Sydney, Sydney, Australia, in 2003. He received the

Bachelor of Science for physics from Peking University, Bejing, P.R.China, in 1988. He is currently a research fellow in the Department of Computing of Macquarie University. He also previously worked in Australia and New Zealand Banking Group Limited as a programmer and in Chinese Academy of Science as a researcher. His current areas of research interest include trust management in service-oriented computing, E-commerce security, security for Internet applications and Web Services.

Index